Lecture Notes in Computer Science 15994

Founding Editors

Gerhard Goos
Juris Hartmanis

AF173569

The series Lecture Notes in Computer Science (LNCS), including its subseries Lecture Notes in Artificial Intelligence (LNAI) and Lecture Notes in Bioinformatics (LNBI), has established itself as a medium for the publication of new developments in computer science and information technology research, teaching, and education.

LNCS enjoys close cooperation with the computer science R & D community, the series counts many renowned academics among its volume editors and paper authors, and collaborates with prestigious societies. Its mission is to serve this international community by providing an invaluable service, mainly focused on the publication of conference and workshop proceedings and postproceedings. LNCS commenced publication in 1973.

Bart Coppens · Bruno Volckaert ·
Vincent Naessens · Bjorn De Sutter
Editors

Availability, Reliability and Security

ARES 2025 International Workshops
Ghent, Belgium, August 11–14, 2025
Proceedings, Part I

 Springer

Editors
Bart Coppens ⓘ
Ghent University
Ghent, Belgium

Bruno Volckaert ⓘ
Ghent University
Ghent, Belgium

Vincent Naessens ⓘ
KU Leuven
Ghent, Belgium

Bjorn De Sutter ⓘ
Ghent University
Ghent, Belgium

ISSN 0302-9743   ISSN 1611-3349 (electronic)
Lecture Notes in Computer Science
ISBN 978-3-032-00629-5   ISBN 978-3-032-00630-1 (eBook)
https://doi.org/10.1007/978-3-032-00630-1

This Springer imprint is published by the registered company Springer Nature Switzerland AG
The registered company address is: Gewerbestrasse 11, 6330 Cham, Switzerland

ARES Workshops 2025 Foreword

Alongside the main track of the 20th International Conference on Availability, Reliability and Security (ARES), the organizers received 17 regular workshop proposals, of which eventually 15 were accepted as workshops. A total of 173 papers were submitted over these workshops, of which 79 were accepted for publication and presentation at ARES 2025. All papers that were not desk rejected received a minimum of 3 double-blind reviews by TPC members, and in the case of conflicts of interest with the workshop organizers, the workshop chairs assigned reviewers and decided on the paper review ranking. As organizers, we believe the resulting workshops will allow for insightful discussions and interesting exchanges of ideas on advances made within the security field.

As workshop chairs we would like to use this space to thank all organizers for their hard work on promoting and managing their workshops. We'd also like to give a special thank you to the TPC members who provided—under strict time constraints—constructive reviews for both accepted and rejected papers. We sincerely believe the workshop programs contribute a lot to maintaining a vibrant ARES community. Therefore, from us to you, a massive thank you.

August 2025

Bart Coppens
Bruno Volckaert
Vincent Naessens
Bjorn De Sutter

ARES Workshops 2025 Organization

General Chair

Bjorn De Sutter   Ghent University, Belgium

General Workshop Chairs

Bart Coppens   Ghent University, Belgium
Bruno Volckaert   Ghent University, Belgium

Proceedings Chairs

Vincent Naessens   KU Leuven, Belgium
Michiel Willocx   KU Leuven, Belgium

Workshop Chairs

Aleksandra Mileva	Goce Delcev University, North Macedonia
Alessandro Aldini	University of Urbino, Italy
Amir Sharif	Fondazione Bruno Kessler, Italy
Amna Shifa	University of Galway, Ireland
Anastasija Collen	University of Geneva, Switzerland
Andrea Saracino	Scuola Superiore Universitaria Sant'Anna di Pisa, Italy
Andrew Marrington	Zayed University, UAE
Angelo Consoli	Scuola Universitaria Professionale della Svizzera Italiana (SUPSI), Switzerland
Artur Janicki	Warsaw University of Technology, Poland
Christoph Schmittner	Austrian Institute of Technology, Austria
Costas Lambrinoudakis	University of Piraeus, Greece
Daniela Pöhn	Universität der Bundeswehr München, Germany
Daniele Canavese	IRIT-CNRS, France
Gregorio Martinez Pérez	University of Murcia, Spain
Günther Pernul	University of Regensburg, Germany
Habtamu Abie	Norwegian Computing Center, Norway

Halvor Holtskog	Norwegian University of Science and Technology, Norway
Hamida Seba	University Lyon 1, France
Helge Janicke	Edith Cowan University, Australia
Javier Lopez	University of Malaga, Spain
Joerg Keller	FernUniversität in Hagen, Germany
Jorge Maestre Vidal	Indra, Spain
Kacper Gradoń	Warsaw University of Technology, Poland
Katarzyna Kamińska	Warsaw University of Technology, Poland
Kim-Kwang Raymond Choo	University of Texas at San Antonio, USA
Leandros Maglaras	De Montfort University, UK
Leonardo Regano	University of Cagliari, Italy
Luca Caviglione	CNR – IMATI, Italy
Mamoona Asghar	University of Galway, Ireland
Mansoor Ahmed	Maynooth University, Ireland
Marco Antonio Sotelo Monge	Indra, Spain
Marco Rasori	National Research Council, Italy
Markus Helfert	Maynooth University, Ireland
Marta Irene García Cid	Indra, Spain
Martin Husák	Masaryk University, Czech Republic
Martin Steinebach	Fraunhofer Institute SIT|ATHENE, Germany
Mauro Conti	University of Padua, Italy
Meriem Benyahya	University of Geneva, Switzerland
Mohamed Ali Kandi	IRIT-University of Toulouse, France
Mohamed-Lamine Messai	University Lyon 2, France
Muhammad Irfan Khalid	University of Agder, Norway
Nadia Kanwal	Keele University, UK
Nils Gruschka	University of Oslo, Norway
Pedro R. M. Inácio	Universidade da Beira Interior, Portugal
Peter Kieseberg	FH St. Pölten, Austria
Philipp Amann	Europol EC3, The Netherlands
Richard Overill	King's College London, UK
Richard Smith	De Montfort University, UK
Salvador Llopis Sanchez	Universitat Politècnica de Valencia, Spain
Sandeep Pirbhulal	Norwegian Computing Center, Oslo, Norway
Simone Fischer-Hübner	Karlstad University, Chalmers University of Technology & Gothenburg University, Sweden
Sokratis Katsikas	Norwegian University of Science and Technology, Norway
Stephen Fisher Davies	Airbus, UK
Steven Furnell	University of Nottingham, UK
Thomas Brandstetter	Limes Security/FHSTP, Austria

Virginia N. L. Franqueira   University of Kent, UK
Wojciech Mazurczyk   Warsaw University of Technology, Poland

ARES Workshops 2025 Organization

Vasilios N. Katos   University of Kent, UK
Wojciech Mazurczyk   Warsaw University of Technology, Poland

AI&CCPS 2025 Preface

Artificial Intelligence (AI) and Cybersecurity had become two of the most prominent topics by 2025, following years of rapid advancements in AI—particularly in Large Language Models (LLMs)—and a steady rise in the number and impact of cyberattacks. In addition, emerging directives, regulations, and legislative acts over recent years had propelled these topics beyond academia into industry and broader society. Although cybersecurity had long been a prolific field for the application of AI techniques, it became increasingly evident that AI itself was turning into a prime target for malicious activities and was also being misused as an attacking agent or facilitator.

The International Workshop on Artificial Intelligence, Cyber and Cyber-Physical Security (AI&CCPS) aimed to explore both the expanding role of AI in addressing security challenges in digital and physical systems, and the need to enhance the robustness and resilience of AI techniques. This workshop brought together researchers and practitioners from both the cybersecurity and artificial intelligence communities to discuss problems and solutions at the intersection of these fields.

AI&CCPS 2025 was the first edition of the workshop and gathered a healthy number of 16 submissions, of which six were accepted for presentation at the workshop and included in the proceedings, leading to an acceptance rate of 37.5%. An additional paper coming from the main track was also included. The technical program committee included 15 researchers from seven different nationalities and the review process benefited from the assistance of seven additional experts who acted as subreviewers. In line with the main conference guidelines, the peer-review process was double-blinded, with every paper undergoing three reviews, and where required a short discussion was motivated prior to taking the final decision.

August 2025

Aleksandra Mileva
Mauro Conti
Pedro R. M. Inácio
Virginia N. L. Franqueira

AI&CCPS 2025 Organization

Workshop Chairs

Aleksandra Mileva	Goce Delcev University, North Macedonia
Mauro Conti	University of Padua, Italy
Pedro R. M. Inácio	Universidade da Beira Interior, Portugal
Virginia N. L. Franqueira	University of Kent, UK

Program Committee

Alberto Giaretta	Orebro University, Sweden
Aleksandar Petrović	Singidunum University, Republic of Serbia
Alessandro Brighente	University of Padova, Italy
Bernardo Sequeiros	Universidade da Beira Interior, Portugal
Isabel Praça	Polytechnic of Porto, Portugal
Jana Dittmann	University of Magdeburg, Germany
João Neves	Universidade da Beira Interior, Portugal
João P. Barraca	Universidade de Aveiro, Portugal
José Inacio Requeno	Universidad Complutense de Madrid, Spain
Simona Bernardi	University of Zaragoza, Spain
Simone Soderi	IMT Lucca, Italy
Stefano Marrone	Università della Campania, Luigi Vanvitelli, Italy
Tiago Cruz	University of Coimbra, Portugal
Tiago Roxo	Universidade da Beira Interior, Portugal
Tomasz Szydlo	Newcastle University, UK

Additional Reviewers

Aleksandar Velinov
Bruno Silva
Joana C. Costa
Rui Pinto
Stefano Cecconello
Vasco Lopes
Vesna Dimitrova

ICS-CSR 2025 Preface

It is our pleasure to present the proceedings of the 8th International Symposium for ICS & SCADA Cyber Security (ICS-CSR), held in Ghent, Belgium on August 13, 2025. This symposium brought together researchers, practitioners, and policymakers from diverse fields to explore critical issues and innovative solutions. The themes addressed at ICS-CSR ranged from Distributed Control Systems (DCS), Supervisory Control and Data Acquisition Systems (SCADA), Industrial Control Systems (ICS), Operational Technology (OT), Cyber Physical Systems (CPS), Industrial Internet of Things (IIoT), Smart City, to Industry 4.0. reflecting the multidisciplinary nature of this vital area of study.

The papers you are reading represent the outcome of rigorous academic effort and dedicated collaboration. We received a total of 8 full papers. Each submission underwent a thorough single-blind peer-review process, with each paper receiving at least 3 independent reviews from members of our Technical Program Committee. This approach ensured that only the highest-quality research was selected for inclusion. Following the review process, 4 full papers were accepted for publication, resulting in an acceptance rate of exactly 50%. ICS-CSR also included a keynote speech entitled "Embedding Security Controls from the Round up: An Asset Owner's Perspective" from Stephen Fisher Davies, a panel discussion on "OT Security" from Larry Vandenaweele, Stephen Fisher Davies and Naghmeh Moradpoor, and the tabletop exercise "Corporates Compromised NISv2" led by Helge Janicke.

The success of ICS-CSR would not have been possible without the tireless efforts of countless individuals. We are immensely grateful to the authors for their valuable contributions, and to the Program Committee members for their insightful critiques. Their commitment to scholarly excellence was instrumental in shaping a high-quality scientific program. We would also like to extend our sincere appreciation to the Organizing Committee for their professional planning and execution, ensuring a smooth and productive conference experience for all participants. Finally, we express our gratitude to our sponsors, whose generous support helped make this event a reality.

We believe that these proceedings will serve as a valuable resource for researchers, practitioners, and anyone interested in advancing the cybersecurity of Cyber Physical Systems. We hope that the ideas and discussions presented herein will inspire further research, foster new collaborations, and contribute to the development of robust and resilient industrial control systems worldwide.

June 2025

Thomas Brandstetter
Stephen Fisher Davies
Helge Janicke
Leandros Maglaras
Richard Smith

ICS-CSR 2025 Organization

Conference Chairs

Thomas Brandstetter	Limes Security/FHSTP, Austria
Stephen Fisher Davies	Airbus, UK
Helge Janicke	Edith Cowan University, Australia
Leandros Maglaras	De Montfort University, UK
Richard Smith	De Montfort University, UK

Program Committee Chairs

Naghmeh Moradpoor	Edinburgh Napier University, UK
Michael Robinson	Airbus, UK

Program Committee

Manos Athanatos	Technical University of Crete, Greece
Nestoras Chouliaras	University of West Attica, Greece
Christos Chrysoulas	Heriot-Watt University, UK
Kubra Duran	Edinburgh Napier University, UK
Vasileios Gkioulos	Norwegian University of Science and Technology, Norway
Andriambelo Ny Hasina	Infosys Limited, France
Helmut Kaufmann	Airbus, UK
Kitty Kioskli	Trustulio, The Netherlands
Dimitrios Kosmanos	University of Thessaly, Greece
Gabor Oesterreicher	FH St. Poelten, Austria
Simon Parkinson	University of Huddersfield, UK
Michael Robinson	Airbus, UK
Panagiotis Sarigiannidis	University of Western Macedonia, Greece
Iqbal H. Sarker	Edith Cowan University, AUS
Yagmur Yigit	Edinburgh Napier University, UK
Nubio Vidal	Airbus, UK
Nida Zeeshan	Edinburgh Napier, UK

SAFER 2025 Preface

The Workshop on Sustainable Security and Awareness For Next Generation Infrastructures (SAFER) was held at Ghent University, Ghent, Belgium, on August 11–14, 2025, in conjunction with the 20th International Conference on Availability, Reliability and Security (ARES).

Cybersecurity poses a significant and ongoing challenge in our increasingly interconnected world, particularly in light of the rapid advancements in the Internet of Things and artificial intelligence. While substantial research is dedicated to enhancing security measures, with many promising developments, the primary focus often remains limited to improving security systems, disregarding their impact on the surrounding environment. This perspective can overlook broader considerations, such as Environmental, Social, and Governance (ESG) factors. For example, the energy requirements of data centers that manage advanced encryption systems or support large-scale neural network training contribute substantially to carbon emissions. The implementation of robust cybersecurity measures can incur significant costs, which may disproportionately affect small and medium-sized enterprises, thereby exacerbating existing inequalities. Socially, security systems—particularly those that incorporate surveillance—can infringe upon individual privacy and diminish public trust. From a governance perspective, emphasizing security without sufficient protections for civil liberties can result in potential abuses of power. These challenges highlight the pressing need to reconsider cybersecurity within a broader context. A more sustainable approach must encompass not only technological resilience but also environmental responsibility, social equity, privacy protection, and ethical governance.

This workshop served as a venue to facilitate the dissemination of research and unite interdisciplinary academics and practitioners at the intersection of cybersecurity and its impact on ESG factors. Authors were asked to submit manuscripts with a maximum length of 18 pages for a double-blind peer review process. We received 10 submissions and we completed the revision process thanks to our Program Committee, composed of 21 experts, and 9 additional reviewers. In the end, each paper was revised by at least three reviewers, and, based on the feedback, we accepted 4 papers for the oral presentation at the workshop (with an acceptance rate of 40%).

We would like to express our gratitude to the authors for submitting their outstanding work, to our reviewers for their prompt and thorough evaluations, and to all our attendees. We sincerely hope that the collaborative efforts to organize this workshop will have a positive impact on cybersecurity worldwide.

August 2025

Daniele Canavese
Mohamed Ali Kandi
Leonardo Regano

SAFER 2025 Organization

Workshop Chairs

Daniele Canavese	IRIT-CNRS, France
Mohamed Ali Kandi	IRIT-University of Toulouse, France
Leonardo Regano	University of Cagliari, Italy

Program Committee

Cataldo Basile	Politecnico di Torino, Italy
Laurent Bobelin	INSA Centre Val de Loire, France
Luca Caviglione	CNR-IMATI, Italy
Paolo Falcarin	Ca' Foscari University of Venice, Italy
Davide Ferraris	University of Málaga, Spain
Giorgio Giacinto	University of Cagliari, Italy
Marko Hölbl	University of Maribor, Slovenia
Youcef Imine	University Polytechnic Hauts-De-France, France
Romain Laborde	IRIT-University of Toulouse, France
Abir Laraba	IRIT-University of Toulouse, France
Davide Maiorca	University of Cagliari, Italy
Luca Mannella	Politecnico di Torino, Italy
Marco Martalò	University of Cagliari, Italy
Antonio Muñoz	University of Málaga, Spain
Francesco Pagano	Università di Verona, Italy
Matteo Repetto	CNR-IMATI, Italy
Rubén Ríos	University of Málaga, Spain
Arianna Rossi	Sant'Anna School of Advanced Studies, Italy
Alessandro Sanna	University of Cagliari, Italy
Fulvio Valenza	Politecnico di Torino, Italy
Ahmad Samer Wazan	Zayed University, UAE

Additional Reviewers

Purbasha Chowdhury
Nicola Deidda
Jonathan Gobbo

Luca Minnei
Lorenzo Pisu
Louis Sahi
Silvia Lucia Sanna
Silvia Sisinni
Mohamed Yacine Touahria Miliani

SecIndustry 2025 Preface

The fourth Industry 4.0 workshop (SecIndustry 2025) was a forum for researchers and practitioners focused on revolutionizing technology and rethinking value-added processes. It includes several critical infrastructures, which are needed to make the different technologies come together to create better products, more effective and efficient production processes. To enhance the security and resilience of Industry 4.0, it is critical to advance our understanding of adversary modelling, foster interdisciplinary collaboration, and refine simulation and testing methods to validate security models under realistic conditions. It is also important to look at the human side of security and privacy when doing digital transformation. Innovation to better understand fast learning, with the use of laboratories, catapult centres and learning factories, applied to real-life security problems, is essential. Using learning factories to simulate and test and set up laboratory production lines, simulating real production lines, gives unprecedented insights into various testing mechanisms and better understanding of the threats and vulnerabilities of Industry 4.0 production lines.

The key technologies that boost Industry 4.0 are the Internet of Things (IoT), Industrial Internet of Things (IIoT), Artificial Intelligence (AI), Cloud Computing, Machine Learning, Security, Big Data, Blockchain, Deep Learning, Digitalization, Digital Twins, Cyber-Physical Systems (CPS), Advanced Analytics, Robotics, and Cognitive Computing. These technologies can expand the attack surface of Industry 4.0. Furthermore, as information technology (IT) and operational technology (OT) become integrated, a new range of security issues can arise, necessitating the defense of both IT and OT. Addressing these security challenges of IT-OT integration is crucial for the implementation of Industry 4.0 technologies.

The workshop garnered the attention of research communities and fostered novel insights and advancements, with a specific focus on cybersecurity threats detection through AI tools for industrial sectors, security and safety for supply chain, digital twin-driven cyber-resilient supply chains, and emerging EU legislations for industry. The 4th Workshop on Cybersecurity in Industry 4.0 (SecIndustry 2025) was held in person. The workshop was organized in conjunction with the 20th International Conference on Availability, Reliability and Security (ARES 2025), Ghent, Belgium, August 11–14, 2025.

A total of eight submissions were received by the workshop, of which seven were subsequently sent for reviews and one desk rejected. As a result of an extensive peer-review process, four papers were selected to be presented at the workshop. The review process primarily emphasized the quality, scientific novelty, and applicability of the papers to safeguarding critical infrastructure and services. The acceptance rate stood at 50%. The accepted articles encompass a diverse range of techniques addressing, monitoring and predicting security threats using AI models in critical infrastructures, additive manufacturing process chains, emerging EU regulations and legislation for industrial sectors.

The workshop consisted of one keynote and technical presentations, with an attendance of approximately 30 individuals. The workshop showcased one significant and thought-provoking keynote on the topics of "Digital Twins for Enhancing Cybersecurity in Industry 4.0".

The workshop was supported by the Center for Research-based Innovation (SFI) Norwegian Centre for Cybersecurity in Critical Sectors (NORCICS) project and the International Alliance for Strengthening Cybersecurity and Privacy in Healthcare (CybAlliance) project. The organizers would like to thank these projects for supporting the SecIndustry 2025 workshop.

The organizers of the SecIndustry workshop would like to extend their heartfelt appreciation to the SecIndustry 2025 Program Committee for their meticulous and punctual review process, which played a crucial role in bringing the workshop to fruition. We would like to express our gratitude to Ghent University, Belgium for graciously hosting the workshop, and extend our appreciation to the ARES 2025 chairs for their invaluable assistance and support.

August 2025   Sandeep Pirbhulal
                                                          Habtamu Abie
                                                          Halvor Holtskog
                                                       Sokratis Katsikas

SecIndustry 2025 Organization

Workshop Chairs

Sandeep Pirbhulal	Norwegian Computing Center, Norway
Habtamu Abie	Norwegian Computing Center, Norway
Halvor Holtskog	Norwegian University of Science and Technology, Norway
Sokratis Katsikas	Norwegian University of Science and Technology, Norway

Program Committee

Cristina Alcaraz	University of Malaga, Spain
Manos Athanatos	Foundation for Research and Technology Hellas, Crete
Sabarathinam Chockalingam	Institute for Energy Technology, Norway
Hervé Debar	Télécom SudParis, France
Sabine Delaitre	BOSONIT, Spain
Vasileios Gkioulos	Norwegian University of Science and Technology, Norway
Ilias Gkotsis	Inlecom Innovation, Greece
Dieter Gollmann	Hamburg University of Technology, Germany
Siv Hilde Houmb	Norwegian University of Science and Technology, Norway
Martin Gilje Jaatun	University of Stavanger, Norway
Basel Katt	Norwegian University of Science and Technology, Norway
Maryline Laurent	Télécom SudParis, France
Wolfgang Leister	Norwegian Computing Center, Norway
Aida Omerovic	The Foundation for Industrial and Technical Research, Norway
Kai Rannenberg	Goethe University Frankfurt, Germany
Reijo Savola	University of Jyväskylä, Finland
Ankur Shukla	Institute for Energy Technology, Norway
Ali Hassan Sodhro	Kristianstad University, Sweden

Mohsen Toorani   University of South-Eastern Norway, Norway
Christos Xenakis   University of Piraeus, Greece
Shouhuai Xu   University of Colorado Colorado Springs, USA

Contents – Part I

**Proceedings of the First Workshop on Sustainable Security and
Awareness For Next Generation Infrastructures (SAFER 2025)**

**Proceedings of the Fourth Workshop on Cybersecurity in Industry
4.0 (SecIndustry 2025)**

Proceedings of the First International Workshop on Artificial Intelligence, Cyber and Cyber-Physical Security (AI&CCPS 2025)

AI&CCPS 2025 Preface

Artificial Intelligence (AI) and Cybersecurity had become two of the most prominent topics by 2025, following years of rapid advancements in AI—particularly in Large Language Models (LLMs)—and a steady rise in the number and impact of cyberattacks. In addition, emerging directives, regulations, and legislative acts over recent years had propelled these topics beyond academia into industry and broader society. Although cybersecurity had long been a prolific field for the application of AI techniques, it became increasingly evident that AI itself was turning into a prime target for malicious activities and was also being misused as an attacking agent or facilitator.

The International Workshop on Artificial Intelligence, Cyber and Cyber-Physical Security (AI&CCPS) aimed to explore both the expanding role of AI in addressing security challenges in digital and physical systems, and the need to enhance the robustness and resilience of AI techniques. This workshop brought together researchers and practitioners from both the cybersecurity and artificial intelligence communities to discuss problems and solutions at the intersection of these fields.

AI&CCPS 2025 was the first edition of the workshop and gathered a healthy number of 16 submissions, of which six were accepted for presentation at the workshop and included in the proceedings, leading to an acceptance rate of 37.5%. An additional paper coming from the main track was also included. The technical program committee included 15 researchers from seven different nationalities and the review process benefited from the assistance of seven additional experts who acted as subreviewers. In line with the main conference guidelines, the peer-review process was double-blinded, with every paper undergoing three reviews, and where required a short discussion was motivated prior to taking the final decision.

August 2025

Aleksandra Mileva
Mauro Conti
Pedro R. M. Inácio
Virginia N. L. Franqueira

AI&CCPS 2025 Organization

Workshop Chairs

Aleksandra Mileva	Goce Delcev University, North Macedonia
Mauro Conti	University of Padua, Italy
Pedro R. M. Inácio	Universidade da Beira Interior, Portugal
Virginia N. L. Franqueira	University of Kent, UK

Program Committee

Alberto Giaretta	Orebro University, Sweden
Aleksandar Petrović	Singidunum University, Republic of Serbia
Alessandro Brighente	University of Padova, Italy
Bernardo Sequeiros	Universidade da Beira Interior, Portugal
Isabel Praça	Polytechnic of Porto, Portugal
Jana Dittmann	University of Magdeburg, Germany
João Neves	Universidade da Beira Interior, Portugal
João P. Barraca	Universidade de Aveiro, Portugal
José Inacio Requeno	Universidad Complutense de Madrid, Spain
Simona Bernardi	University of Zaragoza, Spain
Simone Soderi	IMT Lucca, Italy
Stefano Marrone	Università della Campania, Luigi Vanvitelli, Italy
Tiago Cruz	University of Coimbra, Portugal
Tiago Roxo	Universidade da Beira Interior, Portugal
Tomasz Szydlo	Newcastle University, UK

Additional Reviewers

Aleksandar Velinov
Bruno Silva
Joana C. Costa
Rui Pinto
Stefano Cecconello
Vasco Lopes
Vesna Dimitrova

Profiling Electric Vehicles via Early Charging Voltage Patterns

Francesco Marchiori[1] , Denis Donadel[2]([✉]) , Alessandro Brighente[1] , and Mauro Conti[1]

[1] University of Padova, Padova, Italy
francesco.marchiori@math.unipd.it,
{alessandro.brighente,mauro.conti}@unipd.it
[2] University of Verona, Verona, Italy
denis.donadel@univr.it

Abstract. Electric Vehicles (EVs) are rapidly gaining adoption as a sustainable alternative to fuel-powered vehicles, making secure charging infrastructure essential. Despite traditional authentication protocols, recent results showed that attackers may steal energy through tailored relay attacks. One countermeasure is leveraging the EV's fingerprint on the current exchanged during charging. However, existing methods focus on the final charging stage, allowing malicious actors to consume substantial energy before being detected and repudiated. This underscores the need for earlier and more effective authentication methods to prevent unauthorized charging. Meanwhile, profiling raises privacy concerns, as uniquely identifying EVs through charging patterns could enable user tracking.

In this paper, we propose a framework for uniquely identifying EVs using physical measurements from the early charging stages. We hypothesize that voltage behavior early in the process exhibits similar characteristics to current behavior in later stages. By extracting features from early voltage measurements, we demonstrate the feasibility of EV profiling. Our approach improves existing methods by enabling faster and more reliable vehicle identification. We test our solution on a dataset of 7408 usable charges from 49 EVs, achieving up to 0.86 accuracy. Feature importance analysis shows that near-optimal performance is possible with just 10 key features, improving efficiency alongside our lightweight models. This research lays the foundation for a novel authentication factor while exposing potential privacy risks from unauthorized access to charging data.

Keywords: Electric Vehicles · Profiling · Voltage

1 Introduction

The increasing diffusion of Electric Vehicles (EVs), with total sales forecasted to reach up to 31.1 million by 2030 [10], is a key factor to help fight global warming.

© The Author(s), under exclusive license to Springer Nature Switzerland AG 2025
B. Coppens et al. (Eds.): ARES 2025 Workshops, LNCS 15994, pp. 5–22, 2025.
https://doi.org/10.1007/978-3-032-00630-1_1

At the same time, it opens up to new challenges related to the peculiarity of these devices. Many of these challenges are related to the batteries, how to make a full charge last longer, and how to charge them fast and efficiently, while ensuring the grid stability. The grid leverages communication between vehicles and charging columns by employing the so-called Vehicle-To-Grid (V2G) paradigm. Data exchange usually happens using a power line communication through the control pilot pin of the charging plug and is usually enabled by the ISO 15118 protocol [25]. Through it, EVs can establish a full-featured internet connection with the smart grid, allowing price negotiation, charging time scheduling, authentication handling, and enabling many other services [25]. While this communication comes with high benefits, it could also be exploited by attackers [2,4,9].

Being a Cyber-Physical System (cps), the EV charging infrastructure security must not only rely on the protocol's security but also consider threats from the physical world. In fact, information leakages can happen through the exchange of physical signals. In particular, researchers demonstrated how it is possible to profile an EV by looking at the energy delivered by the charging column [6,7]. This approach collects the charging current in the final part of a full charging process to extract features and characterize each EV. The approach achieves good classification performance and is open to several potential implications, both for attackers who want to trace a vehicle between multiple locations and for defenders as an authentication mechanism. However, since the data are collected during the last part of the charging process (the so-called *tail*), the applicability of this approach is limited to charging processes not reaching 100% of State of Charge (soc), thus potentially missing several profiling chances and making authentication more complicated.

Contributions. In this paper, we analyze a different solution that allows EV profiling by collecting measurements during the early stages of the charging process. In particular, we employ voltage measurements, which are significant in the first part of the charging process, instead of current values, which provide more information in the last part of the charging. Moreover, while similar works consider a dataset coming from a series of charging columns employing an adaptive charging solution (ACN Dataset [17,18]), in this paper, we consider the EVBattery dataset [14,33], which provides a more standard and spread charging management system. Overall, our findings demonstrate that EV authentication can be reliably performed using simple and lightweight models. Our approach achieves an accuracy of up to 0.86, averaged across all vehicle types.

The contribution of this paper can be summarized as follows:

- We analyze the feasibility of profiling a vehicle through measurements of the voltage exchange during the first charging steps.
- We analyze the performance of our framework on a large real-world dataset [33], comprising charges from more than 49 EVs and including three different brands. Our approach is tested on anonymized data, demonstrating its robustness in privacy-preserving scenarios.
- We identify the most relevant features for EV authentication, showing that a small subset of 10 key features is sufficient for high accuracy.

– We make our implementation and code open-source at: https://github.com/spritz-group/EV-Volt-Auth.

Organization. This paper is organized as follows. In Sect. 2 we report related works in the field of EV security and authentication. We then detail the considered system and threat model in Sect. 3, and in Sect. 4 we propose our methodology. We report the results of our evaluation in Sect. 5, and Sect. 6 concludes our work.

2 Related Works

Several research efforts have explored the security and privacy aspects of EVs [2, 13, 24]. Looking at the bigger picture, the need for EV to periodically connect to the grid for charging can threaten the entire power grid. Its stability could be mined by botnets of vehicles [16] and by coordinated attacks [12]. Moreover, the backend connection between control centers and the charging columns opens up several challenges [26]. For instance, the most widely used protocol for backend communications has been proved vulnerable to cyberattacks [1].

Being a CPS, the EV itself exhibits different security risks in addition to traditional petrol-powered cars [5, 31]. Attackers may exploit the physical connection to the charging columns to steal energy from a nearby victim [9] or perform denial of charge attacks, even remotely [4]. Different authentication strategies have been proposed to secure the charging process, investigating also the dynamic charging that allows cars to charge while moving [3, 19, 23]. Brighente at al. [7] first introduced an approach for authentication by employing information from the EV specific charging pattern, which was then expanded in different following works [6, 11]. However, their approach requires a full charge of the EV battery before producing a result, thus reducing the possible applicability of the framework. The same issue holds for authentication methods aimed at lithium-ion batteries, as they can require full battery charges and discharges or sophisticated equipment, making their usability in the context of EVs limited [21].

Privacy aspects of EV charging have also been investigated [30]. However, it is not always easy to prevent CPS from leaking information that an attacker may exploit to mine the user's privacy [32]. Recent work has demonstrated the feasibility of extracting sensitive information—such as user identity, driving style, and trip endpoints purely from battery consumption patterns using Machine Learning (ML) techniques [22]. While this highlights the privacy risks inherent in battery-related telemetry, such approaches focus on post-drive consumption data, typically requiring access to a full trip. In contrast, our work shifts the focus to the early stages of the charging process, showing that brief voltage readings alone can be leveraged for profiling, even without full charging sessions or vehicle usage data. This significantly broadens the threat landscape, as it reduces the time and access requirements for potential adversaries.

3 System and Threat Model

In this section, we describe the system under study (Sect. 3.1), outline the adversarial model (Sect. 3.2), and explore potential use cases of our profiling method (Sect. 3.3). We distinguish between malicious and legitimate applications, highlighting the dual-use nature of EV fingerprinting via voltage traces.

3.1 System Model

Charging an EV requires careful consideration of both the vehicle and the grid. This latter, in particular, must be managed to handle high power requirements from a fleet of EVs, and this is facilitated by the V2G paradigm that creates a bi-directional communication between vehicles and the smart grid. On the other side, EV's battery can be charged at different speeds based on the capabilities of the charging column and the vehicle itself [15].

EVs are usually equipped with batteries containing Lithium-ion (Li-ion) cells. They exhibit a known and peculiar charging pattern where voltage and current levels are correlated to the SoC. In particular, two main behaviors can be identified, as shown in Fig. 1. The charging starts with a *constant current phase* where the voltage slowly increases. At a certain point, usually with SoC values between 60% and 80% of the full charge, a *constant voltage phase* starts, where the current slowly decreases, creating a tail. This behavior is well known and is typical of these kinds of batteries [27].

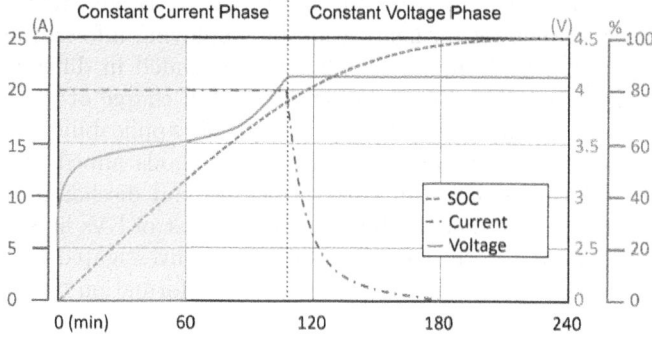

Fig. 1. Charging profile of a Li-ion battery [28]. In this paper, we will show that voltage data from the first part of the constant current phase (highlighted in violet in the graph) are enough for correctly profiling a vehicle.

3.2 Threat Model

In this paper, we consider an entity that can collect measurements during the charging process. In particular, with respect to previous works [6] that collected current levels, we collect voltage levels during the charging process. As we discuss in this paper, this reduces the required collection time to profile a vehicle and does not require a full charge to extract the relevant features. The only other information required by the system is the SoC of the battery, which is used to understand in which part of the charging profile the EV is. All the other data transmitted through the cable, such as the high-level communication transmitted in the control pilot pin, is not collected for this study.

Such profiling could be a double-edged sword and can be applied by different entities for different purposes. An attacker may exploit this methodology to track a vehicle through different locations. A malicious owner of various parking lots with charging columns may track vehicles for advertisement purposes. Another option for an attacker is to install a measurement device as a plug, similar to devices employed in ATM skimming [29], to collect data useful to track a user mining their privacy. On the other side, such data could be employed for good as a second factor or continuous authentication system.

3.3   Applications

We show that it is possible to extract discriminative features from early charging voltage patterns, which are unique enough to allow reliable profiling of a singular vehicle. The ability to fingerprint an EV from voltage measurements can be leveraged in multiple contexts. We highlight both adversarial and defensive uses.

Adversarial Applications.

- **Vehicle tracking across locations:** A malicious entity operating multiple public or semi-public charging stations can silently collect voltage traces and match them across sites to track vehicles over time.
- **Profiling without consent:** An attacker could embed a skimming device within a charging cable or socket to passively collect voltage traces and associate them with a specific vehicle or user, compromising location privacy.
- **Behavioral surveillance:** By linking profiling data with usage patterns, an attacker might infer sensitive behavior (e.g., commuting habits, work location, or home address).

Defensive Applications.

- **Second-factor authentication:** EV profiling can supplement existing user authentication mechanisms, confirming vehicle identity as part of a multifactor security scheme at high-security charging stations.
- **Tamper detection:** Deviations in the expected voltage pattern could be used to detect unauthorized battery replacement or tampering with internal battery components.
- **Anti-theft tracking:** In case of theft, a known voltage fingerprint can serve as a unique signature to detect the vehicle if it is connected to any charging infrastructure.

– **Usage-based insurance or leasing:** Insurance or leasing companies may use this approach to verify the EV's identity under a specific contract, enforcing user-vehicle binding in shared or rental contexts.

These use cases demonstrate that early-stage voltage profiling has a wide range of implications, from privacy threats to enabling lightweight security mechanisms. Our work does not advocate for any particular application but aims to provide a technical foundation and empirical validation for EV identification based on early charging behavior. Depending on who controls the charging infrastructure, this capability may pose a risk to user privacy or be a valuable tool for improving EV security and authentication.

4   Methodology

In this section, we provide a more detailed explanation of the profiling techniques we employ. We first present the dataset and its characteristics (Sect. 4.1). We also discuss our feature extraction process, which is one of the key components of our approach (Sect. 4.2). Next, we present an overview of the ML models used as classifiers and the process of finding their optimal hyperparameters (Sect. 4.3). The overall methodology is summarized in Fig. 2. The first step is collecting charging measurements from EV charging process. From the samples, feature extraction is used to obtain information that can be fed to ML models for classification.

EV Charging   Voltage Data   Feature Extraction   Classification   Prediction

Fig. 2. Pipeline of the proposed profiling framework.

4.1   Dataset

For this work, we created a dataset starting from three EV charging collections, which together consist of over 690,000 charging snippets recorded from 347 distinct EVs [33]. Since the original dataset was designed for anomaly detection, we first remove all potential outliers that exhibit anomalies in the charging process. Next, we extract all charging snippets, which originally are segmented into 128-sample sequences, with each sample recorded once per second. Our primary feature of interest is voltage, though we also incorporate SoC for further processing. To ensure we analyze complete charging events, we concatenate snippets belonging to the same charging session, grouping them based on the car label and segment ID. This process results in complete charge sequences, which we sort by SoC to maintain its natural increasing order. After preprocessing, our dataset consists of voltage and SoC time series, and car labels. From this, we apply two additional filtering steps.

- *SoC Thresholding* – We keep only data where SoC is $\leq 60\%$, as our profiling approach relies on the non-constant voltage phase in the early charging stages (see Fig. 1).
- *Minimum Sample Requirement* – We include only vehicles with at least 100 charging samples, ensuring sufficient data for profiling. Cars with few charging instances are excluded due to insufficient label representation in the dataset.

The final dataset thus contains 36,165 charging snippets constituting 7,408 charging sessions from 49 different EVs. It is worth noting that the voltage data has been perturbed and interpolated as part of the anonymization process applied by the original dataset authors [33]. Despite these modifications, underlying temporal patterns and correlations remain intact, potentially enabling the inference of an EV's identity, an aspect we explore further in Sect. 5.5. After this one-time preprocessing step, we further adapt the dataset dynamically to be used in a classification setup. The final distribution of the dataset is shown in Fig. 3. From now on, we will discuss an authentication scenario, but a malicious user could apply the same process to profile and track a vehicle between charging stations. The only subtle difference is that an attacker may not have access to detailed SoC data since the information could be transmitted encrypted or on channels not under the attacker's control. We will discuss this issue in Sect. 5.3.

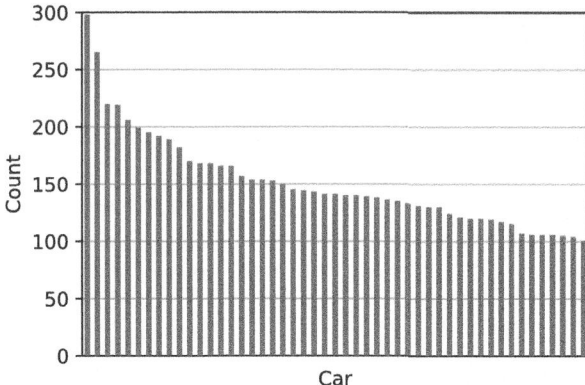

Fig. 3. Distribution of samples for each car in our dataset after pre-processing.

In particular, we set up our systems to first select a vehicle as the authenticated subject for each car label and consider all other vehicles as non-authenticated. This process is repeated for every vehicle in the dataset, ensuring that each car is evaluated as the authenticated one at least once. By structuring the dataset this way, we create multiple binary classification tasks tailored to a specific vehicle's charging behavior.

4.2   Feature Extraction

For each time window, we extract features from the voltage and SoC time series using the `tsfresh` Python package [8]. `tsfresh` automatically computes a wide range of statistical and mathematical characteristics from time series data and selects the most relevant ones for regression or classification tasks. The extracted features include but are not limited to, statistical measures (e.g., mean, variance, skewness, kurtosis), frequency-domain features (e.g., Fourier coefficients, spectral entropy), and time-series properties (e.g., autocorrelation, trend strength, peaks, crossings). We apply this process to the voltage and SoC time series from our processed dataset, ensuring that each driver performs feature extraction separately. This allows us to generate feature representations tailored to each driver's charging behavior, which we then use in a binary classification setting (authenticated vs. non-authenticated). After extracting features, we perform two processing steps.

1. *Feature Imputation* – Some extracted features may contain missing values due to insufficient data in certain time windows. We handle this by imputing missing values, typically by replacing them with appropriate statistical estimates (e.g., mean, median, or interpolation methods), ensuring a complete dataset for classification.

2. *Feature Selection* – Since `tsfresh` generates many features, we apply feature selection to retain only the most informative and discriminative ones. The reduction of feature number is done independently for each EV to maintain the most suited features in each case. This step reduces dimensionality and improves model efficiency, removing noisy or redundant features. Although feature selection is performed independently for each vehicle, we observe a significant overlap in the selected features across different models. This suggests that certain statistical patterns are consistently informative, regardless of the individual EV's characteristics. We further investigate this in Sect. 5.4, where we analyze feature importance and demonstrate that a small set of just 10 common features is sufficient to achieve performance close to that of the full feature set.

4.3   Models

Inspired by previous work on EV authentication [6] and battery authentication [21], we select five lightweight ML models: AdaBoost, Decision Tree (DT), k-Nearest Neighbors (kNN), Neural Network (NN), and Random Forest (RF). These models were chosen not only based on their effectiveness in prior studies but also due to their suitability for real-time deployment. Unlike deep learning approaches, which typically require high computational power and external data processing, these models are lightweight enough to run directly on an

EV charging station without requiring communication with external servers, enhancing security by reducing potential attack vectors associated with remote authentication. We apply an 80/20 split between the training and test sets for model training. Hyperparameter tuning is performed using a grid search approach with 5-fold cross-validation, ensuring that our models generalize well to unseen data. The set of hyperparameters considered for each model is detailed in the Appendix A.1.

5   Evaluation

We now proceed with the evaluation of our models under different settings. In particular, we analyzed the behavior our models when changing the measurement length to extract the features from (Sect. 5.1) and when varying the composition of the dataset (Sect. 5.2). Moreover, we analyzed the importance of the SoC feature in Sect. 5.3, the features employed and the effects on reducing the feature number in Sect. 5.4.

To evaluate our models, we employ two classical metrics, the accuracy and the F1-score, which are defined as follows:

$$Accuracy = \frac{TP + TN}{TP + FP + TN + FN}, \qquad F1 = \frac{2TP}{2TP + FP + FN}, \qquad (1)$$

where:

- *True Positive (TP)*: a sample from the authenticated vehicle is correctly identified.
- *False Positive (FP)*: a sample belonging to the non-authenticated class mistakenly identified as the authenticated vehicle.
- *False Negative (FN)*: a sample belonging to the authenticated driver is mistakenly identified as a non-authenticated driver.
- *True Negative (TN)*: a non-authenticated vehicle is correctly classified as non-authenticated.

5.1   Data Length

One of the most important differences with respect to previous works [6] is that our models do not require a full charge to efficiently profile a vehicle. In fact, since we extract features from the first part of the charging, only a few seconds of charging are sufficient to obtain some results. To understand how much the size of the data capture has an impact on the performance, we tested several options ranging from 16 to 1024 s.

Results are shown in Fig. 4, where Fig. 4a shows the F1-scores, while Fig. 4b the accuracy, both averaged by the ratios (see Sect. 5.2). As we can see, the overall variance between sizes is not very pronounced, and this suggests it is not necessary to wait long to make a decision. In particular, top scores are reached

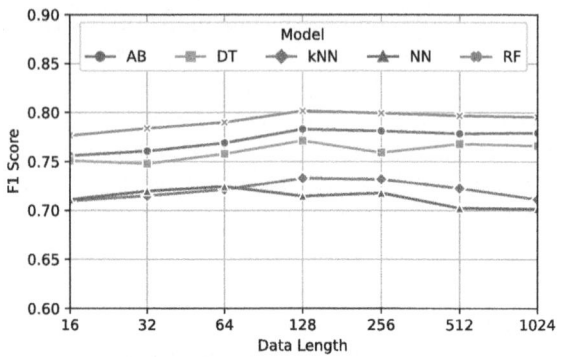

(a) F1 Score of the models.

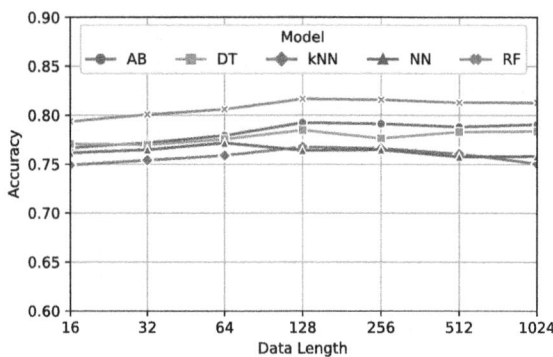

(b) Accuracy of the models.

Fig. 4. Average performance of different data lengths (in seconds).

with a 128-second length by the RF classifier, which overall performed quite better than other models. Another interesting aspect is related to the results of different models within the same data length. The RF models retain an almost constant distance from the second most performing model over all the data lengths. Although kNN and NN represent two very different architectures, they share a curve that sees rising scores up to mid-length (i.e., 64 to 128) and then falling again as length increases.

5.2 Ratio

We conduct several experiments to verify the effect of an unbalanced dataset during training. To analyze it, we tested our models based on different ratios between the data concerning the positive label versus all the others. In particular, a ratio of 5 : 1 indicates that the samples belonging to the selected EV are five times more than samples from all the other vehicles. Conversely, a ratio of 1 : 5

indicates that the dataset contains five times more samples of other vehicles with respect to the selected one. A ratio of 1 : 1 indicates a balanced dataset.

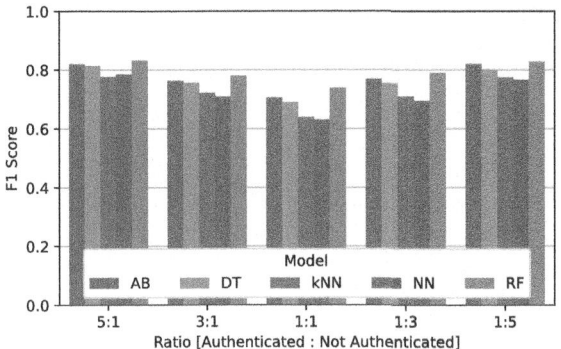

(a) F1 Score of the models.

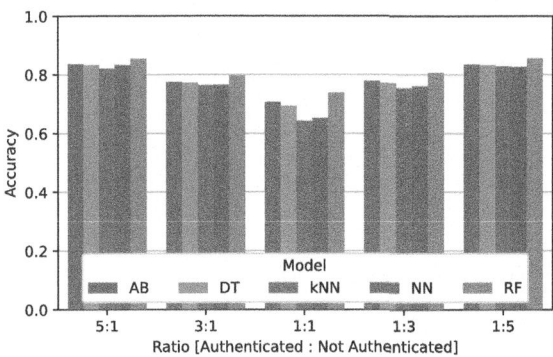

(b) Accuracy of the models.

Fig. 5. Average performance of different ratios (representing the number of authenticated samples vs the number of other samples in the dataset).

The results shown in Fig. 5 clearly indicate unbalanced datasets' capabilities to perform successfully. This is essential in such a scenario where it is usually more difficult to get samples from the authenticated vehicle with respect to data from all the other cars that use the charging column. In particular, we can see how with one-fifth of data related to the target (i.e., ratio 1 : 5), the F1-score surpasses 0.80 for three models out of five. Even in this experiment, RF exhibits the best performances. However, the gap is more pronounced with a balanced dataset, while AdaBoost (AB) almost reaches the F1-Score levels of RF for heavy unbalanced datasets.

5.3   SoC Feature

In our experiments we employ the SoC as a time series for feature extraction through `tsfresh`. This is reasonable since we discussed an authentication scenario where this information should be available to the charging column with a high level of detail. However, in an adversarial scenario, an attacker may only be able to get rough information about the SoC for instance by looking at the charging column display, or by estimating it from the voltage level and the duration of the charging. In this scenario, the attacker could successfully identify if the charging is happening during the constant current phase (see Fig. 1), but cannot use the SoC to extract features. To determine the impact of the absence of the SoC feature, we reproduced our experiments without considering it during the feature extraction, but employing it only to filter out samples with more than 60% of SoC. The results of this analysis are shown in Fig. 6.

As we can see, results are comparable, although the presence of SoC-related features slightly improve the performances of our classifier. Interestingly, we notice a more significant gap in accuracy performance as the considered data length for classification decreases. This suggests that SoC-related features help the model more accurately assess the specific charging phase. However, the model can infer this independently with more considerable data lengths, as suggested by the smaller gap between the accuracy results.

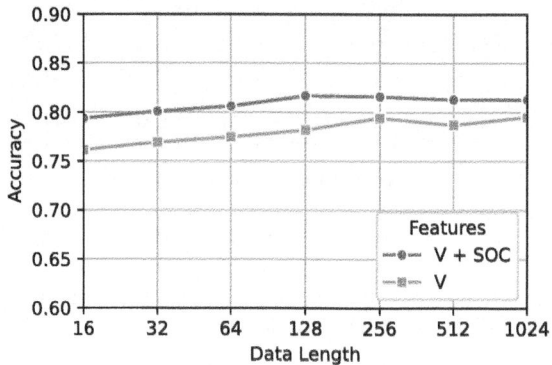

Fig. 6. Average performance of our **RF** model trained on different subsets of features (**V**oltage alone or with **SoC**) at different data lengths.

5.4   Feature Analysis

A complete analysis of the features extracted and employed by `tsfresh` is useful to understand which trait of the charging is more characteristic and thus useful in the profiling. We performed our feature analysis on a subsample of the whole datasets and employed the best-performing model, i.e., the RF model.

We start by analyzing the feature's importance by employing SHapley Additive exPlanations (SHAP), a model-agnostic XAI technique [20]. Figure 7 classify the main features with their importance level, which are explained more into detail in Appendix A.2. The prominence of frequency-domain features among the top 10 highlights the significance of periodic voltage signal behavior in EV authentication. The inclusion of both low- and high-frequency components suggests that variations in power electronics and charging circuit dynamics are distinctive to individual EVs. Additionally, the presence of features such as mean absolute change and standard deviation indicates that, while absolute voltage levels may be comparable across EVs, their dynamic fluctuations provide a unique signature for identification.

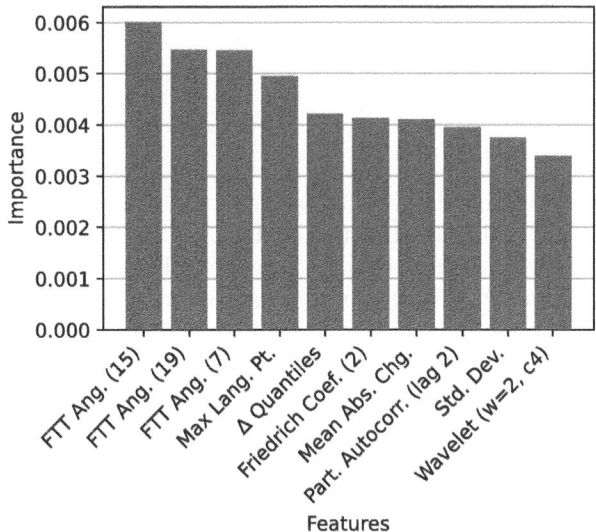

Fig. 7. Top 10 features by importance extracted by SHAP.

After understanding the most significant features, another important aspect is the impact of adding features on the scores. A low number of features reduces the complexity of the model, making it more easy to handle and less exposed to noise. Therefore, we experiment with different numbers of features in a RF model, choosing every time the x most significant features. Results are shown in Fig. 8. They show that increasing the number of features generally improves accuracy, but the rate of improvement diminishes as more features are added, becoming almost negligible from 6 features on. Moreover, the effect varies depending on the data balance ratio. Higher imbalance ratios tend to achieve better performance overall, suggesting that the model benefits from more training samples in the majority class. Even with balanced datasets, accuracy improves until plateauing, showing that a feature subset can achieve near-optimal results while keeping the model efficient.

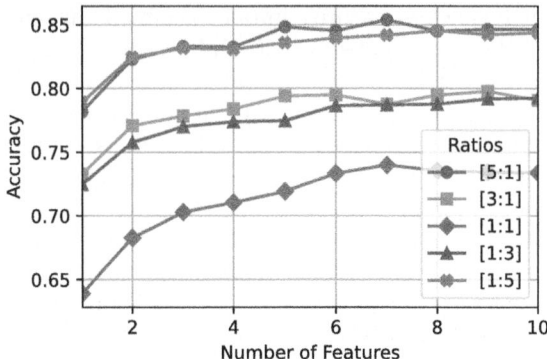

Fig. 8. Accuracy of the classifiers trained on different dataset ratios (i.e., number of authenticated samples vs number of other samples) while increasing the number of features.

5.5   Data Anonymization

The authors of the original dataset [33] applied a series of anonymization steps to protect the identity and characteristics of the EVs. Specifically, they perturbed and interpolated each charging segment's average voltage, current, and temperature values. Additionally, timestamps and mileage values were randomly shifted and scaled. While these anonymization techniques help mask exact values and protect sensitive identifiers, our results show that meaningful patterns remain. In particular, the temporal correlations and statistical structures in the voltage data can effectively be leveraged to infer the EV's identity. This demonstrates the robustness of our methodology not only in idealized settings but also when applied to anonymized real-world data. This highlights the effectiveness of our methodology in both system and threat model scenarios.

- *Benign use case:* When employed for authentication at the charging station level, our method enables privacy-preserving user recognition resilient against side-channel attacks on battery usage [22].
- *Adversarial use case:* When used for malicious profiling, our findings indicate that the current anonymization strategy may be insufficient, pointing to stronger or alternative techniques to prevent identity inference.

6   Conclusions

In this paper, we analyzed the feasibility of profiling an EV during charging by exploiting voltage measurements and the SoC. The data employed are collected during the first part of the charging process, thus allowing vehicle identification during the first stages of the charging, without the need to wait for full charging (i.e., 100% SoC). Our experiments on 49 different vehicles show accuracy up to 0.86, demonstrating the practicality of the approach.

Privacy is an essential requirement in the CPS environment. Looking at potential leakages in the EV scenario is important to defend users against possible misuse of such information. Moreover, in this context, this information could also be employed to enhance the security of the system, providing novel features for authentication. In fact, we foresee future work that can build a fully featured second-factor and continuous authentication system starting from this paper's findings. Using advanced preprocessing can also enhance scores and enable more accurate, robust profiling. Moreover, a larger dataset could allow for investigating the resiliency of the solution to physical properties such as battery aging, seasonality, or time of day.

Open Science and Ethical Considerations

This work builds upon publicly available, pre-processed EV charging data released for research purposes. While raw data remain protected under privacy regulations, the processed dataset includes vehicle identifiers that allow charging sessions to be linked to specific (anonymized) EVs. Our findings demonstrate that even with such limited information, accurate profiling remains feasible— highlighting a broader security and privacy consideration for the community. We believe it is important to share these results to help guide the development of more privacy-preserving data-sharing practices and protocols in future EV infrastructures. All our code is available to promote transparency and reproducibility: https://github.com/spritz-group/EV-Volt-Auth.

Acknowledgment. This work was founded by the European Union under the National Recovery and Resilience Plan (NRRP), Mission 4 Component 2 Investment 1.3 - Call for tender No. 341 of March 15, 2022 of Italian Ministry of University and Research – NextGenerationEU; Code PE00000014, Concession Decree No. 1556 of October 11, 2022 CUP D43C22003050001, Project "SEcurity and RIghts in the CyberSpace (SERICS) - Spoke 7 Infrastructure Security - Visible Light Communication for Secure Vehicle-to-Everything Communication - VisiCar" – Beneficiary's CUP: C99J24000250008.

A Appendix

A.1 Hyperparameters

Table 1 lists the models employed in classification and their hyperparameters.

Table 1. Hyperparameters employed in Grid Search.

Models	Hyperparameters
AdaBoost (AB)	• Number of estimators
Decision Tree (DT)	• Criterion
	• Maximum Depth
k-Nearest Neighbors (kNN)	• Number of neighbors
	• Weight function
Neural Network (NN)	• Hidden layer sizes
	• Activation function
	• Solver
Random Forest (RF)	• Criterion
	• Number of estimators

A.2 Feature Importance

The 10 most important features for the classification of the legitimate EV are the following:

1. *FFT angle (coeff. 15)* – The phase angle of the 15th Fourier coefficient, capturing periodic patterns in the voltage signal.
2. *FFT angle (coeff. 99)* – Similar to the previous feature but for the 99th Fourier coefficient, highlighting high-frequency behaviors.
3. *FFT angle (coeff. 7)* – The phase angle of the 7th Fourier coefficient, indicative of lower frequency components.
4. *Max Langevin point* – A stability indicator derived from stochastic differential equations, estimating system behavior.
5. *Change quantiles (mean)* – Measures the mean absolute change between specific quantiles, capturing shifts in voltage distribution.
6. *Friedrich coefficient (2)* – A coefficient from Friedrich's method, modeling the dynamics of the voltage signal.
7. *Mean absolute change* – Computes the mean of absolute differences between consecutive voltage values, indicating signal variability.
8. *Partial autocorrelation (lag 2)* – Measures the correlation of the voltage signal with its past values at a lag of 2, detecting dependencies.
9. *Standard deviation* – Quantifies the overall dispersion and variation of the voltage signal.
10. *Wavelet coeff. (w=2, coeff. 4)* – Extracted from continuous wavelet transform, capturing multi-scale fluctuations in the voltage signal.

References

1. Alcaraz, C., Cumplido, J., Trivino, A.: OCPP in the spotlight: threats and counter-measures for electric vehicle charging infrastructures 4.0. Int. J. Inf. Secur. **22**(5), 1395–1421 (2023)
2. Antoun, J., Kabir, M.E., Moussa, B., Atallah, R., Assi, C.: A detailed security assessment of the EV charging ecosystem. IEEE Netw. **34**(3), 200–207 (2020)
3. Babu, P.R., Amin, R., Reddy, A.G., Das, A.K., Susilo, W., Park, Y.: Robust authentication protocol for dynamic charging system of electric vehicles. IEEE Trans. Veh. Technol. **70**(11), 11338–11351 (2021)
4. Baker, R., Martinovic, I.: Losing the car keys: wireless PHY-layer insecurity in EV charging. In: 28th USENIX Security Symposium (USENIX Security 19), pp. 407–424. USENIX Association, Santa Clara, CA (2019). https://www.usenix.org/conference/usenixsecurity19/presentation/baker
5. Brighente, A., Conti, M., Donadel, D., Poovendran, R., Turrin, F., Zhou, J.: Electric vehicles security and privacy: challenges, solutions, and future needs. arXiv preprint arXiv:2301.04587 (2023)
6. Brighente, A., Conti, M., Donadel, D., Turrin, F.: EVScout2. 0: electric vehicle profiling through charging profile. ACM Trans. Cyber-Phys. Syst. **8**(2), 1–24 (2024)
7. Brighente, A., Conti, M., Sadaf, I.: Tell me how you re-charge, i will tell you where you drove to: electric vehicles profiling based on charging-current demand. In: Bertino, E., Shulman, H., Waidner, M. (eds.) ESORICS 2021. LNCS, vol. 12972, pp. 651–667. Springer, Cham (2021). https://doi.org/10.1007/978-3-030-88418-5_31
8. Christ, M., Braun, N., Neuffer, J., Kempa-Liehr, A.W.: Time Series FeatuRe Extraction on basis of Scalable Hypothesis tests (tsfresh – A Python package). Neurocomputing **307**, 72–77 (2018). https://doi.org/10.1016/j.neucom.2018.03.067
9. Conti, M., Donadel, D., Poovendran, R., Turrin, F.: EVExchange: a relay attack on electric vehicle charging system. In: Atluri, V., Di Pietro, R., Jensen, C.D., Meng, W. (eds.) European Symposium on Research in Computer Security, pp. 488–508. Springer (2022). https://doi.org/10.1007/978-3-031-17140-6_24
10. Deloitte: Electric vehicles: setting a course for 2030 (2020). https://www2.deloitte.com/us/en/insights/focus/future-of-mobility/electric-vehicle-trends-2030.html
11. Gangwal, A., Jain, A., Conti, M., et al.: On the feasibility of profiling electric vehicles through charging data. In: Inaugural International Symposium on Vehicle Security & Privacy (2023)
12. Ghafouri, M., Kabir, E., Moussa, B., Assi, C.: Coordinated charging and discharging of electric vehicles: a new class of switching attacks. ACM Trans. Cyber-Phys. Syst. (TCPS) **6**(3), 1–26 (2022)
13. Gottumukkala, R., Merchant, R., Tauzin, A., Leon, K., Roche, A., Darby, P.: Cyber-physical system security of vehicle charging stations. In: 2019 IEEE Green Technologies Conference(GreenTech), pp. 1–5 (2019)
14. He, H., et al.: EVBattery: a large-scale electric vehicle dataset for battery health and capacity estimation. arXiv preprint arXiv:2201.12358 (2022)
15. Khalid, M.R., Khan, I.A., Hameed, S., Asghar, M., Ro, J.: A comprehensive review on structural topologies, power levels, energy storage systems, and standards for electric vehicle charging stations and their impacts on grid. IEEE Access **9**, 128069–128094 (2021)
16. Khan, O.G.M., El-Saadany, E., Youssef, A., Shaaban, M.: Impact of electric vehicles botnets on the power grid. In: 2019 IEEE Electrical Power and Energy Conference (EPEC), pp. 1–5. IEEE (2019)

17. Lee, Z.J., Johansson, D., Low, S.H.: ACN-Sim: an open-source simulator for data-driven electric vehicle charging research. 2019 IEEE International Conference on Communications, Control, and Computing Technologies for Smart Grids, Smart-GridComm 2019, pp. 411–412 (2019). https://doi.org/10.1109/SmartGridComm.2019.8909765
18. Lee, Z.J., Li, T., Low, S.H.: ACN-Data: analysis and applications of an open EV charging dataset. In: Proceedings of the Tenth ACM International Conference on Future Energy Systems, pp. 139–149. e-Energy 2019, Association for Computing Machinery, New York, NY, USA (2019)
19. Li, H., Dán, G., Nahrstedt, K.: Portunes+: privacy-preserving fast authentication for dynamic electric vehicle charging. IEEE Trans. Smart Grid 8(5), 2305–2313 (2016)
20. Lundberg, S.M., Lee, S.I.: A unified approach to interpreting model predictions. In: Guyon, I., Luxburg, U.V., Bengio, S., Wallach, H., Fergus, R., Vishwanathan, S., Garnett, R. (eds.) Advances in Neural Information Processing Systems 30, pp. 4765–4774. Curran Associates, Inc. (2017). http://papers.nips.cc/paper/7062-a-unified-approach-to-interpreting-model-predictions.pdf
21. Marchiori, F., Conti, M.: Your battery is a blast! Safeguarding against counterfeit batteries with authentication. In: Proceedings of the 2023 ACM SIGSAC Conference on Computer and Communications Security, pp. 105–119 (2023)
22. Marchiori, F., Conti, M.: Leaky batteries: a novel set of side-channel attacks on electric vehicles. arXiv preprint arXiv:2503.08956 (2025)
23. Mookherji, S., Odelu, V., Prasath, R.: Secure ultra fast authentication protocol for electric vehicle charging. Comput. Electr. Eng. 119, 109512 (2024)
24. Muhammad, Z., Anwar, Z., Saleem, B., Shahid, J.: Emerging cybersecurity and privacy threats to electric vehicles and their impact on human and environmental sustainability. Energies 16(3), 1113 (2023)
25. Mültin, M.: ISO 15118 as the enabler of vehicle-to-grid applications. In: 2018 International Conference of Electrical and Electronic Technologies for Automotive, pp. 1–6 (2018)
26. Nasr, T., Torabi, S., Bou-Harb, E., Fachkha, C., Assi, C.: ChargePrint: a framework for internet-scale discovery and security analysis of EV charging management systems. In: NDSS (2023)
27. Shen, W., Vo, T.T., Kapoor, A.: Charging algorithms of lithium-ion batteries: an overview. In: 2012 7th IEEE Conference on Industrial Electronics and Applications (ICIEA), pp. 1567–1572. IEEE (2012)
28. ThunderSky: Instruction manual for LFP/LCP/LMP lithium power battery. Tech. rep., Thunder Sky (2007)
29. United states secret service: ATM & POS skimming (2024). https://www.secretservice.gov/investigations/skimming
30. Unterweger, A., Knirsch, F., Engel, D., Musikhina, D., Alyousef, A., de Meer, H.: An analysis of privacy preservation in electric vehicle charging. Energy Inf. 5(1), 3 (2022)
31. Ye, J., et al.: Cyber-physical security of powertrain systems in modern electric vehicles: vulnerabilities, challenges, and future visions. IEEE J. Emerg. Sel. Top. Power Electron. 9(4), 4639–4657 (2020)
32. Zhang, H., Shu, Y., Cheng, P., Chen, J.: Privacy and performance trade-off in cyber-physical systems. IEEE Network 30(2), 62–66 (2016)
33. Zhang, J., et al.: Realistic fault detection of LI-ION battery via dynamical deep learning. Nat. Commun. 14(1), 5940 (2023)

ARCeR: An Agentic RAG for the Automated Definition of Cyber Ranges

Matteo Lupinacci[1], Francesco Blefari[1,2], Francesco Romeo[1,2],
Francesco Aurelio Pironti[1], and Angelo Furfaro[1(✉)]

[1] University of Calabria, Rende 87036, Italy
{matteo.lupinacci,francesco.blefari,francesco.romeo,francesco.pironti,
angelo.furfaro}@unical.it
[2] IMT School for Advenced Studies, Lucca 55100, Italy

Abstract. The growing and evolving landscape of cybersecurity threats necessitates the development of supporting tools and platforms that allow for the creation of realistic IT environments operating within virtual, controlled settings as Cyber Ranges (CRs). CRs can be exploited for analyzing vulnerabilities and experimenting with the effectiveness of devised countermeasures, as well as serving as training environments for building cyber security skills and abilities for IT operators. This paper proposes ARCeR as an innovative solution for the automatic definition and deployment of CRs, starting from user-provided descriptions in a natural language. ARCeR relies on the Agentic RAG paradigm, which allows it to fully exploit state-of-art AI technologies. Experimental results show that ARCeR is able to successfully process prompts even in cases that LLMs or basic RAG systems are not able to cope with. Furthermore, ARCeR is able to target any CR framework provided that specific knowledge is made available to it.

1 Introduction

In recent years, the increasing number of threats targeting IT systems has led to a significant focus in the cybersecurity research community on the development of Cyber Ranges (CR) as fundamental tools to train IT professionals in facing cyber threats and attacks. Typically, setting up a CR involves defining its infrastructure and software in a configuration file. A CR platform admin (such as cybersecurity instructors) has to manually design, build and deploy custom scenarios by writing these files, an activity which is both time consuming and prone-to-error. In addition, the complexity of building and maintaining real-world scenarios, both in enterprise and educational settings, is challenging.

This work was partially supported by the SERICS project (PE00000014) under the MUR National Recovery and Resilience Plan funded by the European Union - NextGenerationEU. The work of Francesco A. Pironti was supported by Agenzia per la cybersicurezza nazionale under the 2024–2025 funding program for promotion of XL cycle PhD research in cybersecurity (CUP H23C24000640005).

In the last few years, CR frameworks, as indicated in [1] and [2], have become a widespread solution in assisting the CR development life-cycle. Several frameworks have been proposed, each with distinct features and objectives, that mainly focus on one (or both) of the following two main aspects: (i) enhance the generation of increasingly sophisticated training *scenarios* that accurately reflect real-world threats and (ii) reduce the *time and resources* necessary for the configuration and execution of CR instances (see Sect. 5) by developing framework that provides the necessary infrastructure and establishes connections between machines according to a network topology without the intervention of the instructor.

The use of machine learning (ML) to improve and facilitate CR deployment is explored in [3]. Given a set of pre-existing VMs, this system uses ML to classify VMs and then select the one with the highest feature similarity according to the instructor requests thus reducing the cost of manual selection. The instructor needs to provide a YAML description of the virtual environment that is parsed to deploy the CR.

Among the more innovative approaches, the work by [4] stands out as the first to propose the application of LLM to the CR domain. Their approach transforms the well known and inherent in LLMs 'hallucination' problem into a potential advantage, allowing the creation of complex scenarios that push the boundaries of traditional cybersecurity training.

To the best of our knowledge, this is the first work which proposes the use of Large Language Models (LLMs) and Agentic Retrieval-Augmented Generation (Agentic RAG) [5] systems for the automated definition and deployment of training scenarios compatible with multiple CR platforms.

The devised approach aims to simplify this process by generating CR from natural language descriptions. The ability of Agentic RAGs to plan, use tools external to the LLM, dynamically adapt to responses from the environment, and perform multiple retrieval steps from external-supplied documents enables them to reduce the costs required for fine-tuning an LLM and adapt to multiple CR instantiation platforms.

Furthermore, the use of augmented knowledge empowers the agent to auto-generate valid and randomized CR configuration for a given CR platform. This represents a significant advance compared to previous works [3,4,6] that employed specific techniques for the automatic generation of randomized scenarios. In summary, the main contributions of this paper are:

- the proposal of a novel approach based on Agentic RAG systems for the automated instantiation of CR from natural language text descriptions of the infrastructure that is compatible with multiple CR platforms;
- the support for the autonomous generation of self-devised CR scenarios leveraging RAG systems;
- the design and implementation of ARCER, the first Agentic RAG system for CR definition and deployment (this tool will be made available open-source to foster future research in this area).

The effectiveness of ARCeR has been assessed by testing it with CyRIS [7] CR framework. It has been observed that while the generation of responses based on specific knowledge can generally be accomplished with a pure RAG system, employing an Agentic RAG can enhance the accuracy and integrity of the output while maintaining equivalent complexity.

The remainder of this paper is organized as follows. Section 2 provides the basic background on Cyber Ranges and (AI) Agents. Section 3 presents the proposed approach to the automatic definition and deployment of CR using Agentic RAG. Section 4 discusses the achieved results. Section 5 overviews the related works and Sect. 6 draws the conclusions.

2   Background

2.1   Cyber Ranges

The US National Institute of Standards and Technology (NIST) defines Cyber ranges as *interactive, simulated representations of an organization's local network, system, tools, and applications that are connected to a simulated Internet level environment* [8]. They offer trainees a legal, safe and controlled context for augmenting their cybersecurity skill set through hands-on activities (such as the real-time analysis frameworks for CRs as proposed in [9,10]). CRs are also utilized for the secure emulation and dynamic analysis of new real-world attacks and targeted-malware, where the execution of the malicious code is necessary to determine their purposes.

A CR comprises an IT infrastructure and a suite of selected security features. The infrastructure can include, but is not limited to, machines, networks, storage, and software tools. Security functionalities include the capability to replicate cyberattacks and execute malware in a controlled environment. The orchestration layer of the CR coordinates the diverse technology and service components of the underlying infrastructure and provides isolation from other resources on the host systems. This isolation enables the simulation of complex scenarios without compromising live production systems. A CR may also integrate a Learning Management System (LMS) that allows both instructors and trainees to track and measure progress through a defined training curriculum [11].

The utilization of CRs has undergone a substantial transition, with a shift from their initial adoption by military and government agencies to their current application by a wide array of businesses and organizations including bug-bounty hunters, researchers and students.

According to the NIST, there are four main categories of CRs: (i) simulations, (ii) overlay, (iii) emulation, and (iv) hybrid ranges. These distinctions assume particular significance when aligned with the specific use case of an individual or organization [12].

Simulations ranges entail the establishment of a synthetic network environment that simulates the behavior of real network components within virtual instances (VMs). VMs are used to mimic specific servers or network of various infrastructures. They offer the advantage of quick reconfiguration because they use standardized templates. However, the fidelity of the exercise increases as the simulation closely matches the target infrastructure.

Overlay ranges provide a higher level of fidelity as they directly utilize the actual network infrastructure. However, this increased fidelity comes with notable costs for hardware and the potential risk of compromising the underlying network infrastructure. This type of CRs are often established as global testbeds for research and experimentation.

Emulation is an approach to CR generation that transforms the physical infrastructure into the cyber range itself. It provides closed-network environments that consist of multiple interconnected components and includes traffic generation that emulates various protocols, source patterns, traffic flows and attacks. Emulation gives trainee the authentic experience, rather than pre-programmed actions. A notable example of the use of emulation in CR is the National Cyber Range (NCR) [13].

Hybrid ranges are formed through a customized combination of any of the previously mentioned types that suits specific requirements. A prominent example of Hybrid ranges is the *European Future Internet Research & Experimentation (FIRE)* project. [14]

2.2   Agents

An Agent [15] is defined as a computer system situated in an environment that is capable of acting autonomously in its context in order to reach its delegated objectives.

Autonomy means the ability and requirements to decide how to act to achieve a goal. An agent that can perceive its environment, react to changes that occur in it, take the initiative, and interact with other systems (like other agents or humans) is called an intelligent agent or *AI Agent* (Fig. 1). Another core concept of AI agents is the *memory*. Effective memory management improves an agent's ability to maintain context, learn from past experiences, and make more informed decisions over time.

As pointed out in [16], the emergence of LLMs represents another moment of progress in the realization of AI agents. The substantial advancements made in this direction have culminated in the emergence of *LLM agents*. In particular, LLM agents use LLMs as reasoning and planning cores to decide the control flow of an application while maintaining the characteristics of traditional AI agents. LLM agents enhanced the LLMs by allowing them to invoke external tools for solving specific tasks, such as mathematical calculations or code execution. In the end, the LLM can decide whether the generated answer is sufficient or if more work is needed.

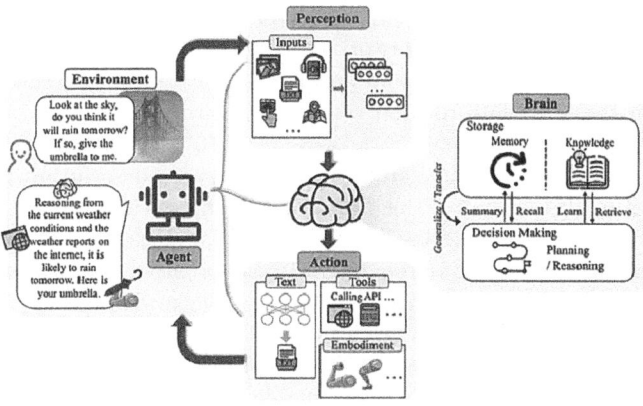

Fig. 1. AI agent structure [16]

2.3   Agentic RAG

Despite their flexibility, general purpose LLMs, and the related LLM agents, often lack the domain-specific knowledge required to solve particular and non-trivial tasks. Such a problem could be solved by re-training or fine-tuning the model; however, the cost of these operations is not negligible.

A possible alternative approach is based on the Retrieval-Augmented Generation (RAG) [17] paradigm where the LLM, in pursuing its goal, cooperates with two external components: (i) a source of domain-specific knowledge (i.e. external-supplied documents) and (ii) a *retriever* which is in charge to search for relevant information in the external knowledge base and to augment the context of the LLM. This operation provides the model what is needed to answer complex questions on specific topic not covered in the training dataset.

In RAG systems, external data are loaded and divided into chunks of the appropriate size. The chunks are then converted into vector representations and stored in data structures for future use. The functioning of a RAG system is typically structured as follows: (i) the user provides a query to the system; (ii) the retriever converts the query into a vector representation and performs a match with the stored embeddings, fetching the most relevant chunks; (iii) the original query is enhanced with the fetched chunks and passed to the LLM; (iv) the context-aware results produced by the LLM are returned to the user.

An agent system that takes advantage of the RAG paradigm is often referred to as *Agentic RAG*. Many state-of-the-art frameworks, such as LangChain [18], LlamaIndex [19], and Langdroid [20], provide easy-to-use interfaces to create custom Agentic RAGs.

3   ARCeR: **Agentic RAG for Cyber Ranges**

Traditional CR instantiation methods require manual configuration because CR platforms receive as input a *description file* containing information about the host running the range and the CR characteristics (e.g., the virtual machines that make up the range and the network topology) with the corresponding image files. Description files are written in specific formats such as YAML [21] and, depending on the CR platform and range specification, they can become very complex to write.

ARCeR leverages Agentic RAG systems to create description files from a high-level textual description of the desired specifications and then for automatic CRs deployment on remote servers. More in detail, ARCeR improves the user-friendliness of the instructor, who can effortlessly create a training environment by simply expressing the desired characteristics in natural language, without the need for concern for the underlying framework's specific syntax requirements. This feature makes CR management accessible to users with different levels of expertise. It allows effective use by enabling advanced attack and defense configurations, adjustable difficulty levels, and full infrastructure customization to meet specific training needs in a fully automated manner.

ARCeR automatically adapts to different CR framework simply by changing the set of documents provided as external knowledge. This ensures a high level of flexibility in that it removes any dependence to specific platforms. This means that alterations in the field, such as the introduction of new configuration patterns or support for novel scenarios, do not necessitate modifications to ARCeR logic. Only a revision of the reference documents is required, thereby facilitating maintenance and adaptation to emerging requirements.

Furthermore, by eliminating the need to fine-tune a model for each framework, ARCeR approach dramatically lowers computational and development costs, making CR generation more affordable, fast, and adaptable to heterogeneous scenarios. Finally, should more efficient LLMs emerge in the future, ARCeR can be upgraded without the need for a complete system rebuild. These characteristics make the Agentic RAG perfectly suited to the ever-changing context of CRs.

This work demonstrates (see Sect. 4) that, while pure RAG systems can indeed address the task of generating responses based on specific documentation with sufficient effectiveness, the Agentic RAG approach of ARCeR leads to enhanced performance.

3.1   ARCeR schema

The overall architecture and the operation of ARCeR are illustrated in Fig. 2. The Agentic RAG structure of ARCeR includes an LLM that operates as a reasoning engine and two external tools: a *RAG subsystem* and a *Checker Tool*. Despite the stateless characteristics of traditional AI agents, ARCeR has effective memory management, thereby conferring to the instructor the flexibility to modify CR features at a subsequent time based on previous interactions.

The *Checker Tool* allows ARCeR to check the generated output during runtime and to perform self-correction of errors if they occur.

The *RAG subsystem* is in charge of completing the retrieval phase of a RAG system using the Maximal Marginal Relevance [22] (MMR) technique, which aims to mitigate redundancy in the extracted chunks from the vector store. This is achieved by selecting the most relevant documents for the query, ensuring those that differ the most from each other, thereby providing the Agentic RAG with a substantial amount of relevant knowledge. Specifically, 20 chunks are initially extracted, and after filtration, only the 8 most relevant ones are transmitted to the LLM. To achieve an optimal balance between relevance and diversity, the specific parameter `lambda_mult` was set to 0.5 [22].

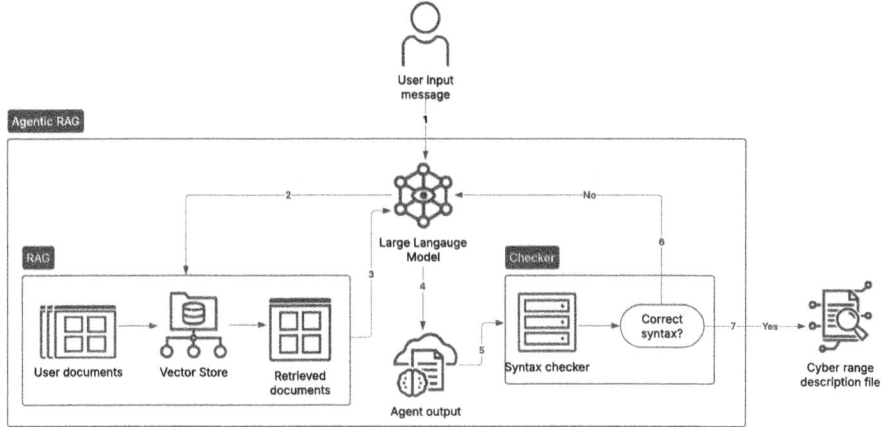

Fig. 2. Overall approach schema

Given ARCeR's support to interact with disparate CR frameworks it employs different vector stores to separately save the embeddings' chunks documents related to different platforms. All documents (e.g., framework usage guides and example configuration files) are stored in a database containing a folder whose name coincides with the name of the specific CR framework. The RAG subsystem exploits format-specific document loaders (e.g., for PDF and YAML) to import them.

In more detail, the steps performed by ARCeR are the following:

(1) The user prompt is fed to the LLM which parses it and evaluates whether it is able to handle it directly or if it needs to call an external tool. In the case it needs to resort to the RAG subsystem it produces a new specific query to be sent to the RAG subsystem. The RAG subsystem identifies the suitable vector store and then it searches for relevant chunks using the MMR technique. On the basis of the additional knowledge contained in these chunks, the LLM produces an initial potential output to the user's query.

(2) The output is sent to an external server that exposes an API to the CR platform component responsible for checking the syntax (and eventually the semantic) of the description file. The verification step is a critical component of the overall process as it ensures the integrity of the generated output.

(3) If the above step is successfully completed, the configuration file is created and subsequently returned to the user. In the event that errors are detected, they are automatically sent back to ARCeR for self-correction and the process starts again from step (1).
(4) At the end of the description file generation phase, ARCeR asks the user whether they want to proceed with the actual instantiation of the CR. If the user agrees, it directly executes the appropriate commands on the host running the CR framework.

3.2   Implementation Details

The current implementation of ARCeR uses Anthropic's *Claude 3.7 Sonnet* [23] as LLM and *Sentence Transformer Model* [24] as embeddings. For the embedding storage an *in-memory vector store* is used. The vector store is populated with chunks of the external-supplied documents of 1000 characters each with an overlap of 200 characters.

The choice of the LLM was made by comparing three different models as detailed in Sect. 4. The MMR metric was selected because it yielded better results with respect to the cosine similarity metric [25] initially used which frequently returned the same chunk multiple times, thereby diminishing the specific knowledge provided to the LLM.

ARCeR has been implemented by using LangChain [18], a framework for the development of applications powered by LLMs, and its extension Lang-Graph [26]. LangChain implements a standard interface not only for LLMs but also for related technologies, such as embedding models and vector stores of hundreds of providers. LangGraph models execution steps as edges and nodes in a graph. LangChain has been chosen because of its popularity in the scientific community and because of its powerful agent-creation libraries. Beyond agents with well-defined high-level interfaces, LangGraph also supports creating agents backed by a low-level, highly controllable API, enabling deep customization of agent logic.

By using the pre-built *ReAct agent constructor* we implemented the retrieval and generation steps of the *RAG* subsystem as a call to external tools. Document chunks, retrieved from the vector store, are incorporated into the message sequence sent to the LLM just as if they were messages obtained from invoking any other external tool. This approach offers the advantage that the model itself generates queries for the retrieval phase, rewriting user messages into more effective search queries. Furthermore, it fully automates direct responses that do not require a retrieval phase, such as responses to generic user greetings.

3.3   A Real Case Study: the CyRIS Framework

CyRIS (Cyber Range Instantiation System) [7] is an open-source tool that provides a flexible, scalable, and low-cost mechanism for managing security training environment. CyRIS supports KVM and AWS virtualization for several guest machines OS, including Ubuntu, CentOS and Windows. The CyRIS input file is structured as a YAML document, which is divided into three sections: `host_settings`, `guest_settings`, and `clone_settings`. It should be noted that CyRIS facilitates the deployment of CR instances to one or more host servers.

We chose CyRIS as CR instantiation framework because it is a platforms that can provide security features even at the CR description stage, such as: (i) traffic capture, (ii) perform attacks and malware emulation, (iii) configure firewall. The GitHub repository [27] is updated and maintained, making it easy to install and use. Moreover, it has a detailed documentation not only on the architecture of the framework, but also on the syntax and semantics to be used when writing configuration file. This aspect, together with the examples of description files already provided by the authors, is an excellent knowledge base for CR generation leveraging Agentic RAG.

The initial documents provided to ARCeR as external knowledge included the most recent version of the paper outlining CyRIS, its user guide, and six CR description files. Despite the adequacy of the documentation, an initial phase of manual document analysis was necessary to remove pages containing information irrelevant to the preparation of the description file. The pages removed included those describing the installation of CyRIS and those documenting performance analysis. To make ARCeR work with CyRIS, we used a total of 28 pages of documentation.

Notwithstanding the present limitations of CyRIS with regard to the supported security features, including the emulation of only a few types of attacks and malware, CyRIS emerged as an excellent framework for testing our approach.

4   Results and Discussion

In this section we evaluate the ARCeR coverage through different methodological strategies. First, a comparative analysis was conducted among the outputs generated: (i) by using only an LLM, (ii) through a RAG system, and (iii) by using ARCeR. The comparative assessment yielded significant discrepancies in accuracy, completeness, and contextual relevance across the three approaches.

Subsequently, we conducted both qualitative and quantitative analyses by generating 20 CR descriptions, of progressively increasing complexity, encompassing all CyRIS characteristics. This test enabled the measurement of the success rate of ARCeR across varying difficulty levels and configuration requirements, thereby providing robust evidence of the system's capabilities under diverse operational scenarios.

Additionally, we evaluated ARCeR's performance using various tool-calling LLMs from different providers: *Claude 3.7 Sonnet* from Anthropic, *Gpt-4o-mini* from OpenAI [28] and *Mistral Large* from Mistral AI [29]. All models successfully completed the task, despite the increasing complexity of the CR to be instantiated. However, minor discrepancies among the models were identified, which ultimately guided the selection of *Claude 3.7 Sonnet* as the primary LLM for ARCeR.

Table 1. Performance Comparison of System Configurations for CR Generation

Metric	Base LLM	RAG	ARCeR
Successful tests	0/10	6/10	10/10
Failure reasons	Lack of framework knowledge despite details provided	Incomplete user requirements Syntax errors	-
Key capabilities	-	Specific CR platform knowledge	RAG capabilities Error correction User interaction Self-devised CR scenarios generation
Main limitations	Ambiguous output Incorrect syntax Failure to meet requirements	Absence of output verification Limited human interaction Knowledge-base quality	Knowledge-base quality

4.1 LLM-Specific Constraints in CR Generation

In order to adequately interface an LLM asking for CR generation, some specific concerns have to be properly addressed. In particular, the amount of required details in the user prompt and the way external tools are invoked both are both specific to the employed LLM. The former concern can be easily resolved by specifying the additional information needed by the specific LLM in the system prompt, so that the user input can be kept as generic as possible. For example, in the case of Gpt-4o-mini, it was necessary to specify in the system prompt a message suggesting that the model first retrieve as much information as possible about the CR framework chosen by the user. In the case of Mistral-Large, it was necessary to specify that each section of the descriptor files for CyRIS begin with the character '-'. These specifications are instrumental in reducing the time required to generate the correct file, but more importantly, they prevent the LLM from performing superfluous computations, thus avoiding reaching the token limit.

The second concern regards the ability of the LLM to independently repeat multiple verification steps on the generated output taking into account the feedback of the checker tool. In contrast to the Anthropic and OpenAI models, which can perform this task autonomously, the Mistral AI model required the explicit implementation of a corresponding loop in its agent code.

4.2 ARCeR vs. LLM and vs. RAG

We carried out tests in three configurations: the base LLM, the RAG subsystem and the full system of ARCeR. Domain experts wrote textual descriptions of 10 low-complexity CR scenarios and submitted them to each of the three configurations. Then we collected, analyzed, and compared produced outputs. During the test involving only the base LLM, additional details regarding the CyRIS framework were explicitly provided to the model to ensure a fairer comparison. The results obtained are summarized in Table 1.

The analysis of LLMs outputs revealed a conspicuous deficiency in their capability to generate correct configuration files, despite the provision of detailed user inputs, making the base LLM incapable of performing the designated tasks. The generated output is often ambiguous and does not align with the specifications of the CR framework stipulated by the user. This outcome underscores the importance for equipping the base LLM with specialized knowledge about the CR framework.

The implementation of a system that is exclusively dependent on RAG signifies a substantial enhancement in the automated generation of description files within a designated CR framework. The integration of knowledge extracted from documents allows the model to produce output that is more closely aligned with the syntax required by the framework, reducing the indeterminacy typical of unconditional generative models. More in detail, in six out of ten tests, the pure RAG system correctly generated configuration files that conformed to both the framework syntax and the user-specified requirements. In the remaining four tests, the failure was attributed to two main factors: (1) incomplete or inaccurate user requirements, in one test, and (2) syntax errors, in the other three tests. In the first case, failures resulted from the user's omission of mandatory information essential for CR instantiation, such as the `entry_point` or the network `topology` attribute required by the CyRIS CR specification format. In the second case, the errors were caused by formatting issues, such as incorrect indentations in the generated output. These issues underscore the inherent limitation of using a pure RAG system. These limitations can be effectively mitigated through the use of Agentic RAG techniques, which introduce mechanisms to automatically verify and correct the LLM generated output at each step.

The Agentic RAG-based approach of ARCeR plays a crucial role in reducing the number of cases in which the system fails to meet user's requests. The LLM can interact directly with a remote server, thereby automatically launching the CR framework and requesting the CR instantiation based on the generated input file. Moreover, using the error messages returned by the framework, ARCeR successfully passed tests that had previously failed due to syntax errors. Furthermore, by leveraging the agent's capacity for iterative interaction with the user, a human-in-the-loop approach can be employed to address the test failed in case (1). In these situations, the agent could ask the user if the missing mandatory parameters should be automatically assigned according to reasonable criteria or if the user would prefer to specify them manually. Adding this interaction enabled the successful generation of a correct output also in this case.

4.3   Quantitative and Qualitative Analysis

In order to assess the current capabilities and limitations of ARCER, 20 textual descriptions of training scenarios, of increasing complexity, were manually written by domain experts. Such descriptions were used as prompts to ARCER requesting it to instantiate them on CyRIS. In writing these scenarios, the experts took care to include of all features supported by CyRIS-based CRs. This was done to evaluate ARCER in the context of different potential user requirements. Furthermore, at least 3 of these scenarios were purposely devised to include all the features supported by CyRIS, in order to evaluate the behavior of ARCER under the most complex descriptions.

The tests were carried out using the configuration described in Sect. 3 using basic subscription accounts to Claude 3.7 Sonnet. The evaluation process entailed a maximum of three retry attempts, with a test considered to be correctly completed if successfully passed within these bounds. Performance evaluation was conducted considering three main factors:

1. *Correct execution of the required task*: the ability to correctly complete the assigned task, which could consist solely of configuration file generation or even automatic deployment to a remote server.
2. *Number of iterations required for completion*: the number of iterations required to correct any errors in the intermediate output.
3. *Semantic validity of the generated output*: since the verification performed by CyRIS via tool calling ensures only the syntactic correctness of the generated file, domain experts manually checked the semantic consistency. They examined the configuration files and their instantiated CRs to determine whether the output was in accordance with the user's requests.

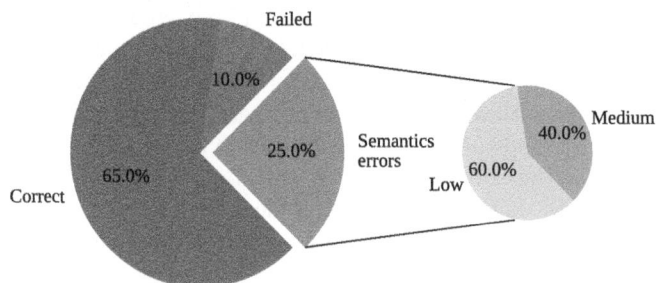

Fig. 3. Performance analysis

The results obtained are presented in Fig. 3. An in-depth analysis of the results yielded the following observations. Of the 18 tasks successfully completed by ARCER, only 4 instances were solved in one ARCER iteration (see Sect. 3.1 for more details about ARCER performed iterations). It should be noted that these 4 instances were the same that would have been correctly addressed also by the pure RAG configuration. For the other instances the initial output contained syntactic errors that necessitated agent iterations to be corrected, see Table 2.

These results corroborate the observations made in the preliminary study and further underscore the need for an Agentic RAG-based approach. Indeed, instances that were successfully completed on the initial attempt correspond to low-complexity scenarios, such as those used in the preliminary tests. However, as the complexity of the user request increased, a pure RAG system proved incapable of completing the task correctly. Of the 3 tests that included all CyRIS features, 2 were successfully completed. The failures observed in the remaining case was mainly due to the *token limit constraints* associated with LLM usage, which prevented the complete generation of the required configuration files.

Table 2. Summary of ARCeR test results

Test category	Count	Percentage (%)
Syntactic successfully tests	**18**	**90%**
Completed in one iteration	4	20%
Completed in two iterations	9	45%
Completed in three iterations	5	25%
Failed tests	**2**	**10%**
Total	20	100%

A secondary consideration pertains to the severity of the identified semantic errors. We identified three categories of errors as follows: (i) *High-Severity errors*: the generated configuration does not include all the virtual machines requested by the user and (or) all the physical hosts required for deployment; (ii) *Medium-Severity Errors*: failure in the emulation set up of important characteristics of the scenario such as attacks or malware emulation; (iii) *Low-Severity errors*: failures that result in the incorrect set up of non-relevant characteristics of the scenario such as alteration of the username on a VM or the failure to execute a program that is of marginal relevance to the scenario under investigation.

The analysis revealed that of the 5 tests in which domain experts detected semantic errors, none were of the highest severity, 2 errors were classified as medium-severe, while the others 3 had minimal impact. This substantiates the reliability of the employed approach (see Table 3).

In all the tests the semantic correctness of the output was evaluated just after the agent has completed the task within a maximum of three attempts. Nevertheless, it is important to highlight that any identified semantic errors could have been easily rectified by a user with basic familiarity with the CR platform. This can be accomplished through interaction with the agent, where the user can issue an additional request to correct the generated configuration. Such corrections are facilitated by the memory mechanism embedded within

ARCER architecture, which enables the system to maintain context and adapt to the user's requests.

Finally, a notable consideration is related to the distinctive feature of ARCER to autonomously conceive a simulation scenario and generate the corresponding configuration file without explicit user specification. Given a prompt requesting the creation of a CR based on a specific platform (e.g., CyRIS), ARCER was able to ideate a meaningful scenario, reasonably configure the virtual machines (e.g., installing appropriate programs and executing coherent scripts), and sensibly connect them within a network. This level of autonomy marks a significant advancement over previous approaches based on random scenario generation, offering platform-adapted outputs. An example of CyRIS-based CR defined and deployed using ARCER is shown in A.

Table 3. Completed tests with semantic errors

High severity errors	**0**
Medium severity errors	**2**
Completed in two iterations	1
Completed in three iterations	1
Low severity errors	**3**
Completed in two iterations	2
Completed in three iterations	1
Total	**5**

5   Related Work

Among the proposed CR systems, several have gained prominence. Nautilus [30] is a CR platform that provides a training environment along with a *marketplace* platform allowing to share scenarios, scripts or other pre-implemented vulnerabilities and CVEs. Nautilus leverages cloud technologies to semi-automate deployment of vulnerable systems. Furthermore, it provides a graphical interface to initialize/terminate a training scenario through a remote virtual console available in the Nautilus Web Interface. Real-life scenarios can be written either in a custom Scenario Definition Language or by using the web interface.

A novel lightweight framework for CR orchestration is CyExec* [6], a Docker based CR that encompasses a system that automatically generates multiple scenarios with the same learning objectives utilizing DAG (Directed Acyclic Graph)-based scenario randomization. It leverages container-type virtualization, which offers a lightweight execution environment to run multiple virtual instances efficiently and reducing overall costs using the power of dockerfiles and `docker-compose` for topology generation.

Further advancements in CR verification were introduced in [31], where the authors are the first to propose a method to formally verify the non-contradictory of the scenario. Their framework relies on the virtual scenario description language (VSDL), a domain-specific language for defining high-level features of the desired infrastructure while hiding low-level details. The VSDL specification is then converted into an SMT problem. If this problem is found to be satisfiable, a model is returned that can be used to create the infrastructure.

Despite these advances, many of the proposed solutions have proven viable only for specific CR frameworks for which they were designed. Therefore, ARCeR is the first Agentic RAG for the configuration and deployment of CRs compatible with multiple CR framework. This implies that ARCeR can be employed to generate CRs based on different frameworks, thus enabling instructors to leverage the specific advantages offered by each platform.

The present study is situated within the emerging body of research that explores the application of LLMs agents in the domain of cybersecurity. Specifically, our approach aligns with recent studies that leverage the reasoning and generation capabilities of LLM agents for threat intelligence, vulnerability detection, malware and anomaly detection, fuzz and program repair, LLM assisted attack and (in)secure code generation, as reported in [32]. In [33] the authors show that LLM agents can autonomously hack websites, performing tasks as complex as blind database schema extraction and SQL injections without human feedback and without the need to know the vulnerability beforehand. This capability is uniquely enabled by the use of the tool and leveraging the extended context. Similar is the work presented in [34] where the authors presented that LLM agents powered by GPT-4 can autonomously exploit one-day vulnerabilities in real-world systems given the CVE description.

The use of multi-agent systems for cybersecurity goals is explored using SecurityBot [35], a mechanism to enable effective collaboration between LLM agents and pre-trained RL agents that supports cybersecurity operations for red-team and blue-team tasks.

6   Conclusion and Future Works

In this work ARCeR has been presented as a Agentic RAG-based solution for the automatic definition and deployment of CR starting from a textual description, in a natural language, of the desired scenario. ARCeR is designed to be independent of any specific CR platform and can interact with different CR frameworks by simply adapting the set of documents provided as augmented knowledge to the RAG component. ARCeR ensures better performance compared to a pure RAG approach, while maintaining the same level of system complexity. Furthermore, ARCeR successfully completed the generation of 90% of the tested simulation scenarios, confirming the validity and effectiveness of the proposed approach.

The most relevant current limitation is that ARCeR cannot determine a priori whether the user's request is within the capabilities of the CR framework. To illustrate this point, consider the case of CyRIS. The system is unable to independently detect whether the user is requesting an unsupported network topology, such as a configuration other than the only one currently implemented bus topology. This failure can result in attempts to generate configuration files that can lead to subsequent failures during the CR instantiation phase. To address this challenge, a potential future development involves integrating a mechanism for prior validation of the user's request. This mechanism would be based on structured knowledge of the target framework, thereby enabling the agent to identify any inconsistencies prior to output generation. Following this identification, the agent would then communicate the inconsistencies to the user.

A further extension for future development involves enhancing the Agentic RAG to enable it to correct semantic errors within the generated configuration. This would provide a more comprehensive solution by allowing the system to autonomously address issues related to the configuration that do not adhere to the user's specifications. Another important direction is to test our approach using open-source LLMs, with the goal of identifying the model of the least dimensionality within a family of models that supports RAG interaction and tool invocation, yet is capable of correctly completing the tasks. This development aims to demonstrate that the Agentic RAG approach incurs minimal cost while maintaining optimal performance, further validating the efficiency and scalability of the system.

A   Appendix A: ARCER Execution Example

User Prompt

Create a CyRIS-based CR distributed over two physical hosts that use the user account "cyuser". The first use as management address "localhost" and communicates with guest VMs thorough the virtual bridge "192.168.122.1"; the second use as management address "172.16.5.2" and the virtual bridge "192.168.122.1". The CR is composed of 3 Ubuntu VMs whose KVM configuration file is "/cyris/basevm.xml." The first is named "desktop". Create a 'pcap' file '/home/traffic.pcap' containing traffic from a 'ddos' attack with low noise level. The second is 'attacker' and install the ping tool. The third is 'webserver' and runs the nginx program, installed via the package manager. Clone an instance of the environment on each physical host, each containing an instance of each guest VM. The "attacker" VM is the entry point of the CR. The network topology defines a segment called "virtual_lab" which includes all machines, each connected to its own network interface.

Tool Processing

Step 1: Knowledge retrieval for CyRIS file format
→ Tool Calls: `retrieval(query: "CyRIS cyber range description file format example")`
Step 2: Initial configuration generation
Step 3: Configuiration validation
→ Tool Calls: `verify_cyris_description_file(file_content)` Errors detected:

- Unknown tag 'interpreter' in guest_settings/tasks/install_package
- Missing 'topology' tag in clone_settings/hosts/guests
- Misplaced 'topology' section in clone_settings

Step 4: Error correction and re-validation
→ Tool Calls: `verify_cyris_description_file(file_content)` CORRECT CONFIG

Final Configuration

```
- host_settings:                          - id: webserver
  - id: host_1                              basevm_host: host_1
    mgmt_addr: localhost                    basevm_config_file: /cyris/basevm.xml
    virbr_addr: 192.168.122.1               basevm_type: kvm
    account: cyuser                         basevm_os_type: ubuntu
  - id: host_2                              tasks:
    mgmt_addr: 172.16.5.2                     - install_package:
    virbr_addr: 192.168.122.1                   - package_manager: apt-get
    account: cyuser                             name: nginx
- guest_settings:                       - clone_settings:
  - id: desktop                           - range_id: 1
    basevm_host: host_1                     hosts:
    basevm_config_file: /cyris/basevm.xml   - host_id: host_1, host_2
    basevm_type: kvm                          instance_number: 1
    basevm_os_type: ubuntu                    guests:
    tasks:                                      - guest_id: desktop
      - emulate_traffic_capture_file:             number: 1
        - format: pcap                          - guest_id: attacker
          file_name: /home/traffic.pcap           number: 1
          attack_type: ddos_attack                entry_point: true
          noise_level: low                      - guest_id: webserver
  - id: attacker                                  number: 1
    basevm_host: host_1                     topology:
    basevm_config_file: /cyris/basevm.xml   - type: custom
    basevm_type: kvm                          networks:
    basevm_os_type: ubuntu                    - name: virtual_lab
    tasks:                                      members: desktop.eth0,
      - install_package:                                 attacker.eth0,
        - package_manager: apt-get                       webserver.eth0
          name: iputils-ping
```

References

1. Grimaldi, A., Ribiollet, J., Nespoli, P., Garcia-Alfaro, J.: Toward next-generation cyber range: a comparative study of training platforms. In: Katsikas, S., et al. (eds.)Computer Security. ESORICS,: International Workshops. Springer Nature Switzerland, pp. 271–290 (2024). https://doi.org/10.1007/978-3-031-54129-2_16

2. Gustafsson, T., Almroth, J.: Cyber range automation overview with a case study of CRATE. In: LNCS, pp. 192–209. Springer International Publishing (2021). http://dx.doi.org/10.1007/978-3-030-70852-8_12

3. Zhou, S., et al.: Automating the deployment of cyber range with Openstack. Comput. J. **67**, 851–863 (2023). http://dx.doi.org/10.1093/comjnl/bxad024

4. Yamin, M.M., Hashmi, E., Ullah, M., Katt, B.: Applications of LLMs for generating cyber security exercise scenarios. IEEE Access **12**, 143806–143822 (2024)

5. Singh, A., Ehtesham, A., Kumar, S., Khoei, T.T.: Agentic retrieval-augmented generation: a survey on agentic rag. (2025). https://dx.doi.org/10.48550/ARXIV.2501.09136

6. Nakata, R., Otsuka, A.: Cyexec*: a high-performance container-based cyber range with scenario randomization. IEEE Access **9**, 109095–109114 (2021)

7. Beuran, R., Pham, C., Tang, D., Chinen, K.I., Tan, Y., Shinoda, Y.: Cybersecurity education and training support system: Cyris. IEICE Trans. Inf. Syst. **E101.D**(3), 740–749 (2018)

8. NIST: Cyber ranges (2018). https://www.nist.gov/system/files/documents/2018/02/13/cyber_ranges.pdf

9. Blefari, F., Pironti, F.A., Furfaro, A.: Toward a log-based anomaly detection system for cyber range platforms. In: ARES 2024 Association for Computing Machinery (2024). https://doi.org/10.1145/3664476.3669976

10. Romeo, F., Blefari, F., Pironti, F.A., Furfaro, A.: Unveiling attack patterns from CTF network logs with process mining techniques. In: (ITASEC & SERICS 2025) (2025)
11. Taylor, H.: What is a cyber range? Learn hands-on cybersecurity skills (2023). https://cybersecurityguide.org/resources/cyber-ranges/
12. NIST: The cyber range: a guide (2023). https://www.nist.gov/system/files/documents/2023/09/29/The%20Cyber%20Range_A%20Guide.pdf
13. Ferguson, B., Tall, A., Olsen, D.: National cyber range overview. In: IEEE Military Communications Conference, vol. 2014, pp. 123–128 (2014)
14. Gavras, A., Karila, A., Fdida, S., May, M., Potts, M.: Future internet research and experimentation. ACM SIGCOMM Comput. Commun. Rev. **37**, 89–92 (2007). http://dx.doi.org/10.1145/1273445.1273460
15. Wooldridge, M.: An Introduction to MultiAgent Systems, 2nd edn. Wiley (2009)
16. Xi, Z., et al.: The rise and potential of large language model based agents: a survey. Sci. China Inf. Sci. **68**, 121101:1–121101:44 (2025)
17. Lewis, P., et al.: Retrieval-augmented generation for knowledge-intensive NLP tasks. In: Advances in Neural Information Processing Systems (2020)
18. Chase, H.: Langchain (2022). https://github.com/langchain-ai/langchain
19. Liu, J.: Llamaindex (2022). https://github.com/jerryjliu/llama_index
20. Chalasani, P., Jha, S.: Langdroid. https://github.com/langroid/langroid
21. Ingy döt Net, C.E., Ben-Kiki, O.: YAML (2001). https://yaml.org/about.html
22. Goldstein, J., Carbonell, J.: Summarization: (1) using MMR for diversity-based reranking and (2) evaluating summaries. In: TIPSTER TEXT PROGRAM PHASE III: Proceedings of a Workshop held at Baltimore, Maryland, October 13-15, 1998. Association for Computational Linguistics, pp. 181–195 (1998). https://aclanthology.org/X98-1025/
23. Anthropic: Claude 3.7 sonnet system card (2025). https://assets.anthropic.com/m/785e231869ea8b3b/original/claude-3-7-sonnet-system-card.pdf
24. Reimers, N., Gurevych, I.: Sentence-BERT: sentence embeddings using Siamese BERT-networks. In: Proceedings of the 2019 Conference on Empirical Methods in Natural Language Processing. Association for Computational Linguistics (2019)
25. Steck, H., Ekanadham, C., Kallus, N.: Is cosine-similarity of embeddings really about similarity? In: Proceedings of WWW 2024: The ACM Web Conference 2024, pp. 887–890. ACM (2024)
26. Nuno, C., Vadym, B., William, F.: LangGraph. https://github.com/langchain-ai/langgraph
27. Beuran, R.: CYB3RLAB/CYRIS. https://github.com/cyb3rlab/cyris
28. GPT-4o system card (2024). https://arxiv.org/abs/2410.21276
29. Mistral AI team: Mistral large 2 (2024). https://mistral.ai/news/mistral-large-2407
30. Bernardinetti, G., Iafrate, S., Bianchi, G.: Nautilus: a tool for automated deployment and sharing of cyber range scenarios ARES21, pp. 1–7 (2021)
31. Costa, G., Russo, E., Armando, A.: Automating the generation of cyber range virtual scenarios with VSDL. arXiv preprint arXiv:2001.06681 (2020)
32. Zhang, J., et al.: When LLMs meet cybersecurity: a systematic literature review. Cybersecurity (2025). http://dx.doi.org/10.1186/s42400-025-00361-w
33. Fang, R., Bindu, R., Gupta, A., Zhan, Q., Kang, D.: LLM agents can autonomously hack websites. arXiv (2024). https://arxiv.org/abs/2402.06664
34. Fang, R., Bindu, R., Gupta, A., Kang, D.: LLM agents can autonomously exploit one-day vulnerabilities. arXiv preprint arXiv:2404.08144, 2024
35. Yan, Y., Zhang, Y., Huang, K.: Depending on yourself when you should: mentoring LLM with RL agents to become the master in cybersecurity games. arXiv preprint arXiv:2403.17674 (2024)

Edge Virtual Fence for Smart Airport Physical Security: A Case Study

Alberto Giaretta$^{(\boxtimes)}$ and Hadi Banaee

Department of Computer Science, Örebro University, Örebro, Sweden
{alberto.giaretta,hadi.banaee}@oru.se

Abstract. The growing digitisation of airport operations has paved the way for the smart airports of the future. One key challenge faced by smaller hubs is minimising the time spent by skilled operators on boring, repetitive tasks, and allowing them to be assigned to more critical duties. One such task is the monitoring of restricted areas to prevent unauthorized access by individuals, vehicles, or wildlife. This paper presents the design and deployment of an Edge-based virtual fence system at a Swedish regional airport, as a case study in implementing privacy-preserving and automated surveillance. Our system integrates off-the-shelf components, such as IP cameras and AI-powered Edge devices, to detect and respond to trespassing events. Furthermore, we analyse the system's robustness against potential cybersecurity and physical security threats and present our considerations regarding design choices and techniques for mitigating such threats.

Keywords: Virtual fence · Edge computing · Airport security · Privacy-preserving surveillance · AI-based surveillance

1 Introduction

Thanks to the latest technological improvements, many facilities face an increasing rate of modernisation and digitisation, ranging from warehouses to factories. Airports are no exception. Among other advancements, improvements in unmanned aerial vehicles (UAVs) and artificial intelligence (AI) are driving the transition from semi-automated to fully automated ones, also known as smart airports.

One of the critical duties that airport personnel must undertake is to monitor different areas to ensure physical safety and security. Passengers should not have access to limited zones within the airport, and wildlife should be kept away from the landing strips. In general, living beings should not trespass areas, both to prevent health hazards but also to prevent access to restricted areas (e.g., unauthorized personnel should not be able to step on conveyor belts to bypass locked doors).

To remain sustainable, small regional airports must operate on a limited amount of workforce, therefore employees are required to wear different hats

© The Author(s), under exclusive license to Springer Nature Switzerland AG 2025
B. Coppens et al. (Eds.): ARES 2025 Workshops, LNCS 15994, pp. 41–54, 2025.
https://doi.org/10.1007/978-3-032-00630-1_3

throughout their day-to-day duties. Many airports are already equipped with closed-circuit television (CCTV) cameras, but assigning one (or more) employees to the task of monitoring the cameras to detect suspicious activities is a costly investment. An investment that can be avoided by implementing virtual fences (also known as electronic fences), through the deployment of devices that allow for automatic detection of activities. With adequate recognition routines, virtual fences can be used for detecting unexpected trespassing, distinguishing between animals, people, and vehicles, as well as for data-driven ranking of areas according to likelihood of trespassing.

However, deploying new devices and algorithms to achieve virtual fences, comes with a cybersecurity price in terms of an enlarged attack surface. Whenever new technologies are added to previously existing systems, careful evaluations of cybersecurity consequences must be conducted, in particular in the case of highly critical environments like airports. Not only devices and algorithms should be chosen wisely, but they should also be configured following state-of-the-art policies and best practices. In particular, virtual fence architectures that rely on cameras must take into account individual users' privacy. Careful consideration should be given to all phases involving the use and manipulation of raw camera data, including acquisition, communication, elaboration, and storage.

In this paper, we report a real case study involving the deployment of an Edge-based virtual fence at a Swedish regional airport. Based on our experience and on previous literature, we report challenges and opportunities that arise from instantiating virtual fences in future smart airports. Last, we evaluate the robustness of our virtual fence system, for what it concerns its cybersecurity properties.

This paper is organised as follows. In Sect. 2, we provide an overview on the relevant research in the topic of virtual fencing. In Sect. 3, we propose a general architecture for implementing a virtual fence, discussing essential components and requirements, while in Sect. 4 and Sect. 5 we discuss the case study analysed in this paper, and how we have instanced the general architecture to fit the case study goals. In Sect. 6 we discuss the security properties and challenges that could be encountered, when implementing a virtual fence following our general architecture. Finally, in Sect. 7, we draw our conclusions.

2   Related Work

Virtual fence is a technology that has been previously studied in different contexts and applications. One prominent field of applications is free-ranging livestock management. The basic principle of virtual fencing consists in restraining living beings within defined boundaries or preventing access to restricted zones using different techniques for detecting, identifying, and deterring.

Umstatter [1] defines a virtual fence as a structure serving as an enclosure, a barrier, or a boundary without a physical barrier. Although Umstatter focuses her research on virtual fencing for livestock management, which is not the focus of this paper, she lays out an important take that transcends the field of application. Among other benefits, she highlights how virtual fencing is especially interesting, because it allows manual labour to be transformed into cognitive labour and improves employees' lifestyles. This benefit is particularly relevant for other applications, such as virtual fencing within smart airports. That being said, techniques used for livestock management require attaching sensors to animals, which is impractical for monitoring humans and wildlife in airport environments. Virtual fences for livestock management rely on the use of sensors (such as radio ear tags or GPS receivers) mounted on the animals. The spatial information output by these sensors is used to monitor their position with respect to the virtual fence, and deterring signals (such as electric stimuli or audio cues) are output. It is self-evident that such sensors cannot be mounted neither on human beings nor on the entire wildlife surrounding the area to monitor. For this reason, for the scope of this paper, we neglect the corpus of research that focuses on virtual fencing for cattle management. Instead, we focus on the literature work that replaces physically-mounted sensors with ambient sensors, in particular cameras.

Chen et al. [2] propose a virtual fence system for detecting trespassers in outdoor wide areas, composed of four main components. The first two modules are an IP video camera that transmits the images of an outdoor area, and a video analysis module that uses Gaussian Mixture Model (GMM) and AdaBoost for performing human detection. The last two are a communication module that transmits trespassing text messages to the assigned guards, and a human-computer interaction (HCI) module that allows the administrator to redefine the virtual fence by drawing on-screen a polygonal bounding region.

Yong et al. [3] developed a method that adopts stereo cameras for monitoring a zone and triggering an alarm in case of trespassing into the area. The authors, inspired by the binocular parallax characteristic of human vision, position two stereo cameras on the same horizontal axis and mimic human vision for extracting depth information. Their model consists of a preprocessing phase that extracts the background, followed by the actual foreground object detection.

Stewart et al. [4] noted that traditional cameras produce a large amount of data that must be transferred and processed for each and every frame. In their work, they describe the creation of Edge-based virtual fence devices, composed of a Raspberry P4B and a neuromorphic camera, also known as an event camera. Contrary to traditional ones, neuromorphic cameras only record the variation when light hits individual pixels. This allows to detect of new events ensuring low latency ($\sim 1ms$), fine-grained temporal resolution($\sim 1\mu$), and low bandwidth consumption. For reference, with equal resolution and FPS, a neuromorphic camera generates 99% less data than a regular camera for recording background information. Besides, the fact that a neuromorphic camera records events in the foreground against the background information, it requires considerably less processing. In their paper, the authors' goal is to identify Class-1 drones invading airspace, discerning such drones from other flying objects that might fly by, such as birds or thrown objects. Their experiments show that it is feasible to create a virtual fence by using a neuromorphic camera, showing that the total power consumption does not exceed $6.75W$. However, the authors note that current neuromorphic cameras deliver a fairly low resolution of 346×240 pixels, which restricts the maximum distance useful for detection up to $9m$. In a continuation study, Stewart et al. [5] switched to a higher resolution neuromorphic camera and introduced a neural network for increasing the recognition performance of the virtual fence system. Their experiments showed that the increased resolution allows for detecting objects at a higher distance, improving from $9m$ of their previous work to a maximum distance of $19m$.

Zhang et al. [6], starting from the observation that trespassing is the leading cause of railroad fatalities, highlight the need for an automatic detection of dangerous trespassing events. The paper proposes a framework that monitors potential trespassers at dangerous regions of interest (ROIs), using standard IP cameras, and utilises the You Only Look Once (YOLO) object detection algorithm for identifying the trespassers. Using the COCO object detection dataset for training their algorithm, the authors not only can detect trespassing events, but they can also classify the nature of the trespasser.

Huang et al. [7], using an Edge-computing camera and a network digital video recorder (NVR) for image storage, developed an Edge-based solution for monitoring ROI areas and trigger warnings in case of trespassing. Although less refined than Zhang et al. solution, Huang et al. system is capable of discerning between humans and other trespassers and, in the former case, triggering a warning and storing the snapshot of the trespassing event in the NVR.

Russomanno et al. [8] developed a method that relies on a set of active near-IR sensors, deployed as a sparse vertical array, for creating an electronic fence. Their proof-of-concept, which uses a classification algorithm based on the Mahalanobis distance, shows that the technology has the capability of detecting (and discriminating among) humans, animals, and vehicles. Although the use of near-IR sensors allows the system to be privacy-preserving, their placement at ground level increases the likelihood for the system to face physical tampering.

3   General Architecture and Requirements

To deploy a generic virtual fence system, it is trivial to infer that two main components are essential: a field sensor, and a computing device for data processing and user visualisation. However, such a system requires transmitting raw data from the sensor to the computing device, usually located in a remote control room. It also requires storing raw data within the server, at least for as long as the processing phase requires the data.

In the case of a virtual fence that uses cameras and, at the same time, strives to preserve users' privacy, a fundamental requirement must be fulfilled: raw image data should not leave the Edge environment where it is captured. Therefore, it is necessary to decouple the visualisation and storage phases from the preprocessing phase. This can be achieved by enriching the system architecture with an additional Edge machine, entrusted with data aggregation and processing tasks.

In the architectural diagram in Fig. 1, we show a general model that can be used as a blueprint for deploying a virtual fence. On the top left figure of this

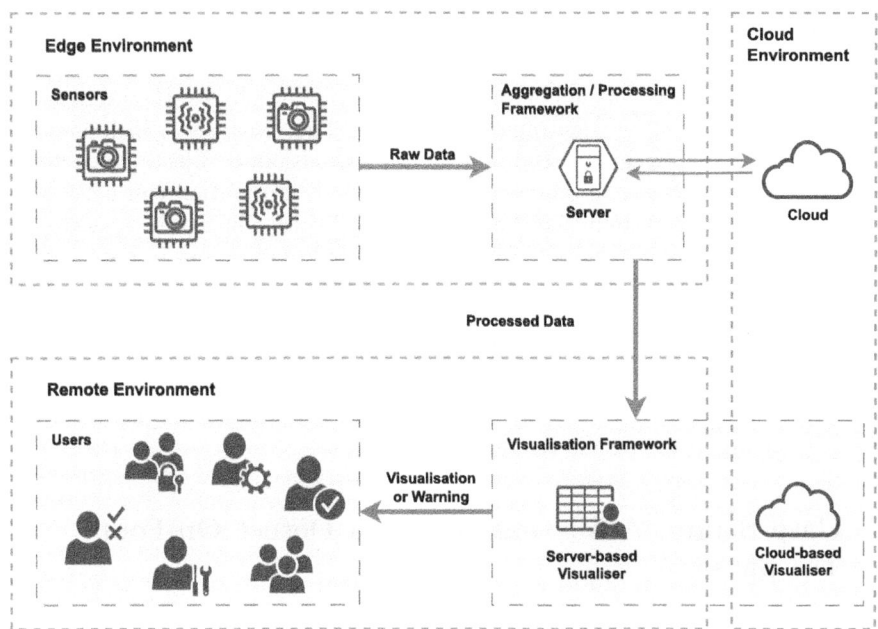

Fig. 1. General architectural diagram for developing Edge-based virtual fences. The light grey boxes represent the physical environments: the area where the virtual fence camera is deployed and the control room where the visualisation computer sits. In light blue, the devices that compose the architecture (e.g., sensors and Edge devices). In the Aggregation/Processing Framework, the raw data preprocessing can be either performed only by a local server, or preprocessed by the server (to enforce privacy) and refined by a Cloud service. In the Visualisation Framework, the visualiser could be either hosted locally, or on the Cloud. (Color figure online)

architecture, at the Edge environment, we have the field sensors that could be of different nature (e.g., cameras, NFC sensors) and used in cooperation for achieving a heterogeneous infrastructure. The raw data collected by these devices is then passed to the processing framework, where it is elaborated by the Edge server and processed to detect the object's positions, trajectories, and velocity. To ensure a functional virtual fence that allows users to visualise relevant information, the processed data should provide three components. First, the nature of the detected object (e.g., a vehicle or a person). Second, the trajectory of the object, is necessary to understand whether it is entering or leaving the virtually-fenced area. Third, the speed of the object, to detect dangerous situations, such as a reckless driver. We envision the possibility of relying on Cloud services, to offload part of the processing loads and keep under control the costs of acquiring a powerful Edge server. However, to satisfy our requirement for a privacy-preserving architecture, raw data cannot be computed directly by the Cloud and a minimal Edge server is required. This server transforms the raw data into anonymised data, which can be later processed by the Cloud service to elaborate (or refine) objects' trajectories. After the Cloud processing, the data is sent back to the Edge server.

Once that the data has undergone all the processing phases, the Edge server forwards this information to a remote visualiser. The visualiser, which could be either server-based or cloud-based, allows users to visualise objects' trajectories in an intuitive interface. In addition, the processed information can be used to automate a warning system that, based on a set of rules, alarms the operators of trespassing events. For example, if no vehicles should be present in a pedestrian area, the system can be programmed to trigger a warning at any time a vehicle enters the virtual fence area. This makes it possible for the system to operate in total autonomy, without requiring a human operator to monitor the visualiser.

In the next section, we discuss a real case study that shows how using this general architecture, it is possible to implement a virtual fence instance and tweak it according to specific requirements.

4   Case Study: A Virtual Fence to Detect On-Foot Trespassers

The case study airport, is a Swedish regional airport and a critical cargo flight hub, located in the centre of Sweden. Being a local regional airport, the number of employees is limited, and the staff must cover different roles throughout the day, depending on the arrivals and departures timetable. To guarantee people's safety, the airport has the necessity to monitor the runway area and prevent anyone from trespassing the safety zone. Given the limited availability of staff, dedicating an employee to this passive (and admittedly boring) task is a waste of human resources. A virtual fence could allow the airport to automate the task and free up precious time.

The airport staff identified a particular area of the airport, enclosed between two buildings, that yields a high risk of trespassing. Based on the assessment, we have defined with the staff an imaginary safety line that forms the basis for our case study virtual fence.

In Fig. 2, we highlight the components of the virtual fence: the red trapezoid represents the area that we continuously monitor with our deployed system, and the purple line marks the virtual line that triggers the trespassing warnings. The goal is to develop and implement a system that monitors the red trapezoid area without any human supervision. Moreover, the system must be able to discern between pedestrians and vehicles and trigger the warning only in case pedestrians cross the purple virtual line. In case of vehicles crossing the line, no warnings should be triggered. This is justified by the fact that only service vehicles are allowed in the airport, and these vehicles must cross the line multiple

Fig. 2. Top: Aerial view of the monitored area showing the virtual fence implementation zone (red trapezoid) and the security boundary line (purple), as defined in the system design. Bottom: Ground-level camera point of view of the same area, illustrating the physical environment corresponding to the fenced zone. (Color figure online)

times a day to perform authorized duties. Pedestrian traffic across this line is restricted because it typically indicates unauthorized access or a security protocol deviation. At the same time, there is the possibility, albeit small, for walking visitors to sneak around the airport.

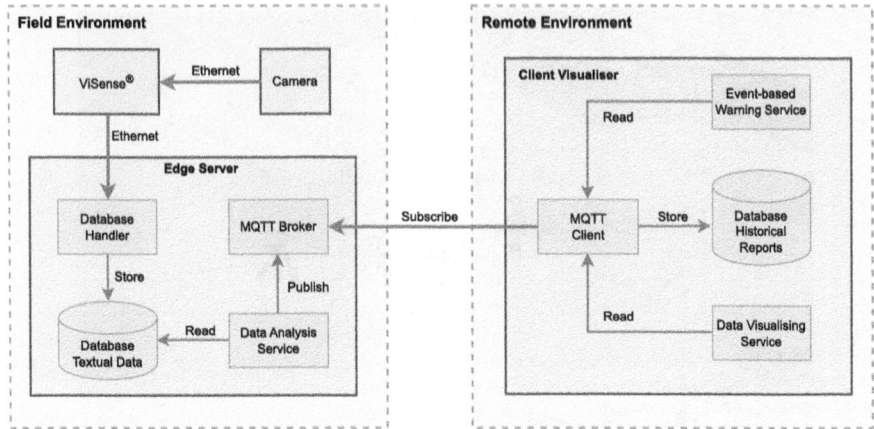

Fig. 3. System architecture diagram of the virtual fence deployed in our project. The light grey boxes represent the physical environments: the area where the virtual fence camera is deployed and the control room where the visualisation computer sits. In light blue, the devices that compose the architecture (e.g., sensors and Edge devices). In light orange, are the services that the different devices host and offer. (Color figure online)

5   Implementation

In this section, we present the architectural design and the implementation choices we have taken for developing and deploying our virtual fence. To demonstrate that building virtual fences and reaping their many benefits can be easy and intuitive, a first important requirement for our system is to rely solely on off-the-shelf components. A second requirement is that the system should be privacy-preserving, limiting the amount of information that could be leaked. Therefore, we opt for an Edge-based architecture that does not rely on a central server to collect and analyse data, but rather performs the analysis at the Edge node. We show the resulting architecture in Fig. 3.

To implement the architecture, we selected the following components. For the camera, an AXIS M42 IP Camera [9] is powered via a power-over-Ethernet (PoE) switch. For analysing the images, we chose the ViSense® from ViNotion [10], a device that takes as input camera images, applies machine learning algorithms, and outputs textual information that includes object type (e.g., discerning vehicles from pedestrians), speed, and positions. The textual information is collected in a mini computer that sits locally at the Edge, and every device is connected via Ethernet using a generic router.

Beyond collecting data, the mini computer has the task of analysing the textual information received as input from the ViSense, defining the perimeter that constitutes the virtual fence, triggering trespassing events, and collecting historical logs. Last, the mini computer is connected to a secure wireless network; sitting in one of the airport's control rooms, a remote computer communicates with the minicomputer on the same secure wireless network. The Edge mini computer transfers the data analysis results to the remote computer using Mosquitto a widely used MQTT broker, which facilitates communication between Edge devices and the remote computer. The system preserves privacy by processing all video data at the edge, extracting only object type and trajectory information, without storing or transmitting personally identifiable visual data.

The data analysis service will retrieve the types and positions of all objects in the scene continuously (about 6 positions per object per second), and construct the trajectory of the object. Then, in a real-time analysis of such trajectories, the service will identify whether the present objects are humans or not, along with detecting their direction of movement. In case any of the trajectories approach the virtual fens, the alarm detection system will trigger a warning and mark the trajectory as a potentially hazardous action violating the security zone. In the real world, based on predefined security rules, this procedure can be used to identify e.g. a passenger took a wrong path towards an unauthorised area of the airport.

Besides the real-time event-based warnings and alarm detection, the service also analyses historical data. The model uses AI-based methods to determine the patterns in the recorded trajectories and recognises the typical behaviour of the objects. In this way, the service is able to detect abnormal trajectories in real-time as well. Note that the detected anomalies do not necessarily indicate a security breach, but they provide useful insights for the end user to monitor suspicious or potentially dangerous behaviours. For example, assume there is a gas station in one corner of the trapezoid and the data analysis shows that *normally there are trajectories towards this station during the day*. Then, if the service observes *an object moving towards the station at midnight*, then it annotates the object's trajectory as abnormal behaviour and triggers a warning.

After the data analysis service processes trajectories and detects potential security violations, this information is transmitted to the remote environment using the MQTT protocol. A Streamlit-based web application handles visualization and monitoring, offering a simple and interactive interface for real-time updates.

Streamlit was chosen for its ability to rapidly develop interactive applications with minimal code. The application continuously subscribes to the MQTT broker running on the Edge server, receiving live updates on detected objects, their trajectories, and security violations. The interface presents a dynamic map view of the monitored area, marking the virtual fence boundary and overlaying real-time trajectories. Pedestrian and vehicle paths are colour-coded, with automatic alerts highlighting trespassing incidents.

Figure 4 illustrates the visualization interface, where the trapezoid monitoring area is shown with the virtual fence boundary (orange lines). Vehicle trajectories appear in blue, pedestrian paths in red, and trespassing events trigger alerts for immediate attention. This streamlined approach enhances situational awareness while minimizing operator workload.

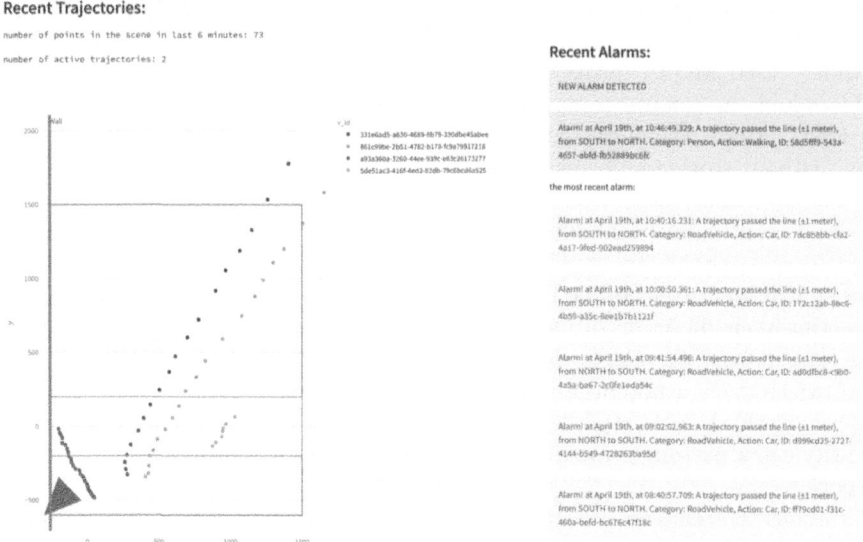

Fig. 4. Real-time visualization interface of the monitored area, including virtual fence boundaries and detected trajectories, with trespassing alerts.

6 Security Properties and Challenges

In this section, first, we describe a set of basic assumptions that circumscribe the system operations. Then, we provide a threat model that considers the architecture we designed and its potential weak points, encompassing cybersecurity and physical security aspects. Finally, using this model, we discuss possible directions to explore, for tackling the identified challenges.

6.1 Model Assumptions

For the scope of this paper, we establish the following assumptions:

- The Edge devices (i.e., the ViSense and the Edge computer) are considered trustworthy, operate in an isolated subnetwork, and perform their operations as expected;
- Cameras are semi-trustworthy, meaning that they transmit the video data reliably, but are vulnerable to physical tampering that could alter what appears in their field of view;
- Information exchanged between devices is encrypted and cannot be read or altered by an attacker.

6.2 Threat Model

Most architectures are not immune to cybersecurity weaknesses, and ours is no exception. Let us refer to the architectural diagram previously described in Fig. 3. We assume that a malicious cyber-attacker can perform the following actions:

– Reach and communicate with the client in the Remote environment;
– Observe and interfere with the communication channel established between the Edge environment and the Remote environment.

With regard to the physical security of our virtual fence, we consider that a malicious physical attacker can:

– Obstruct totally or partially the camera;
– Attempt to hide or disguise themselves, to prevent detection.

6.3 Cyber-Physical Security Challenges

Based on the threat model previously defined, we envision a few strategies that a malicious attacker could use, in an attempt to compromise or elude our virtual fence. We also mention possible strategies to mitigate these risks.

DDoS Attacks. Among the classical attacks that can be struck against an IT system, we have distributed denial-of-service (DDoS) attacks. In our architecture, a malicious party could try to impede our operations by overwhelming the services. For example, they could DDoS the communication channel between the processing server in the Edge environment and the visualiser in the Remote environment, creating critical communication delays between the MQTT Broker and the MQTT Client. This would result, in practice, in the visualiser not receiving any trajectory data from the processing server. Although various strategies exist for mitigating DDoS attacks, many open challenges still exist and no definitive solution is available [11].

Replay Attacks and Man-in-the-Middle Attacks. As aforementioned, we assume that the data exchanged between devices is encrypted, in such a way that a third party cannot read nor modify the information. However, different encryption strategies achieve different results. MQTT provides users with a functionality named *payload encryption*, where only the content of the message is encrypted, while the metadata is available in plain text. Payload encryption finds uses in situations where Transport Layer Security (TLS) cannot be used, due to its high demand for resources: for example, TLS over MQTT has been shown to use 4 times the energy of plain MQTT communication [12]. However, while TLS protects communications from replay and Man-in-the-Middle (MitM) attacks, MQTT payload encryption does not offer the same assurances.

Let us take as an example a replay attack against MQTT payload encryption. An attacker could eavesdrop on the MQTT communications between the processing server and the visualiser during the night, when none is around, hence when cameras do not register any trajectory. During the day, the attacker could intercept and drop the legitimate messages, substituting them with the messages recorded during the night. This would result in the visualiser receiving no trajectories at all (i.e., a correct representation of what happened during the night), allowing trespassers to freely roam in the virtual fence area. This is possible because MQTT payload encryption, unlike TLS, has no mechanism to verify packet sequence legitimacy. Even if the payload of the message is encrypted, the attacker does not need to read it or tamper with it. The attacker just knows that the packet sequence represents the camera recording during the night, when (most certainly) no trajectories were detected, and that is enough for the attack to succeed. To avoid replay and MitM attacks, where possible, TLS should be enabled on every connection, included MQTT ones.

Concealing Behind Other Objects. Broadly speaking, we could define the act of concealing themselves behind other moving objects as a physical attack against a virtual fence. For example, a trespasser could pass through the virtual fence by walking behind a work vehicle. By interposing the moving vehicle between themselves and the camera, the trespasser trajectory would not be perceived and registered. Although this does not affect directly the camera, nor any other device, we can consider it a physical attack, as it renders useless the purpose of the virtual fencing system. A simple solution to mitigate this issue would be to install multiple cameras for covering various angles, but that might not be enough.

A technical solution could be offered by object anchoring techniques, which allow keeping track of occluded object. For example, Persson et al. [13] proposed an anchoring matching function that maintains object entities in space and time, and integrates a probabilistic object tracker that tracks occluded objects through probabilistic reasoning. Once an object has been detected by the camera, the framework is capable of distinguishing whether the object left the camera field of vision or it is occluded behind another object. Clearly, the technique cannot handle situations in which an object was occluded before entering the field of vision and never shows on camera. However, it can handle any scenario in which, at any given point, an object appears in the field of vision, and help strengthen the virtual fence resilience to concealing scenarios.

7   Conclusions

In this paper, we have discussed the design, implementation, and deployment of an Edge-based virtual fence system as a practical implementation that contributes to the ongoing digitalization of airport operations. Our system automates the detection of unauthorized access, minimizing the reliance on human operators, and ensuring both privacy and safety. By leveraging off-the-shelf AI-based hardware, the virtual fence system offers an efficient, scalable, and privacy-conscious solution for regional airports with limited resources.

Our analysis highlighted the importance of robust architectural choices, including localized data processing and secure communication protocols, to safeguard against cybersecurity threats such as replay and DDoS attacks. Additionally, we explored physical security challenges, such as the risk of trespassers concealing behind objects, and we proposed mitigations such as probabilistic object tracking.

This case study demonstrates how virtual fences can provide efficient security monitoring in specific airport zones, potentially serving as one component in comprehensive smart airport security systems. At the same time, our paper highlights that the adoption of such systems requires careful consideration of security, privacy, and adaptability to evolving operational demands.

Acknowledgment. This work has been partially supported by Sweden's Innovation Agency (Vinnova), as part of the project System of Autonomous Airport Systems - The Future for the Cargo Airports (2022-02678), and by the Wallenberg AI, Autonomous Systems and Software Program (WASP) funded by the Knut and Alice Wallenberg Foundation.

References

1. Umstatter, C.: The evolution of virtual fences: a review. Comput. Electron. Agri. **75**(1), 10–22 (2011). https://www.sciencedirect.com/science/article/pii/S0168169910001997
2. Chen, J.H., Tseng, T.H., Lai, C.L., Hsieh, S.T.: An intelligent virtual fence security system for the detection of people invading. In: 2012 9th International Conference on Ubiquitous Intelligence and Computing and 9th International Conference on Autonomic and Trusted Computing, pp. 786–791 (2012)
3. Yong, Y.S., Hon, H.W., Osman, Y.S., Chan, C.H., Then, S.J., Chau, S.W.: Virtual fence for a surveillance system. In: Köppen, M., Kasabov, N., Coghill, G. (eds.) ICONIP 2008. LNCS, vol. 5507, pp. 808–815. Springer, Heidelberg (2009). https://doi.org/10.1007/978-3-642-03040-6_99
4. Stewart, T., Drouin, M.A., Gagne, G., Godin, G.: Drone virtual fence using a neuromorphic camera. In: International Conference on Neuromorphic Systems 2021, ser. ICONS 2021. New York, NY, USA: Association for Computing Machinery (2021). https://doi.org/10.1145/3477145.3477264
5. Stewart, T., Drouin, M.A., Picard, M., Djupkep Dizeu, F.B., Orth, A., Gagné, G.: A virtual fence for drones: efficiently detecting propeller blades with a DVXplorer event camera. In: Proceedings of the International Conference on Neuromorphic Systems 2022 ICONS 2022. New York, NY, USA: Association for Computing Machinery (2022). https://doi.org/10.1145/3546790.3546800
6. Zhang, Z., Zaman, A., Xu, J., Liu, X.: Artificial intelligence-aided railroad trespassing detection and data analytics: methodology and a case study. Accident Anal. Prevention **168**, 106594 (2022). https://www.sciencedirect.com/science/article/pii/S0001457522000306
7. Huang, W., Wang, C.-S., Chang, Y.-F., Yeh, C.-M., Lin, J.: An electronic fence application in in mass rapid transit station scenarios with the edge-Computing approach. In: 2020 IEEE 2nd Eurasia Conference on Biomedical Engineering, Healthcare and Sustainability (ECBIOS), pp. 119–121 (2020)

8. Russomanno, D.J., Chari, S., Jacobs, E.L., Halford, C.: Near-IR sparse detector sensor for intelligent electronic fence applications. IEEE Sens. J. **10**(6), 1106–1107 (2010)
9. AXIS M42 Dome Camera Series. https://www.axis.com/products/axis-m42-series. Accessed 07 Jan 2025
10. ViSense®for urban crowds and traffic, intelligent video interpretation at the edge. https://vinotion.com/urban-crowds-and-traffic/visense/. Accessed on 07 Jan 2025
11. Hoque, N., Bhattacharyya, D.K., Kalita, J.K.: Botnet in DDOS attacks: trends and challenges. IEEE Commun. Surv. Tutorials **17**(4), 2242–2270 (2015)
12. Paris, I., Habaebi, M.H., Zyoud, A.M.: Implementation of SSL/TLS security with MQTT protocol in IoT environment. Wireless Pers. Commun. **132**(1), 163–182 (2023)
13. Persson, A., Zuidberg Dos Martires, P., De Raedt, L., Loutfi, A.: Semantic relational object tracking. IEEE Trans. Cognit. Dev. Syst. **12**(1), 84–97 (2020)

Evaluating Explanation Quality in X-IDS Using Feature Alignment Metrics

Mohammed Alquliti$^{(\boxtimes)}$ [ID], Erisa Karafili [ID], and BooJoong Kang [ID]

School of Electronics and Computer Science, University of Southampton,
Southampton, UK
{M.H.Alquliti,E.Karafili,B.Kang}@soton.ac.uk

Abstract. Explainable artificial intelligence (XAI) methods have become increasingly important in the context of explainable intrusion detection systems (X-IDSs) for improving the interpretability and trust-worthiness of X-IDSs. However, existing evaluation approaches for XAI focus on model-specific properties such as fidelity and simplicity, and neglect whether the explanation content is meaningful or useful within the application domain. In this paper, we introduce new evaluation metrics measuring the quality of explanations from X-IDSs. The metrics aim at quantifying how well explanations are aligned with predefined feature sets that can be identified from domain-specific knowledge bases. Such alignment with these knowledge bases enables explanations to reflect domain knowledge and enables meaningful and actionable insights for security analysts. In our evaluation, we demonstrate the use of the proposed metrics to evaluate the quality of explanations from X-IDSs. The experimental results show that the proposed metrics can offer meaningful differences in explanation quality across X-IDSs and attack types, and assess how well X-IDS explanations reflect known domain knowledge. In cases where explanations consistently show weak alignment, this may point to limitations in the current domain knowledge used for evaluation. The findings of the proposed metrics provide actionable insights for security analysts to improve the interpretability of X-IDS in practical settings.

Keywords: Explainability · XAI · Explanation Evaluation · IDS

1 Introduction

Nowadays, cyber threats continuously increase in complexity to evade intrusion detection systems (IDSs). This has led to the use of machine learning-based intrusion detection systems (ML-IDSs). ML-IDSs have shown potential in improving detection capabilities by analysing and adapting to complex patterns and anomalies in network traffic [3]. Despite their advantages, many ML-IDSs act as black boxes and lack transparency in explaining the reasoning why detected activities are deemed suspicious [3,20,28]. This leaves security analysts, and consequently subsequent response mechanisms, with insufficient information about detected

B. Coppens et al. (Eds.): ARES 2025 Workshops, LNCS 15994, pp. 55–72, 2025.
https://doi.org/10.1007/978-3-032-00630-1_4

suspicious activities. This problem requires explainable IDSs (X-IDSs) that combine ML-IDSs with explainable AI (XAI) methods [15]. Several recent studies have begun to integrate XAI methods into IDS frameworks to enhance transparency and trustworthiness [1,3,14–17,19,21,22,26,27]. In practice, common XAI methods such as local interpretable model-agnostic explanations (LIME) [5] and Shapley additive explanations (SHAP) [12] can highlight which network flow features have most influenced the prediction of ML-IDSs.

As XAI methods are increasingly applied to X-IDSs, evaluating the quality of explanations becomes critical, since analysts rely on clear and understandable explanations to make decisions effectively [17]. There have been XAI evaluation methods focusing on generic properties, such as how well it mimics the model's behaviour (fidelity) [2], or how concise it is (simplicity) [11]. However, there has been a lack of research on developing evaluation methods focusing on the quality of explanations in the domain-specific context. As a result, current evaluation methods do not account for whether an explanation aligns with domain expectations or highlights indicators of known attack patterns [17,20].

To address this gap, we propose new evaluation metrics that assess the quality of explanations in the cybersecurity context, more specifically, X-IDSs. The aim of the proposed metrics is to quantitatively evaluate how well explanations capture domain-informed features that support the analyst's understanding of the detected attack. They are based on comparing the top-k features identified in an explanation with a predefined set of domain-informed features that are considered important to detect a specific type of attack. These sets are used by our metrics to assess whether the X-IDS is highlighting the features that matter most from a cybersecurity perspective. The proposed metrics are: Feature Alignment Precision (FAP), Feature Alignment Recall (FAR), and Feature Alignment F1 (FAF1). In essence, these metrics measure the alignment between the explanation of an X-IDS and the domain-informed features of an attack derived from cybersecurity knowledge domain resources. The FAP measures the proportion of an explanation top features that are relevant according to domain knowledge. The FAR measures the proportion of the domain-informed features that the explanation of an X-IDS managed to capture. The FAF1 provides a balanced single measure of explanation quality in terms of domain alignment.

To evaluate these metrics, we applied them to explanations generated by three X-IDSs: Random Forest (RF) [1], Deep Neural Network (DNN) [1], and Convolutional Neural Network with Bidirectional Long Short-Term Memory (CNN-BiLSTM) [25]. These models were selected to reflect a diverse range of architectures commonly used in intrusion detection, from traditional ensemble methods to deep learning. All models were trained on the CICIDS2017 benchmark intrusion detection dataset [23]. The goal of the evaluation was to determine how well each explanation aligned with domain-informed feature sets across different types of attacks. We assessed alignment at three levels of evaluation: instance level (individual explanations), attack class level (aggregated by attack type), and dataset level (overall performance across all examples). Our findings show that explanation quality varies across models and attack types. For example, the DNN and CNN-BiLSTM achieved higher FAP and FAR at lower values of k. This suggests that these X-IDSs are more effective at identifying most of the domain-informed features earlier in the explanation process. These results show that the proposed metrics can effectively distinguish explanation quality across X-IDSs and assess whether an X-IDS highlights the features that matter most for the detection.

In the remainder of this paper, we start with an overview of the related work on X-IDS in Sect. 2. In Sect. 3, we present our methodology, where each metric is introduced along with its calculation and evaluation. In Sect. 4, we present our experimental setup and results to illustrate how our metrics reveal differences in explanation quality across various X-IDSs. We conclude the paper and discuss future potential research directions in Sect. 5.

2   Related Work

In this section, we review prior work in three foundational areas. First, we examine X-IDS, focusing on the nature of their explanations and the need for interpretability for end-users like security analysts. Second, we explore how frameworks such as MITRE ATT&CK and D3FEND contextualise security tasks. Finally, we summarise recent methods for evaluating explanation quality in XAI, highlighting the lack of metrics addressing alignment with domain knowledge.

2.1   Explainable Intrusion Detection Systems

Recently, a growing emphasis has been placed on the need for XAI methods to provide explanations tailored to end-users, rather than solely interpretable by developers and researchers. In [15], authors argue that many XAI methods produce low-level explanations, typically in the form of numerical feature importance vectors. These low-level explanations are useful for developers and researchers to understand the internal behaviour of models. However, they lack the contextual interpretation needed for end-users (e.g., security analysts). In contrast, high-level explanations aim to relate model outputs to broader security concepts, such as known attack tactics or behaviours, making them more accessible to security analysts. Such explanations provide the contextual clarity and actionable insights that security analysts need. For example, [9] presents Auto-Encoder (AE)-pvalues, an explanation method for unsupervised network IDSs that identifies abnormal network traffic using autoencoder-based anomaly scores. However, the explanations remain low-level as they highlight numerical deviations in features without indicating their operational relevance. The authors of [9] indicate that this limitation is derived from factors such as high feature correlations, dataset biases, and the model's focus on individual network connections without contextual information about expected values. Similarly, [24] presents an explainable Deep Learning (DL)-based IDS aimed at enhancing the transparency and robustness of DL-based IDSs. This solution applies SHAP and LIME techniques to generate low-level explanations in the form of numerical

feature importance vectors, supporting analysts in the following steps or processes. As these studies [9,15,24] highlight that low-level explanations may not
be meaningful to security analysts, this limitation highlights the lack of alignment between explanations and the domain-specific knowledge that analysts rely
on during investigations. To address this, [24] emphasised the necessity of collaborative efforts in advancing XAI to communicate results effectively to non-AI
experts. Furthermore, incorporating domain-specific knowledge into XAI methods is crucial for improving model interpretability and elevating explanations to
high-level and actionable insights [28]. Additionally, based on [28], it is essential
to go beyond mere identification of feature importance and pursue conceptual-
level explanations by incorporating domain-specific knowledge. Existing work
demonstrates the need for explanations to reflect such domain knowledge. Our
work builds on this foundation by introducing metrics to evaluate how well
explanations, produced by SHAP, align with domain-specific knowledge.

2.2   Domain Knowledge Frameworks

As high-level explanations are needed, standardised domain-specific knowledge
bases to encode domain expertise are increasingly leveraged. For example,
MITRE ATT&CK can help to contextualise the IDS outputs. The MITRE
ATT&CK matrix serves as a repository of tactics and techniques [4,13]. Mapping
the IDS detections to these known tactics and techniques can make explanations
more actionable for security analysts. Arreche et al. [1] recently demonstrated
this approach by referencing network attack classes with relevant ATT&CK
tactic and technique for IDs. For instance, Denial of Service (DoS) attack in
CICIDS2017 dataset can be labelled as Network Denial of Service [MITRE
ATT&CK ID: T1498]. This alignment allows an IDS to explain alerts in terms
of the existing offensive techniques in MITRE. This approach can bridge the
gap between low-level features and high-level detection explanations. Similarly,
the idea of linking IDS detections to MITRE ATT&CK is becoming popular,
e.g., [18] uses automation to label network IDS signatures with the appropriate MITRE ATT&CK tactics and techniques. This approach ensures that alerts
generated by these rules include an explanation of the adversarial technique. Furthermore, MITRE D3FEND offers a complementary knowledge base of defensive
techniques and countermeasures [7]. It provides and links defensive actions to the
ATT&CK techniques they mitigate, enabling the definition of domain-informed
features based on established knowledge. Our proposed explanation evaluation
metrics assess how well the most influential features identified by an X-IDS correspond to these domain-informed features.

2.3   Evaluation of Explanations

Evaluating the quality of explanations from XAI methods has been addressed
through qualitative approaches, typically through human-centred studies [22,29].
However, many surveys note that formal evaluation for explanation quality is
frequently assumed or judged rather than measured [16,22,29]. Despite the lack

of generalised accepted metrics to evaluate XAI approaches, qualitative metrics have the potential to ultimately establish a standardised and quantified means of evaluation [6,21,22]. In [6], the authors provided a set of five distinct properties for evaluation: *faithfulness, robustness, localisation, randomisation*, and *complexity*. Properties like faithfulness (e.g., how the model's influencing features truly affect its explanation changes) and robustness (e.g., how stable a model's explanation remains with minimal changes to input) focus merely on the XAI method behaviour. In IDS context, [1] presented an end-to-end framework for evaluating both global and local explanations using SHAP and LIME, and defines six metrics for explanation quality, i.e., descriptive accuracy/fidelity, efficiency, stability, sparsity, robustness, and completeness. The metrics used in [10] are closer to our work as they compare the identified features of the XAI method to a ground truth of important features. [10] provides a score similar to precision-recall, but lacks the division between correctness and completeness.

The above metrics do not explicitly verify whether explanations align with domain-specific knowledge, particularly in the IDS context. To address this gap, we introduce formally defined metrics, namely *FAP, FAR*, and *FAF1*. In our related experiments, we compare outputs of the explanation method using these metrics and analyse the alignment at various levels (per instance, per attack class, and across the entire dataset).

3   Methodology

This section introduces the proposed evaluation metrics that assess the quality of explanations produced by X-IDSs. These X-IDSs utilise ML/DL-based IDS models with post hoc explanation techniques, such as LIME and SHAP, which identify the reasoning behind a model's predictions by highlighting the most influential features, as illustrated in Fig. 1. We check how well the most influential features align with domain-specific knowledge. Our proposed metrics evaluate this alignment by comparing the explanations of the model against predefined sets of domain-informed features for specific attack classes.

To use our evaluation metrics, we require predefined sets of domain-informed features for each attack class. These feature sets capture domain knowledge and can be derived from domain-specific knowledge bases, expert knowledge, or security frameworks. In this work, we use feature sets derived from the MITRE ATT&CK and D3FEND frameworks as a representative example. The procedure used to construct these sets is described in the experimental setup (Sect. 4.1).

3.1   System Model

This section formalises the structure of an X-IDS used in our work by defining the components involved in generating and evaluating explanations, including the dataset, prediction model, explanation method, and the reference feature sets used to assess explanation relevance.

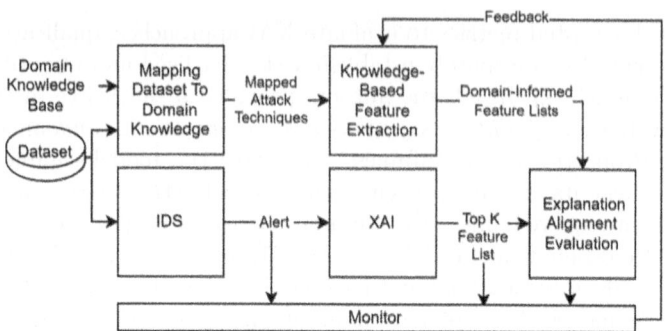

Fig. 1. High-level overview of the explanation evaluation process.

Let $\mathcal{D}$ denote the dataset used for training an ML-IDS. Each instance $d \in \mathcal{D}$ is defined as $d = \{f_1, f_2, \ldots, f_n, c\}$ where $f_1, f_2, \ldots, f_n$ are the features of the instance (e.g., the characteristics of a network traffic record), and c is the class assigned to the instance (e.g., a specific attack type or benign). Here, we denote the feature vector of an instance d as $x = \{f_1, f_2, \ldots, f_n\}$, and let $\mathcal{X}$ be the set of all feature vectors in the dataset and let $\mathcal{C}$ be the set of all corresponding classes. For training and evaluation, let $\mathcal{X}^{\text{train}} \subseteq \mathcal{X}$ and $\mathcal{X}^{\text{test}} \subseteq \mathcal{X}$ denote the disjoint training and testing sets, respectively. The corresponding classes denoted as $\mathcal{C}^{\text{train}} \subseteq \mathcal{C}$ and $\mathcal{C}^{\text{test}} \subseteq \mathcal{C}$.

A classifier f learns a mapping from feature vectors to corresponding classes, denoted as $f : \mathcal{X} \rightarrow \mathcal{C}$. A classifier f is trained on the feature vectors in $\mathcal{X}^{\text{train}}$ and corresponding classes in $\mathcal{C}^{\text{train}}$. Once trained, the classifier produces predictions $f(x) = \hat{c}$ for the feature vector of an instance $x \in \mathcal{X}^{\text{test}}$, where $\hat{c}$ is the predicted class. Also, let $\mathcal{C}^{\text{attack}} \subseteq \mathcal{C}$ denote the set of all attack classes considered for evaluation, excluding the benign class.

To make the prediction $\hat{c}$ interpretable, an XAI method is applied. An XAI method $g(f, x) = E_x$ takes a trained classifier f and a feature vector of an instance $x \in \mathcal{X}$ and returns an ordered set of features E_x that most influenced the classifier's prediction for instance x. The features in E_x are ordered by their importance scores, which reflect how much each feature contributed to the model's decision. An X-IDS often select the top-k features from E_x denoted as $E_x(k)$ where $E_x(k) \subseteq E_x$.

3.2   Explanation Evaluation Metrics

This section introduces our evaluation metrics used to evaluate the quality of the explanations produced by X-IDSs. These evaluation metrics quantify how well explanations of an X-IDS correspond to the domain-informed feature sets defined by security domain knowledge. The FAP metric measures the fraction of the top-k most influential features that are relevant to the sets of domain-informed features defined by security domain knowledge. In other words, it counts how many of the top-k features from the explanation are present in predefined sets of domain-informed features. The FAR metric measures the fraction of the domain-informed features that are present in the top-k features produced by the X-IDS. It measures how well the explanation covers the critical indicators identified by security domain knowledge. The FAF1 metric offers a balanced overall score that captures both the correctness and the completeness of the explanations.

In evaluating the quality of the explanations, the set of top-k features $E_x(k)$ is compared against a set of domain-informed features associated with the predicted class. Let F_c denote the set of domain-informed features that are associated with a class $c \in C^{\text{attack}}$. These feature sets must be predefined and can be derived from structured cybersecurity knowledge bases, expert input, or relevant examples. They are used as a reference to assess how well the explanation $E_x(k)$ aligns with domain knowledge. Comparing $E_x(k)$ and F_c enables the computation of our proposed evaluation metrics.

Each metric can be evaluated at three different levels: instance, class, and dataset levels. First is the instance level, which focuses on a single instance x. Second is the class level, which considers subsets of test instances that share the same label c, denoted as $\mathcal{X}_c^{\text{test}} \subseteq \mathcal{X}^{\text{test}}$. Lastly, the dataset level evaluation uses all instances in the test set, denoted by $\mathcal{X}^{\text{test}}$.

Our methodology evaluates the quality of $E_x(k)$, the explanation for instance x, by computing against F_c, the set of domain-informed features for the true class c. This comparison enables us to assess how well the model's explanation aligns with domain-informed indicators. Below, we formally define the key concepts and present how each of our evaluation metrics is calculated.

Feature Alignment Precision

FAP measures the correctness of the explanation of an X-IDS according to a set of domain-informed features. It quantifies how many of the top-k features selected by the explanation method are also present in the reference set of domain-informed features for a given attack class. We define this metric at the instance, class, and dataset levels.

The *instance-level FAP* captures how well the explanation for an individual feature vector of an instance x aligns with the domain-informed features expected for its true class c. It is defined as:

$$\text{FAP}_I(x, k) = \frac{|E_x(k) \cap F_c|}{|E_x(k)|} \tag{1}$$

where $E_x(k)$ is the set of top-k features produced by the explanation method for the feature vector of an instance x, and F_c is the set of domain-informed features corresponding to class c. A higher $\text{FAP}_I(x, k)$ value indicates that a greater proportion of the selected features are relevant, which suggest better explanation quality for that instance.

The *class-level FAP* evaluates explanation correctness within a specific class label for more detailed scores. It is computed as the average instance-level FAP across all test samples belonging to a class c:

$$\mathrm{FAP}_C(c, k) = \frac{1}{|\mathcal{X}_c^{\mathrm{test}}|} \sum_{x \in \mathcal{X}_c^{\mathrm{test}}} \mathrm{FAP}_I(x, k) \tag{2}$$

where k is the specified number of top features, $\mathcal{X}_c^{\mathrm{test}}$ the set of test instances correctly predicted as the class c, and $\mathrm{FAP}_I(x, k)$ is the instance-level FAP.

The *dataset-level FAP* provides a high-level overview of the explanation quality across all attack classes for the evaluated X-IDS. This FAP value provides a single overall number across the entire dataset's performance, excluding benign traffic. It is computed as the average of class-level FAP scores over all classes used in the evaluation:

$$\mathrm{FAP}_D(k) = \frac{1}{|\mathcal{C}^{\mathrm{attack}}|} \sum_{c \in \mathcal{C}^{\mathrm{attack}}} \mathrm{FAP}_C(c, k) \tag{3}$$

where k is the specified number of top features, $\mathcal{C}^{\mathrm{attack}}$ denotes the set of classes considered for evaluation. Each $\mathrm{FAP}_C(c, k)$ is the average precision for class c.

Feature Alignment Recall

FAR measures how many of a set of domain-informed features are captured in the produced explanations. It reflects the completeness of the produced top-k in covering the set of domain-informed features. Similarly to FAP, FAR is computed at the instance, class, and dataset levels.

The *instance-level FAR* for the feature vector of an instance x with the correctly predicted as the class c is computed as:

$$\mathrm{FAR}_I(x, k) = \frac{|E_x(k) \cap F_c|}{|F_c|} \tag{4}$$

where $E_x(k)$ is the top-k features from the XAI method for the feature vector of instance x, and F_c the domain-informed features for true class c. A higher $\mathrm{FAR}_I(x, k)$ indicates better completeness of the explanation for that instance.

The *class-level FAR* is calculated by averaging the instance-level $\mathrm{FAR}_I(x, k)$ over all test instances that belong to a specific class c:

$$\mathrm{FAR}_C(c, k) = \frac{1}{|\mathcal{X}_c^{\mathrm{test}}|} \sum_{x \in \mathcal{X}_c^{\mathrm{test}}} \mathrm{FAR}_I(x, k) \tag{5}$$

where $\mathcal{X}_c^{\mathrm{test}}$ is the subset of test instances that are correctly predicted as the class c.

The *dataset-level FAR* provides a high-level overview of how well explanations cover the domain-informed feature sets across all attack classes. It is computed as the average of class-level FAR scores as follows:

$$\mathrm{FAR}_D(k) = \frac{1}{|\mathcal{C}^{\mathrm{attack}}|} \sum_{c \in \mathcal{C}^{\mathrm{attack}}} \mathrm{FAR}_C(c, k) \tag{6}$$

where k is the specified number of top features, and $\mathcal{C}^{\text{attack}}$ is the set of classes included in the evaluation.

Feature Alignment F1

Similar to the traditional F1-score in classification, FAF1 reflects a harmonic mean of FAP and FAR into a single score. FAF1 provides a balanced measure that captures both the correctness and the completeness of the top-k explanations. We define this metric at the instance, class, and dataset levels.

The *instance-level FAF1* is computed as the harmonic mean of instance-level FAP and FAR for each feature vector of instance x:

$$\text{FAF1}_I(x, k) = \frac{2 \cdot |E_x(k) \cap F_c|}{|E_x(k)| + |F_c|} \tag{7}$$

where $E_x(k)$ is the set of top-k features produced by the XAI method for the feature vector of instance x, and F_c is the domain-informed feature set for its class c. A high $\text{FAF1}_I(x, k)$ score indicates that the explanation captures a greater proportion of the domain-informed feature set while minimising the inclusion of irrelevant ones.

The *class-level FAF1* is defined as the average instance-level FAF1 across all test instances with class c defined below.

$$\text{FAF1}_C(c, k) = \frac{1}{|\mathcal{X}_c^{\text{test}}|} \sum_{x \in \mathcal{X}_c^{\text{test}}} \text{FAF1}_I(x, k) \tag{8}$$

The *dataset-level FAF1* aggregates the class-level FAF1 scores over all attack classes as follows:

$$\text{FAF1}_D(k) = \frac{1}{|\mathcal{C}^{\text{attack}}|} \sum_{c \in \mathcal{C}^{\text{attack}}} \text{FAF1}_C(c, k) \tag{9}$$

where k is the specified number of top features, $\mathcal{C}^{\text{attack}}$ denotes the set of evaluated classes, and $\text{FAF1}_C(y, k)$ is the class-level FAF1 for class c.

3.3   Perspectives of Our Explanation Evaluation Metrics

Although we use the terms "precision", "recall" and "F1" in our metrics (e.g., Eqs. 1-9), their interpretation differs from the conventional precision, recall, and F1 that are used in standard classification tasks. In standard classification, precision measures the proportion of correctly classified instances among all predicted positives, while recall measures the proportion of correctly classified instances among all true positives. In contrast, our *explanation evaluation* metrics assess the quality of explanations by comparing the top-k most influential features E_x produced by an XAI method to a set of domain-informed features F_c. Rather than evaluating correctness at the instance level, our metrics evaluate correctness and completeness at the feature level. In other words, our metrics focus on whether the explanation highlights features that align with the domain-informed feature set. A high FAP means that most of the features selected by the model belong to the set of domain-informed features E_x, while a high FAR means we are capturing most of the domain-informed features that matter.

4 Evaluation

The evaluation aims to measure how well explanations generated by X-IDSs align with domain-specific knowledge bases in the intrusion detection context. In this section, we present the details of our evaluation process and results. In the experimental setup, we introduce the derivation of the domain-informed feature sets using the MITRE ATT&CK and D3FEND frameworks [4,7]. We continue by explaining the dataset, ML-IDS, and XAI method used in the evaluation. Finally, we analyse the experimental results from comparing the most influential features of each model against the domain-informed feature sets using our evaluation metrics at different levels.

4.1 Experimental Setup

Our evaluation includes two key components: (1) generating domain-informed feature sets that reflect what should be relevant for each attack type, and (2) extracting the top-k features from the explanations that was generated by X-IDS to compare and assess them against the domain-informed feature sets.

To construct the domain-informed feature sets, we mapped each attack class in the dataset to its corresponding offensive techniques in the MITRE ATT&CK framework. The identified techniques were linked to defensive tactics in MITRE D3FEND to derive domain-informed feature sets. In particular, we focused on the detect tactics, which outline specific indicators that security analysts can use to identify malicious behaviour. We enriched these sets by using contextual ATT&CK resources, such as detection recommendations, mitigation strategies, and real-world examples, to enhance feature extraction per attack. The derived feature sets were used as the domain-specific knowledge to evaluate the quality of the explanations generated by the X-IDS. While we rely on this process to produce domain-informed feature sets, the primary aim of this study is not to propose a new derivation method, but rather to evaluate the effectiveness of our explanation metrics using these sets as a baseline.

To evaluate the metrics, our experiments are based on the CICIDS2017 benchmark intrusion detection dataset [23]. A balanced subset was extracted using undersampling [8] to mitigate the impact of class imbalance. This prepro-cessed dataset was used to train three ML/DL-IDSs:RF and DNN [1], and a hybrid CNN-BiLSTM architecture [25]. RF was selected as a traditional, inter-pretable model that performs robustly and can be easily explained using feature-based methods, while DNN was chosen as a strong deep learning baseline that offers higher detection accuracy but requires post hoc explanation due to its complexity. The CNN-BiLSTM model was included as it combines convolutional and bidirectional LSTM layers to capture both spatial and temporal patterns in network traffic. These models demonstrated robust and consistent detection capabilities across attack classes in their original studies [1,25].

All three used ML/DL-IDS are followed by an XAI method, SHAP, for the explainability part [1]. SHAP is a post hoc model-agnostic ML explainability approach that can be used after the AI models and assigns to each feature a score that represents the feature contribution to the reached prediction [12]. We used the generated explanations against the domain-informed feature sets using the proposed explanation evaluation metrics presented in Sect. 3.2.

4.2   Experimental Results

The performance of the explanation evaluation metrics is evaluated on three X-IDS (RF and DNN [1], and CNN-BiLSTM [25]). We assess how well their explanations align with domain-informed features derived from MITRE frameworks. In particular, we generated SHAP explanations for each model's prediction on the test set and compared the top-k features of the explanations to the MITRE-based feature sets for the corresponding attack class. The evaluation is performed at multiple levels (instance level, class level, and dataset level) to provide a comprehensive view of the explanations' quality. We introduce in Table 1 and Fig. 2 each model's overall alignment performance on the full dataset. The results provide a direct comparison of how well explanations aligned with domain-informed feature sets. We provide FAP, FAR, and FAF1 values for each model under varying k-values (number of top influential features considered). Different values of k allow us to examine the model's explanation alignment when considering concise or extensive feature sets from the XAI method.

Table 1. The dataset level explanation evaluation metrics (FAP, FAR, FAF1) for RF, DNN, and CNN-BiLSTM X-IDSs, evaluated across varying top-k values.

Top-k	RF [1]			DNN [1]			CNN-BiLSTM [25]		
	FAP	FAR	FAF1	FAP	FAR	FAF1	FAP	FAR	FAF1
5	0.09	0.04	0.06	0.30	0.18	0.23	0.17	0.09	0.12
10	0.07	0.06	0.07	0.23	0.25	0.24	0.16	0.16	0.16
20	0.09	0.25	0.13	0.21	0.44	0.28	0.18	0.35	0.24
40	0.11	0.63	0.19	0.17	0.70	0.27	0.20	0.82	0.32

Dataset Level Explanation Evaluation Results: We compute the dataset-level evaluation metrics: FAP, FAR, and FAF1, by averaging across all attack classes in the evaluation in order to provide a single overall measure. This measure represents the quality of the explanation for each X-IDS at each k. As shown in Table 1, the DNN and CNN-BiLSTM X-IDSs have consistently higher alignment scores across k values compared to the RF X-IDS. This indicates that the explanations of the deep learning X-IDS (DNN and CNN-BiLSTM) are more aligned with the domain-informed features than the RF X-IDS. For example, at a small cutoff number of features $k = 5$, the DNN reaches a FAP of 0.30, where RF is 0.09. This means that 30% of the top features in DNN are relevant to the attack according to the set of domain-informed features, while only 9% for the RF features. Similarly, FAR at $k = 5$ shows that DNN is quicker in covering more of the domain-informed features (0.18) compared to RF, which covers 0.04 of the expected features. The CNN-BiLSTM also outperforms RF at $k = 5$ (FAP 0.17, FAR 0.09), but not to the extent of DNN. Furthermore, we notice that the DNN X-IDS provides the highest alignment at smaller k, while the CNN-BiLSTM reaches DNN when k grows larger, as illustrated in Fig. 2. The DNN achieves the highest FAF1 score at $k = 5$ and 10 (0.23 and 0.24), compared to CNN (0.12 and 0.16) and RF (0.06 and 0.07). This indicates that with fewer top influential features from the XAI method, the DNN X-IDS can identify critical domain-informed features that provide a more balanced combination of correctness (FAP) and completeness (FAR). This can provide a practical value as security analysts can utilise quick and accurate insights based on the most influential features in a model prediction.

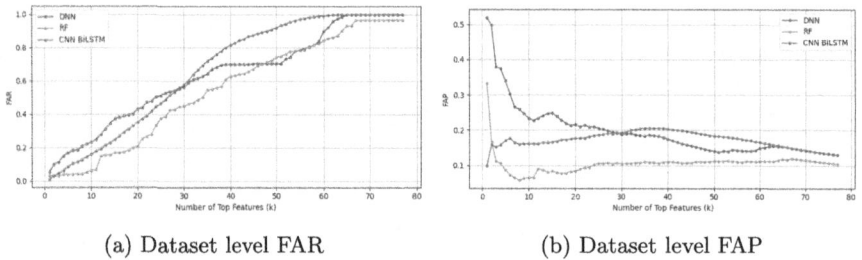

(a) Dataset level FAR   (b) Dataset level FAP

Fig. 2. (a) FAR and (b) FAP at various top-k cutoffs for DNN, RF, and CNN-BiLSTM X-IDSs. These metrics show how well each X-IDS's top-k features align with the set of domain-informed features *across the entire dataset*.

Class Level Explanation Evaluation Results: We also compute the class level FAP, and FAR by averaging the instance-level scores for each attack class. This provides a detailed view of how well each model explanation aligns with the domain-informed feature sets for individual attack types at different k values. To better understand how explanation alignment varies across different types of attacks, we visualise class level FAR and FAP with respect to k across multiple attack classes in the dataset, as illustrated in Fig. 3. Each curve corresponds to a different attack class. In Fig. 3a, attack classes such as DDoS/DoS, Brute Force, and Web Attack show improvement in FAR as k increases. For these attacks, a larger portion of the domain-informed features is captured in the explanation gradually through k. We see that certain attacks reach high FAR with smaller k. For example, the PortScan attack class can capture more domain-informed features at $k = 4$ with higher FAR. This indicates that the FAR curve rises quickly for attack classes with a small set of domain-informed features, compared to attack classes with a richer set of domain-informed features, such as DDoS/DoS. In contrast, infiltration and bot attack classes consistently show zero FAR as the predefined domain-informed feature set indicates no features to compare against. In Fig. 3b, we observe that FAP generally decreases as k increases, which is an expected trend since the comparison of top influential features of explanation at certain k against the predefined domain-informed feature set will decrease (after exceeding the maximum number of the existing predefined features in the corresponding set). For Web Attack and Brute Force, FAP starts high and gradually declines, indicating strong alignment at lower k values. The trends across attack classes show that our metrics are influenced by the number of domain-informed features per attack. This variation helps security analysts identify which attack types are well-explained by the model.

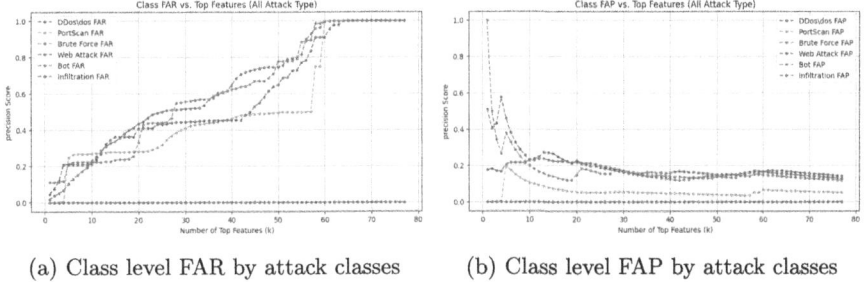

(a) Class level FAR by attack classes   (b) Class level FAP by attack classes

Fig. 3. Class level explanation evaluation metrics across attack types for the DNN model. (a) FAR trends showing how many of the domain-informed features are captured as k increases. (b) FAP trends showing how many of domain-informed features are captured by the explanations at each k.

Alignment Trends and Trade-Off Analysis: To further examine how well the top-k features produced by each X-IDS align with the domain-informed feature sets, we analyse two aspects: (1) the overall balance of explanation correctness and completeness using the FAF1 metric, and the trade-off between FAP and FAR using a precision-recall style curve. These plots allow us to visually compare how each model performs across different values of k. For clarity, we focus on the DDoS/DoS class as a representative example, since it has one of the largest domain-informed feature sets (10 expected features), and the class level view makes it easier to observe how models behave around a known threshold (i.e., number of expected features), especially when visualising FAP and FAR together where k is implicit.

FAF1 trend analysis: Fig. 4a shows the FAF1 curves for the DDoS/DoS class. This plot provides an overall view of alignment quality as k increases. We observe that the DNN model maintains higher FAF1 values for small k where it peaks at $k = 15$. This indicates an optimal balance of correctness and completeness at that point. The FAF1 curve of DNN starts to decline gradually as more irrelevant features are introduced. On the other hand, the CNN-BiLSTM curve for FAF1 gradually exceeds DNN, however, this happens slowly at a larger number of k. The RF curve for FAF1 reflects poor balance as it remains the lowest across all k values. This indicates that it does not capture the MITRE-based features effectively at any point. Overall, FAF1 plot offers a holistic view that helps to illustrate the balance of both completeness (FAR) and correctness (FAP) and highlight the overall quality of alignment for each model.

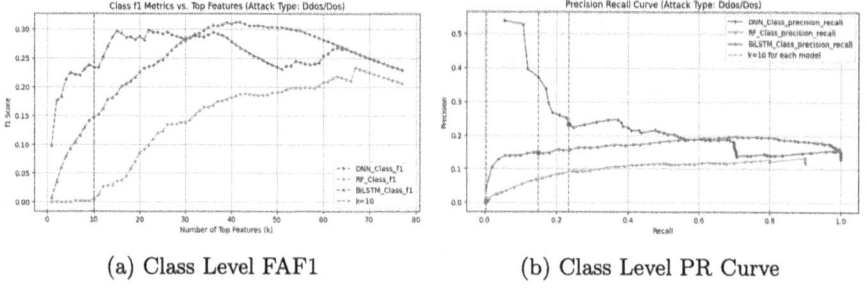

(a) Class Level FAF1   (b) Class Level PR Curve

Fig. 4. (a) Class Level FAF1 curve illustrating how each model's top-k features balance correctness (FAP) and completeness (FAR) with respect to the MITRE-based features. (b) Class Level Feature alignment Precision-Recall (FPR) curve, showing how FAP varies with FAR for different k values.

FAP-FAR trade-Off Analysis: Figure 4b shows another perspective that represents a FAP against FAR for each model. It provides a precision-recall style view of the alignment by directly plotting FAP (precision) against FAR (recall) for the DDoS/DoS class. Each curve represents the values of FAP and FAR values at each k that is implicitly shown by the number of points. The FAP-FAR comparison curve highlights how each model balances FAP and FAR across various values of k, with vertical lines highlight particular cuttoffs at $k = 10$, which corresponds to the number of domain-informed features for the evaluated attack class. The DNN model, for example, begins with a high FAP at a modest FAR. This indicates that more expected features are retrieved and covered in the early top features generated by the most influential features. The FAP-FAR comparison curve is important because it highlights the potential trade-off between FAP and FAR for each model in a single view. Compared to the separated plots of FAP and FAR over k, the combined curve allows us to assess how the model is efficiently retrieving domain-informed features with merely the values of FAP and FAR. As k values are not explicitly shown, vertical reference lines can help indicate key cutoff points for comparing model behaviour at meaningful thresholds. This curve offers an intuitive view of the trade-off between FAP and FAR to identify how well a model retrieves domain-informed features.

4.3 Key Insights and Implications

The above results demonstrate that explanations for X-IDSs can be quantitatively evaluated against domain knowledge using our evaluation metrics. The DNN and CNN-BiLSTM X-IDSs show a better alignment with MITRE-informed features than the RF. This shows that an X-IDS's ability to align explanations with domain knowledge is key to explanation quality and varies across models. For security analysts, higher alignment means more useful, interpretable alerts, enabling faster understanding and response.

An important factor influencing explanation quality is the value to consider for the top-k features. Our evaluation across multiple k shows how the quality of each explanation differs. The patterns of different models suggest that explanations can offer meaningful insight with relatively few features when those features are highly aligned with domain knowledge. At lower k, a higher FAP indicates that the most influential features included are highly relevant. Similarly, a higher FAR value shows more complete coverage of the expected feature set. For each attack type, the minimal value of k can initially be set based on the number of its corresponding domain-informed features. In cases where fewer features are considered (i.e., k is less than the domain-informed set size), this can still be meaningful, particularly when using weighted averages that account for the relative importance of individual features. In particular, this perspective is best observed through the FAF1 curve, which reveals the effectiveness of explanation's quality across different cutoffs to determine the most appropriate k value. This has a practical use when deciding whether to show analysts a very concise explanation or include more features. Thus, we can choose k based on the trade-off presented in FAF1 and the FAP-FAR comparison curve.

In addition to FAF1, we plot FAP-FAR comparison curves across different k to show the trade-off between explanation correctness (FAP) and completeness (FAR). Unlike the standard Precision-Recall (PR) curve that relies on a continuous probability threshold, our version depends on discrete k to calculate FAR and FAP values. Consequently, when we plot multiple models together, the progression along k may differ in how quickly or gradually models retrieve relevant features. As a result, the comparison can be visually misleading if one model adds relevant features earlier than another. Although both axes still run from 0 to 1 for FAP and FAR in the PR-curve, the stepwise progression of each model can be visually confusing. To address this challenge, we mark key k values, such as when k equals the number of expected features for a specific attack label (e.g., k equals 10 for DDoS/DoS), so the relative performance of different models at meaningful thresholds becomes easier to interpret.

Another insight relates to the quality of the domain-informed feature sets themselves. It is important to evaluate the results in the context of the quality and completeness of the predefined domain-informed feature sets. However, in cases such as the infiltration and bot attacks curves, we observed low alignment scores. Such low alignment scores suggest that the domain-informed features derived from expert knowledge may not fully capture relevant indicators or may not generalise well to the dataset used. Due to this mismatch, we find that the predefined domain-informed feature sets may require additional fine-tuning to align with features in the selected dataset. Consequently, the score of the alignment metrics can be affected. Therefore, it needs to include a user feedback loop in order to adjust the feature sets when necessary.

Finally, our current evaluation metrics aggregate FAP and FAR using the arithmetic mean. Consequently, averaging the values provides a single and intuitive number that shows how well the performance is across all instances. Although the arithmetic mean is straightforward and easy to interpret, it does treat each instance as equally important. This makes it vulnerable to outliers in a skewed distribution. In such cases, alternative aggregation techniques, such as median, weighted, or trimmed averages, can offer more robust and reliable evaluation, especially when the class or dataset level distributions contain outliers.

Overall, our findings show that the proposed explanation evaluation metrics (FAP, FAR, FAF1) can serve in several purposes. First, they effectively differentiate between X-IDSs based on how well their explanations align with domain knowledge. This differentiation makes it easier to identify which X-IDS produce more meaningful outputs. Second, by analysing how the explanations quality are changing across k, the metrics offer insights on how many top-k features should be shown to analysts. Finally, consistently low scores for certain attack classes may suggest that the domain-informed feature sets need refinement. Thus, these metrics help assess explanation quality during X-IDS development and improve how explanations are presented to analysts in real-world use.

5   Conclusion

In this paper, we present three novel metrics to evaluate the explanations generated by X-IDSs with domain-specific knowledge in the context of IDSs. We analyse our three explanation evaluation metrics for a popular XAI technique (i.e., SHAP). These three evaluation metrics are Feature Alignment Precision (FAP), which quantifies the correctness of the output of the XAI method based on defined indicators from domain-specific knowledge, Feature Alignment Recall (FAR), which quantifies how well the most important features capture all defined domain knowledge, and Feature Alignment F1 (FAF1), which quantifies the harmonic means between FAP and FAR. Our metrics enable the explanation evaluation at three different levels: instance, class, and dataset levels in order to capture the quality of the explanation, respectively, for individual predictions, across specific attack types, and obtain an overall measure of interpretability.

We applied our metrics to explanations generated for three X-IDS RF, DNN, CNN-BiLSTM) trained on a balanced subset of the CICIDS2017 dataset. The experimental results demonstrated how our metrics provide a richer and more actionable view of explanation quality. Specifically, our findings highlight that X-IDS can offer higher alignment with expected features at lower values of k, which makes their explanations more suitable for operational use. At the same time, consistently low scores for certain attack types may indicate that the domain-informed feature sets are incomplete or require refinement.

As future work, we plan to investigate alternative aggregation strategies, such as weighted averages, as we recognise that our approach assumes every instance contributes equally and could be heavily influenced by outliers. Additionally, we aim to apply the proposed evaluation metrics across various machine learning models and explanation methods to better understand their alignment with domain knowledge.

Acknowledgements. The work of Mohammed Alquliti was supported by King Abdulaziz University, Jeddah, Saudi Arabia.

References

1. Arreche, O., Guntur, T., Abdallah, M.: XAI-IDS: toward proposing an explainable artificial intelligence framework for enhancing network intrusion detection systems. Appl. Sci. **14**(10), 4170 (2024)
2. Arya, V., Bellamy, R.K., Chen, et al.: One explanation does not fit all: a toolkit and taxonomy of AI explainability techniques. arXiv preprint arXiv:1909.03012 (2019)
3. Capuano, N., Fenza, G., Loia, V., Stanzione, C.: Explainable artificial intelligence in cybersecurity: a survey. IEEE Access **10**, 93575–93600 (2022)
4. Cybersecurity and Infrastructure Security Agency (CISA): Best practices: Mitre ATT&CK® mapping. CISA Insights (2023). https://www.cisa.gov/news-events/news/best-practices-mitre-attckr-mapping. Accessed 12 Apr 2025
5. Dieber, J., Kirrane, S.: Why model why? Assessing the strengths and limitations of lime. arXiv preprint arXiv:2012.00093 (2020)
6. Hedström, A., Weber, L., Krakowczyk, D., Bareeva, D., Motzkus, et al.: Quantus: an explainable AI toolkit for responsible evaluation of neural network explanations and beyond. J. Mach. Learn. Res. **24**(34), 1–11 (2023)
7. Kaloroumakis, P.E., Smith, M.J.: Toward a knowledge graph of cybersecurity countermeasures. MITRE Corporation **11**, 2021 (2021)
8. Kostas, K.: Anomaly detection in networks using machine learning. Res. Proposal **23**, 343 (2018)
9. Lanvin, M., Gimenez, P.F., Han, Y., Majorczyk, et al.: Towards understanding alerts raised by unsupervised network intrusion detection systems. In: Proceedings of the 26th International Symposium on Research in Attacks, Intrusions and Defenses, pp. 135–150 (2023)
10. Lin, Y.S., Lee, et al.: What do you see? Evaluation of explainable artificial intelligence (XAI) interpretability through neural backdoors. In: Proceedings 27th ACM SIGKDD Conference on Knowledge Discovery and Data Mining, pp. 1027–1035 (2021)
11. Lopes, P., Silva, E., Braga, C., Oliveira, et al.: XAI systems evaluation: a review of human and computer-centred methods. Appl. Sci. **12**(19), 9423 (2022)
12. Lundberg, S.M., Lee, S.I.: A unified approach to interpreting model predictions. In: Advances in Neural Information Processing Systems, vol. 30 (2017)

13. MITRE corporation: Mitre ATT&CK® knowledge base, v16.1 (release 2024-10-31). MITRE ATT&CK Insights (2024). https://attack.mitre.org/. Accessed 19 Apr 2025

14. Mohale, V.Z., et al.: A systematic review on the integration of explainable artificial intelligence in intrusion detection systems to enhancing transparency and interpretability in cybersecurity. Front. Artif. Intell. **8**, 1526221 (2025)

15. Moustafa, N., Koroniotis, N., Keshk, M., Zomaya, A.Y., Tari, Z.: Explainable intrusion detection for cyber defences in the internet of things: opportunities and solutions. IEEE Commun. Surv. Tutorials **25**(3), 1775–1807 (2023)

16. Nauta, M., Trienes, J., Pathak, S., Nguyen, E., Peters, et al.: From anecdotal evidence to quantitative evaluation methods: a systematic review on evaluating explainable AI. ACM Comput. Surv. **55**(13s), 1–42 (2023)

17. Neupane, S., et al.: Explainable intrusion detection systems (X-IDS): a survey of current methods, challenges, and opportunities. IEEE Access **10**, 112392–112415 (2022)

18. Nir, D., Kaiser, F.K., Giladi, S., Sharabi, et al.: Labeling network intrusion detection system (NIDS) rules with MITRE ATT&CK techniques: machine learning vs. large language models. Big Data Cognit. Comput. **9**(2), 23 (2025)

19. Patil, S., Varadarajan, V., Mazhar, S.M., Sahibzada, et al.: Explainable artificial intelligence for intrusion detection system. Electronics **11**(19), 3079 (2022)

20. Pawlicki, M., Pawlicka, A., Kozik, R., Choraś, M.: The survey on the dual nature of XAI challenges in intrusion detection and their potential for AI innovation. Artif. Intell. Rev. **57**(12), 1–32 (2024)

21. Rosenfeld, A.: Better metrics for evaluating explainable artificial intelligence. In: Proceedings of the 20th International Conference on Autonomous Agents and Multiagent Systems, pp. 45–50 (2021)

22. Schwalbe, G., Finzel, B.: A comprehensive taxonomy for explainable artificial intelligence: a systematic survey of surveys on methods and concepts. Data Min. Knowl. Disc. **38**(5), 3043–3101 (2024)

23. Sharafaldin, I., Lashkari, et al.: Toward generating a new intrusion detection dataset and intrusion traffic characterization. ICISSp **1**(2018), 108–116 (2018)

24. Shtayat, M.M., Hasan, M.K., Sulaiman, R., Islam, S., Khan, A.U.R.: An explainable ensemble deep learning approach for intrusion detection in industrial internet of things. IEEE Access **11**, 115047–115061 (2023)

25. Sinha, J., Manollas, M.: Efficient deep CNN-BILSTM model for network intrusion detection. In: Proceedings of the 2020 3rd International Conference on Artificial Intelligence and Pattern Recognition, pp. 223–231 (2020)

26. Tritscher, J., Krause, et al.: Feature relevance XAI in anomaly detection: reviewing approaches and challenges. Front. Artif. Intell. **6**, 1099521 (2023)

27. Tritscher, J., Wolf, M., Hotho, A., Schlör, D.: Evaluating feature relevance XAI in network intrusion detection. In: Longo, L. (eds.) World Conference on Explainable Artificial Intelligence, pp. 483–497. Springer, Cham (2023). https://doi.org/10.1007/978-3-031-44064-9_25

28. Wu, Z., Chen, J., Li, Y., Deng, Y., Zhao, H., Hsieh, et al.: From black boxes to actionable insights: a perspective on explainable artificial intelligence for scientific discovery. J. Chem. Inf. Model. **63**(24), 7617–7627 (2023)

29. Zhou, J., Gandomi, A.H., Chen, et al.: Evaluating the quality of machine learning explanations: a survey on methods and metrics. Electron. **10**(5), 593 (2021)

A Multi-dataset Evaluation of Models for Automated Vulnerability Repair

Zanis Ali Khan$^{(\boxtimes)}$, Aayush Garg$^{(\boxtimes)}$, and Qiang Tang

Luxembourg Institute of Science and Technology (LIST), Esch-sur-Alzette,
Luxembourg
{zanis-ali.khan,aayush.garg,qiang.tang}@list.lu

Abstract. Software vulnerabilities pose significant security threats,
requiring effective mitigation. While Automated Program Repair (APR)
has advanced in fixing general bugs, vulnerability patching—a security-
critical aspect of APR—remains underexplored. This study investigates
pre-trained language models, CodeBERT and CodeT5, for automated
vulnerability patching across six datasets and four languages. We evaluate their accuracy and generalization to unknown vulnerabilities. Results
show that while both models face challenges with fragmented or sparse
context, CodeBERT performs comparatively better in such scenarios,
whereas CodeT5 excels in capturing complex vulnerability patterns.
CodeT5 also demonstrates superior scalability. Furthermore, we test fine-
tuned models on both in-distribution (trained) and out-of-distribution
(unseen) datasets. While fine-tuning improves in-distribution performance, models struggle to generalize to unseen data, highlighting challenges in robust vulnerability detection. This study benchmarks model
performance, identifies limitations in generalization, and provides actionable insights to advance automated vulnerability patching for real-world
security applications.

Keywords: code patching · vulnerability patching · large language
models · automated program repair

1 Introduction

Software vulnerabilities remain a constant threat to contemporary software systems, leaving them susceptible to exploitation by malicious actors. These vulnerabilities, which include problems like injection flaws and memory management
errors, can result in unauthorized access, data breaches, and service interruptions [34]. Addressing these issues is essential to ensure the reliability and security of software systems [1]. However, the manual effort required to detect and fix
these vulnerabilities is time-consuming, prone to errors, and struggles to match
the growing complexity and scale of today's software ecosystems [23].

Automated Program Repair (APR) has gained traction as a promising approach to tackle this issue, employing computational methods to autonomously

B. Coppens et al. (Eds.): ARES 2025 Workshops, LNCS 15994, pp. 73–87, 2025.
https://doi.org/10.1007/978-3-032-00630-1_5

generate fixes for software bugs [3]. While APR has achieved notable progress in addressing general software defects, the specialized area of vulnerability-focused program repair—which deals with the unique challenges of security vulnerabilities—remains underdeveloped. Unlike general-purpose bug fixes, patches for vulnerabilities often require addressing the flaw in a way that is not only functionally correct but also generalizable across variations of the vulnerability [9]. This makes vulnerability patching a more nuanced subset of Automated Program Repair (APR), where the ability to generate broadly applicable fixes becomes especially important.

Existing techniques in vulnerability-focused Automated Program Repair (APR) predominantly depend on either static analysis tools or traditional machine learning models trained on specific vulnerability patterns. Although these approaches have demonstrated potential in identifying vulnerabilities, their capacity to generate meaningful and effective patches remains limited. For instance, static analysis tools are highly effective at detecting vulnerabilities but often struggle to produce practical fixes [36]. Similarly, conventional machine learning models are hindered by their dependence on restricted datasets [14], which limits their generalizability and effectiveness across a wide range of programming languages and vulnerability types [38].

Recent advancements in deep-learning have paved the way for automated vulnerability patching, particularly with the emergence of pre-trained language models tailored for code. Models like CodeBERT [12] and CodeT5 [39] utilize large-scale code corpora to capture both syntactic and semantic structures, facilitating tasks such as code generation, summarization, and translation [17]. Their ability to discern patterns from extensive datasets makes them a promising tool for vulnerability-focused program repair. However, the practical application of these models remains challenging. Due to substantial differences in syntax, semantics, and vulnerability characteristics across programming languages, existing pre-trained models, which are often designed for monolingual or domain-specific tasks, may struggle with generalization [8]. Evaluating their performance across diverse languages is therefore a crucial yet underexplored area of research [19].

This paper systematically evaluates the performance of pre-trained language models in vulnerability-focused program repair, specifically analyzing Code-BERT and CodeT5 in generating patches for known vulnerabilities across six datasets covering four programming languages. We assess their effectiveness using *CodeBLEU* and *CrystalBLEU* scores and explore their generalizability by evaluating performance on both in-distribution and out-of-distribution datasets, providing insights into their strengths and limitations.

Our results show that while both models excel in generating vulnerability patches, they exhibit distinct limitations. CodeT5 generally outperforms Code-BERT in accuracy, especially on datasets with complex vulnerability patterns. However, both models struggle with fragmented contexts and sparse data, which limits their ability to produce correct fixes in such settings. Additionally, while fine-tuning improves performance on in-distribution datasets, both models face challenges in generalizing to out-of-distribution datasets, highlighting limitations in detecting and patching vulnerabilities in unseen scenarios.

Hence, our contributions in this paper are threefold:

- We provide an evaluation of CodeBERT and CodeT5 for vulnerability-focused program repair, covering a diverse set of 6 datasets across multiple programming languages.
- We establish benchmarks for model performance in generating vulnerability patches, serving as a foundation for evaluating pre-trained models in dataset-driven vulnerability patching scenarios.
- We identify key limitations in model generalization, particularly the challenges of fine-tuning and performance on out-of-distribution datasets.

2   Related Work

Software vulnerabilities refer to security gaps or defects within code that can be leveraged by malicious actors to compromise systems [33]. One notable example is the buffer overflow vulnerability, which arises when a program tries to write more data into a buffer than it can hold, leading to the overflow spilling into neighboring memory areas. This can allow attackers to inject and execute harmful code [18]. As these vulnerabilities grow more complex, they pose substantial obstacles to developing and deploying robust countermeasures.

While vulnerability detection has been extensively studied, significantly less attention has been given to generating patches. Traditional static analysis tools have long been used for detection, but their reliance on predefined rules often makes it difficult to identify complex patterns [2]. In contrast, AI-driven methods have gained traction for their ability to process vast codebases and uncover intricate security flaws. Models like *CodeBERT* [13] and *GraphCodeBERT* [21] have proven effective in analyzing source code, contributing to advancements in vulnerability detection and assessment [16]. Additionally, large language models (LLMs) such as OpenAI's GPT-4, Meta AI's Llama2, and Mistral AI's Mistral have demonstrated strong adaptability in tackling vulnerability detection tasks [22].

Conversely, creating effective patches continues to be a significant challenge. The majority of research on automated patch generation is centered on fixing general code defects rather than targeting vulnerabilities directly. The subsequent sections will explore methodologies within this broader context.

2.1   Traditional Approaches to Code Repair

Automated code repair traditionally falls into two categories: heuristic-based and constraint-based [20]. Heuristic methods search for patches that pass all tests, often using transformation schemas for efficiency [29]. Approaches like GenProg [28] and PAR [27] leverage genetic programming, while others use random or deterministic strategies to refine the search.

Constraint-based methods employ symbolic execution [5] to guide patch generation by exploring multiple execution paths. Tools such as SemFix [31] and Angelix [30] derive repair constraints, while techniques like Nopol [41] target specific cases, such as repairing conditional expressions.

2.2 ML-Based Code Repair

Machine learning has emerged as a key technique for automating code repair, generating patches for software vulnerabilities and bugs. Early efforts relied on Neural Machine Translation (NMT) with encoder-decoder architectures, such as SequenceR [7] and CODIT [6], which used attention mechanisms to prioritize critical regions during decoding.

More recently, transformer-based models have excelled at capturing long-range dependencies and nuanced context, leveraging attention to focus on relevant code segments. Ding *et al.* [10] highlighted their transformative potential, paving the way for broader adoption in program repair.

Further expanding these approaches, large language models (LLMs) such as CodeBERT [12] and CodeT5 [39] have shown promise for code-related tasks, benefiting from pretraining on large code corpora. While prior work has explored their capabilities in general code generation and repair, their effectiveness for vulnerability-specific patching remains underexplored. This motivates our evaluation of both models in this context.

Nevertheless, patching vulnerabilities is distinct from fixing general bugs. It requires highly contextual, security-focused modifications and robust generalization across complex scenarios. Current solutions emphasize fine-tuning LLMs and advancing techniques to enhance adaptability for various datasets and security-specific demands.

3 Methodology

In this section, we outline our experimental workflow, from dataset preparation and preprocessing to splitting the data for training and testing, followed by model selection and fine-tuning strategies.

3.1 Dataset Preparation and Pre-processing

For this study, we collected six publicly available datasets containing code samples with known vulnerabilities and their corresponding patches. These datasets comprises of multiple programming languages, including Go, Java, PHP, and C, ensuring diverse code structures and vulnerability patterns. The inclusion of diverse datasets allowed us to evaluate the models' ability to generalize across varied programming contexts. Details about these datasets, including their references are provided in Sect. 4.1, offering a comprehensive overview of their sources. This diversity in datasets not only enhances the robustness of our evaluation but also reflects real-world scenarios where vulnerabilities span multiple languages and coding paradigms.

We preprocessed the raw datasets to standardize their structure and enhance model compatibility. Given the noise in real-world vulnerability datasets [14,26], our preprocessing aimed to reduce inconsistencies and improve data quality, as emphasized in studies on noisy datasets [15,25]. By ensuring uniformity, we created a robust foundation for reliable model training and evaluation. These steps were critical for noise reduction and dataset preparation.

i. **Token Length Filtering.** Code exceeding *512* tokens was truncated/excluded due to model limits.
ii. **Comment Removal.** Language-specific regex removed comments, focusing on functional code.
iii. **Normalization.** Fixed formatting inconsistencies (whitespace, line breaks) for uniform datasets.

Table 1. Datasets

Dataset	I_{rows}	$R_{tok.}$	$R_{comm.}$	$R_{norm.}$	T_{rows}
Go	1,472	551	357	0	921
PHP	6,696	335	4,923	1	6,360
MegaVul_C_2023	17,975	3,147	0	302	14,526
MegaVul_C_2024	17,975	3,147	0	302	14,526
Vul4J	1,790	3	0	0	1,790
CodeParrot	69,420	19,420	1,505	0	50,000

3.2 Training and Testing Split

The datasets were partitioned into *85%* for training and *15%* for testing, a widely adopted ratio that provides a robust balance between model learning and evaluation [42]. This split ensures sufficient data for effective training while reserving enough samples to yield meaningful test results. To avoid data leakage and maintain the integrity of the evaluation, all overlapping or duplicate instances were excluded.

3.3 Model Selection and Fine-Tuning

We utilized and fine-tuned *CodeBERT* and *CodeT5* for vulnerability patching, leveraging their strengths in code understanding and generation. CodeBERT, tailored for programming tasks, adapted to detect vulnerabilities and their fixes, while CodeT5, optimized for code generation, improved handling diverse code structures. Despite alternatives like *TFix*, these models were chosen for their versatility, robustness, and real-world applicability.

4 Experimental Setup

In this section, we detail the computational environment and methodologies used for training and evaluating our models on a range of vulnerable code scenarios. All experiments were conducted on a High-Performance Computing (HPC) cluster with nodes featuring *2.20GHz Intel Xeon Silver 4210* processors and *NVIDIA Tesla V100-PCIE-32GB* GPUs. Model training and evaluation were performed using the *PyTorch 2.0.1* framework with *CUDA 12* compatibility.

Table 2. Accuracy Scores

Dataset	CodeBLEU		CrystalBLEU	
	CodeBERT	*CodeT5*	*CodeBERT*	*CodeT5*
Go	0.7641	0.6499	0.6557	0.5264
PHP	0.7351	0.6924	0.4624	0.3727
MegaVul_C_2023	0.8396	0.8549	0.7893	0.8131
MegaVul_C_2024	0.8395	0.8549	0.7893	0.8131
Vul4J	0.3737	0.9373	0.1229	0.8985
CodeParrot	0.997	0.9973	0.9595	0.9603

4.1 Datasets

To address the research questions outlined in Sect. 5, we leveraged publicly available datasets that contain comprehensive collections of vulnerable source code along with their corresponding fixed versions, which served as our ground truth. Specifically, we utilized six datasets, including Go and PHP[1], MegaVul_C_2023, and MegaVul_C_2024[2], Vul4J[3] [4], and also CodeParrot[4]. These datasets encompass a variety of programming languages, including C, Java, Go, and PHP, offering a well-rounded foundation for evaluation. Prior to their use, we implemented preprocessing steps as outlined in Sect. 3.1

Table 1 reports on the size of our datasets, in terms of the number of rows (I_{rows}), rows affected by tokenization ($R_{tok.}$), rows affected by comment removal ($R_{comm.}$), rows affected by normalization ($R_{norm.}$), and the total number of rows remaining after pre-processing ($T_{rows.}$).

4.2 DL Models

For vulnerability patching, we employed *CodeBERT* [12] and *CodeT5* [39], widely used for code analysis and vulnerability detection due to their strong performance in handling code semantics and structure.

CodeBERT [12] bridges programming and natural languages, enhancing tasks like code completion, summarization, and vulnerability detection. Built on a transformer architecture, it captures syntactic and semantic relationships from codeâĂŞlanguage pairs, enabling precise vulnerability identification and remediation at scale.

CodeT5 [39] is a T5-based model for code generation and understanding, excelling in vulnerability detection and patching. It generates context-aware patches, preserves code intent, and supports multiple languages. Pre-trained on

---

[1] Go and PHP–https://doi.org/10.5281/zenodo.13870382.

[2] MegaVul_C_2023, and MegaVul_C_2024–https://github.com/Icyrockton/Mega Vul.

[3] Vul4J–https://github.com/tuhh-softsec/vul4j.

[4] https://huggingface.co/datasets/codeparrot/github-code-clean.

extensive programming data, it performs well on benchmarks, improving software security and code quality. It also preserves semantics in decompilation, advancing vulnerability repair frameworks [40].

4.3 Evaluation Metrics

We evaluated the LLMs using *CrystalBLEU* [11] and *CodeBLEU* [37]. CrystalBLEU refines BLEU [35] by addressing n-gram limitations in programming languages, focusing on trivially shared n-grams for better code evaluation. CodeBLEU enhances BLEU by combining n-gram matching with AST-based structures and semantic data flow, making it ideal for assessing code quality. Together, these metrics provide accurate evaluations by considering both syntactic and semantic aspects of generated code.

5   Results

In this section, we present our findings, focusing on how effectively CodeBERT and CodeT5 generate accurate patches for both known and unknown vulnerabilities across diverse datasets.

5.1   RQ1: How Effectively do CodeBERT and CodeT5 Generate Accurate Patches for Known Vulnerabilities Across Diverse Datasets?

In this research question, we evaluated the effectiveness of CodeBERT and CodeT5 in generating patches by fine-tuning them on the same dataset. Our analysis spans six datasets across four programming languages, following the methodology outlined in Sect. 3.2. Table 2 displays the CodeBLEU, and CrystalBLEU scores of CodeBERT and CodeT5 across six datasets used in our evaluation. Examining the performance of both models on these datasets reveals key insights into how pre-training data diversity and model architecture impact the models' effectiveness in vulnerability patching tasks. CodeT5 consistently outperforms CodeBERT in VUL4J and CodeParrot datasets, with less difference on MegaVul_C_2023 and MegaVul_C_2024 datasets but still demonstrates a clear advantage over CodeBERT when evaluated using both CodeBLEU and CrystalBLEU accuracy scores. This result aligns with the fact that CodeT5 has been pre-trained on diverse data that spans a variety of programming languages and textual formats, enabling it to capture more generalized patterns and nuances in code. On Go, and PHP, CodeBERT performs better than CodeT5 using CodeBLEU and CrystalBLEU metrics. By analyzing these two datasets, we observed that they often contain incomplete functions or isolated snippets lacking full context. This could potentially lead to lower performance for CodeT5, as it relies on contextual understanding from diverse sources that might not align well with fragmented or incomplete code. Conversely, CodeBERT, which is also trained on

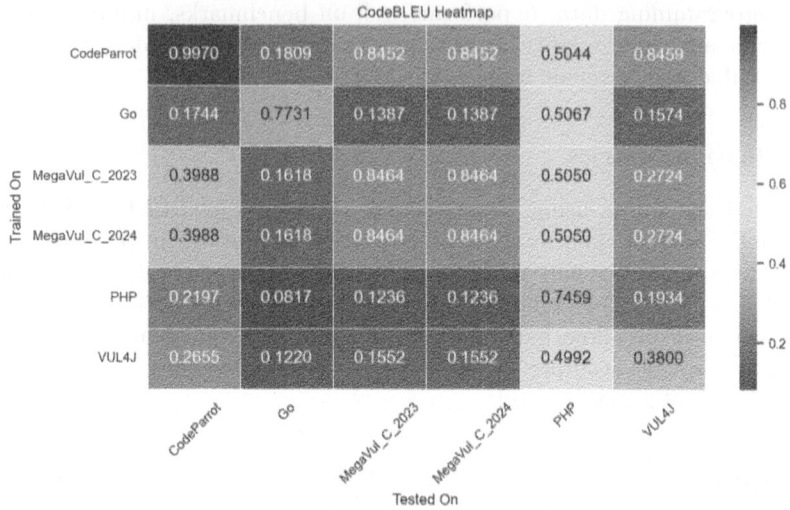

(a) CodeBLEU for CodeBERT

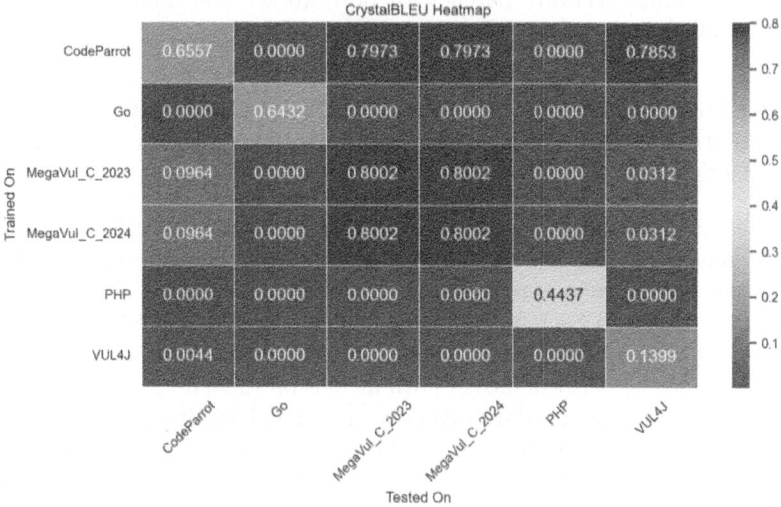

(b) CrystalBLEU for CodeBERT

Fig. 1. Heatmaps for CodeBERT

a broad variety of programming languages, may still benefit from its fine-tuned focus on code structure, making it more adaptable to such fragments.

These findings suggest that CodeBERT's architecture might be inherently more robust when handling incomplete or context-limited code, a factor that could contribute to its better performance on Go and PHP. Moreover, despite

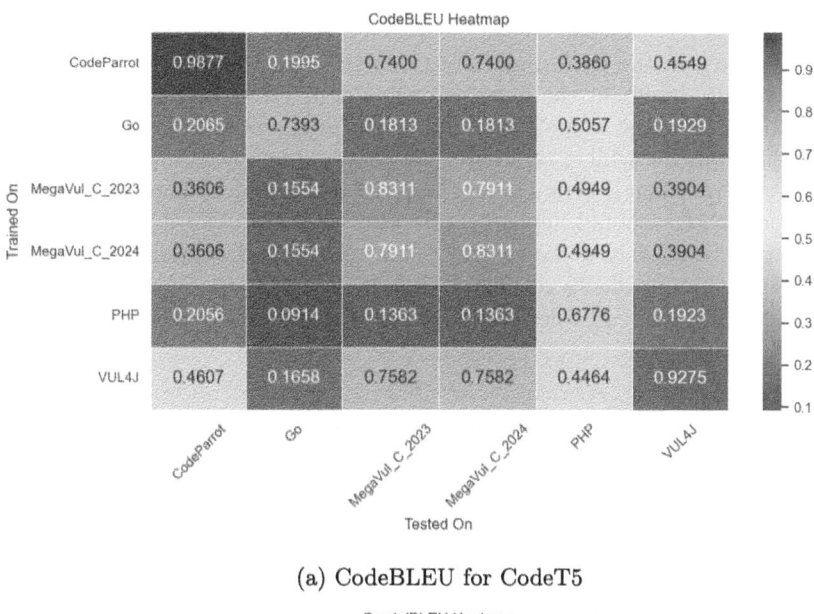

(a) CodeBLEU for CodeT5

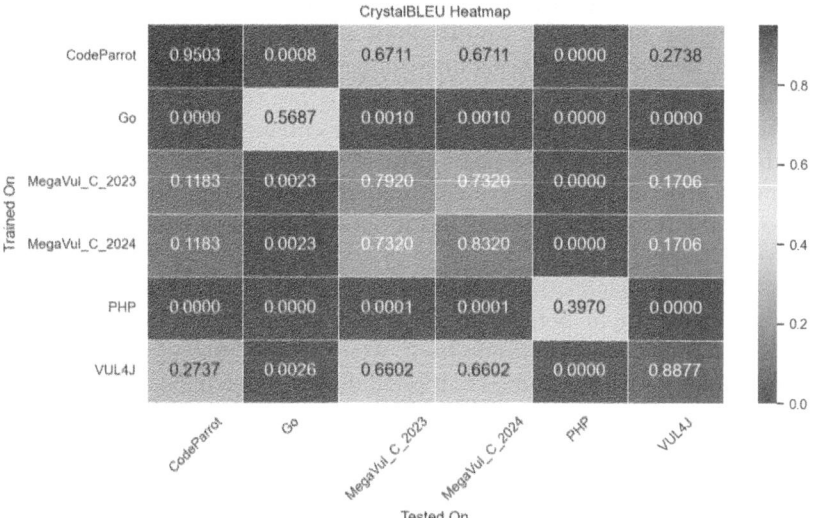

(b) CrystalBLEU for CodeT5

Fig. 2. Heatmaps for CodeT5

CodeBERT generally being outperformed by CodeT5, lacking the extensive pre-training diversity of CodeT5, can still achieve near-competitive results in certain domains, particularly for language-specific tasks. This observation underscores the need for further investigation to better understand the interplay between dataset characteristics and metric sensitivity, rather than drawing generalized conclusions about the performance of CodeBLEU or CrystalBLEU.

Our results highlight the benefits of model diversity in deep learning-based vulnerability patching. CodeT5's broad pre-training excels on datasets with complex vulnerabilities, while CodeBERT's focused design performs well on datasets with more traditional, syntactically constrained samples. These insights show that model choice should depend on dataset characteristics. CodeBERT's simpler architecture likely makes it less reliant on context, while CodeT5 handles diverse inputs more effectively. Thus, while CodeT5 is suited for complex, varied data, CodeBERT is valuable in environments with incomplete or non-standard code snippets.

5.2   RQ2: How Effectively do CodeBERT and CodeT5 Generate Accurate Patches for Unknown Vulnerabilities Across Diverse Datasets?

Figures 1 and 2 show the results for RQ2, where we evaluated the fine-tuned CodeBERT and CodeT5 models. For each model, we fine-tuned them on one dataset and tested their performance on two types of datasets: (1) the same dataset used for fine-tuning (in-distribution testing) and (2) all remaining datasets that were not used during fine-tuning (out-of-distribution testing). This setup allowed us to analyze whether fine-tuning pre-trained models (i.e., CodeBERT and CodeT5) on high-quality datasets enhances their ability to detect vulnerabilities, including previously unknown ones. Specifically, we aimed to determine if fine-tuning improves the models' generalization capabilities compared to their pre-trained versions, both on datasets they were trained on and on unseen datasets.

In Sect. 5.1, we demonstrated the performance of pre-trained models (CodeBERT and CodeT5) in detecting vulnerabilities accurately on datasets they were trained or fine-tuned on. For RQ2, we extended this analysis to evaluate their performance on both in-distribution and out-of-distribution datasets. From Fig. 1 and Fig. 2, we observe that both models perform significantly better on in-distribution datasets, with almost similar results and only minor percentage differences compared to their performance in Sect. 5.1 or RQ1. This behavior is expected, as fine-tuning allows models to adapt to the specific characteristics of the training data, leading to higher accuracy on familiar datasets.

However, when tested on out-of-distribution datasets, the models exhibit a noticeable drop in accuracy. Notably, when a model trained on a specific programming language is tested on the same language—for example, trained on Megavul_C_2023 and tested on Megavul_C_2024—the accuracy remains high. A similar trend is observed for Vul4J and CodeParrot, as both are Java-based datasets. In contrast, for CodeBERT, training on Vul4J and testing on Vul4J results in lower accuracy. This is due to the same reason mentioned in Sect. 5.1. These findings suggest that while fine-tuning enhances performance on datasets similar to the training data, it does not generalize well to entirely new datasets.

Additionally, the models exhibit non-deterministic behavior (e.g., small variations in accuracy even on in-distribution datasets), which is common in large language models (LLMs) like CodeBERT and CodeT5. This variability can be attributed to factors such as randomness in weight initialization, optimization processes, or inherent fluctuations in the models' predictions.

6   Discussion

Fine-tuning on well-characterized datasets substantially boosts CodeBERT and CodeT5 performance in-distribution tests. However, this advantage drops sharply on out-of-distribution data, especially when the code differs in language or structure. Such declines reflect overfitting, as models learn dataset-specific signals rather than broader security principles.

Additionally, we observe sporadic variability across executions, caused by random weight initialization and hyperparameter sensitivity. Repeated training can alleviate these fluctuations, but consistent checkpointing and parameter tuning remain critical for stable outcomes.

A key lesson is that diverse datasets foster more generalizable repair models. Narrow data coverage may yield high accuracy for certain vulnerability types but struggles with unseen threats. Beyond standard fine-tuning, future work could explore meta-learning, multi-task strategies, and data augmentation to improve cross-domain robustness and ensure patches address genuine security concerns.

7   Threats to Validity

Construct Validity. We evaluate "correct" patches using CodeBLEU and CrystalBLEU, which primarily gauge syntactic and limited semantic cues. Although these metrics are well-suited for code-focused tasks, they may overlook deeper security implications and potential exploit vectors. Moreover, the labeled "patched" instances within our datasets may not fully represent truly secure fixes, raising the risk of overestimating model performance.

Internal Validity. Our findings are sensitive to model randomness (e.g., weight initialization) and hyperparameter settings. Even minor fluctuations in these variables can skew comparative outcomes. Additionally, data preprocessing steps such as token truncation and comment removal may eliminate vital context needed to generate security-relevant patches. These factors, if not uniformly controlled, limit the consistency and interpretability of our experimental results.

External Validity. While this work involves six datasets in four languages, real-world projects frequently rely on specialized libraries and domain-specific coding styles. The observed performance drop on out-of-distribution datasets highlights limited cross-domain generalizability. To enhance broader applicability, future work should consider more diverse datasets and investigate meta-learning approaches that better capture variability across language ecosystems and security contexts.

8 Conclusion

Our findings illustrate the promise of large language models for automated vulnerability repair while underscoring significant generalization challenges. Code-BERT and CodeT5 both excel when confronted with familiar vulnerability patterns, yet exhibit performance gaps on unseen datasets and in cross-language contexts. Achieving robust, production-grade vulnerability repair will demand more than simple fine-tuning; it calls for richer datasets, more advanced training paradigms, and continuous adaptation to evolving security threats. By addressing these gaps, future research and practice can more confidently integrate automated patch generation into real-world software development pipelines.

Acknowledgments. This research received funding from the European Commission through the Horizon Europe Programme as part of the LAZARUS project (https://lazarus-he.eu/) (Grant Agreement No. 101070303). The content of this article represents the sole responsibility of the authors and does not necessarily reflect the official views of the European Union.

Data Availability Statement. In support of Open Science, the source code and datasets used in our study are publicly available on Zenodo [24].

References

1. Albanese, M., Çam, H., Jajodia, S.: Automated cyber situation awareness tools and models for improving analyst performance. In: Cybersecurity Systems for Human Cognition Augmentation, Advances in Information Security, vol. 61, pp. 47–60. Springer (2014). https://doi.org/10.1007/978-3-319-10374-7_3
2. Arusoaie, A., Ciobâca, S., Craciun, V., Gavrilut, D., Lucanu, D.: A comparison of open-source static analysis tools for vulnerability detection in C/C++ code. In: 2017 19th International Symposium on Symbolic and Numeric Algorithms for Scientific Computing (SYNASC), pp. 161–168 (2017). https://doi.org/10.1109/SYNASC.2017.00035
3. Bui, Q., Paramitha, R., Vu, D., Massacci, F., Scandariato, R.: APR4VUL: an empirical study of automatic program repair techniques on real-world java vulnerabilities. Empir. Softw. Eng. **29**(1), 18 (2024). https://doi.org/10.1007/S10664-023-10415-7
4. Bui, Q.C., Scandariato, R., Ferreyra, N.E.D.: VUL4J: a dataset of reproducible java vulnerabilities geared towards the study of program repair techniques. In: 2022 IEEE/ACM 19th International Conference on Mining Software Repositories (MSR), pp. 464–468 (2022). https://doi.org/10.1145/3524842.3528482
5. Cadar, C., Dunbar, D., Engler, D.: Klee: unassisted and automatic generation of high-coverage tests for complex systems programs. In: 8th USENIX Conference on Operating Systems Design and Implementation, p. 209–224. OSDI'08, USENIX Association, USA (2008)
6. Chakraborty, S., Ding, Y., Allamanis, M., Ray, B.: Codit: code editing with tree-based neural models. IEEE Trans. Software Eng. **48**(4), 1385–1399 (2018). https://doi.org/10.1109/TSE.2020.3020502

7. Chen, Z., Kommrusch, S., Tufano, M., Pouchet, L.N., Poshyvanyk, D., Monperrus, M.: Sequencer: sequence-to-sequence learning for end-to-end program repair. IEEE Trans. Software Eng. **47**(09), 1943–1959 (2021). https://doi.org/10.1109/TSE.2019.2940179

8. Dang, N.N.H., Thanh, T.Q., Nguyen-Duc, A.: BERTVRepair: on the adoption of CodeBERT for automated vulnerability code repair, pp. 173–196. Springer Nature Switzerland, Cham (2024). https://doi.org/10.1007/978-3-031-55642-5_8

9. de-Fitero-Dominguez, D., García-López, E., García-Cabot, A., Martínez-Herráiz, J.J.: Enhanced automated code vulnerability repair using large language models. Eng. Appl. Artif. Intell. **138**, 109291 (2024). https://doi.org/10.1016/J.ENGAPPAI.2024.109291

10. Ding, Y., Ray, B., Devanbu, P., Hellendoorn, V.J.: Patching as translation: the data and the metaphor. In: Proceedings of the 35th IEEE/ACM International Conference on Automated Software Engineering, pp. 275–286. ASE 2020, Association for Computing Machinery, New York, NY, USA (2021). https://doi.org/10.1145/3324884.3416587

11. Eghbali, A., Pradel, M.: CrystalBLEU: precisely and efficiently measuring the similarity of code. In: Proceedings of the 37th IEEE/ACM International Conference on Automated Software Engineering, pp. 1–12 (2022)

12. Feng, Z., et al.: CodeBert: a pre-trained model for programming and natural languages. arXiv preprint arXiv:2002.08155 (2020)

13. Feng, Z., Guo, D., Tang, D., et al.: CodeBert: a pre-trained model for programming and natural languages. In: Findings of the Association for Computational Linguistics: EMNLP 2020, pp. 1536–1547. Association for Computational Linguistics (2020). https://doi.org/10.18653/v1/2020.findings-emnlp.139

14. Garg, A., Degiovanni, R., Jimenez, M., Cordy, M., Papadakis, M., Traon, Y.L.: Learning to predict vulnerabilities from vulnerability-fixes: a machine translation approach. CoRR abs/2012.11701 (2020). https://arxiv.org/abs/2012.11701

15. Garg, A., Degiovanni, R., Jimenez, M., Cordy, M., Papadakis, M., Traon, Y.L.: Learning from what we know: how to perform vulnerability prediction using noisy historical data. Empir. Softw. Eng. **27**(7), 169 (2022). https://doi.org/10.1007/S10664-022-10197-4

16. Garg, A., Degiovanni, R., Papadakis, M., Traon, Y.L.: Vulnerability mimicking mutants. CoRR abs/2303.04247 (2023). https://doi.org/10.48550/ARXIV.2303.04247

17. Garg, A., Degiovanni, R., Papadakis, M., Traon, Y.L.: On the coupling between vulnerabilities and LLM-generated mutants: A study on vul4j dataset. In: IEEE Conference on Software Testing, Verification and Validation, ICST 2024, Toronto, ON, Canada, May 27-31, 2024, pp. 305–316. IEEE (2024). https://doi.org/10.1109/ICST60714.2024.00035

18. Garg, A., Patsakis, C., Khan, Z.A., Tang, Q.: Payload analysis of adversaries' tooling: automated identification of fuzzers. techrxiv preprint (2024). https://doi.org/10.36227/techrxiv.173385946.65994728/v1

19. Gharibi, R., Sadreddini, M.H., Fakhrahmad, S.M.: T5APR: empowering automated program repair across languages through checkpoint ensemble. J. Syst. Softw. **214**, 112083 (2024). https://doi.org/10.1016/J.JSS.2024.112083

20. Goues, C.L., Pradel, M., Roychoudhury, A.: Automated program repair. Commun. ACM **62**(12), 56–65 (2019). https://doi.org/10.1145/3318162

21. Guo, D., et al.: GraphCodeBert: pre-training code representations with data flow. In: 9th International Conference on Learning Representations, ICLR 2021, Virtual

Event, Austria, May 3-7, 2021. OpenReview.net (2021). https://openreview.net/forum?id=jLoC4ez43PZ

22. Guo, Y., Hu, Q., Tang, Q., Traon, Y.L.: An empirical study of the imbalance issue in software vulnerability detection. In: Tsudik, G., Conti, M., Liang, K., Smaragdakis, G. (eds.) European Symposium on Research in Computer Security, pp. 371–390. Springer (2023). https://doi.org/10.1007/978-3-031-51482-1_19

23. Khan, S., Parkinson, S.: Review into state of the art of vulnerability assessment using artificial intelligence. In: Guide to Vulnerability Analysis for Computer Networks and Systems - An Artificial Intelligence Approach, pp. 3–32. Computer Communications and Networks, Springer (2018). https://doi.org/10.1007/978-3-319-92624-7_1

24. Khan, Z.A., Garg, A., Tang, Q.: Artifact for a multi-dataset evaluation of models for automated vulnerability repair (2025). https://doi.org/10.5281/zenodo.15599983

25. Khan, Z.A., Shin, D., Bianculli, D., Briand, L.C.: Guidelines for assessing the accuracy of log message template identification techniques. In: 44th IEEE/ACM 44th International Conference on Software Engineering, ICSE 2022, Pittsburgh, PA, USA, May 25-27, 2022, pp. 1095–1106. ACM (2022). https://doi.org/10.1145/3510003.3510101

26. Khan, Z.A., Shin, D., Bianculli, D., Briand, L.C.: Impact of log parsing on deep learning-based anomaly detection. Empir. Softw. Eng. **29**(6), 139 (2024). https://doi.org/10.1007/S10664-024-10533-W

27. Kim, D., Nam, J., Song, J., Kim, S.: Automatic patch generation learned from human-written patches. In: Proceedings of the 2013 International Conference on Software Engineering, pp. 802–811. ICSE 2013, IEEE (2013). https://doi.org/10.1109/ICSE.2013.6606626

28. Le Goues, C., Dewey-Vogt, M., Forrest, S., Weimer, W.: A systematic study of automated program repair: fixing 55 out of 105 bugs for $8 each. In: 34th International Conference on Software Engineering (ICSE), pp. 3–13 (2012). https://doi.org/10.1109/ICSE.2012.6227211

29. Liu, K., Koyuncu, A., Kim, D., Bissyandé, T.F.: TBAR: revisiting template-based automated program repair. In: Proceedings of the 28th ACM SIGSOFT International Symposium on Software Testing and Analysis, pp. 31–42. ISSTA 2019, Association for Computing Machinery, New York, NY, USA (2019). https://doi.org/10.1145/3293882.3330577, https://doi-org.proxy.bnl.lu/10.1145/3293882.3330577

30. Mechtaev, S., Yi, J., Roychoudhury, A.: Angelix: scalable multiline program patch synthesis via symbolic analysis. In: 38th International Conference on Software Engineering (ICSE), pp. 691–701 (2016). https://doi.org/10.1145/2884781.2884807

31. Nguyen, H.D.T., Qi, D., Roychoudhury, A., Chandra, S.: SemFix: program repair via semantic analysis. In: 35th International Conference on Software Engineering (ICSE), pp. 772–781 (2013). https://doi.org/10.1109/ICSE.2013.6606623

32. Ni, C., Shen, L., Yang, X., Zhu, Y., Wang, S.: MegaVul: A c/c++ vulnerability dataset with comprehensive code representations. In: Proceedings of the 21st International Conference on Mining Software Repositories. MSR 2024, Association for Computing Machinery, New York, NY, USA (2024). https://doi.org/10.1145/3643991.3644886

33. Ogata, M., Franklin, J., Voas, J., Sritapan, V., Quirolgico, S.: Vetting the security of mobile applications. Tech. rep., National Institute of Standards and Technology (2019). https://doi.org/10.6028/NIST.SP.800-163r1

34. Okutan, A., et al.: Empirical validation of automated vulnerability curation and characterization. IEEE Trans. Software Eng. **49**(5), 3241–3260 (2023). https://doi.org/10.1109/TSE.2023.3250479

35. Papineni, K., Roukos, S., Ward, T., Zhu, W.J.: BLEU: a method for automatic evaluation of machine translation. In: Proceedings of the 40th Annual Meeting of the Association for Computational Linguistics, pp. 311–318 (2002)

36. Piskachev, G., Becker, M., Bodden, E.: Can the configuration of static analyses make resolving security vulnerabilities more effective? - A user study. Empir. Softw. Eng. **28**(5), 118 (2023). https://doi.org/10.1007/S10664-023-10354-3

37. Ren, S., et al.: CodeBLEU: a method for automatic evaluation of code synthesis. arXiv preprint arXiv:2009.10297 (2020)

38. Risse, N., Böhme, M.: Uncovering the limits of machine learning for automatic vulnerability detection. In: 33rd USENIX Security Symposium, USENIX Security 2024, Philadelphia, PA, USA, August 14-16, 2024. USENIX Association (2024). https://www.usenix.org/conference/usenixsecurity24/presentation/risse

39. Wang, Y., Wang, W., Joty, S., Hoi, S.C.: Codet5: identifier-aware unified pre-trained encoder-decoder models for code understanding and generation. arXiv preprint arXiv:2109.00859 (2021)

40. Wu, Y., et al.: How effective are neural networks for fixing security vulnerabilities. In: Proceedings of the 32nd ACM SIGSOFT International Symposium on Software Testing and Analysis, ISSTA 2023, Seattle, WA, USA, July 17-21, 2023, pp. 1282–1294. ACM (2023). https://doi.org/10.1145/3597926.3598135, https://doi.org/10.1145/3597926.3598135

41. Xuan, J., et al.: Nopol: automatic repair of conditional statement bugs in java programs. IEEE Trans. Software Eng. **43**, 34–55 (2017). https://doi.org/10.1109/TSE.2016.2560811

42. Zhao, R., Wang, J., Zheng, X., Wen, J., Rao, L., Zhao, J.: Maritime visible image classification based on double transfer method. IEEE Access **8**, 166335–166346 (2020)

Adversarial Robustness of Machine Learning-Based Access Control

Javier Martínez Llamas$^{(\boxtimes)}$ ⓘ, Matthias Van Hoof, Davy Preuveneers ⓘ,
and Wouter Joosen

DistriNet, KU Leuven, Leuven, Belgium
javier.martinezllamas@kuleuven.be

Abstract. As technological systems grow in complexity, the task of managing authorisation and access control becomes increasingly challenging. Machine learning (ML) has emerged as a solution capable of adapting to this landscape by leveraging insights from historical data and promptly determining who should be granted access to specific resources. The integration of machine learning into authorisation and access control systems yields numerous benefits. However, it also introduces new vulnerabilities, notably adversarial attacks. A malicious actor could potentially gain unauthorised access to a resource by manipulating an access request. This paper examines the robustness of Machine Learning-based Access Control (MLBAC) systems against evasion attacks. More specifically, it investigates the feasibility of adversarial attacks in the context of access control and examines the importance of attributes in crafting such requests. Our findings indicate that the access control models we examined exhibit a high susceptibility to adversarial examples. This will serve as a foundation for enhancing the robustness of MLBAC systems through adversarial training. This technique results in a significant improvement in robustness, as evidenced by a reduction in evasion rates of *circa* 40%. The promising results contribute towards addressing one of the primary challenges associated with MLBAC systems, improving their safety, security and robustness, and contribute to a wider acceptance.

Keywords: access control · machine learning · adversarial attacks · evasion · robustness

1 Introduction

Traditional access control systems are an essential security component of software and organisations. They regulate access to information and resources by enforcing policies specifying the criteria under which access should be granted. These systems, including Discretionary Access Control (DAC) [37], Role-based Access Control (RBAC) [13], and Attribute-Based Access Control (ABAC) [19], are commonly rule-based and rely on a predefined set of policies to make access

B. Coppens et al. (Eds.): ARES 2025 Workshops, LNCS 15994, pp. 88–105, 2025.
https://doi.org/10.1007/978-3-032-00630-1_6

decisions. Nonetheless, the rapid evolution and increasing complexity of organisations have rendered traditional access control systems less effective and challenging to maintain [5,6,39,43]. For instance, a common practice in real-world systems is to grant users more permissions than necessary to reduce the number of policies and prevent potential conflicts. This tendency facilitated broken access control to rank at the top of the OWASP Top 10 [34] web application vulnerabilities. Within the array of challenges confronting traditional systems, the most notable ones include managing uncertainty and policy misconfiguration.

As a response to these emerging obstacles, Artificial Intelligence (AI) has been proposed as a complementary enhancement to conventional access control mechanisms [22,24,33]. It has demonstrated notable efficiency, flexibility, and adaptability in addressing access control tasks. The benefits include the ability to monitor loopholes in access control policies, account for uncertainties (e.g. time or location) and anomalies, and facilitate the mining of complex and large-scale policies. This approach reduces human error, expedites verification procedures, and enhances the scalability and effectiveness of access control systems in complex environments.

Nonetheless, Machine Learning (ML) and Deep Learning (DL) models are known to be susceptible to adversarial evasion attacks [21,26,35]. These attacks aim to deceive the ML models by introducing perturbations to the input data, leading to misclassification by the model. As illustrated in Fig. 1, within an access control setting, this attack could culminate in a malicious actor obtaining access to restricted resources that would otherwise be unauthorised.

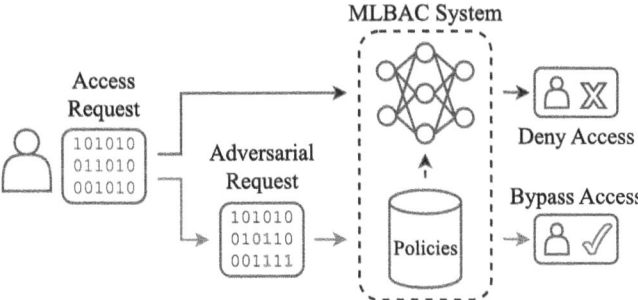

Fig. 1. Adversarial attack on an MLBAC system. An attacker performs adversarial perturbations to a benign access request in order to bypass the system.

The key problem we want to address in this paper is the lack of an exhaustive comprehension of the safety, security and robustness of Machine Learning-based Access Control (MLBAC) systems. To that end, this paper explores (1) the susceptibility of MLBAC systems to evasion attacks and (2) how attack knowledge can contribute to their robustness. To the best of our knowledge, this is the first work to study the robustness of MLBAC systems.

The main contributions are as follows:

– We study the feasibility and risks of evasion attacks on MLBAC systems.
– We explore the use of adversarial training in order to increase the robustness of access control models against evasion attacks.
– We validate our research on top of real-world access control data.

The remaining sections of this paper are structured as follows. Section 2 reviews related work. Section 3 introduces our methodology. Section 4 covers the evasion attacks and threat model. Section 5 investigates the robustness of MLBAC systems. Section 6 discusses the challenges and limitations of our work. Section 7 presents our conclusions.

2 Related Work

In this section, we review related work on the integration of AI into the field of access control, and the vulnerability of ML models to adversarial attacks.

2.1 Enhancing Rule-Based Access Control

The first efforts to integrate ML in the access control domain are motivated by the need to streamline, optimise and validate traditional access control systems. With the advancement of AI capabilities, there is an emerging trend in access control focused on optimising policy mining. Xu and Stoller [44] exploit ML capabilities to mine ABAC policies from Access Control Lists (ACLs). Frank et al. [14] propose a probabilistic model for role mining in RBAC. Cotrini et al. [12] propose an ABAC mining algorithm that reduces man-made policies duplicities and over-permissiveness. Alohaly et al. [2] use a Long-Short Term Memory (LSTM) network to extract ABAC attributes from free text policies. Polisma framework [1] learns ABAC policies from logs combined with external sources such as Lightweight Directory Access Protocol (LDAP) directories.

A similar trend is observed in the domains of administration and verification, where research efforts are directed towards minimising human workload and reducing the likelihood of errors in these processes. Gumma et al. [16] address the problem of administration of traditional systems through ML. Implementing and comparing various models for ABAC policy administration, creating new rules, and extending existing ones based on change requests. Similarly, Luciano et al. [4] detect and leverage behavioural anomalies exhibited by users in order to refine and update ABAC policies. Hu [18] explores a ML model to verify and enhance the quality of access control policies. Xiang et al. [42] introduce a tool designed to monitor access control policies, identify unintended policy modifications, and facilitate post-mortem forensic analysis following security breaches.

2.2 Machine Learning for Access Decision

The increasing popularity of ML has spurred its adoption as a decision-making engine, transcending its traditional role as a supportive tool. Liu, Aodi, Xuehui Du, and Na Wang [24] implement a Random Forest (RF) model for request classification, highlighting the scarcity of real-world access control data. Nobi et al. [33] consider the potential application of DL, evaluating several Convolutional Neural Network (CNN) architectures functioning as decision engines. The inherent rigidity of traditional access control systems is also taken into consideration. Chang et al. [10] propose a method leveraging access timestamps for decision-making, employing a Support Vector Machine (SVM) model.

This nascent line of research underscored the parallelism between MLBAC and rule-based access control, emphasising the necessity for a comprehensive security evaluation. Karimi and Abdelhakim [22] consider the problem of administering these MLBAC systems through a reinforcement learning model for ABAC synthetic data. Simultaneously considering its viability as a decision engine and its incremental administration through a reward function. Another study [32] addresses the administration problem of ML models by comparing a RF and a residual neural network (ResNet). The authors evaluate the retraining and incremental training of such models. Similarly, Llamas et al. [25] explored this adaptation to new policies as well as the implications of unlearning in vulnerability correction.

2.3 Adversarial Attacks

Traditional adversarial attacks have historically concentrated on Deep Learning (DL) models and domains such as image recognition [7,35,36,40]. However, the swift proliferation of AI has prompted the exploration of such attacks in the space of tabular data. Ballet et al. [41] propose an imperceptible adversarial attack for tabular data through a gradient-based method. Cartella et al. [9] present an adversarial attack tailored to imbalanced tabular data, within the fraud detection domain. Mathov et al. [27] propose a framework for adversarial examples in heterogeneous tabular data, they validate their approach using three datasets from different content domains. Nobi et al. [31] introduces the threat of adversarial attacks in the context of access control models. Their study, employing synthetic data, demonstrates the susceptibility of MLBAC models to such attacks in a white-box scenario. However, the evaluation of the robustness of MLBAC systems remains unexplored, as well as the exploration of more intricate and realistic adversarial settings, alongside an.

2.4 Robustness Against Adversarial Examples

The concept of adversarial robustness was first introduced by Huang et al. [20], followed by Goodfellow et al. [15]. The posterior work by Madry et al. [26] represents a seminal contribution to the field, as it is the first to empirically demonstrate robustness against adversarial examples. This robustness is achieved through the process of adversarial training, wherein the model is trained using adversarial examples generated by an attacker. Specifically, the attacker utilises Projected Gradient Descent (PGD) to explore the space of adversarial perturbations; creating a set of adversarial examples that the model learns to withstand.

While the majority of adversarial robustness research has concentrated on image and text domains, the work of Kireev et al. [23] extends this inquiry to the domain of tabular data, highlighting the unique challenges it presents. The authors argue that the differences between tabular data and other domains are significant, and techniques effective in one domain cannot be directly transferred to another. They assert that in the context of tabular data, the notion of imperceptibility is less critical compared to the cost of generating adversarial examples, as their generation for tabular data is notably more inefficient.

2.5   Bridging the Gap

Despite the increasing research interest in MLBAC, it remains a nascent field. The critical importance of access control systems necessitates a comprehensive evaluation and risk assessment of MLBAC systems, an area that has largely remained unexplored. In response to this gap, our study seeks to contribute to the broader adoption of MLBAC systems by investigating the adversarial robustness of such systems.

3   Methodology

In this section, we detail (1) the access control datasets, (2) the data augmentation and preprocessing and (3) the experimental setup.

3.1   Access Control Datasets

As it is common in the security domain, publicly available access control datasets are scarce due to their sensitive nature. We perform our experiments on two real-world datasets provided by Amazon [3,29]. The first one, hosted at Kaggle [3], comprises real historical data collected from 2010 to 2011, where employees are manually granted or denied access to certain resources. The dataset, which consists of 32769 access tuples with access data of 9560 users and 7517 resources, includes users' attributes and the resource being accessed for a total of 10 features. The second dataset [29], hosted at University of California Irvine (UCI) Machine Learning Repository, is presented in an sparse structure, which we processed to resemble that of the first dataset. The resulting dense dataset consists of a total of 13 features and 111390 access tuples.

For illustrative purposes, we outline the features present in the Kaggle dataset, with the intention of referencing this explanation in subsequent sections. Nevertheless, the same principles are applicable to both samples.

An access request r_i is formally given by the tuple $r_i = (r_{i_1}, \ldots, r_{i_9}, t_i, y_i)$, where r_{i_j} are the categorical features of the user, t_i the target resource, and y_i the access decision for that user-resource pair. The nature of the target label models a binary problem $\forall i : y_i \in \{0, 1\}$, representing a decision for access granted (1) and access denied (0).

The different features r_{i_j} are as follows: MGR_ID, or the ID of the manager of the current employee, ROLE_ROLLUP_1, or company role grouping category ID 1 (e.g. US Engineering), ROLE_ROLLUP_2, or company role grouping category ID 2 (e.g. US Retail), ROLE_DEPTNAME, or company role department description (e.g. Retail), ROLE_TITLE, or company role business title description (e.g. Senior Engineering Retail Manager), ROLE_FAMILY_DESC, or company role family extended description (e.g. Retail Manager, Software Engineering), ROLE_FAMILY, or Company role family description (e.g. Retail Manager), ROLE_CODE, or company role code, unique to each role (e.g. Manager).

3.2 Data Preprocessing

These datasets, which are commonly used in access control literature, have one major limitation: they have a highly imbalanced target distribution. For instance, in the Kaggle set, 94% of the total available access control tuples belong to the positive class (access granted). To mitigate this, we apply Synthetic Minority Over-sampling Technique (SMOTE) [11] to increase the sample size of the minority class (deny). Oversampling the negative class is straightforward in this scenario, as it corresponds to a deny decision; the default action for a security system would be to reject any unauthorised request. Conversely, in scenarios involving a larger sample of denied accesses, it becomes essential to assess the associated security risks or explore alternative approaches, such as downsampling.

In an access control setting, models might result in biased access decisions, favouring or discriminating against users with certain traits. This notion of fairness [28] might include characteristics such as location, gender or age; which can prejudice users even within the same policy. This potential problem is encountered with a "Manager ID" column in both datasets (e.g. MGR_ID). This feature connects the user to their corresponding manager, potentially utilising the manager's set of permissions to guide decision-making. To prevent this, we drop in both sets any information related to the manager of the user at subject.

Additionally, since the features of both datasets are, in its entirety, categorical, we apply binary encoding [38] to the data, where an integer is assigned to each of the categories and subsequently transformed to binary.

In order for the model to generalise, the following data partition is defined: a training subset (80% of the total sample) and a test subset (20% of the total sample). The split is performed randomly due to (1) the absence of temporal information beyond the order of accesses in the Amazon Kaggle set, and (2) the sparsity of certain policies, which would cause an ordinal division to allocate them exclusively to a single set.

3.3 Experimental Setup

Decision Engine. The model takes as input the attributes of the user and the resource to be accessed, and return an access decision to the requested resource. To evaluate the impact and generalisability of the results, we opt for four different models: (1) *ResNet* [17] for its popularity in MLBAC literature [30,33]. With a total depth of 10 layers and batch size of 32, the model is trained for a total of 20 epochs. The learning rate is set to 1e−3. The loss function used is Binary Cross Entropy. (2) *Multi-layer Perceptron* (MLP), (3) *Decision Tree* (DT), and (4) *Random Forest* (RF). All models except ResNet are trained with default parameters.

Metrics. To evaluate the model performance the following metrics are used: True Positive Rate (TPR), False Positive Rate (FPR), True Negative Rate (TNR), False Negative Rate (FNR) and F_1 Score. To measure robustness, we use the evasion rate. Specifically, we evaluate the model's accuracy against adversarial examples by measuring the number of adversarial negative examples (formerly denied requests) that are still correctly classified by the model. Conversely, we assess the number of adversarial requests that successfully deceive and evade the model relative to the total number of adversarial requests.

4   Evasion Attacks

In this section, we detail (1) the threat model, and (2) the experimental methodology for the evasion attacks.

4.1   Threat Model

This paper considers a threat model [8]. In this context, it is necessary to assume the attacker's goal, knowledge and capabilities. Each assumption is designed to prioritise the evaluation of robustness over the representation of real-world characteristics.

Goal. Evasion attacks aim at the deception of ML models, where the objective is to induce misclassification by presenting perturbed malicious inputs. In the context of access control systems, such perturbations would imply altering an access request so that the attacker gains access to a restricted resource. That is, the attacker modifies its own attributes before requesting access to the target resource. Naturally, this approach is only meaningful if the initial access request is denied, as a user deliberately blocking their own access would be unrealistic. Therefore, the goal of the attacker is defined as an evasion attack, which involves identifying one or multiple successful attacks for a particular target resource and user. Formally, for a machine learning model $f()$ and a benign access request r_i, where the output access decision $f(r_i) = 0$, the objective is to identify an adversarial request r_i' such that $f(r_i') = 1$.

Knowledge. We require the attacker to have limited knowledge about the system. We assume the success of the attack, given the tabular nature and low complexity of the data, is independent of the ML model architecture. Consequently, the attacker has no knowledge about the underlying model. However, the attacker is knowledgeable about the access control attributes and the allowed values. We assume these values are publicly available to all users. For instance, accessible through the graphical interface of the user profile configuration, where a user can select their attributes. While this scenario may not be faithful to most real-world access control systems, it is critical to assume the most vulnerable scenario and a most capable attacker for a rigorous security evaluation. This assumption serves as a baseline for advanced scenarios. No access to the MLBAC model training dataset is needed by the attacker.

Capabilities. An evasion attack is only possible if the attacker can modify the set of user attributes. We assume that the attacker can perform an unlimited number of requests to the access control system, without the risk of being detected or blocked by it. As previously mentioned, in a real-world scenario, this level of exposure would not be feasible due to the presence of additional layers of defence. However, the evaluation of a comprehensive security pipeline is beyond the scope of this paper. Our analysis is confined to MLBAC models. Additionally, the malicious actor should be able to modify its own set of user attributes. In the majority of access control systems, users will have limited control over their attributes, whereas administrators will control the majority of them. In order to consider this real-world constraint, the attacker will be able to only modify one attribute per request.

4.2   Attack Scenarios

In order to assess the vulnerability of MLBAC models against adversarial attacks we define two different scenarios and constraints:

No Limitation. As described in the threat model, the attacker is able to (1) perform an unlimited number of requests, (2) modify only one attribute per request and (3) to select any allowed value. A value is considered to be allowed if it is present in the dataset. We opt for this definition due to the absence of numeric features and the specific nature of access control attributes. Consider ROLE_TITLE; only values such as "Retail Manager" or "Software Engineer" are permitted, as entries like "adversarial123" or 0xA1 would not be allowed by the system. If such values were permitted, they would be indicative of adversarial behaviour.

Limited Value Set. Extending the previous scenario, the attacker is restricted to sampling attribute values from a predefined set of allowed options. These allowed values are defined as the 15 most frequent values per feature. The rationale for this restriction is that less frequent values are typically associated with special roles (e.g. higher management) and are therefore inaccessible to the attacker.

4.3   Crafting Adversarial Requests

The categorical and tabular nature of the data precludes the application of well-established adversarial techniques, such as Projected Gradient Descent (PGD) [26], which is commonly used in the image recognition domain. In response to this limitation, and based on our threat model wherein all features and values are publicly accessible, we define the following procedure for crafting adversarial requests:

A random subset of 500 observations from the denied class is selected for perturbation. For each feature of these observations, the target feature is modified while keeping the others fixed. A new value, distinct from the original, is randomly selected, and the adversarial request is recorded. This process is repeated five times for each feature—excluding resource and target—before proceeding to the next.

Consider an access request $r_i = (r_{i_1}, r_{i_2}, \ldots, r_{i_m}, t_i, y_i)$, where $r_i \in U$, and U is a random subset of the denied access requests set D with $|U| = 500$ and $y_i = 0$. For each request r_i, a set of adversarial requests R_i is generated by perturbing each feature r_{i_j} $(j = 1, 2, \ldots, m)$ while keeping the remaining features fixed. The set R_i is defined as:

$$R_i = \bigcup_{j=1}^{m} \{(r_{i_1}, \ldots, r_{i_{j-1}}, r'_{i_j}, r_{i_{j+1}}, \ldots, r_{i_m}, t_i) \mid r'_{i_j} \neq r_{i_j},$$

where r'_{i_j} is a randomly sampled value from the sample space of r_{i_j}. For each feature r_{i_j}, five adversarial samples are generated, resulting in $|R_i| = 5 \cdot m$. The complete adversarial dataset is then $R = \bigcup_{i=1}^{|U|} R_i$.

This procedure is performed twice: once without sample space limitations R^α and once with a restricted set of values R^β, as described in the previous section.

Perturbation Size. In other domains, adversarial attacks often consider the size of the perturbation to ensure that the attack remains inconspicuous. However, this approach is not feasible in the context of access control, where the only meaningful measure of perturbation size is the number of altered features. A significant perturbation would result in modifying a request to the point where it becomes an entirely different one. That is, $\exists r_k \mid r'_i \approx r_k, \ k \neq i$. Naturally, if $f(r_k) = 1$, where $f()$ is the MLBAC model, the request would no longer be considered adversarial, but rather a benign request that complies with an enforced policy.

5   Robustness of MLBAC Systems

5.1   Evasion Evaluation

To provide a clearer understanding of the impact of adversarial requests, Table 1 presents the various metrics for the non-robust baseline models. These models are trained as outlined in Sect. 3, using the training set without the application of additional measures.

Table 1. Non-robust models' performance metrics (%).

Model	F_1	TPR	FPR	TNR	FNR
Kaggle					
ResNet	95.38	94.58	3.71	96.29	5.42
RF	97.23	98.40	3.96	96.04	1.60
DT	93.99	92.10	3.83	96.17	7.90
MLP	95.38	94.29	3.38	96.62	5.71
UCI					
ResNet	90.60	88.34	6.78	93.23	11.66
RF	91.98	91.62	7.68	92.32	8.38
DT	87.45	83.32	7.33	92.67	16.68
MLP	90.97	89.02	6.79	93.21	10.98

To evaluate the effectiveness of the crafted adversarial requests and the vulnerability of the MLBAC models, we test the crafted sets R^α and R^β against the various models. As noted, this is accomplished by modifying one attribute at a time, which allows us to assess the vulnerability of each feature individually. The results are depicted in Fig. 2 and Table 2.

Table 2. Non-robust models' average performance comparison against adversarial attacks.

Data	Model	Set	Evasion Rate (%)	Accuracy (%)
Kaggle	DT	R^α	49.22	50.78
		R^β	42.46	57.54
	MLP	R^α	52.34	47.66
		R^β	37.29	62.71
	RF	R^α	53.46	46.54
		R^β	41.65	58.35
	ResNet	R^α	39.03	60.97
		R^β	26.39	73.61
UCI	DT	R^α	25.24	74.76
		R^β	22.42	77.58
	MLP	R^α	38.25	61.75
		R^β	32.27	67.73
	RF	R^α	23.00	77.00
		R^β	18.11	81.89
	ResNet	R^α	29.92	70.08
		R^β	23.32	76.68

The first notable observation is that the degree of vulnerability is independent of the model architecture, with ResNet showing lower evasion rates but still remaining exposed. Similarly, while imposing additional constraints, such as the limited value set, improves the results, all models remain susceptible to attacks and are unsuitable for real-world deployment. Furthermore, the higher data complexity of the UCI dataset leads to slightly more robust models by default.

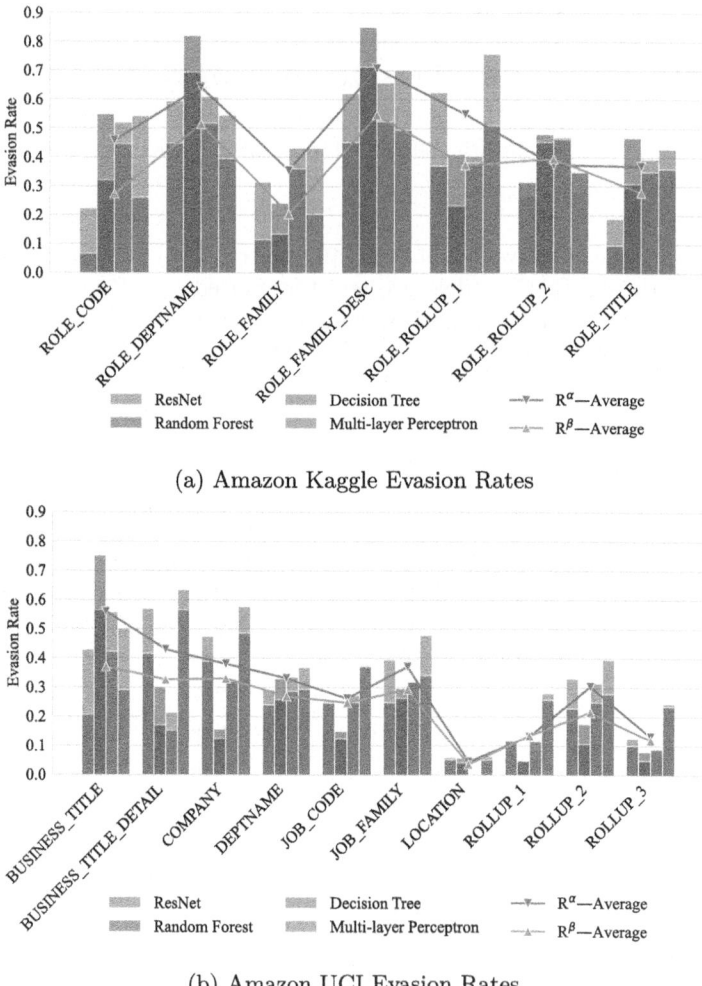

(a) Amazon Kaggle Evasion Rates

(b) Amazon UCI Evasion Rates

Fig. 2. Evasion rates for the different MLBAC features for the two scenarios: limited value set and no limitation.

5.2   Adversarial Training

In adversarial training [26], the model is presented during training with adversarial examples to maximise its resistance to perturbations. By exposing the model to these adversarial inputs during training, the model learns robust and generalisable features, enhancing its performance on unseen data and its resilience to potential attacks. In the context of access control, adversarial training will ensure the model only enforces allowed policies.

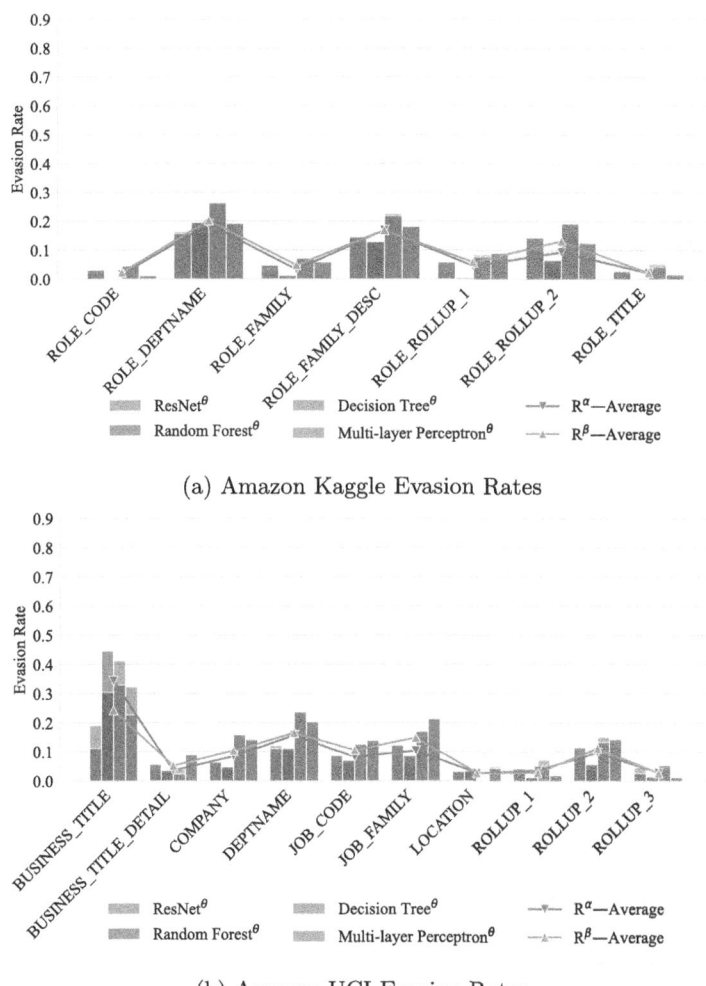

(a) Amazon Kaggle Evasion Rates

(b) Amazon UCI Evasion Rates

Fig. 3. Evasion rates for the different MLBAC features for the two robust scenarios: limited value set and no limitation.

We generate a new pair of sets, $R^{\alpha'}$ and $R^{\beta'}$, following the procedure outlined in Sect. 4.3, to be used for adversarial training. These sets are then incorporated into the original training data, and the new robust models are re-trained from scratch. The sets R^α and R^β are subsequently utilised for evaluation.

5.3   Robustness Evaluation

We conduct the same evaluation as performed for the non-robust models. As a baseline, Table 3 presents the metrics of the robust models trained alongside the adversarial examples. The performance of these models is comparable to that of the non-robust models, with only a slight reduction in performance.

Table 3. Robust models' performance metrics (%).

Model	F_1	TPR	FPR	TNR	FNR
Kaggle					
ResNet$^\theta$	94.01	91.65	3.29	96.71	8.35
RF$^\theta$	96.82	97.35	3.71	96.29	2.65
DT$^\theta$	92.86	89.86	3.64	96.36	10.14
MLP$^\theta$	93.58	90.77	3.19	96.81	9.23
UCI					
ResNet$^\theta$	89.19	84.50	5.04	94.96	15.50
RF$^\theta$	91.81	91.21	7.58	92.42	8.79
DT$^\theta$	86.11	81.04	7.27	92.73	18.96
MLP$^\theta$	89.41	86.61	7.22	92.78	13.39

The robust models, when evaluated against the original adversarial sets R^α and R^β, demonstrate a significant increase in robustness. As shown in Fig. 3 and Table 4, adversarial training results in a reduction of evasion rates by approximately 40% across all models and datasets. Notably, the impact of a constrained sample space (R^β) is less pronounced compared to the non-robust models. This suggests that additional defensive measures, such as restricting user inputs, inherently enhance the robustness of MLBAC models.

Despite the notable improvements in robustness, the models remain susceptible to adversarial requests. This vulnerability is evident in the feature importance. As depicted in Fig. 3, and especially in Fig. 3b, different attributes are affected unequally by adversarial training. Nonetheless, this approach and its findings can assist system administrators in gaining a deeper understanding of MLBAC models and developing potential defensive strategies.

Another benefit of adversarial training is the reduction in the minimum number of attempts required by an attacker to bypass an access control model. To evaluate this, 100 requests are randomly sampled, and for each request, five adversarial requests are generated per feature, following the procedure described in Sect. 4.3. The resulting R_i array is then randomly shuffled, and its requests are

Table 4. Robust models' average performance comparison against adversarial attacks.

Data	Model	Set	Evasion Rate (%)	Accuracy (%)
Kaggle	DT^θ	R^α	11.55	88.45
		R^β	12.41	87.59
	MLP^θ	R^α	7.49	92.51
		R^β	10.38	89.62
	RF^θ	R^α	4.53	95.47
		R^β	5.78	94.22
	$ResNet^\theta$	R^α	7.09	92.91
		R^β	9.10	90.90
UCI	DT^θ	R^α	13.34	86.66
		R^β	12.26	87.74
	MLP^θ	R^α	11.73	88.27
		R^β	11.65	88.35
	RF^θ	R^α	9.07	90.93
		R^β	6.98	93.02
	$ResNet^\theta$	R^α	8.40	91.60
		R^β	7.37	92.63

sequentially tested against the MLBAC model. The number of attempts required to successfully bypass access is recorded.

As shown in Fig. 4, adversarial training not only enhances overall resilience to attacks but also increases the minimum number of attempts required for successful breaches. This is particularly significant in real-world deployments, where users are limited in the number of requests they can perform, thereby reducing the likelihood of unauthorised access. In the Amazon Kaggle dataset, there is a notable decrease in attacks requiring only one attempt, from 70.75% of the requests to 43.30%. Similarly, in the Amazon UCI dataset, a smaller but still significant reduction is observed, from 56.53% to 51.77%.

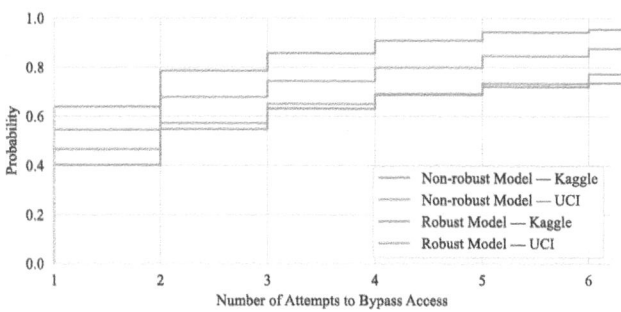

Fig. 4. Cumulative Distribution Function (CDF) of the minimum number of attempts needed to bypass the MLBAC models on average.

6   Discussion

In this section, we examine the implications and limitations of our results, while also exploring potential areas for future research.

6.1   Validity Threats

Generalisability of Results. The sensitive nature of security information significantly contributes to the scarcity of publicly available datasets. This scarcity is particularly pronounced in the access control domain, where datasets are not only limited in quantity but also in the detail and complexity of the data they contain. Therefore, the generalisability of our results can be limited by this scarcity. In this paper, we attempted to mitigate the absence of policy knowledge by extracting such information from access logs. However, it is important to acknowledge that this extracted data may not entirely replicate the intricacies and complexity of real-world access control policies and it is necessary to consider these limitations when applying the results to real-world applications. Future work would need to collect complex and up-to-date real-world data to offer a more comprehensive representation of access control environments. Alternatively, leveraging complex synthetic datasets could provide a more realistic simulation of real-world scenarios.

Threat Model Assumptions. The devised threat model does not consider the notion of imperceptibility and magnitude of the perturbations. This is intrinsically linked with the limitations found in the data, where only categorical values are available and it is not possible to discern the relationship between attributes. This assumption is valid for the majority of attributes in access control systems, as they are typically categorical. Nonetheless, there could be numerical attributes, such as timestamps or aggregated features (e.g. the number of accesses within specific time windows), where the notion of imperceptibility may become relevant.

Under the threat model, we assume that the attacker has certain capabilities, such as unlimited requests, modification of the attributes and access to the system. These assumptions are made to rigorously evaluate the security of the MLBAC models. Consequently, implementing additional and necessary security measures will limit the success of adversarial attacks. Notably, this is the case with hybrid access control systems with both a ML-based component and a rule-based component. Future work should consider the feasibility and applicability of adversarial attacks against such systems.

7   Conclusion

This paper explores the robustness of Machine Learning-based Access Control systems through two distinct phases: (1) examining the susceptibility of MLBAC systems to adversarial attacks and (2) enhancing their robustness. Initially, a threat model was defined to capture real-world attack scenarios, providing insights into how adversarial attacks impact MLBAC models. We demonstrate the risk adversarial requests pose to such models, with evasion rates ranging from 20% to 50%, as well as the importance of features. Subsequently, the paper explored adversarial training to enhance the robustness of MLBAC systems. A major decrease in evasion rate was demonstrated when compared to the baseline non-robust models, with a drop of *circa* 40% in evasion rates. These findings contribute significantly to the security of MLBAC systems and foster broader acceptance and understanding of their efficacy.

Acknowledgements. This research is partially funded by the Research Fund KU Leuven, and by the Flemish Research Programme Cybersecurity. This paper was also partially supported by the AIDE project funded by the Belgian SPF BOSA under the programme "Financing of projects for the development of artificial intelligence in Belgium" with reference number 06.40.32.33.00.10.

References

1. Abu Jabal, A., Bertino, E., Lobo, J., Law, M., Russo, A., Calo, S., Verma, D.: Polisma - A framework for learning attribute-based access control policies. In: Chen, L., Li, N., Liang, K., Schneider, S. (eds.) ESORICS 2020. LNCS, vol. 12308, pp. 523–544. Springer, Cham (2020). https://doi.org/10.1007/978-3-030-58951-6_26

2. Alohaly, M., Takabi, H., Blanco, E.: Towards an automated extraction of ABAC constraints from natural language policies. In: Dhillon, G., Karlsson, F., Hedström, K., Zúquete, A. (eds.) SEC 2019. IAICT, vol. 562, pp. 105–119. Springer, Cham (2019). https://doi.org/10.1007/978-3-030-22312-0_8

3. Amazon, Kaggle: Amazon.com - Employee access challenge (2014). https://www.kaggle.com/competitions/amazon-employee-access-challenge/data. Accessed 20 Jan 2025

4. Argento, L., Margheri, A., Paci, F., Sassone, V., Zannone, N.: Towards adaptive access control. In: Kerschbaum, F., Paraboschi, S. (eds.) DBSec 2018. LNCS, vol. 10980, pp. 99–109. Springer, Cham (2018). https://doi.org/10.1007/978-3-319-95729-6_7

5. Bauer, L., Cranor, L.F., Reeder, R.W., Reiter, M.K., Vaniea, K.: Real life challenges in access-control management. In: Proceedings of the SIGCHI Conference on Human Factors in Computing Systems, pp. 899–908 (2009)

6. Bauer, L., Garriss, S., Reiter, M.K.: Detecting and resolving policy misconfigurations in access-control systems. ACM Trans. Inf. Syst. Secur. (TISSEC) **14**(1), 1–28 (2011)

7. Biggio, B., Corona, I., Maiorca, D., Nelson, B., Šrndić, N., Laskov, P., Giacinto, G., Roli, F.: Evasion attacks against machine learning at test time. In: Blockeel, H., Kersting, K., Nijssen, S., Železný, F. (eds.) ECML PKDD 2013. LNCS (LNAI), vol. 8190, pp. 387–402. Springer, Heidelberg (2013). https://doi.org/10.1007/978-3-642-40994-3_25

8. Carlini, N., et al.: On evaluating adversarial robustness. arXiv preprint arXiv:1902.06705 (2019)

9. Cartella, F., Anunciacao, O., Funabiki, Y., Yamaguchi, D., Akishita, T., Elshocht, O.: Adversarial attacks for tabular data: application to fraud detection and imbalanced data. arXiv preprint arXiv:2101.08030 (2021)

10. Chang, C.C., Lin, I.C., Liao, C.T.: An access control system with time-constraint using support vector machines. Int. J. Netw. Secur. **2**(2), 150–159 (2006)

11. Chawla, N.V., Bowyer, K.W., Hall, L.O., Kegelmeyer, W.P.: Smote: synthetic minority over-sampling technique. J. Artif. Intell. Res. **16**, 321–357 (2002)

12. Cotrini, C., Weghorn, T., Basin, D.: Mining ABAC rules from sparse logs. In: 2018 IEEE European Symposium on Security and Privacy (EuroS&P), pp. 31–46. IEEE (2018)

13. Ferraiolo, D., Cugini, J., Kuhn, D.R., et al.: Role-based access control (RBAC): features and motivations. In: Proceedings of 11th Annual Computer Security Application Conference, pp. 241–48 (1995)

14. Frank, M., Basin, D., Buhmann, J.M.: A class of probabilistic models for role engineering. In: Proceedings of the 15th ACM conference on Computer and communications security, pp. 299–310 (2008)

15. Goodfellow, I.J., Shlens, J., Szegedy, C.: Explaining and harnessing adversarial examples. arXiv preprint arXiv:1412.6572 (2014)

16. Gumma, V., Mitra, B., Dey, S., Patel, P.S., Suman, S., Das, S.: Pammela: policy administration methodology using machine learning. arXiv preprint arXiv:2111.07060 (2021)

17. He, K., Zhang, X., Ren, S., Sun, J.: Deep residual learning for image recognition. In: Proceedings of the IEEE Conference on Computer Vision and Pattern Recognition, pp. 770–778 (2016)

18. Hu, V.C., Hu, V.C.: Machine learning for access control policy verification. US Department of Commerce, National Institute of Standards and Technology (2021)

19. Hu, V.C., Kuhn, D.R., Ferraiolo, D.F., Voas, J.: Attribute-based access control. Computer **48**(2), 85–88 (2015)

20. Huang, L., Joseph, A.D., Nelson, B., Rubinstein, B.I., Tygar, J.D.: Adversarial machine learning. In: Proceedings of the 4th ACM Workshop on Security and Artificial Intelligence, pp. 43–58 (2011)

21. Jagielski, M., Oprea, A., Biggio, B., Liu, C., Nita-Rotaru, C., Li, B.: Manipulating machine learning: Poisoning attacks and countermeasures for regression learning. In: 2018 IEEE symposium on security and privacy (SP), pp. 19–35. IEEE (2018)

22. Karimi, L., Abdelhakim, M., Joshi, J.: Adaptive ABAC policy learning: a reinforcement learning approach. arXiv preprint arXiv:2105.08587 (2021)

23. Kireev, K., Kulynych, B., Troncoso, C.: Adversarial robustness for tabular data through cost and utility awareness. arXiv preprint arXiv:2208.13058 (2022)

24. Liu, A., Du, X., Wang, N.: Efficient access control permission decision engine based on machine learning. Secur. Commun. Netw. **2021**, 3970485 (2021)

25. Llamas, J.M., Preuveneers, D., Joosen, W.: Effective machine learning-based access control administration through unlearning. In: 2023 IEEE European Symposium on Security and Privacy Workshops (EuroS&PW), pp. 50–57. IEEE (2023)

26. Madry, A., Makelov, A., Schmidt, L., Tsipras, D., Vladu, A.: Towards deep learning models resistant to adversarial attacks. arXiv preprint arXiv:1706.06083 (2017)

27. Mathov, Y., Levy, E., Katzir, Z., Shabtai, A., Elovici, Y.: Not all datasets are born equal: On heterogeneous tabular data and adversarial examples. Knowl. Based Syst. **242**, 108377 (2022)

28. Mehrabi, N., Morstatter, F., Saxena, N., Lerman, K., Galstyan, A.: A survey on bias and fairness in machine learning. ACM Comput. Surv. (CSUR) **54**(6), 1–35 (2021)

29. Montanez, K.: Amazon access samples. UCI Machine learning repository (2011). https://doi.org/10.24432/C5JW2K

30. Nobi, M.N., Gupta, M., Praharaj, L., Abdelsalam, M., Krishnan, R., Sandhu, R.: Machine learning in access control: a taxonomy and survey. arXiv preprint arXiv:2207.01739 (2022)

31. Nobi, M.N., Krishnan, R.: Adversarial attacks in machine learning based access control. In: Italian Conference on Big Data and Data Science (ITADATA2022) (2022)

32. Nobi, M.N., Krishnan, R., Huang, Y., Sandhu, R.: Administration of machine learning based access control. In: Computer Security–ESORICS 2022: 27th European Symposium on Research in Computer Security, Copenhagen, Denmark, September 26–30, 2022, Proceedings, Part II, pp. 189–210. Springer (2022). https://doi.org/10.1007/978-3-031-17146-8_10

33. Nobi, M.N., Krishnan, R., Huang, Y., Shakarami, M., Sandhu, R.: Toward deep learning based access control. In: Proceedings of the Twelveth ACM Conference on Data and Application Security and Privacy, pp. 143–154 (2022)

34. OWASP Foundation: OWASP Top Ten (2021). https://owasp.org/www-project-top-ten/. Accessed 20 Jan 2025

35. Papernot, N., McDaniel, P., Goodfellow, I.: Transferability in machine learning: from phenomena to black-box attacks using adversarial samples. arXiv preprint arXiv:1605.07277 (2016)

36. Papernot, N., McDaniel, P., Goodfellow, I., Jha, S., Celik, Z.B., Swami, A.: Practical black-box attacks against machine learning. In: Proceedings of the 2017 ACM on Asia Conference on Computer and Communications Security, pp. 506–519 (2017)

37. Sandhu, R., Munawer, Q.: How to do discretionary access control using roles. In: Proceedings of the Third ACM Workshop on Role-Based Access Control, pp. 47–54 (1998)

38. Seger, C.: An investigation of categorical variable encoding techniques in machine learning: binary versus one-hot and feature hashing (2018)

39. Servos, D., Osborn, S.L.: Current research and open problems in attribute-based access control. ACM Comput. Surv. (CSUR) **49**(4), 1–45 (2017)

40. Shokri, R., Stronati, M., Song, C., Shmatikov, V.: Membership inference attacks against machine learning models. In: 2017 IEEE Symposium on Security and Privacy (SP), pp. 3–18. IEEE (2017)

41. Vincent, B., Xavier, R., Jonathan, A., Thibault, L., Pascal, F., Marcin, D.: Imperceptible adversarial attacks on tabular data. arXiv preprint arXiv:1911.03274 (2019)

42. Xiang, C., et al.: Towards continuous access control validation and forensics. In: Proceedings of the 2019 ACM SIGSAC Conference on Computer and Communications Security, pp. 113–129 (2019)

43. Xu, T., Naing, H.M., Lu, L., Zhou, Y.: How do system administrators resolve access-denied issues in the real world? In: Proceedings of the 2017 CHI Conference on Human Factors in Computing Systems, pp. 348–361 (2017)

44. Xu, Z., Stoller, S.D.: Mining attribute-based access control policies. IEEE Trans. Dependable Secure Comput. **12**(5), 533–545 (2014)

Towards Robust Artificial Intelligence: Self-supervised Learning Approach for Out-of-Distribution Detection

Wissam Salhab[✉], Darine Ameyed, Hamid Mcheick, and Fehmi Jaafar

555 University of Quebec at Chicoutimi, Quebec, G7H 2B1, Canada
{wissam.salhab1,dameyed,hamid_mcheick,fehmi.jaafar}@uqac.ca

Abstract. Robustness in AI systems refers to their ability to maintain reliable and accurate performance under various conditions, including out-of-distribution (OOD) samples, adversarial attacks, and environmental changes. This is crucial in safety-critical systems, such as autonomous vehicles, transportation, or healthcare, where malfunctions could have severe consequences. This paper proposes an approach to improve OOD detection without the need of labeled data, thereby increasing the AI systems' robustness. The proposed approach leverages the principles of self-supervised learning, allowing the model to learn useful representations from unlabeled data. Combined with graph-theoretical techniques, this enables the more efficient identification and categorization of OOD samples. Compared to existing state-of-the-art methods, this approach achieved an Area Under the Receiver Operating Characteristic Curve (AUROC) = 0.99.

Keywords: Trustworthy AI · Reliability · Robustness · OOD Detection · AI Safety

1 Introduction

The rapid advancement of AI-driven systems has significantly impacted decision-making in various domains, including healthcare, finance, transportation, and security. However, AI systems often struggle with handling data from diverse sources, structures, and distributions, raising concerns about their robustness in real-world applications. Ensuring AI robustness is crucial, as these systems must consistently deliver reliable and accurate outputs under diverse conditions to maintain user trust and facilitate safe deployment and secure integration across multiple domains. This need is particularly pressing in high-stakes systems, where errors or incorrect decisions can have severe consequences and pose significant risk to human safety [7].

A key aspect of AI robustness is the ability to detect OOD samples, thereby preventing unreliable predictions. Simply put, OOD occurs when input data differs from the training distribution. OOD samples can originate from various

© The Author(s), under exclusive license to Springer Nature Switzerland AG 2025
B. Coppens et al. (Eds.): ARES 2025 Workshops, LNCS 15994, pp. 106–121, 2025.
https://doi.org/10.1007/978-3-032-00630-1_7

sources, often arising from unseen situations the model has not encountered during training. Moreover, they can also result from adversarial attack inputs deliberately designed to mislead the model. Consequently, understanding how OOD samples impact AI systems is essential to making them adaptable to dynamic input data.

Thus, ODD detection involves identifying inputs that differ significantly from the training distribution, including previously unseen classes, random noise, or adversarial attacks. However, OOD detection remains a significant challenge. Many existing methods often struggle to accurately detect these outliers, especially when deep neural networks exhibit overconfidence, resulting in the misclassification of OOD data.

We propose a self-supervised method for extracting embeddings from unlabeled images using graph theory, which enables nuanced representations of both in-distribution and OOD data.

This study suggests a new OOD detection approach connecting self-supervised contrastive learning, graph-based clustering, and Mahalanobis distance. Unlike previous methods, our approach is completely unsupervised, requires only in-distribution unlabeled data, which improves scalability and is targeted in real-world scenarios.

The integration of Graph clustering addresses the limitations of distance by modeling the distribution of data as a mixture of Gaussians, thereby improving the detection of near OOD samples. Compared to Maple [21], which depends on label data and Gaussian assumption, our approach leverages the graph theory of capturing local data structures, and relative to SSD [15], in contrastive learning but lacks clustering, our approach enhances robustness through graph representations, achieving superior AUROC score of 0.99 on benchmark datasets (CIFAR-10, CIFAR-100, SVHN).

The rest of this paper is structured as follows. Section 2 reviews related work in this field. Section 3 provides a detailed explanation of the proposed approach, followed by an experiment presented in Sect. 4. The challenges and limitations are addressed in Sect. 5. Finally, we conclude the paper in Sect. 6, highlighting future research directions.

2   Related Works

OOD detection has been an active area of research. As we propose a self-supervised approach for ODD detection, this section reviews relevant related works in the field.

2.1   Mahalanobis-Based OOD Detection

Mahalanobis distance (MD) is the distance between a data point and a distribution, and has been widely used in the literature for anomaly detection applications [12,22]. In OOD detection, MD is frequently employed to distinguish far

OOD samples from in-distribution samples, which differ greatly in meaning and style.

However, MD frequently fails to classify OOD samples close to the decision boundary and semantically similar to in-distribution samples [3]. To address this limit, a straightforward solution known as the relative Mahalanobis distance (RMD) has been implemented as a more robust alternative. RMD enhances performance and increases resilience to hyperparameter fluctuations [12]. RMD relies on predefined statistical assumptions that often do not generalize well across diverse datasets or complex OOD situations. Its effectiveness also decreases in high-dimensional settings where estimating function correlations is difficult.

2.2 OOD Detection Using Supervised Classifiers

OOD classifiers help discover and classify data points that significantly deviate from a given data distribution [10]. This is typically achieved by training a model using binary or multi-class classification approaches [18]. The authors of [21] introduced MAPLE, which enhances OOD detection through predictive probability calibration. MAPLE dynamically clusters non-Gaussian class representations into multiple Gaussian distributions. The approach involves training a CNN using cross-entropy and triplet loss functions, combined with MD-based classification.

Their reliance on labeled data limits the effectiveness of many OOD detection methods, as they struggle to identify OOD instances that do not align with learned distributions. Additionally, the flexibility of these methods often relies on Gaussian assumptions, which may not always apply. This underscores the need for more adaptable OOD detection techniques that minimize the dependence on labeled data or rigid distribution assumptions. Contrastive learning models, for example, require large and diverse datasets to perform well and are sensitive to the selection of negative samples. Similarly, methods such as Maximum Mean Discrepancy (MMD) can be less effective in high-dimensional spaces, where distance metrics become unreliable. These issues underscore the necessity of developing robust OOD detection techniques that can effectively handle unlabeled datasets.

2.3 OOD Detection Using Contrastive Learning

Self-supervised contrastive learning has gained significant attention, especially in computer vision and natural language processing tasks [5]. The main objective of contrastive learning is to learn a representation of similar embedding in the feature space by grouping similar samples while pushing dissimilar ones apart [20].

Sehwag et al. [15] present SSD, a self-supervised system that utilizes unlabeled in-distribution data for ODD detection. SSD also incorporates training data labels and introduces enhancements for few-shot OOD detection.

Moreover, the authors of [4] proposed CADet, a fully self-supervised anomaly detection method that leverages contrastive learning and the Maximum Mean Discrepancy (MMD) metric. CADet examines whether two independent sample sets originate from the same distribution by combining contrastive learning with MMD, utilizing mean-based analysis.

2.4 OOD Detection Using Graph

Liu et al. [9] proposed a new approach for detecting OOD samples in graph-structured data. Their primary objective is to identify OOD graphs using unlabeled in-distribution data. They utilized the concept of contrastive learning to identify OOD graphs without the need for ground-truth labels [9]. Whereas, other methods make use of Graph neural networks (GNN) to detect OOD samples within graph data [17].

Although these methods adapt OOD detection to graph structures, they face several challenges. GNN-based methods, in particular, require extensive tuning and often struggle with the complexity of high-dimensional graphs. Additionally, they often encounter scalability issues when handling large, densely connected graphs.

2.5 Limitations of Previous Methods

In this paper, we employ contrastive learning to extract embeddings from images in a self-supervised manner, enabling OOD detection without relying on labeled OOD samples. The proposed approach offers numerous advantages, including its ability to effectively capture feature correlations and maintain robustness in high-dimensional spaces without requiring labeled data. We summarize the limitations of existing methods and highlight our contributions in Table 1. By eliminating the requirement for labeled data, reducing dependence on the Gaussian assumption, and optimizing computational efficiency through KNN-based graph constructions, our method provides a scalable and robust solution to detect OOD.

3 Proposed Approach

In this section, we provide a detailed explanation of our proposed approach. We present the proposed approach in Fig. 1. It consists of two phases: The In-Distribution data representation phase and the OOD inference phase. It provides a schematic overview of the proposed approach, clarifying the workflow from embedding extraction to OOD classification. These visualizations highlight the method's ability to capture meaningful semantic structures, which supports its superior AUROC.

Table 1. Comparison of OOD Detection Methods

Method	Labeled Data	Gaussian Assupmtion	AUROC (CIFAR10 vs SVHN)
MAPLE [21]	Yes	Yes	0.996
SSD [15]	No	No	0.996
Deep Ensemble [6]	Yes	Yes	-
ViTB16 [12]	Yes	No	-
Ours	No	No	0.999

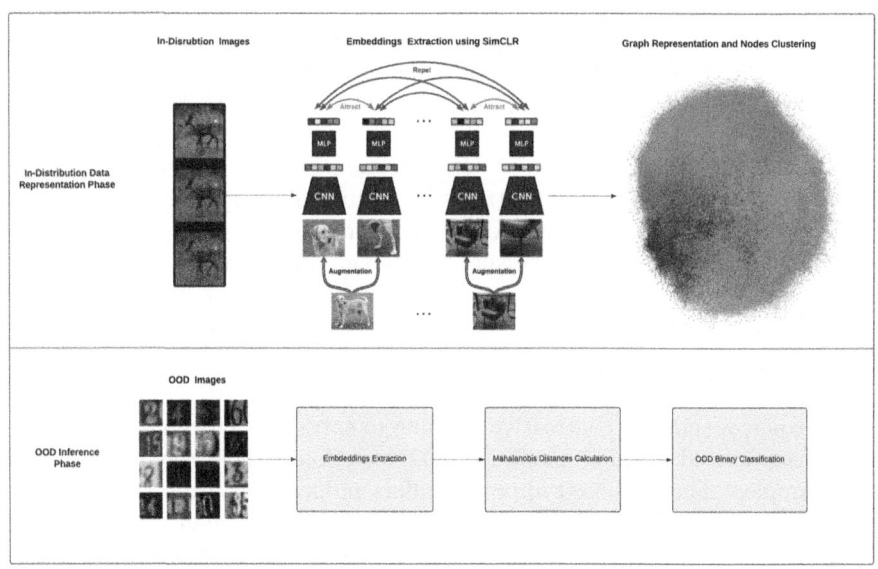

Fig. 1. The proposed approach includes two phases: **In-Distribution Data Representation Phase**: This phase involves extracting embeddings and creating a clustered graph based on these embeddings. **OOD Inference Phase**: This phase consists of extracting OOD embeddings, calculating the Mahalanobis distances to the in-distribution clusters, and performing binary classification for OOD detection.

3.1   Phase 1: In-Distribution Data Representation Phase

This phase aims to group the in-distribution unlabeled samples into distinct clusters. It achieves this by extracting embeddings from input samples, constructing a representative clustered graph.

Embeddings Extraction: We employ self-supervised contrastive learning, a practical approach that enables models to differentiate between augmented versions of the same image and other distinct images, thereby learning strong representations from unlabeled data [16].

Furthermore, SimCLR is a well-known framework that uses a contrastive learning approach [11]. It simplifies contrastive self-supervised learning algorithms without the need for memory banks or specific architectures. SimCLR uses the infoNCE loss presented in Eq. (1):

$$\ell_{i,j} = -\log \frac{\exp(\text{sim}(z_i, z_j)/\tau)}{\sum_{k=1}^{2N} 1_{[k \neq i]} \exp(\text{sim}(z_i, z_k)/\tau)} \tag{1}$$

$$= -\text{sim}(z_i, z_j)/\tau + \log \left[\sum_{k=1}^{2N} 1_{[k \neq i]} \exp(\text{sim}(z_i, z_k)/\tau) \right] \tag{2}$$

where the batch size is represented as N, and τ represents the temperature parameter, z_i and z_j are two enhanced perspectives of the same case, and $\text{sim}(.,.)$ represents the similarity function between two examples. The similarity between these embeddings is then calculated using cosine similarity, which forms the basis of the loss function.

In this study, we use SimCLR to extract image embeddings. SimCLR outperforms supervised methods when fine-tuned with a limited amount of labeled data [15].

However, embedding can be high-dimensional and still contain redundant information, leading to higher computation cost and model performance degradation [8]. After extracting the high-dimensional embedding, we employ Principal Component Analysis (PCA) to represent the latent space in lower dimensions, which reduces computational costs and mitigates performance degradation.

Graph Representation and Nodes Clustering: Once the embeddings are extracted, we construct the representation graph, where each node represents an embedding and is connected to all other nodes. To simplify the graph, we remove nodes that have no edges. However, this method presents computational challenges, as a fully dense graph is inefficient and costly. To address this issue, we employ K-nearest neighbors (KNN) to reduce the number of edges in the graph, allowing each node to connect only to its nearest neighbors. The edges of the graph are weighted using cosine similarity as follows:

$$\text{cosine similarity} = \frac{E_i \cdot E_j}{\|E_i\| \|E_j\|} \tag{3}$$

$E_i \cdot E_j$ represents the dot product of the two embedding vectors E_i and E_j, $\|E_i\|$ and $\|E_j\|$ stand for magnitude of the two vectors.

After constructing the graph, the Louvain method was used to group nodes within a graph into distinct clusters. This approach leverages modularity optimization to uncover the underlying structure of the graph, making it especially valuable for analyzing complex relationships and clusters [1].

3.2   Phase 2: OOD Inference

After identifying the clusters in phase 1, phase 2 focuses on classifying new samples as in-distribution or OOD samples. In this phase, we extract embeddings from new samples and calculate Mahalanobis distances from each embedding point to the centroids of the clusters identified in phase 1. This involves binary classification of data points that exhibit significant deviations from the established in-distribution data.

Embeddings Extraction: After we train the SimCLR model on the dataset, we extract embeddings from the OOD data during the inference phase. This method enables us to capture patterns and features without requiring labeled data, and it facilitates the calculation of Mahalanobis distances to the centroids of in-distribution clusters.

Mahalanobis Distances Calculation: Unlike Euclidean distance, MD considers the covariance between the variables as shown in Eq. (4). In this study, md is the distance between an input and the nearest centroid of the in-distribution clusters.

$$md = \sqrt{(\mathbf{x} - \mu)^T \mathbf{S}^{-1}(\mathbf{x} - \mu)} \tag{4}$$

$\mathbf{x}$ is the input vector, μ is the centroid of the cluster, and $\mathbf{S}$ is the covariance matrix of the cluster. We use MD to calculate the distance of the samples from the centroid of the in-distribution clusters.

OOD Binary Classification: While a threshold is commonly used for practical classification, it is essential to differentiate between its role in decision-making and overall performance evaluation. Following the approach outlined in [14], the authors demonstrated the effectiveness of setting the threshold at the 95th percentile of distances within the in-distribution dataset. In our study, we also set the threshold at the 95th percentile of the in-distribution data, solely to evaluate classification accuracy within this dataset. Although this specific threshold helps assess in-distribution classification accuracy, we use the AUROC as the primary evaluation metric for OOD detection. Unlike threshold-based methods, the AUROC is threshold-independent and measures the classifier's ability to distinguish between in-distribution and OOD data across various thresholds. This provides a more comprehensive assessment of the Mahalanobis distance-based OOD classifier.

3.3   Theoretical Justification for Graph Clustering and Mahalanobis Distance

The proposed approach is integrated to enhance contrastive learning and graph-based clustering for OOD detection, utilizing the Mahalanobis distance. This section provides a theoretical foundation for why graph clustering enhances

Mahalanobis-based OOD detection. Graph clustering, achieved through the Louvain method, involves grouping different in-distribution embeddings into distinct groups based on their latent space similarity. This process captures the underlying structure of the data and addresses the limits of the Mahalanobis distance in high-dimensional settings. The Mahalanobis distance is considered for a single Gaussian distribution of data, which may fail when the data exhibits multi-model or non-Gaussian characteristics [3]. Concerts we implement, effectively modeling assumptions as a mixture of Gaussians, where each cluster represents a local Gaussian component. This means that the Mahalanobis distance is calculated with respect to the nearest cluster centroid, which improves the sensitivity of OOD tests near the decision limits. By reducing md in Eq. 4 on all clusters, we choose the nearest cluster, which improves the strength of distributional shifts. The Louvain method optimizes modularity, ensuring that clusters are closely connected while being externally connected, and interact with the perception that they disassemble the data into units. This grouping reduces the effect of high-dimensional covariance estimation errors, as S is calculated on small, more homogeneous groups. In addition, the use of KNN reduces the graph calculation complexity by limiting the connection to the nearest neighbors, which minimizes the graph from $O(n^2)$ to $O(n^K)$. These savings preserve the local neighborhood.

4   Experimental Results

Our primary results confirm the effectiveness of our proposed approach. Across several datasets, we observe a significant increase in the AUROC, achieving a maximum value of 0.999.

4.1   Datasets

We validate our approach using well-used datasets in computer vision and machine learning, including CIFAR10, CIFAR100, and SVHN.

CIFAR10: consists of 60,000 images classified into 10 classes, each containing 6,000 photos. It includes 10,000 test images and 50,000 training images. This dataset is a commonly used resource for training computer vision and machine learning algorithms. In this study, no labeled training images were used.

CIFAR100: This dataset comprises of 60,000 photos, each measuring 32×32 pixels, divided into 100 classes with 600 photos in each class. It includes 50,000 training images and 10,000 test images. The training images without labels were used in this study.

SVHN: This dataset includes 600,000 images of house numbers from Google Street View, including 73,257 training images and 26,032 images as the testing dataset [19]. The training images without labels were used in this study. The code and results of this study are available on GitHub [13].

4.2   Experiment Setup

The SimCLR model is trained using a batch size 256 to extract image embeddings. The temperature parameter is set to $\tau = 0.1$, and the learning rate to

0.0001. A weight decay of $1e^{-4}$ is applied and the training lasts over 300 epochs. We utilize 4 GPUs, including an NVIDIA 8GB V100, which completes the training in 8.795 h. The process involves transforming the input images using various techniques, including Random Horizontal Flip, Random Resized Crop, Color Jitter, and Random Grayscale. These transformations adjust the images' brightness, contrast, saturation, and hue. The ResNet50 architecture serves as the base encoder, with an output dimension of 2048. The final layer of this model consists of a multi-layer perceptron (MLP), which includes a linear layer followed by a rectified linear unit (ReLU) activation function. The last layer functions as a projection layer with a dimension of 128. Before extracting features for the downstream task, we remove the projection head from the model. KNN was used for graph construction; we used k = 7 to balance cluster accuracy and computational efficiency (see Tables 2 and 3).

4.3   Results

Embeddings Extraction: The result of SimCLR training with this setup is shown in Fig. 2, which indicates an accuracy of 0.982 for top-5 validation on the CIFAR10 dataset. After extracting embeddings, we utilize PCA to reduce dimensionality. Following the SimCLR training on CIFAR-10, we leverage the learned representations to extract embeddings for all other datasets. These embeddings are then utilized to evaluate the model's performance on downstream tasks, specifically clustering and OOD detection. The results confirm that these learned representations effectively capture meaningful semantic information despite domain shifts between datasets.

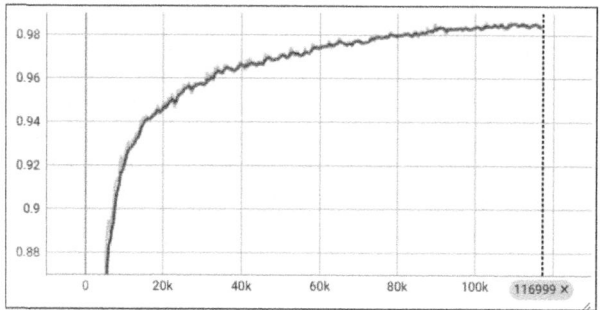

Fig. 2. Top-5 validation accuracy chart. The model reaches a top-5 validation accuracy of 98.2% after 117000 steps for the CIFAR10 dataset. A top-5 accuracy indicates that the true labels are among the five highest predicted probabilities.

Graph Building and Clustering: Choosing 'k' neighbors in KNN is essential as it establishes the graph structure. Instead of calculating and storing the full

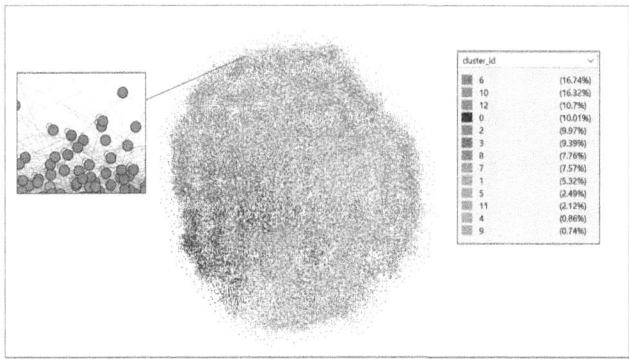

Fig. 3. Clustered Graph: Each node in the graph represents an image embedding in latent space. We obtained 13 clusters (differentiable via colors in this image) out of 10 clusters.

adjacent matrix, we connect each data point to its closest neighbors. This graph reduces the calculation costs and the memory required to store the graph representation. This approach provides a sufficient efficiency advantage by reducing the density of the edges.

After creating the graph, we use the Louvain method to identify clusters within it. This method is designed to recover non-overlapping communities from large networks [2]. It involves calculating the degree to which the nodes in a cluster are more densely linked than they would be in a random network. Figure 3 shows us the graph after performing Louvain clustering.

Moreover, we test the number of neighbors to consider in the KNN with several values of 'k'. The findings for CIFAR100 are shown in Table 2. When the number of neighbors 'k' increases from 5 to 9, the number of edges rises from 180480 to 335785, while the number of clusters decreases from 167 to 90. Overall, the graph presents a total of 109 clusters at k = 7, which is close to the target of 100 clusters, the ground truth in the case of CIFAR100. At k = 7, the graph contains 258,385 edges and 50,000 nodes. The results for the CIFAR10 graph are presented in Table 3. As the number of neighbors, 'k', increases from 5 to 11, the number of clusters first decreases from 16 to 13. However, when 'k' reaches 11, the number of clusters increases to 14. The selection of k = 7 resulted in a graph with 180,451 edges, 50,000 nodes, and 13 clusters, which is closest to 10, the ground truth in CIFAR-10. In contrast, k = 9 had 335,773 edges and the same number of clusters (13), but with more edges, resulting in a higher computational cost.

OOD Detection Results: We present the results of the OOD detection in Table 4. When we train the model on CIFAR10 (In-Distribution) and test it on CIFAR100 and SVHN (OOD datasets), our proposed approach achieves nearly the best AUROC and AUPR scores of 0.999 on both OOD datasets, significantly outperforming MAPLE [21], Deep Ensemble [6], SSD [15], and even

Table 2. Using different k-values for KNN **with cifar100** dataset, The optimal value of k is 7, resulting in 109 clusters, the closest to the ground truth in CIFAR100 clusters.

K	Nodes	Edges	Clusters
k = 5	50000	180480	167
k = 7	50000	258385	109
k = 9	50000	335785	90

Table 3. Using different k-values for KNN with **cifar10** dataset, The optimal value of k = 7 results in 13 clusters, closest to the ground truth of CIFAR10 clusters.

K	Nodes	Edges	Clusters
k = 5	50000	258280	16
k = 7	50000	180451	13
k = 9	50000	335773	13
k = 11	50000	412678	14

the competitive Vision Transformer (ViT-B16) [12]. Similarly, when trained on CIFAR100 (In-Distribution) and evaluated on CIFAR10 and SVHN (out-of-distribution datasets), the proposed approach maintains exceptional performance with AUROC scores of 0.999 and 0.997 for CIFAR10 and SVHN, respectively (Table 5), again surpassing all comparative methods. The proposed approach consistently exhibits substantial improvements across both evaluation scenarios, underscoring its robustness and effectiveness in distinguishing OOD samples.

Table 4. The performance of our approach compared to existing methods on the same datasets: **CIFAR10 (In-Distribution), CIFAR100 and SVHN (ODD).**

Method	ID Accuracy	OOD (AUROC)		OOD (AUPR)	
		CIFAR100	SVHN	CIFAR100	SVHN
MAPLE [21]	0.956 ± 0.01	0.926 ± 0.01	0.996 ± 0.01	0.918 ± 0.01	0.997 ± 0.01
Deep Ensemble [6]	0.964 ± 0.01	0.864 ± 0.01	-	0.885 ± 0.01	-
SSD [15]	-	0.906	0.996	0.892	-
SSD_k (k = 5) [15]	-	0.931	0.997	0.919	-
ViT-B_16 [12]	-	0.998	-	-	-
Our	0.95	0.999	0.999	0.999	0.999

Table 5. The performance of our approach compared to existing methods on the same datasets: **CIFAR100 (In-Distribution), CIFAR10 and SVHN (ODD).**

Method	ID Accuracy	OOD (AUROC)		OOD (AUPR)	
		CIFAR10	SVHN	CIFAR10	SVHN
MAPLE [21]	0.789 ± 0.01	0.793 ± 0.01	-	0.799 ± 0.01	-
Deep Ensemble [6]	0.796 ± 0.01	0.798	-	0.792 ± 0.01	-
SSD [15]	-	0.696	0.949	0.645	-
SSD_k(k = 5) [15]	-	0.782	0.991	0.772	-
ViT-B_16 [12]	-	0.9442	-	-	-
Our	0.97	0.999	0.997	0.999	0.997

4.4   Discussion

The results of our proposed approach demonstrate significant advancements in addressing OOD detection challenges. Our method begins by constructing a graph from embeddings through self-supervised learning, eliminating the need for labeled data. This graph-based structure effectively captures the local neighborhood relationships between data points, providing a more nuanced understanding of the underlying manifold and enhancing the discriminative power for tasks such as clustering and OOD detection.

However, while the self-supervised approach significantly improves the incremental robustness of AI systems in detecting OOD, it is not without drawbacks. Its effectiveness heavily depends on the quality and diversity of the raw data. The integration of graph-based clustering proves highly beneficial, enabling more effective grouping of data points. By uncovering underlying structures within the dataset that traditional methods may overlook, our approach reveals patterns that can inform better decision-making in OOD detection scenarios.

Furthermore, leveraging Mahalanobis distance for similarity measurement with a graph enhances the robustness of our classification strategy. This metric provides precise distance calculations between data points and their respective clusters, enabling the model to maintain high classification performance even when encountering distributional shifts.

Overall, our findings underscore the practical applicability of the proposed approach. It offers a scalable and efficient solution tailored for real-world OOD detection challenges, paving the way for more reliable and practical machine learning applications across various domains.

5   Challenges and Limitations

OOD detection poses several challenges and limitations that hinder its implementation and efficiency in different applications. Understanding these barriers is crucial for developing more effective OOD detection methods.

One major challenge lies in the process of generating OOD samples, which remains poorly understood. This ambiguity creates significant obstacles in building reliable systems.

Another critical issue is setting an appropriate threshold for the in-distribution that effectively flags OOD examples without increasing the risk of false positives or false negatives. This remains challenging when dealing with unlabeled datasets. Calibrating a threshold that is both sensitive enough to detect OOD samples and precise enough to prevent misclassification is a complex task, especially when dealing with an unlabeled dataset. Moreover, failing to detect an OOD input can lead to poor decision-making or system errors, which is particularly critical in safety-sensitive applications. Conversely, the computational requirements for the OOD detection method increase with model complexity and the size of the data. For instance, the complexity Louvain method alone used in this study ranges from $O(N \log N)$ to $O(N^2)$, with memory usage reaching $O(N^2)$ due to the adjacency matrix, posing scalability challenges for extra large datasets that are resource-intensive.

Moreover, the effectiveness of an OOD detection model is closely tied to the quality and diversity of the training dataset. This limitation highlights the need for comprehensive and representative datasets to enhance the model's ability to identify a wide range of OOD scenarios.

6   Conclusion and Future Work

We highlight the significant progress in enhancing the trustworthiness of AI systems, especially through advances brought by self-supervised learning. We delve into the challenges faced by AI and propose a novel approach for out-of-distribution detection, based on Mahalanobis distance, graph theory, and contrastive learning. We emphasize the critical role of OOD detection in ensuring the robustness of AI systems without the need for labeled data.

For future work, we plan to integrate our proposed approach with uncertainty estimation methods and existing AI systems, particularly those deployed in safety-critical applications. This integration aims to further enhance the trustworthiness of AI systems in real-world scenarios. Ensuring the robustness and reliability of AI systems is essential for their widespread adoption and long-term success across various industries.

A   Ablation Study

In this Section, we tried to isolate the effect of the clustering algorithm and confirm the importance of graph-based embedding representations.

A.1   Supervised OOD Detection Using KNN Without Graph Representation

In this section, we implemented a direct neighbor (KNN) algorithm on raw data without performing any embedding extraction or graph representation. The purpose was to evaluate the performance of KNN in differentiating between the in-distribution data (CIFAR-10) and the OOD (CIFAR-100) data and to emphasize the role of embedding extraction on OOD classification. We used values ranging from 1 to 14 with different K values and calculated the AUROC for each value. The consequences summarized in Table 6 indicate that the AUROC scores improve but are still limited, reaching a maximum of 0.54 at K = 15 for CIFAR10 and CIFAR100. This indicates that many neighbors can provide more effective discrimination between the two classes in this context.

Table 6. AUROC Scores for Different Values of K

k neighbors	CIFAR10(ID) vs CIFAR100(OOD)	CIFAR100(ID) vs CIFAR10(OOD)
5	0.5292	0.5292
7	0.5319	0.5318
9	0.5360	0.5360
11	0.5381	0.5380
13	0.5392	0.5392
15	0.54219	0.5406

A.2   K-Means for Node Clustering

In this section, we attempted to implement K-means as the clustering algorithm instead of the Louvain method. However, the efficiency remains high, as demonstrated in Table 7 while the in-distribution accuracy decreased from 0.97 to 0.95. The same holds for other datasets; the impact of the clustering algorithm was minimal. This confirms the robustness of our proposed approach, which relies on graph representation for data embedding to detect OOD instances.

Table 7. The performance of our approach compared to existing methods on the same datasets: **CIFAR100 (In-Distribution), CIFAR10 and SVHN (ODD)**, using K-means where k = 109 (same k as the number of clusters obtained via the Louvain method)

ID Accuracy	OOD (AUROC)		OOD (AUPR)	
	CIFAR10	SVHN	CIFAR10	SVHN
0.95	0.999	0.99	0.999	0.99

A.3   Effect of K-Neighbors on OOD Detection

In this subsection, we explored the impact of varying the number of neighbors (k) on the AUROC.

To evaluate the sensitivity of our approach to neighboring parameters, we tested the entire out-of-distribution (OOD) pipeline using values of K = 5, 7, and 11 during the detection process. We obtained the same AUROC score of 0.999, with only a minor difference of 7×10^{-6}. This indicates that as long as the graph remains connected, varying the number of neighbors (K) within this range does not impact the performance of OOD detection. Therefore, we can fix K without requiring further hyperparameter tuning.

Table 8. Overall classification accuracy as a function of percentile threshold τ applied to Mahalanobis distances.

Percentile Threshold	Accuracy
80	0.90
85	0.92
90	0.95
95	0.97
99	0.91

A.4 Effect of Threshold on Accuracy

While a threshold is often used for practical classification purposes, it is essential to distinguish between its role in decision-making and its role in overall performance evaluation. We tested different thresholds to evaluate their impact on accuracy as shown in Table 8. The adjustment from 80 to 99 confirms that our detector's accuracy is significantly stronger in the exact specified area, with an optimal range identified between 85% and 95%. Accuracy improves from 80% to 90% and reaches 95.5%. This increase reflects a better performance; however, when we push the threshold closer to 99%, the detector becomes overly conservative; for instance, valid CIFAR-10 images begin to be rejected, causing the overall accuracy to drop to 91.5%.

References

1. Combe, D., Largeron, C., Géry, M., Egyed-Zsigmond, E.: I-Louvain: an attributed graph clustering method. In: Fromont, E., De Bie, T., van Leeuwen, M. (eds.) IDA 2015. LNCS, vol. 9385, pp. 181–192. Springer, Cham (2015). https://doi.org/10.1007/978-3-319-24465-5_16
2. De Meo, P., Ferrara, E., Fiumara, G., Provetti, A.: Generalized Louvain method for community detection in large networks. In: 2011 11th International Conference on Intelligent Systems Design and Applications, pp. 88–93. IEEE (2011)
3. Fort, S., Ren, J., Lakshminarayanan, B.: Exploring the limits of out-of-distribution detection. In: Ranzato, M., Beygelzimer, A., Dauphin, Y., Liang, P., Vaughan, J.W. (eds.) Advances in Neural Information Processing Systems, vol. 34, pp. 7068–7081. Curran Associates, Inc. (2021)

4. Guille-Escuret, C., Rodriguez, P., Vazquez, D., Mitliagkas, I., Monteiro, J.: Cadet: fully self-supervised anomaly detection with contrastive learning. CoRR (2022)

5. Jaiswal, A., Babu, A.R., Zadeh, M.Z., Banerjee, D., Makedon, F.: A survey on contrastive self-supervised learning. Technologies **9**(1), 2 (2020)

6. Larsson, M., Stenborg, E., Toft, C., Hammarstrand, L., Sattler, T., Kahl, F.: Fine-grained segmentation networks: self-supervised segmentation for improved long-term visual localization. In: Proceedings of the IEEE/CVF International Conference on Computer Vision, pp. 31–41 (2019)

7. Li, B., Qi, P., Liu, B., Di, S., Liu, J., Pei, J., Yi, J., Zhou, B.: Trustworthy AI: from principles to practices. ACM Comput. Surv. **55**(9), 1–46 (2023)

8. Liu, G., Yan, S.: Latent low-rank representation for subspace segmentation and feature extraction. In: 2011 International Conference on Computer Vision, pp. 1615–1622. IEEE (2011)

9. Liu, Y., Ding, K., Liu, H., Pan, S.: Good-d: On unsupervised graph out-of-distribution detection. In: Proceedings of the Sixteenth ACM International Conference on Web Search and Data Mining, pp. 339–347 (2023)

10. Mohseni, S., Pitale, M., Yadawa, J., Wang, Z.: Self-supervised learning for generalizable out-of-distribution detection. In: Proceedings of the AAAI Conference on Artificial Intelligence, vol. 34, pp. 5216–5223 (2020)

11. Oord, A.v.d., Li, Y., Vinyals, O.: Representation learning with contrastive predictive coding. arXiv preprint arXiv:1807.03748 (2018)

12. Ren, J., Fort, S., Liu, J., Roy, A.G., Padhy, S., Lakshminarayanan, B.: A simple fix to mahalanobis distance for improving near-OOD detection (2021)

13. Repository, G.: Emperical study code on Github (2024). https://github.com/wiseresearch/Towards-Robust-AI-OOD-using-Contrastive-learning-and-Mahalanobis-distance

14. Sastry, C.S., Oore, S.: Detecting out-of-distribution examples with gram matrices. In: International Conference on Machine Learning, pp. 8491–8501. PMLR (2020)

15. Sehwag, V., Chiang, M., Mittal, P.: SSD: a unified framework for self-supervised outlier detection (2021)

16. Sohn, K.: Improved deep metric learning with multi-class n-pair loss objective. In: Advances in Neural Information Processing Systems, vol. 29 (2016)

17. Song, Y., Wang, D.: Learning on graphs with out-of-distribution nodes, pp. 1635–1645. KDD 2022, Association for Computing Machinery, New York, NY, USA (2022). https://doi.org/10.1145/3534678.3539457

18. Sun, J., et al.: Gradient-based novelty detection boosted by self-supervised binary classification. In: Proceedings of the AAAI Conference on Artificial Intelligence, vol. 36, pp. 8370–8377 (2022)

19. SVHN: Street view house number (SVHN) dataset, available online (2024). https://www.kaggle.com/datasets/stanfordu/street-view-house-numbers

20. Tsai, Y.H.H., Wu, Y., Salakhutdinov, R., Morency, L.P.: Self-supervised learning from a multi-view perspective. arXiv preprint arXiv:2006.05576 (2020)

21. Venkataramanan, A., Benbihi, A., Laviale, M., Pradalier, C.: Gaussian latent representations for uncertainty estimation using mahalanobis distance in deep classifiers. In: Proceedings of the IEEE/CVF International Conference on Computer Vision, pp. 4488–4497 (2023)

22. Zhang, Y., Du, B., Zhang, L., Wang, S.: A low-rank and sparse matrix decomposition-based mahalanobis distance method for hyperspectral anomaly detection. IEEE Trans. Geosci. Remote Sens. **54**(3), 1376–1389 (2015)

Proceedings of the Eighth International Symposium for Industrial Control System & SCADA Cyber Security Research (ICS-CSR 2025)

ICS-CSR 2025 Preface

It is our pleasure to present the proceedings of the 8th International Symposium for ICS & SCADA Cyber Security (ICS-CSR), held in Ghent, Belgium on August 13, 2025. This symposium brought together researchers, practitioners, and policymakers from diverse fields to explore critical issues and innovative solutions. The themes addressed at ICS-CSR ranged from Distributed Control Systems (DCS), Supervisory Control and Data Acquisition Systems (SCADA), Industrial Control Systems (ICS), Operational Technology (OT), Cyber Physical Systems (CPS), Industrial Internet of Things (IIoT), Smart City, to Industry 4.0. reflecting the multidisciplinary nature of this vital area of study.

The papers you are reading represent the outcome of rigorous academic effort and dedicated collaboration. We received a total of 8 full papers. Each submission underwent a thorough single-blind peer-review process, with each paper receiving at least 3 independent reviews from members of our Technical Program Committee. This approach ensured that only the highest-quality research was selected for inclusion. Following the review process, 4 full papers were accepted for publication, resulting in an acceptance rate of exactly 50%. ICS-CSR also included a keynote speech entitled "Embedding Security Controls from the Round up: An Asset Owner's Perspective" from Stephen Fisher Davies, a panel discussion on "OT Security" from Larry Vandenaweele, Stephen Fisher Davies and Naghmeh Moradpoor, and the tabletop exercise "Corporates Compromised NISv2" led by Helge Janicke.

The success of ICS-CSR would not have been possible without the tireless efforts of countless individuals. We are immensely grateful to the authors for their valuable contributions, and to the Program Committee members for their insightful critiques. Their commitment to scholarly excellence was instrumental in shaping a high-quality scientific program. We would also like to extend our sincere appreciation to the Organizing Committee for their professional planning and execution, ensuring a smooth and productive conference experience for all participants. Finally, we express our gratitude to our sponsors, whose generous support helped make this event a reality.

We believe that these proceedings will serve as a valuable resource for researchers, practitioners, and anyone interested in advancing the cybersecurity of Cyber Physical Systems. We hope that the ideas and discussions presented herein will inspire further research, foster new collaborations, and contribute to the development of robust and resilient industrial control systems worldwide.

June 2025

Thomas Brandstetter
Stephen Fisher Davies
Helge Janicke
Leandros Maglaras
Richard Smith

ICS-CSR 2025 Organization

Conference Chairs

Thomas Brandstetter	Limes Security/FHSTP, Austria
Stephen Fisher Davies	Airbus, UK
Helge Janicke	Edith Cowan University, Australia
Leandros Maglaras	De Montfort University, UK
Richard Smith	De Montfort University, UK

Program Committee Chairs

Naghmeh Moradpoor	Edinburgh Napier University, UK
Michael Robinson	Airbus, UK

Program Committee

Manos Athanatos	Technical University of Crete, Greece
Nestoras Chouliaras	University of West Attica, Greece
Christos Chrysoulas	Heriot-Watt University, UK
Kubra Duran	Edinburgh Napier University, UK
Vasileios Gkioulos	Norwegian University of Science and Technology, Norway
Andriambelo Ny Hasina	Infosys Limited, France
Helmut Kaufmann	Airbus, UK
Kitty Kioskli	Trustulio, The Netherlands
Dimitrios Kosmanos	University of Thessaly, Greece
Gabor Oesterreicher	FH St. Poelten, Austria
Simon Parkinson	University of Huddersfield, UK
Michael Robinson	Airbus, UK
Panagiotis Sarigiannidis	University of Western Macedonia, Greece
Iqbal H. Sarker	Edith Cowan University, AUS
Yagmur Yigit	Edinburgh Napier University, UK
Nubio Vidal	Airbus, UK
Nida Zeeshan	Edinburgh Napier, UK

Performance Evaluation of Quantum-Resistant Algorithms on Industrial Embedded Systems

Leonie Reichert[(✉)] [ID], Nicolas Coppik [ID], and Soeren Finster [ID]

ABB Corporate Research Center, Mannheim, Germany
Leonie.reichert@de.abb.com

Abstract. Quantum computers will change the world of computation, especially in the field of cryptography. In preparation, the NIST recently released a set of standards for quantum-resistant cryptography. These new standards are already influencing industry practices as suppliers move towards integrating these new algorithms into their products to ensure regulatory compliance and future-proof their systems. To assess the practical implications of these standards in the field of Industrial Automation and Control Systems (IACS), we analyze the practicability of the standardized algorithms across different classes of industrial devices. To this end, first, relevant applications for quantum-resistant algorithms as well as corresponding challenges in the ecosystems of IACS are identified. Next, we benchmark these algorithms and compare their performance against traditional cryptographic methods. Our evaluation is conducted on three representative embedded platforms: an ARM Cortex-53 and an ARM Cortex-R5 on the Xilinx Zynq UltraScale+ MPSoC as well as an ARM Cortex-7 on the STM32H753ZI board, representing devices using application processors, real-time processors, and microcontrollers, respectively. The results show that quantum-resistant algorithms such as ML-KEM and ML-DSA can outperform their classical counterparts in terms of speed. However, ML-DSA in particular requires significantly more memory than the traditional ECDSA, which presents a challenge for resource-constrained devices.

Keywords: Post-Quantum Cryptography (PQC) ·
Quantum-Resistant Algorithms · Embedded Platforms · Benchmark ·
Industrial Automation and Control Systems

1 Introduction

Quantum computers are expected to transform the field of computation once they become a reality. However, even the threat of their arrival has already begun reshaping the landscape of cryptography and cybersecurity. Since Peter Shor published his paper on algorithms for quantum computing in 1994 [25], it has been clear that the mathematical foundations of modern cryptography are

B. Coppens et al. (Eds.): ARES 2025 Workshops, LNCS 15994, pp. 127–148, 2025.
https://doi.org/10.1007/978-3-032-00630-1_8

vulnerable. To keep sensitive information secret, alternative mathematical problems must be leveraged to create the foundation of a post-quantum or *quantum-resistant cryptography.*

While usable quantum computers are nowadays still far from being powerful enough to break currently used cryptography, standardization of quantum-resistant cryptography by US National Institute of Standards and Technology (NIST) has now finalized the first algorithms [15–17]. At the same time, early adopters already move to quantum-resistant cryptography. For example, OpenSSH uses a quantum-resistant key exchange algorithm by default since 2022 [19] and added support for standardized algorithms shortly after publication by NIST. Without users even noticing, they might already be using quantum-resistant cryptography to log into their computer systems.

Regulatory requirements will drive the adoption of quantum-resistant cryptography across a wide range of industries. In the field of *Industrial Automation and Control Systems* (IACS), regulations like the IEC 62443 [6] reference the NIST Special Publication (SP) 800-57 [4] for guidance on cryptographic key management. The latest version of the SP 800-57, published in 2020, indicates that updates are expected to incorporate recommendations for quantum-resistant algorithms. As a result, quantum-resistant security requirements are likely to be introduced into IACS standards in the near future. This shift poses particular challenges for embedded systems, which are the foundation of IACS.

While the integration of post-quantum algorithms may appear straightforward for projects like OpenSSH, the transition becomes more complex in resource-constrained environments. Quantum-resistant cryptographic algorithms differ significantly from those currently in use. Not only are CPU demands larger, but also memory usage, code complexity, key sizes, and signature lengths change.

To illustrate how different these properties can be, observe that the public key sizes for quantum-resistant signature schemes range from 752 Byte up for padded Falcon to almost 7,856 kB for SL-DSA at the lowest security level [18]. For the highest security level, signature sizes can grow to as much as 50 kB per signature. In contrast, the widely adopted ECDSA algorithm provides comparable security against classical (non-quantum) attacks with a signature size of just 64 Byte. An increase in key size even of a few orders of magnitude is little more than a nuisance on desktop or server-grade hardware. However, it can be problematic or even prohibitive for a transition to quantum-resistant cryptography with hardware platforms we find, e.g., in field devices. With limited resources, a software upgrade to quantum-resistant cryptography might already be impossible simply for the fact, that there is not enough room for the new kind of keys in RAM and storage or the CPU is not capable enough to handle the computations for the new cryptographic primitives.

In this paper, we first identify the relevant applications in the ecosystem of embedded platforms for IACS that need to be adapted when transitioning to quantum-resistant cryptography. We then proceed to analyze the challenges that arise in relation to both hardware and software during such a transition.

In order to understand the impact of the standardized algorithms on different embedded platforms, we compare traditional algorithms to quantum-resistant algorithms for key encapsulation and digital signatures on three embedded platforms: an ARM Cortex-53 and an ARM Cortex-R5 on the Xilinx Zynq UltraScale+ MPSoC as well as an ARM Cortex-7 on the STM32H753ZI board. These platforms have been selected to represent a range of different classes of industrial devices such as application processors, real-time processors, and microcontrollers.

In the following section, Sect. 2, begins by exploring the rationale behind the need for quantum-resistant cryptography. Then, the standardization efforts of the NIST are outlined and the two types of cryptographic primitives, key encapsulation mechanisms and digital signatures, for which quantum-resistant alternatives have been selected are introduced. In Sect. 3, related works are presented. Applications and challenges of implementing quantum-resistant algorithms in IACS are discussed in Sect. 4. Then the benchmarking setup is described in Sect. 5. The results of this evaluation are presented and discussed in Sect. 6.

2   Background

This section discusses the need for quantum-resistant cryptography and the standardization efforts conducted by the NIST. To this end, the concepts of *key encapsulation mechanisms* (KEM) and *digital signatures* (DSA) are introduced.

2.1   Quantum-Resistant Cryptography and Standardization

In the 1990 s, two significant quantum algorithms were published that showed that current cryptography is threatened by capable quantum computers which are nowadays refered to as *Grover's algorithm* [8] and *Shor's algorithm* [25]. Grover's algorithm significantly speeds up unstructured search, affecting symmetric-key cryptography by accelerating brute-force, collision, and pre-image attacks. However, its impact is limited, as increasing key lengths can maintain security. For instance, AES-256 is considered secure in a quantum context if AES-128 is secure classically.

Shor's algorithm finds the prime factors of an integer in polynomial time. This impacts asymmetric-key cryptography since many cryptographic protocols are based on the difficulty of factoring large integers or related problems, such as the *discrete logarithm problem* and the *elliptic curve discrete logarithm problem*. The classical computational power needed to factor large integers rises exponentially with the length of these numbers. The key length of 3072 bits in the RSA cryptosystem seems comfortably out of reach for contemporary and future classical computation. Shor's algorithm, however, scales in polynomial time and, given a sufficiently capable quantum computer, can factor the necessary numbers to break a key in relatively short time.

The key question is no longer whether quantum computers can break current asymmetric cryptographic systems as Shor's algorithm has already proven this.

The real concern is when quantum computers will be powerful enough to pose a practical threat. Transitioning to quantum-resistant cryptography is a complex task that involves research, cryptoanalysis, standardization, and widespread implementation, with challenges such as varying key lengths.

Predicting the timeline for quantum computing is difficult, and experts remain cautious. A report from the Quantum Threat Timeline [13] suggests a 34% likelihood of a cryptographically relevant quantum computer within a decade. The German Federal Office for Information Security estimates a serious threat to classical cryptography by quantum computers in the early 2030s [5].

The US National Institute of Standards and Technology (NIST) initiated a standardization process for quantum-resistant cryptography in 2016. In August 2024, NIST released standardization for three algorithms. Nonetheless, the standardization process is still ongoing.

Instead of defining the strength of quantum-resistant algorithms using precise estimates of the number of "bits of security", NIST defines a collection of broad security strength categories. Each category is specified by a reference primitive (either AES or SHA), whose security serves as a floor for a wide variety of metrics that NIST deems potentially relevant to practical security. A given cryptosystem may be instantiated using different parameter sets in order to fit into different categories. During the standardization process, the NIST focused on finding replacements for two use cases where asymmetric cryptographic primitives are unavoidable: key encapsulation and digital signatures.

2.2   Key Encapsulation Schemes

When two parties, often called Alice and Bob, want to privately communicate over a public channel, they require some form of secret key to encrypt their communication. This key does not need to be preset but can be established by publicly exchanging information without the risk of an eavesdropper being able to efficiently derive the correct key. The concept of key encapsulation mechanism (KEM) formalizes such methods for key exchange [2]. A KEM consists of the following phases:

1. **Key Generation**: Alice generates a decapsulation key d and an encapsulation key e. She transmits e to Bob. The decapsulation key needs to remain private.
2. **Key Encapsulation**: Bob uses e to generate a shared secret s and an corresponding ciphertext c. He sends c to Alice.
3. **Key Decapsulation**: Alice derives s by using her decapsulation key d and ciphertext c.

After the decapsulation, both Alice and Bob will hold the shared secret s and can use it to either encrypt their communication or derive an appropriate encryption key. A KEM requires at least two subsequent messages to derive a shared key. If a *public-key infrastructure* (PKI) is present, Bob can use it to retrieve Alice's pk. This reduces the number of required messages. In this case, if Alice and Bob hold the same shared secret and use it for communication, then Bob can be certain that the Alice he communicates to is the same one as listed in the PKI.

With FIPS 203, the NIST standardized a quantum-resistant algorithm for KEM, called *modular-lattice key encapsulation mechanism* (ML-KEM). [16]. It leverages the hardness of the *Module Learning with Error* (MLWE) problem. Here, a set of equations are given for which the solution is secret. Small amounts of noise are added to each equation to ensure that algorithms like the Gaussian elimination mechanism do not find a solution. Such a set of equations is easy to set up and to verify when given a solution. The core assumption making module lattices suitable for cryptography is that such a solution to a noisy linear system of equations can not be guessed in efficient time. The solution can be seen as a private key, while the linear equations represent the public key. By means of constructing a public-key encryption scheme from MLWE, a KEM can be created with the functionalities described above.

An attentive reader might have noticed that the commonly used *Diffie-Hellman key agreement* does not fall under the definition of a KEM. For the Diffie-Hellman key agreement, both parties transmit data over the public channel that does not depend on input from the other party. This also requires two messages to be sent over a public channel, however, they can be sent at the same time. Unlike KEM algorithms, Diffie-Hellman first generates a shared secret and then derives a key. RSA-KEM [2] is a standardized KEM algorithm and a candidate for hybrid operation with quantum-resistant KEM algorithms [20]. The phases of RSA-KEM are as follows: For key generation, Alice generates an RSA key pair (pk, sk). She sends public key pk to Bob. For key encapsulation, Bob generates a shared secret s, encrypts it with pk, and sends the resulting ciphertext c to Alice. For key decapsulation, Alice uses her secret key sk to decrypt ciphertext c and obtain the shared secret. This secret can then be used to symmetrically encrypt all following messages between Alice and Bob.

2.3   Digital Signature Schemes

Digital signatures allow the recipient of a message to verify the identity of the sender and check whether the message has been changed during transport. Digital signature schemes are used as follows [11]:

1. **Key Generation:** Alice generates a public-private key pair (pk, sk) and communicates pk to Bob. This can happen through an existing public-key infrastructure.
2. **Message Signing:** Alice now wants to send a message m to Bob. She first produces a message digest h, for example by hashing the message. She produces a signature σ by signing h with her private key sk. Then, both m and σ are sent to Bob.
3. **Signature Verification:** Bob has received m, σ and knows Alice's pk. He computes h from m with the same method Alice used. Using the pk and h, he then verifies the signature σ. If verification is successful, he will know that Alice has sent the message and it has not been tampered with. Otherwise, he will reject the message.

A commonly used signature scheme is DSA which relies on the discrete logarithm problem [11]. Due to the increased computation capabilities of modern computers, DSA signature need to be rather long to provide suitable security. As a result, ECDSA has become increasingly popular. It also relies on the discrete logarithm problem but on elliptic curves and allows shorter key lengths at the same security level [4].

Two digital signature algorithms have been standardized by the NIST, *Stateless Hash-Based Digital Signature Algorithm* (SLH-DSA) [17] and *Module-Lattice Digital Signature Algorithm* (ML-DSA) [15]. As of May 2025, a third candidate called *Falcon* is not yet fully standardized. As the name implies, ML-DSA is based on the above-mentioned MLWE problem, utilizing modern but still not well-understood cryptographic foundations. In contrast, the SLH-DSA scheme relies on the well-established security of cryptographic hash functions like SHA-2. Its core assumption is that, given a hash value produced by a secure hash function, it is computationally infeasible for an attacker to determine the original input.

These new algorithms, ML-KEM, ML-DSA, and SLH-DSA, are expected to replace standard cryptographic algorithms. During the transition period, a hybrid approach is anticipated, in which both conventional and quantum-resistant keys and signatures are used in parallel.

3   Related Work

A number of existing works touch on the topic of benchmarking quantum-resistant algorithms on embedded systems. However, the authors of these papers either used different platforms with less relevance to industrial embedded systems or analyzed different algorithms.

Kannwischer et al. [10] benchmarked the last round standardization candidates Kyber (the predecessor of ML-KEM), Dilithium (the predecessor of ML-DSA) as well as Falcon and SPHINCS+ (standardized with slight changes as SLH-DSA [17]). For their benchmarks, they used the STM32L4R5ZI board which provides an Arm Cortex-M4 and 640 KB of RAM. The authors also optimized the code of five submissions to the NIST to the M4 platform. They analyzed the runtime and memory requirements of the different algorithms. However, they did not consider the corresponding non-quantum-resistant algorithms.

Howe and Westerbaan [9] analyzed the two last-round candidates for digital signatures, Dilithium and Falcon, on an ARM Cortex M7 using the STM32F767ZI NUCLEO-144. They only compared quantum-resistant algorithms against one another and did not consider the corresponding traditional algorithms.

Paul et al. [21] propose solutions for integrating quantum-resistant cryptography in the industrially relevant OPC UA communication protocol. In addition to the extensive work on proving the security of their solution, they also include a performance evaluation. However, their performance evaluation is done on a Raspberry Pi 3 and focuses on their protocol solution and not on the cryptographic primitives.

Fitzgibbon and Ottaviani [7] analyze the performance impact of quantum-resistant algorithms on IoT devices for protocols such as TLS. As benchmarking platform, they used a Raspberry Pi 4 and analyzed the standardization candidates Kyber, Dilithium, and Falcon. The authors discuss the challenges of quantum-resistant algorithms for the TLS handshake, but do not compare these to their traditional cryptographic equivalent for key agreement and digital signatures.

Zheng et al. [27] provide optimizations for quantum-resistant cryptography in the context of TLS and provide an ML-KEM implementation with significant speedup. However, the implementation and evaluation focus on desktop or server-grade hardware using hardware features that are not common on industrial-grade hardware for smaller devices.

4 Transitioning to Quantum-Resistant Cryptography

Cryptographic functions are used in various parts of the ecosystem of IACS. In the following, we highlight key applications where cryptography is essential, including software package verification, secure boot processes, secure manufacturing, user and device authentication, and secure communication protocols. For each of these applications, we identify the specific cryptographic operations that require transitioning to quantum-resistant alternatives.

4.1 Applications

Software Verification. When introducing new software to a system, the authenticity and integrity of this software need to be guaranteed. This could be a new firmware, that needs to be flashed or a software module that provides extended functionality. In any case, software that gets executed on the device itself and/or is persisted is a valuable target for attackers and therefore needs to be authenticated and protected against tampering. A common way to achieve this is to equip entities that need to securely receive software with the public part of a trusted root key. This public key can then be used to either verify the signature on the received software directly or it can be used to verify a chain of certificates that, in the end, authenticate the key that was used to provide the signature on the software. The tasks on the receiving device are relatively straightforward and involve hashing of the software to be verified and verifying a signature using a pre-distributed public key or a certificate chain with a pre-distributed root.

Quantum-Relevance: public key storage, signature verification.

Secure Boot and Secure Manufacturing. Secure boot is a feature related to software verification. But instead of verifying software once, secure boot verifies incrementally each piece of software that is used during the boot process of the device. In many embedded devices, this can include 1st and 2nd stage bootloaders, firmware for auxiliary processors (e.g., power management controllers), operating system kernels, and global configuration files. To arrive at a securely booted operating system, the embedded device starts from a trusted state (reset), executes first trusted code (stored in ROM), and then verifies a signature on each following software that takes over execution. For example, after reset, ROM code would verify the signature of the bootloader which is found in a well-known location using a public key which, again, is found in a well-known location. To prevent tampering with the root public key, it is often stored immutably (e.g., using ROM or eFuses) in the device. After successful signature verification, the bootloader is executed and takes over control. The bootloader, in turn, follows the same strategy to verify the operating system kernel before it hands over execution to it. When producing field devices, one or more hashes of public keys need to be burnt into eFuses to ensure the public key used for secure boot has not been tampered with. Secure manufacturing ensures that third-party contractors provision the correct public keys to the product and can not modified before written. Provisioning stations in third-party factories need to be able to process quantum-resistant key material

Quantum Relevance: public key storage, signature verification.

User and Device Authentication. Many systems offer some form of login option where users need to authenticate themselves before executing operations on the system. In addition to the authentication of the user by the system, the system itself must authenticate itself to the user. One common example is the SSH daemon, which offers remote login functionality. To achieve this, users can store their public key on the system which will then be used by SSH to authenticate the user. To assure the users that they are logging in to the correct system, SSH stores a permanent private key on the system. If users know the matching public key, they can authenticate the system before logging in. In SSH, this is usually done using a concept called Trust-On-First-Use (TOFU). If the system key is yet unknown, the user gets prompted to acknowledge the one offered upon connection. If the user approves, the key is permanently stored on the user's system and automatically used for system authentication in future connections. In addition to the authentication of user and system, SSH also provides a secure communication protocol. This will be the focus of the next example.

Quantum Relevance: public key storage, private key storage, key generation, signature verification, signing.

Secure Communication Protocols. The most common secure communication protocol today is Transport Layer Security (TLS), which provides security guarantees in most of the applications one can find on the Internet or the World-Wide-Web (e.g., HTTPS, Email, Instant Messaging, Voice-over-IP, etc.) It is a client-server protocol that is designed to prevent eavesdropping and tampering of messages passing through untrusted networks. TLS offers both server authentication and client authentication. On the Internet, TLS is often found as a building block of HTTPS which only performs server authentication. There are many secure communication protocols beyond TLS. Most use the same primitives as TLS to arrive at their goal. From the OT world, OPC UA is a prominent example that offers comparable security guarantees as TLS with comparable implementation details. However, one notable difference is that OPC UA by default requires mutual authentication of both endpoints ensuring client and server authentication at the same time. For securing communication, TLS uses a public key infrastructure for the authentication of servers and/or clients, a key exchange mechanism to arrive at session keys, and symmetric encryption of the communication using the session keys. A notable feature of TLS is the flexibility in using different cryptographic primitives to achieve these goals. A pre-defined combination of cryptographic primitives is called a cipher suite. Client and server negotiate the usage of a specific cipher suite during connection establishment.

Quantum Relevance: public key storage, private key storage, key generation, signature verification, signing, key encapsulation.

4.2 Challenges

There are many challenges when transitioning to quantum-resistant cryptography in IACS, which we will explore in the following.

Hardware Not Capable Enough. As will be shown in Sect. 6, quantum-resistant cryptography is not necessarily more demanding on hardware than classical cryptography. However, resource usage is not uniform among the different standardized and non-standardized quantum-resistant algorithms. It is not always possible to select the most fitting candidate. For example, the standardization of quantum-resistant cryptography for a specific secure communication protocol might not include the desired candidate. If this protocol needs to be supported, the selected algorithm must be implemented. There are several roadblocks one might encounter. First, the processor is too slow and cryptographic operations take too much time for the functional requirements of the application (e.g., results arrive too late to be useful) or for non-functional requirements of the protocol (e.g., timeouts get triggered and connections get reset). Cryptographic operations might block normal execution for too long, resulting in decreased functionality of the device (e.g., gaps in measurement series).

Second, the cryptographic operations might require too much RAM. A mitigation might be to use slower memory (e.g., external RAM) to mitigate this. However, this often comes at a performance penalty that could prologue cryptographic operations and cause the same symptoms like a processor that is too slow.

Last, but not least, the code required for the new cryptographic operations does not fit into the available space on the device. Although code storage is usually less of a bottleneck than processor speed and RAM, it still is a scarce resource in many resource-constrained devices. However, the situation could be somewhat mitigated, if the introduction of the new cryptographic primitives comes together with the removal of the old cryptographic primitives. Regarding backwards compatibility, however, this is unlikely.

Algorithms and Keys Are Anchored in Hardware. In some systems, cryptography is deeply integrated with hardware, which makes transitioning to quantum-resistant algorithms particularly challenging. For instance, resource-constrained devices often rely on specialized hardware to handle the computational demands of traditional cryptographic methods. RSA, for example, is frequently implemented using a dedicated chip. Additionally, certain security standards require that private keys be usable but never extractable. This is typically enforced by separate hardware components designed for that purpose.

Some cryptographic operations may also be optimized through hardware implementations, either directly within the processor or via separate hardware components. When system design, and thus resource allocation, depends on these hardware optimizations, transitioning to new cryptographic standards can become particularly difficult. Moreover, implementing security at levels below the operating system often involves fixed, unchangeable properties, further complicating such transitions. Secure boot, for example, is often implemented by performing the first checks using algorithms in ROM or hardware with burned-in public keys.

The integration of cryptographic algorithms in hardware alone does not prevent the transition of quantum-resistant alternatives. However, its presence is indicative of the challenges. The main system resources could be insufficient to support computationally intensive cryptography. In case the resources are sufficient they might be otherwise bound, for example through timing requirements. Specialized features of external solutions, such as unextractable private keys, might be required. In all these cases, a pure software upgrade to quantum-resistant cryptography is not possible.

Applications Do Not Support New Cryptographic Primitives. A major challenge in transitioning to quantum-resistant cryptography is that some applications may be difficult or impossible to modify. For instance, a communication protocol may use only one key agreement algorithm, with no negotiation option. Changing the protocol would break backward compatibility. Since negotiation is not possible, a new separate protocol that implements the new cryptographic primitives would be required. Modern protocols exercise *crypto-agility*, a practice for designing information security protocols and standards in a way such that they can support multiple cryptographic primitives and algorithms. An example of this is the usage of cipher suites in TLS. This, in theory, would allow for a quick change to quantum-resistant cryptography.

But even with crypto-agility, there can be challenges. For example, during the TLS handshake, packets are exchanged that include cryptographic payload, for example, digital certificates. When new quantum-resistant cryptography requires signatures to be much larger, a TLS handshake would need more packets to exchange this information. This could result in a significant increase in the time necessary for connection establishment.

5 Benchmarking

In the previous section, we discussed the challenges of quantum-resistant cryptography in IACS. Now, we analyze how these challenges impact different industrial devices, starting with an introduction to the benchmarked platforms, evaluation methodology, and selected algorithms.

5.1 Evaluation Platforms

Our evaluation is based on platforms that represent key categories of industrial embedded systems. The following categories were evaluated:

- **Application Processor (AP)**: An Ultra96v2 board, based on the Xilinx Zynq UltraScale+ MPSoC and equipped with 2 GiB of LPDDR4 memory [3], using the ARM Cortex-A53 processor.
- **Real-Time Processor (RP)**: The same Ultra96v2 board that is used for the AP, using the ARM Cortex-R5 real-time processor.
- **Microcontroller Processor (MP)**: An STM32H753ZI microcontroller, equipped with a Cortex-M7 MCU and 1 MiB of RAM [26].

These platforms were chosen to reflect the spectrum of industrial devices, from resource-constrained microcontrollers (MP) and systems with real-time processing demands (RP) to high-performance embedded devices (AP).

5.2 Implementation

The PQClean library [24] provides reference implementations of quantum-resistant algorithms. It includes three versions: a "clean" C version and two optimized versions for ARM and x86 processors. For the STM32 and RPs, the "clean" version was used. On the AP, both the "clean" and `aarch64` versions were tested, and we found that the `aarch64` version was slower and used more stack for ML-KEM than the "clean" version, with slight performance drops for ML-DSA. All results are presented using the "clean" version.

PQClean offers NIST-standardized ML-KEM and ML-DSA algorithms at three security levels, but does not yet provide a compliant SLH-DSA [23]. The MbedTLS library [12] was used for comparison. It provides cryptographic primitives like RSA and ECDSA and is optimized for embedded systems with a small memory footprint. Code was built in release mode with GCC optimization level 3.

5.3 Measurement Methodology

To measure the time taken by each algorithm, the AP uses the CNTPCT register running at 100 MHz with 10 ns resolution. The RP uses the TTC1 counter at 3.125 MHz for 320 ns resolution, while the MP uses TIM2 at 1 MHz for 1 μs resolution.

FreeRTOS, a real-time OS for embedded platforms, was used for benchmarking. It's available on various devices, widely used in industrial applications, and has built-in functions for memory usage analysis. The function xPortGetFreeHeapSize help measure heap usage, while stack usage is measured via uxTaskGetStackHighWaterMark. Each algorithm phase was executed once for memory consumption estimation as they are static, and runtime was averaged over 100 repetitions per phase.

5.4 Algorithm and Parameter Selection

Comparing quantum-resistant algorithms with traditional ones is challenging, especially in selecting appropriate counterparts. For ML-DSA, deterministic ECDSA is the reference algorithm due to its faster performance, small key sizes, and suitability for devices that lack access to high-quality randomness [22]. To compare ML-KEM with an equivalent non-quantum secure algorithm, we selected RSA-KEM as described in Sect. 2.2 as it is a candidate for hybrid operation with quantum-resistant KEM algorithms [20].

Another challenge is selecting the appropriate security level. The strength of quantum-resistant algorithms is defined relative to that of different symmetric algorithms [14–16]. Level 1 corresponds to the effort required to break AES-128, while Level 5 equates to the effort needed to break AES-256 [14]. Given that practical quantum computers capable of breaking traditional cryptography have not yet been realized, these security levels provide a foundation for selecting parameters for both quantum-resistant algorithms and their classical counterparts [4].

To account for the restricted performance of the selected reference platforms, the lowest security level is selected for each quantum-resistant algorithm. For ML-KEM, Level 1 (equivalent to AES-128 security) is chosen, with RSA-KEM 3072-bit as a corresponding classical algorithm. The lowest level for ML-DSA provides Level 2 security (equivalent to SHA-256 security). For this reason, ECDSA 256 with SHA-256 and the Secp256r1 NIST curve is selected as the reference.

5.5 Limitations Summary

Selecting the appropriate algorithms and algorithm pairing to compare for an evaluation can be challenging. For comparison with ML-DSA, RSA-KEM is used. However, in practice it is more common to use an authenticated Diffi-Hellmann key agreement to set up a symmetric key for communication.

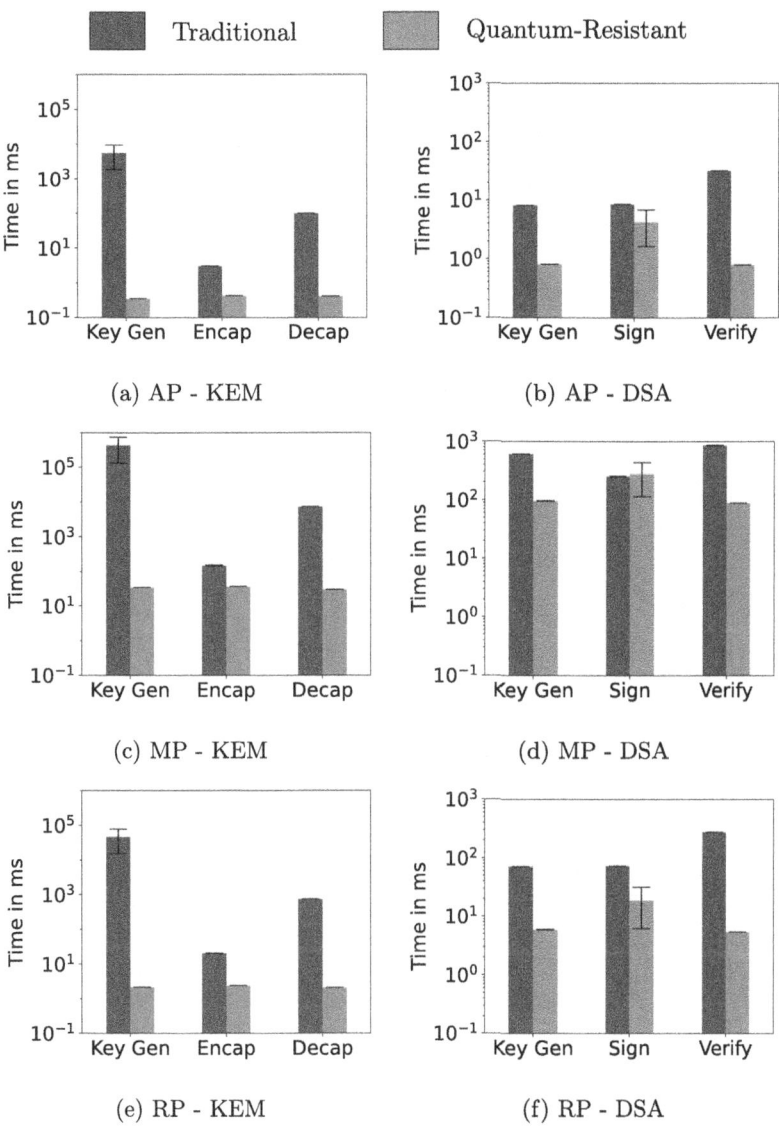

Fig. 1. Comparison of the runtime of traditional and quantum-resistant algorithms for key encapsulation mechanisms (left) and digital signatures (right) on different embedded platforms. For KEM algorithms, the phases key generation, key encapsulation, and key decapsulation are compared for RSA-KEM 3072 and ML-KEM 512. For DSA algorithms, the phases key generation, message signing, and signature verification are compared for ECDSA 256 and ML-DSA 44. The embedded platforms are an application processor (AP), a microcontroller (MP), and a real-time processor (RP). The time is reported on a **logarithmic** scale. Error bars are present on all bars of this figure (but very small in most cases) and represent the standard deviation.

Our method for pairing standard and quantum-resistant algorithms can also be seen as a limitation, as it is generally difficult to establish such a pairing. We use the comparison with symmetric algorithms as a clutch. We also only look at the weakest security level for the quantum-resistant algorithms. To increase security against increasingly strong standard computers, higher security levels are needed. This benchmark only evaluates standardized algorithms and ignores the not-yet fully standardized SLH-DSA algorithm.

Last, but not least, we used the "clean" implementation of quantum-resistant algorithms from the PQClean library as the "aarch64" implementation displayed irregularities in the reported runtime.

6   Evaluation

In this section, we compare standardized quantum-resistant algorithms with their counterparts based on traditional cryptographic assumptions. We begin by presenting runtime measurements for both Key Encapsulation Mechanism (KEM) algorithms and Digital Signature Algorithms (DSA). Next, we discuss overall memory usage, including both heap and stack, as well as key sizes. The concrete values for Fig. 1 and Fig. 2 can be found in Appendix A.

6.1   Runtime

KEM Algorithms. The left column of Fig. 1 presents runtime measurements for the selected representative processors.

The figure allows comparing RSA-KEM with 3072 bit keys with ML-KEM 512 for different algorithm phases across different types of devices.

It can be seen that the individual algorithmic phases such as key generation, key encapsulation, and key decapsulation take a similar amount of time for ML-KEM 512 across all platforms. For RSA 3072 on the other hand all three phases behave differently, with key generation taking the longest. To better understand the overall performance difference between the boards, the absolute runtimes of RSA key generation are reported, as it is very inefficient. While the AP takes "only" about 5.6 s, the RP takes 46.7 s, and the MP requires about 7.9 min. This highlights the need for more efficient cryptographic algorithms on low-performance embedded systems.

The speed-ups for using ML-KEM are as follows. Key generation is 12,769 times to 21,530 times faster. Encapsulation is between 4 times and 9 times faster. Decapsulation is 243 times to 354 times faster.

Across all boards, especially key generation benefits from the use of quantum-resistant algorithms. This suggests that ML-KEM is a well-suited choice for restricted devices in environments where new keys need to be generated regularly. The speedup might even facilitate encrypted communication in settings where this is currently not possible due to resource constraints.

DSA Algorithms. The right column of plots in Fig. 1 shows the benchmark results for the signature algorithms ECDSA 256 and ML-DSA 44 for the selected platforms. The results are presented for the three main phases of the algorithms: key generation, signing messages, and verifying signatures. For both signing and verifying with ECDSA, the measurement includes computing the message hash to ensure it is comparable to ML-DSA.

Regarding the time required to execute a single phase, it can be seen that ML-DSA outperforms ECDSA in almost all cases on all platforms. This effect is the lowest for the message signing phase, which also displays a comparatively large standard deviation. For key generation and signature verification, the quantum-resistant algorithm is at least one order of magnitude faster on all boards. This performance improvement is especially relevant when considering that verifying signatures is a process that can easily be utilized by attackers to mount resource-exhaustion attacks.

Key generation is 6 to 12 times faster. Signing is 10% (so 1.1 times) slower for the RP, but 2 times faster on the AP and 4 times faster on the RP. Verification is between 10 and 51 times faster. Overall, ML-DSA 44 is faster than ECDSA 256 in almost all cases.

6.2   Memory

Memory consumption is a key concern on embedded platforms with limited RAM and static memory. The stack manages data for program execution, growing as functions are called and shrinking when they return. Stack overflows can cause unpredictable behavior, so even lightweight operating systems like FreeRTOS include overflow detection.

The heap is used for dynamic memory allocation, but issues like allocation failure or fragmentation can cause program termination or inefficient memory use. Common errors, like failing to free memory, can lead to memory leaks and eventual failure.

To avoid heap-related issues, the PQClean library avoids heap usage entirely, placing even large arrays on the stack. In contrast, MbedTLS uses both heap and stack. Comparing the memory consumption of algorithms from these libraries requires considering both types of memory usage.

KEM Algorithms. The left-hand side of Fig. 2 presents plots for the memory usage for RSA-KEM 3072 and ML-KEM 512 across the selected representative platforms.

The plots consist of both heap and stack measurements for different algorithmic phases. The bar charts show clearly the different patterns and design approaches of PQClean and MbedTLS regarding stack and heap usage. Proportionally to the overall memory usage, PQClean requires more stack than heap while MbedTLS heavily uses the heap. Despite the large key sizes of quantum-resistant algorithms such as ML-KEM, total memory usage for key generation is similar to RSA.

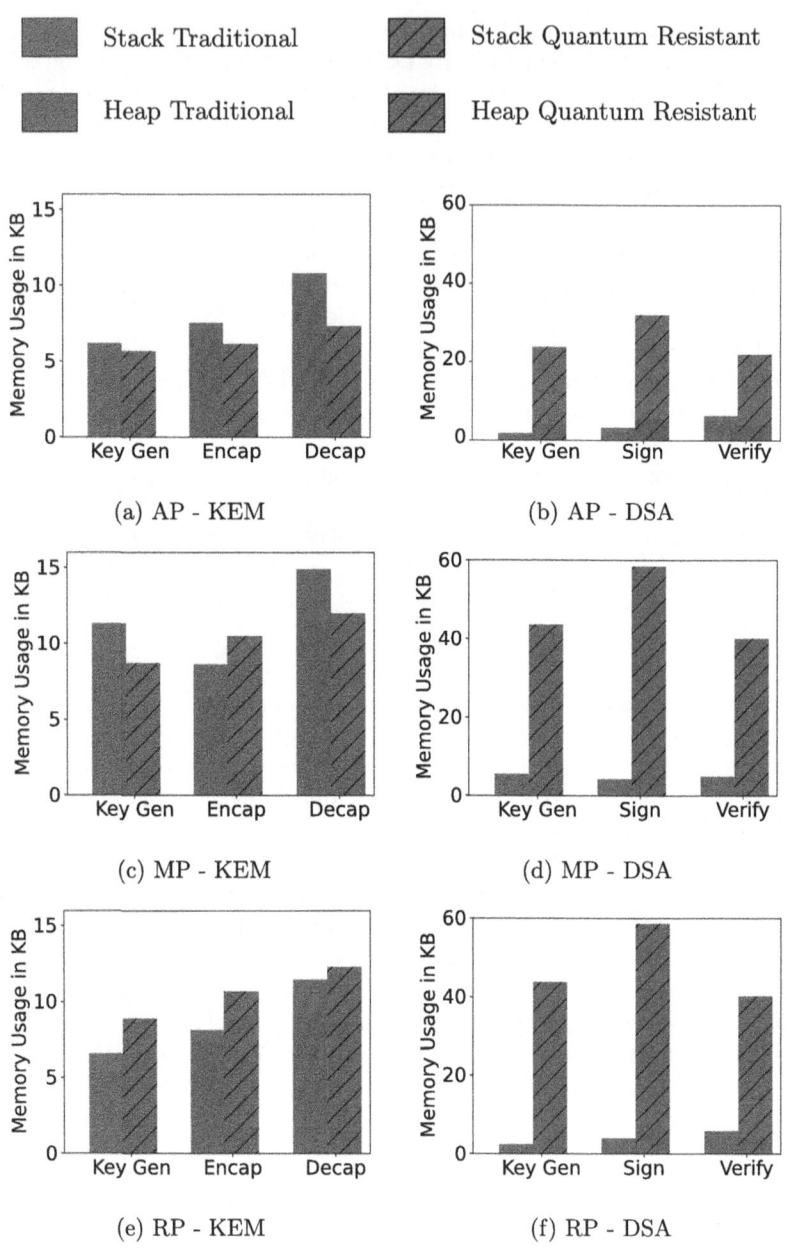

Fig. 2. Comparison of total memory usage of traditional cryptographic algorithms and quantum-resistant algorithms for key encapsulation mechanisms (left) and digital signatures (right) on different embedded platforms. For KEM algorithms the phases key generation, key encapsulation, and key decapsulation are compared for RSA-KEM 3072 and ML-KEM 512. For DSA algorithms the phases key generation, message signing, and signature verification are compared for ECDSA 256 and ML-DSA 44. The embedded platforms are an application processor (AP), a microcontroller (MP), and a real-time processor (RP).

Table 1. Comparison of key sizes, signature size, and ciphertext size the analyzed traditional and quantum-resistant algorithms in Bytes. The values for ML-DSA 44 and ML-KEM 512 are taken from the PQClean code [24], values for RSA-KEM are derived from calls to MbedTLS code [12] and values for ECDSA are taken from [1]. (*) The shared secret's size was set to 32 Byte in our evaluations for RSA-KEM to emulate ML-KEM behavior.

	RSA 3072	ML-KEM 512	Factor	ECDSA 256	ML-DSA 44	Factor
Public Key	384	800	2	64	1312	21
Private Key	384	1632	4	32	2560	80
Signature	-	-	-	64	2420	38
Ciphertext	384	768	2	-	-	-
Shared Secret	32(*)	32	2	-	-	-

The memory usage of ML-KEM slightly increases for encapsulation and decapsulation. This increase can also be seen for RSA-KEM but at greater rates. On the AP, key generation, encapsulation, and decapsulation require 2%, 11%, and 36% percent more memory, respectively. On the MP this trend is not as clear anymore. For key generation and decapsulation, the traditional algorithms use 30.4%, respectively 24%, more memory than the quantum-resistant alternative. Encapsulation, on the other hand, requires 21.7% more memory for ML-DSA. For the RP, the trend is slightly reverted. Here, key generation, encapsulation, and decapsulation require more memory for ML-DSA. The corresponding values are, respectively, 35%, 31%, and 7% more memory.

A portion of the memory used during execution can be attributed to the generated keys and ciphertexts. The sizes for these outputs differ between RSA 3072 and ML-KEM. Table 1 shows how both algorithms differ for this metric. We can see that private keys for ML-KEM are 4 times larger than the RSA 3072 equivalent. Ciphertexts and public keys, which both need to be transmitted over the network, are 2 times larger for ML-KEM.

DSA Algorithms. While quantum-resistant algorithms have outperformed traditional algorithms so far, this changes when looking at memory usage for DSA algorithms. In Fig. 2, the plots on the right-hand side compare the total memory usage of ECDSA 256 and ML-DSA 44. To ensure comparability, the values for signing and verifying with ECDSA include hashing a message with SHA-256.

The plot shows clearly how ML-DSA requires up to 13 times more memory than ECDSA for the AP. This corresponds with 23.9 KB of memory being allocated, to most parts on the stack. Signing requires 10 times more memory on the AP and verifying is at 4 times more memory. For the RP and MP, this trend becomes even more visible. On the MP, ML-DSA requires 8 times more memory for key generation, 14 times more memory for signing, and 8 times more memory for signature verification. Compared to the MP, key generation is cheaper for ECDSA on the RP. As the numbers for ML-DSA remain approximately the same, the percentages shift. It follows that key generation requires 18 times more memory for ML-DSA on the RP. Signing is at 15 times and verifying at 7 times more memory. The highest value is signing on the RP with ML-DSA 44, which uses 58.9 KB.

A portion of the memory consumed during the execution of the various algorithmic phases can be attributed to the generated keys and signatures. Table 1 provides a comparison of these values. In both categories, key size and signature size, ML-DSA requires significantly more data compared to ECDSA. This is particularly important for signatures, which are often transmitted over the network alongside messages to authenticate the sender and ensure message integrity.

The results indicate that messages using quantum-resistant signatures may exceed the maximum packet size (also known as the Maximum Transmission Unit (MTU))on certain networks, leading to packet fragmentation. In such cases, the network splits a large packet into multiple smaller fragments to facilitate transmission. This fragmentation introduces a drawback: if any fragment is lost, the entire packet must be retransmitted. Moreover, the other NIST-standardized quantum-resistant signature algorithm not included in our benchmarks, SLH-DSA, performs even worse in this regard, with signature sizes up to seven times larger than those of ML-DSA [10]. So while runtime is not a concern when it comes to quantum-resistant algorithms, both for key encapsulation and digital signatures, memory consumption introduces new challenges for the adoption in IACS.

7   Conclusion

To understand the influence of the newly released NIST standards for quantum-resistant cryptographic algorithms on industrial automation and control systems (IACS), we first motivated the need for such algorithms. We then introduced key encapsulation and digital signatures as common cryptographic primitives and examined their roles in IACS applications where quantum-resistant alternatives will be necessary.

To understand the performance impact of these alternatives, we benchmarked these standardized algorithms across three classes of embedded platforms: an application processor (ARM Cortex-A53 on the Xilinx Zynq Ultra-Scale+ MPSoC), a real-time processor (ARM Cortex-R5 on the same board), and a microcontroller (ARM Cortex-M7 on the STM32H753ZI). Our benchmarks focused on runtime and memory usage, comparing the quantum-resistant ML-KEM and ML-DSA against their classical counterparts, RSA-KEM and ECDSA, respectively.

Our findings show that ML-KEM not only matches but in most cases outperforms RSA-KEM in terms of speed and memory efficiency, simplifying the overall transition to a quantum-resilient alternative in embedded environments. Especially applications that require frequent key generation for secure communication can profit from the use of ML-KEM. ML-DSA also demonstrates faster performance than ECDSA. Memory consumption remains a significant challenge when using ML-DSA. While ECDSA-256 requires less than 5 KB of memory during signature generation, ML-DSA-44 may demand up to 59 KB, posing difficulties for resource-limited platforms. When possible symmetric algorithms should be used for ensuring integrity and authenticity, limiting the amount of quantum-resistant signatures that need to be verified.

Based on the challenges discussed in Sect. 4, our results show that concerns about hardware being insufficient for handling quantum-resistant cryptography are largely unfounded. While software updates can introduce support for new cryptographic primitives, the more significant challenge lies in enabling hardware support for quantum-resistant algorithms. This involves replacing or redesigning existing cryptographic co-processors and ensuring that quantum-resistant keys can be securely anchored in hardware, for example, during the secure manufacturing process.

A   Measurements

Table 2 shows the values for runtime measurements for RSA-KEM and ML-KEM. Table 3 shows the values for heap and stack measurements.

Table 2. Exact values for KEM and DSA runtime. All values in milliseconds, given as mean $\pm$ standard deviation. A speedup of 1 means that both algorithms take the same amount of time.

Algorithm	Board	Standard	Quantum-resistant	Speedup
KEM-Key Gen	AP	$(5.57 \pm 3.74) \times 10^3$	$(3.51 \pm 0.06) \times 10^{-1}$	15,882
	MP	$(4.43 \pm 3.11) \times 10^5$	$(3.47 \pm 0.08) \times 10^1$	12,769
	RP	$(4.68 \pm 3.14) \times 10^4$	2.17 ± 0.01	21,530
KEM-Encap	AP	3.03 ± 0.03	$(4.28 \pm 0.004) \times 10^{-1}$	3
	MP	$(1.48 \pm 0.06) \times 10^2$	$(3.67 \pm 0.10) \times 10^1$	4
	RP	2.05 ± 0.04	2.41 ± 0.01	8
KEM-Decap	AP	$(9.99 \pm 0.01) \times 10^1$	$(4.11 \pm 0.005) \times 10^{-1}$	100
	MP	$(7.35 \pm 0.02) \times 10^3$	$(3.01 \pm 0.12) \times 10^1$	244
	RP	$(7.43 \pm 0.02) \times 10^2$	2.10 ± 0.01	354
DSA-Key Gen	AP	8.17 ± 0.02	0.81 ± 0.00	10
	MP	610.01 ± 2.85	95.87 ± 0.93	6
	RP	71.54 ± 0.10	5.95 ± 0.05	12
DSA-Sign	AP	8.49 ± 0.02	4.26 ± 2.63	2
	MP	251.35 ± 3.12	277.39 ± 163.41	0.91
	RP	73.21 ± 0.12	18.79 ± 12.58	4
DSA-Verify	AP	32.24 ± 0.11	0.79 ± 0.00	41
	MP	865.56 ± 9.69	88.44 ± 0.01	10
	RP	277.58 ± 0.28	5.43 ± 0.01	51

Table 3. Exact values for KEM and DSA memory measurements. All values in KB. An increase of 1 means the standard and the quantum-resistant algorithm have the same memory consumption.

Algorithm	Board	Standard		Quantum Resistant		Increase
		Heap	Stack	Heap	Stack	
KEM-Key Gen	AP	5.6	0.6	2.7	3.0	0.9
	MP	8.9	2.5	2.4	6.3	0.8
	RP	5.4	1.2	2.7	6.2	1.4
KEM-Encap	AP	7.2	0.4	1.9	4.3	0.8
	MP	6.6	2.1	1.6	8.9	1.2
	RP	7.2	0.9	1.8	8.9	1.3
KEM-Decap	AP	9.7	1.1	2.7	4.7	0.7
	MP	11.6	3.3	2.4	9.6	0.8
	RP	9.4	2.1	2.6	9.7	1.1
DSA-Key Gen	AP	1.2	0.7	4.1	19.8	12.6
	MP	4.2	1.2	3.9	39.8	8.0
	RP	1.0	1.4	4.1	39.8	18.0
DSA-Sign	AP	2.2	1.1	5.5	26.5	9.6
	MP	2.0	2.2	5.2	53.2	13.9
	RP	1.9	2.1	5.5	53.2	14.6
DSA-Verify	AP	5.3	1.0	4.2	17.8	3.5
	MP	3.3	1.5	4.0	36.1	8.3
	RP	4.3	1.5	4.2	36.0	6.9

References

1. Adalier, M., Teknik, A.: Efficient and secure elliptic curve cryptography implementation of curve P-256. In: Workshop on Elliptic Curve Cryptography Standard. NIST (2015). https://eprint.iacr.org/2019/1361
2. Alagic, G.: Recommendations for key-encapsulation mechanisms. Tech. Rep. NIST SP 800-227 ipd, NIST, Gaithersburg, MD (2025). https://doi.org/10.6028/NIST.SP.800-227.ipd
3. AMD: AMD Zynq^{TM} UltraScale+^{TM} MPSoCs. https://www.amd.com/en/products/adaptive-socs-and-fpgas/soc/zynq-ultrascale-plus-mpsoc.html
4. Barker, E.: Recommendation for key management: part 1 - general. Tech. Rep. NIST SP 800-57pt1r5, NIST, Gaithersburg, MD (2020). https://doi.org/10.6028/NIST.SP.800-57pt1r5
5. Bundesamt für Sicherheit in der Informationstechnik (BSI): Kryptografie Quantensicher Gestalten. Tech. Rep. BSI-Bro21/01 (2021)
6. Commission, I.E.: Security for industrial automation and control systems – Part 4-2: Technical security requirements for IACS components. Tech. Rep. 62443–4, IEC (2019)

7. Fitzgibbon, G., Ottaviani, C.: Constrained device performance benchmarking with the implementation of post-quantum cryptography. Cryptography **8**(2), 21 (2024). https://doi.org/10.3390/cryptography8020021

8. Grover, L.K.: A fast quantum mechanical algorithm for database search. In: STOC 1996.,pp. 212–219. ACM Press, Philadelphia, Pennsylvania, United States (1996). https://doi.org/10.1145/237814.237866

9. Howe, J., Westerbaan, B.: Benchmarking and analysing the NIST PQC lattice-based signature schemes standards on the ARM cortex M7. In: AFRICACRYPT 2023, pp. 442–462. Springer Nature Switzerland, Cham (2023). https://doi.org/10.1007/978-3-031-37679-5_19

10. Kannwischer, M.J., Krausz, M., Petri, R., Yang, S.Y.: PQM4: benchmarking NIST additional post-quantum signature schemes on microcontrollers. In: Fifth PQC Standardization Conference. NIST (2024). https://eprint.iacr.org/2019/844

11. Katz, J., Lindell, Y.: Introduction to Modern Cryptography: Principles and Protocols. Chapman and Hall/CRC, New York (2007). https://doi.org/10.1201/9781420010756

12. MbedTLS project: Mbed-TLS (2025). https://github.com/Mbed-TLS/mbedtls

13. Mosca, M., Piano, M.: Quantum Threat Timeline Report 2024. Quantum Threat Timeline Report (Dec 2024)

14. NIST: Call for proposals - post-quantum cryptography (2017). https://csrc.nist.gov/Projects/post-quantum-cryptography/post-quantum-cryptography-standardization/Call-for-Proposals

15. NIST: Module-lattice-based digital signature standard. Tech. Rep. NIST FIPS 204, NIST, Washington, D.C. (2024). https://doi.org/10.6028/NIST.FIPS.204

16. NIST: Module-lattice-based key-encapsulation mechanism standard. Tech. Rep. NIST FIPS 203, NIST, Washington, D.C. (2024). https://doi.org/10.6028/NIST.FIPS.203

17. NIST: Stateless hash-based digital signature standard. Tech. Rep. NIST FIPS 205, NIST (2024). https://doi.org/10.6028/NIST.FIPS.205

18. Open quantum safe: Algorithms in liboqs. https://openquantumsafe.org/liboqs/algorithms/

19. OpenSSH project: OpenSSH release notes. https://www.openssh.com/releasenotes.html

20. Ounsworth, M., Gray, J., Pala, M., Klaußner, J., Fluhrer, S.: Composite ML-KEM for use in X.509 public key infrastructure and CMS. Internet-Draft draft-ietf-lamps-PQ-composite-kem-06, IETF (2025). https://datatracker.ietf.org/doc/draft-ietf-lamps-pq-composite-kem/06/, Work in Progress

21. Paul, S., Scheible, P., Wiemer, F.: Towards post-quantum security for cyber-physical systems: integrating PQC into industrial M2M communication. J. Comput. Secur. **30**(4), 623–653 (2022). https://doi.org/10.3233/JCS-210037

22. Pornin, T.: Deterministic Usage of the digital signature algorithm (DSA) and Elliptic Curve Digital Signature Algorithm (ECDSA). Tech. Rep. RFC 6979, IETF (2013). https://doi.org/10.17487/RFC6979

23. PQClean: Update SPHINCS+/SLH-DSA to be compliant with FIPS205, Issue #562. https://github.com/PQClean/PQClean/issues/562

24. PQClean: PQClean/PQClean (2025). https://github.com/PQClean/PQClean

25. Shor, P.: Algorithms for quantum computation: discrete logarithms and factoring. In: FOCS 1994, pp. 124–134. IEEE Comput. Soc. Press, Santa Fe, NM, USA (1994). https://doi.org/10.1109/SFCS.1994.365700, http://ieeexplore.ieee.org/document/365700/

26. STMicroelectronics: STM32H753ZI. https://www.st.com/en/microcontrollers-microprocessors/stm32h753zi.html
27. Zheng, J., et al.: Faster Post-quantum TLS 1.3 Based on ML-KEM: implementation and Assessment. In: ESORICS 2024, pp. 123–143. Springer (2024). https://doi.org/10.1007/978-3-031-70890-9_7

TADFICS: A Threat-Aware Digital Forensics Data Model for ICS

Alexios Karagiozidis[✉] and Martin Gergeleit

University of Applied Sciences RheinMain, Wiesbaden 65195, Germany
alexios.karagiozidis@gmail.com, martin.gergeleit@hs-rm.de

Abstract. The convergence of IT and Operational Technology (OT) increases risks for industrial control systems (ICS), as Internet connectivity enables attackers to remotely issue commands that can disrupt operations or damage equipment. Investigating such attacks requires identification, collection, examination, and analysis of relevant data. However, the mix of IT and OT components, such as field controllers, propertiary, and different technologies, limit the applicability of IT forensics knowledge and results in a lack of defined forensic data in OT environments. In addition, the implementation specific differences between ICS vendors makes finding general approaches difficult, while ICS forensic research remains limited. To address this, we propose TADFICS, a threat-aware forensic relational data model for ICS. The model provides general ICS data types in conjunction with threat knowledge that must be mapped to implementation-specific ICS data, while also specifying the interrelations and attributes of the actual ICS data to be considered. Therefore, our approach enables the systematic identification and mapping of forensically relevant or required data, including the forensic capabilities of an ICS. Once the model is initialized and the mapping completed, it supports in determining the forensic readiness. Furthermore, it assists in an incident, e.g. how specific ICS data can be acquired or examined, by representing the identified data in a way that supports forensic analysis in ICS while taking the forensic challenges into account. We evaluate our model and demonstrate its applicability by executing a Denial-of-Service (DoS) attack against a PLC of a real-world productive Distributed Control System (DCS) based on the ABB 800xA suite of an operational electrical utility. Our work contributes a novel structured approach to enhance forensic readiness and response by allowing system-specific data alignment with threat-informed forensic aspects, covering preparatory and execution forensic phases.

Keywords: Industrial Control Systems · Operational Technology · Digital Forensics · Distributed Control Systems

1 Introduction

In an ICS, devices such as Programmable Logic Controllers (PLCs) and field controllers supervise and control physical processes via sensors and actuators. Data

B. Coppens et al. (Eds.): ARES 2025 Workshops, LNCS 15994, pp. 149–171, 2025.
https://doi.org/10.1007/978-3-032-00630-1_9

is exchanged with other components, such as Human-Machine Interfaces (HMIs) in the control room, where operators monitor the system. If an adversary gains network access or compromises a component, they can manipulate sensor readings or inject malicious commands [12,19]. Tracing such incidents requires identifying, collecting and analyzing data from both the IT and OT domains [4,9]. The existing forensic data models developed for IT [4] are not applicable to OT environments due to proprietary protocols, specialized hardware, and physical processes [27]. This results into different data to be considered than in IT environments. However, with the increasing convergence of IT and OT, IT forensics remains relevant in ICS contexts. A key challenge in developing broadly applicable approaches lies in the vendor-specific and implementation-specific variability of available data. TADFICS addresses this challenge by providing a data model compatible with both IT and OT environments while incorporating existing ICS attacks, making it threat-aware. The model defines the required ICS data types and supports their mapping to vendor-specific data sources. By specifying relationships and attributes through a relational data model, it enables the structured representation of all vendor-specific data, including forensic capabilities. This allows for a systematic identification of data and capabilities. Furthermore, in addition to forensic preparation, it assists in execution by allowing the model to be queried for forensic questions, such as which data can be acquired and how. Through these features, TADFICS can be applied in various ICS environments while considering implementation-specific differences. Its structured interrelations and constraints between required and actual data enable the identification of data sources, along with their forensic attributes and capabilities, necessary to trace known ICS attacks. We use the MITRE ATT&CK framework [21] for ICS, which catalogs known tactics, techniques, and procedures (TTPs) against ICS. This paper begins by outlining the foundational concepts of digital forensics and ICS. We then review related work that has influenced the development of TADFICS. The proposed model is introduced alongside an analysis of how the ICS data relates to relevant MITRE TTPs. Finally, we evaluate the model by applying it to a real-world Distributed Control System (DCS) of an operational electrical utility and demonstrate how TADFICS can be used in tracing an attack executed by an authorized adversary.

2   Background

In the following, we introduce the general proceedings of a forensic investigation according to the forensic guides of the German Information Security Authority (BSI) [4] and the National Standard Institute [18].

2.1   Digital Forensics

The goal of digital forensics is to trace an incident by collecting, examining, and analyzing evidence to find answers to the questions of what happened when, why and where [4,18].

Digital Forensics Phases and TADFICS. A digital forensic process typically consists of the main phases of data collection, examination, and analysis, while the BSI additionally explicitly defines the strategic and operational preparation. In the following, we introduce the phases and how TADFICS assists in these.

1. *Strategic Preparation*: This phase is executed before any incident to enable forensics. During strategic preparation, existing data and forensic capabilities are determined. The relational data model of TADFICS assists in mapping the required data to actual ICS data by providing general data types and relevant attributes that need to be evaluated. Through TADFICS, it is also possible to map how these data can be acquired and examined. Furthermore, TADFICS provides interrelations between these data and MITRE ATT&CK techniques, enabling an assessment of which attacks can be traced based on the available data making it threat-aware.

2. *Operational Preparation*: This phase is triggered by an initial trigger and prepares the actual forensic investigation for an incident. TADFICS helps here by enabling to query which data is available and can be acquired by the existing methods with further aspects that need to be considered. This assists, e.g., in creating a prioritized list with data to be acquired and their suitable methods.

3. *Data collection*: All relevant data is acquired by using the previous created list of required data. TADFICS, once initiated, can specify how the data can be further examined, while providing all relevant attributes, such as acquisition *tool, asset, location, etc.*, as required by forensic guidelines [4,18].

4. *Examination*: Collected data of the previous phase is now examined for additional artefacts or evidence and data. For example, commands or statuses are extracted from traffic recordings of the field controllers and HMIs. This includes a conversion of binary data to human-readable. Here, TADFICS can indicate which further data in the acquired data can be examined, including the corresponding tools. Furthermore, TADFICS defines the correlation of the data examined or extracted as evidence for specific MITRE TTPs.

5. *Analysis*: In the last phase, a hypothesis of the incident is formed. This phase is not covered by our model, as it focuses on a formal representation and the capabilities of the available and theoretically necessary data. However, the resulting artifacts of the model can still be of use in the analysis.

2.2   ICS Components

Figure 1 shows a minimal ICS architecture based on the established PERA or Purdue ICS model [26,28] which is covered by TADFICS. The Purdue model consists of multiple levels which are introduced in the following.

Enterprise Network (Level 4). The enterprise network, comprising conventional office IT [20], is already well addressed by existing IT forensic frameworks. Therefore, it is out of the scope of our work.

Control Center (Level 3). The control center consists of both IT and OT components and serves as a central hub for controlling and monitoring physical processes by exchanging data with multiple field sites. The fundamental components of an ICS are outlined in the following section.

- **Engineering Workstation (EWS)**: The EWS utilizes project planning or engineering software to manage and configure field devices, such as creating control logic and downloading it to these.
- **Human Machine Interface (HMI)**: The HMI visualizes the physical process and allows an operator to monitor and control the process.
- **Data Historian (DH)**: The data historian is a centralized database that stores and archives operational data, e.g. measured values or events of an ICS.
- **Control Server (CS)**: The control server is usually a software instance on an IT server that uses different protocols to communicate or interact with the ICS components of the field sites.

Field Sites and Physical Process (Level 1/2). The remote field site is not covered by established IT forensics, as interconnected embedded systems with actuators and sensors are used. They directly control and monitor a physical process. As field controllers, usually PLCs and remote terminal units (RTUs) are used. PLCs primarily focus on local control and automation, while the latter is used to exchange telemetry and control data.

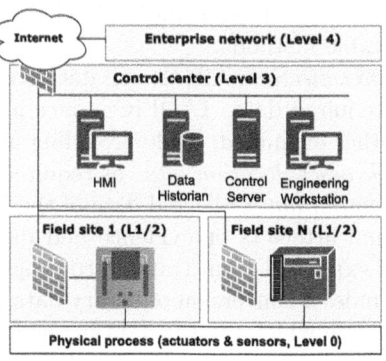

Fig. 1. Minimalistic Purdue Architecture.

2.3 Challenges Related to Data of ICS

Due to the nature of ICS environments, primarily monitoring and controlling physical processes, several challenges arise for ICS forensics. In this section, we outline the specific forensic challenges of ICS, which our proposed model, TADFICS, takes into account.

- **Heterogeneity**: Due to the mixed components of IT and OT components as well as new and older technologies, there is a high heterogeneity of data and components. This results in many different proprietary formats and different forensic capabilities for each ICS. Our model provides all forensically relevant attributes and data types applicable to all ICS that need to be assessed in conjunction with existing attacks.

- **Live**: A further challenge is that data must be acquired from an ICS without affecting the running components. If these are impaired, the safety of the physical process is no longer provided, as the operating and monitoring capabilities of the control room are restricted, including an impact on the productivity of the ICS. TADFICS is designed in such a way that, after the model is initialized and the data is mapped, it can be used to assess which existing live methods are most suitable, based on the data and ICS state.
- **Data Complexity**: A lot of related data is distributed across various ICS components in different formats. This applies, for example, devices configuration and program. These are located on the devices themselves and on the EWS that configures these. Moreover, ICS environments consist of data types that differ from those in traditional IT systems, since ICS have the sole function of controlling and monitoring a physical process. TADFICS aims to address this challenge by defining generally applicable data types and offering a relational data model that represents how implementation-specific data, in conjunction with known attacks, is available.
- **Physical Process**: A further significant difference from IT is an existing physical process that is monitored and controlled by the ICS software and hardware. Depending on the specific process (such as power generation or a sorting facility), there can be a high rate and volume of real-time data which might be relevant for a forensic investigation. Here, our model establishes the relevant relationships between the physical process and IT/OT components.
- **Lack of forensic capabilities and operational constraints**: Since ICS components are mainly developed with a focus on safety and functional requirements related to physical processes, their forensic capabilities remain limited, and there are few tools for the acquisition and analysis of data from such systems [9]. In addition, ICS in operational environments can be minimally or not at all modified from an operators perspective, making it crucial to determine how existing data can be acquired and examined by vendor default tools. Here, our model defines types of assets and tools (e.g., vendor diagnostic tools, engineering software, traffic sniffers, etc.), enabling targeted searches based on these categories within the ICS system.

TADFICS is established with these challenges in mind, aiming to enhance or provide guidance in forensic investigations and incident response within ICS environments. Specifically, it supports the identification of critical ICS data with their forensically relevant attributes, allowing a more effective and structured forensic investigation within existing ICS systems.

3   Related Work

In 2020, the MITRE ICS ATT&CK catalog [22] was introduced and has since been expanded with new attack techniques targeting ICS. The catalog classifies adversarial behavior into tactics and techniques (TTPs). To make our model, TADFICS, threat-aware based on existing attacks, we incorporate relevant MITRE TTPs. The data types provided by TADFICS are intended to aid in tracing these. In 2022, NIST published a Digital Forensics and Incident Response (DFIR) framework for operational technology (OT) environments [13]. Although this framework outlines the procedural aspects of forensic investigations, it addresses required data only briefly without reference to existing attacks. In 2023, a survey on ICS forensics was published [7], in which the authors summarize *previously reported data artefacts based on various studies*. However, these data artefacts are only a small portion of the survey and are not explicitly covered. In the same year, the work *A Digital Forensic Taxonomy for PLC Data Artefacts* [25] was introduced. It provides a structured classification of PLC related data along with their relationships and characteristics to support forensic investigation of attacks against PLCs. Although both of these studies are incorporated into TADFICS or our work, their scope is limited to PLCs, leaving other standard ICS components including the process control system (PCS), such as the control server, unaddressed. Moreover, these studies also do not consider known or existing ICS attacks, lacking of threat awareness. To establish TADFICS, we extend the determined data in the related work by determining forensically relevant data from ICS components beyond PLCs, which have remained largely unaddressed in existing research. It is therefore the first approach to comprehensively consider both PCS and PLCs, including the identification and representation of forensically relevant data and capabilities of an ICS environment. This assists in executing a forensic investigation within ICS as well.

4   Analysis of the Data Types and Introduction of the Forensic Data Model

In this chapter we present the forensic relational model of TADFICS after a discussion of general ICS data in conjunction with related MITRE TTPs. We also present the relational data model of TADFICS. We refer to artefacts as specific data sources (based on data types) that provide potential evidence.

4.1   Analysis of Required ICS Data

To achieve compatibility with IT forensics by enabling the integration of known IT forensic data, we assign relevant conceptual ICS forensic data to the data categories provided by the BSI IT forensics guide [4]. Simultaneously, we extend the BSI data categories by introducing ICS-specific categories, allowing for a more effective integration of ICS forensically relevant data and ensuring ICS compatibility. Following this, we examine and specify which data types can provide information to trace which MITRE TTP to achieve a threat awareness.

Forensic Artefacts or Data Types in ICS. In Table 1 we provide the ICS specific data types assigned to the BSIs data categories with their source assets. The data types in are based on the related work work [7,8,20,25]. In addition, we extend the data types by including data from non-covered assets, such as the control server, based on our own analysis of related standards and guides [1, 13–15, 26].

We further extend the BSIs categories by *Diagnostics, Physical Process, Documentation* for better applicability to the ICS domain. A data type may contain multiple or other data types that must be identified and extracted during the examination phase [4]. For example, project files can be obtained from an acquired hard drive image. In the following, we discuss the addition categories we have added for the ICS applicability.

Table 1. Selected data types assigned to extended BSI categories.

Data Category	Data Type	Assets with Data Types	Data Category	Data Type	Assets with Data Types
Hardware	Disk images	EWS, CS, DH	Session	Uploads/downloads	EWS, PLC, HMI
	Firmware	PLC, HMI		Project changes	EWS, CS
	Device metadata	PLC, HMI		Operators interactions	HMI
	Device information	PLC, HMI		Screen recording	HMI
	I/O modules	PLC		Event logs	EWS, CS, PLC, HMI
	Actuators/sensors	PLC		Audit logs	EWS, CS, PLC, HMI
Raw	RAM image	EWS, CS, DH, HMI	User	Project files	EWS, PLC, HMI
	Operational databases	CS, DS		Application code	EWS, PLC, HMI
	Memory binary	PLC, HMI		Variables	EWS, PLC, HMI
	I/O data	PLC		Setpoints	EWS, PLC, HMI
				Faceplates	EWS, HMI
Metadata	Industrial software filetypes	EWS, CS, DH, HMI	Diagnostics	Live or indicated tags	EWS, CS, PLC, HMI
	Industrial software files	EWS, CS, DH, HMI		Live or indicated values	
	Project files metadata	EWS, CS		Error buffer and logs	
	Available devices/stations	PLC, HMI		Health monitoring data	
	Device meta data	PLC, HMI			
Configuration	User configuration	All	Physical Process	Alarms/events	HMI, DH, CS
	Device configuration	EWS, PLC, HMI		Process image	
	Security settings	All		Analog readings	
	Alarm and event settings	EWS, CS		Digital readings	
	Backup settings	EWS, CS, DH		Historical data	
				Plant Site area	
				Physical component	
Communication	Industrial protocol	All	Documentation	Operators logbook	N/A
	Uploads/downloads	EWS, PLC, HMI		Operators shiftbook	
	Transmitted tags and values	CS, DH, HMI, PLC		Witness report	
	Read/write requests	CS, HMI, PLC		Plant documentation	
	Commands/acknowledgments			Photos	
	Communication drivers	EWS, CS, HMI		Maintenance logs	
Process	Industrial software activity	EWS, CS, DH, HMI			
	Industrial software drivers				
	Industrial software services				

- **Diagnostics**: Due to the lack of forensic capabilities and the proprietary nature of ICS, diagnostic data are essential for ICS forensics [9, 11]. These are often the only available information of system-internal data, ranging from specific error messages to status information such as the health of an ICS component.
- **Physical Process**: The physical process is a major difference from IT, which is why we explicitly categorize it. This includes all data related to the physical process, such as control and monitoring data, as well as alarms/events but also the HMI's process visualization [20]. This further includes the plant site area

(e.g., self-consumption control) of an ICS, along with its physical components (such as circuit breakers or transformers), which might be affected by an attack.

- **Documentation**: This category includes data that might not be found on any of the assets but is still important. E.g. this includes a witness report or operators log- and shiftbook.

Analysis of ICS Data in Relation to MITRE TTPs. Table 2 assigns the data types of Table 1 to MITRE ICS TTPs they can potentially provide evidence for. We limit ourselves to OT exclusive MITRE TTPs that have been observed in real-world attacks or can affect control room operations and visibility making them safety-critical.

To find answers to the forensic objectives *what happened, when where and why* all related data types must be considered [7]. This also results from the distinction between direct and indirect evidence. Direct evidence is the data generated directly by the attacker, while indirect evidence contains evidence about the impact of the attacks on the ICS. The latter also results from an analysis as a correlation between multiple data types with the same context.

In particular, communication data can provide potential evidence for many of the attacks, as a lot of the TTPs are network-related. Furthermore, our analysis determined that *alarms/events* can provide valuable information for tracing any critical attack. This is due to the fact that ICS, by default and for compliance reasons, must log all events related to the physical process and its automation system [6]. Therefore, alarms/events were essential in tracing all real-world attacks, such as those described in [10,24]. Since these can be manipulated during an attack [21], it is essential to consider additional data types for comparison or cross-validation.

The assignment of Table 2 supports the idea that when a MITRE TTP is suspected, all associated data types can be considered for acquisition and examination. This also allows for an assessment of which MITRE TTPs are forensically covered by the available data and capabilities, making the TADFICS threat aware.

4.2   Relational Data Model of TADFICS

In Fig. 2 the relational data model of TADFICS is presented. Due to its extent, we include the entities without their attributes. We uploaded a full ERD with attributes (including primary and foreign keys) on GitHub [17].

Type Entities. The types are applicable to all ICS, regardless of the vendor, as they cover all general types that need to be identified or assigned to the actual ICS. As we introduced the data types in relation with MITRE TTPs in the prior section, we skip those here. Asset types include the Purdue components of the ICS together with other relevant types as *security* and *forensics* assets.

Table 2. Selected Data Types mapped to MITRE TTPs they can assist tracing.

	T0816 Device Restart/ Shutdown	T0835 Manipulate I/O Image	T0856 Spoof Reporting Message	T0858 Change Operating Mode	T0878 Alarm Suppression	T0803 Block Command Message	T0804 Block Reporting Message	T0838 Modify Alarm Settings	T0855 Unauth. Command Message	T0814 Denial of Service	T0881 Service Stop	T0889 Modify Program
Hardware:												
Firmware												X
Device metadata	X			X				X			X	X
Raw:												
RAM image			X			X	X			X		
Operational databases			X	X	X	X	X	X				X
Memory binary		X										X
I/O data		X	X	X	X	X	X		X			
Metadata:												
Project files metadata								X				X
Available devices/stations			X							X		
Configuration:												
Device configuration			X					X				X
Alarm and event settings				X				X				
Communication:												
Industrial protocol	X	X	X		X	X	X		X	X		X
Uploads/downloads												X
Transmitted tags and values		X	X		X	X	X		X	X		
Read/write requests		X	X		X	X	X	X	X			
Commands									X			
Process:												
Process activity			X		X	X	X		X	X	X	X
Session:												
Uploads/downloads												X
Operators interactions			X						X			
Screen recording			X			X	X		X	X		
Event logs					X	X	X	X	X	X	X	X
User:												
Project files								X				X
Application code								X				X
Faceplates								X				X
Documentation:												
Witness report			X	X	X				X	X		
Maintenance logs				X				X			X	X
Physical Process:												
Alarms/events	X	X	X	X	X	X	X	X	X	X		
Process image	X	X	X	X	X	X	X		X	X	X	
Diagnostics:												
Live tags/values			X		X	X	X		X	X		
Error buffer and logs	X			X	X	X	X	X	X	X	X	X

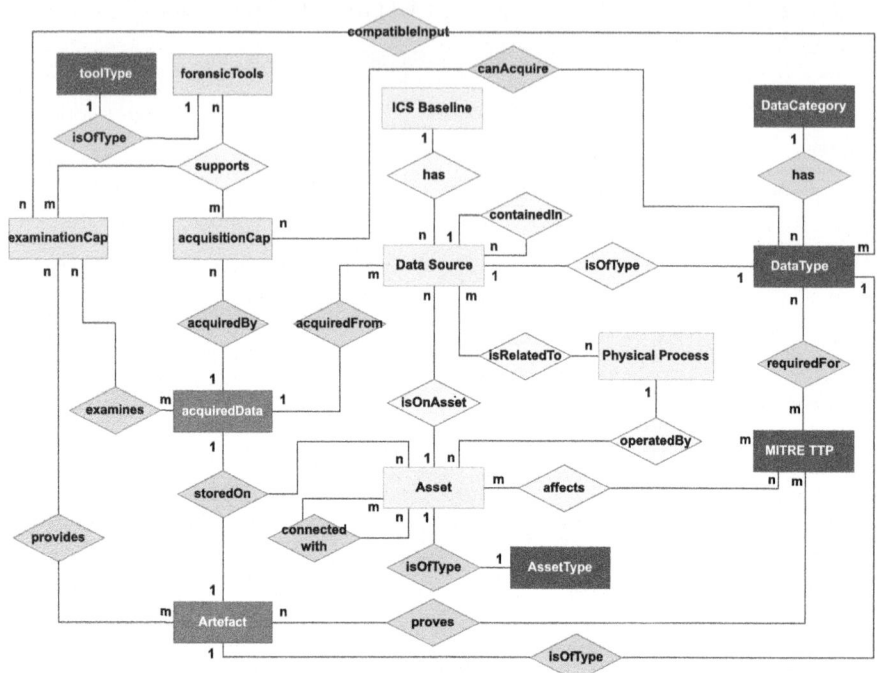

Fig. 2. Relational forensic data model of TADFICS.

The tool types include *vendor diagnostic tools* and *vendor default tools* next to security and analysis tools, while the types can be extended as needed. This representation enables the identification and indication of the location of the data and their associations with other assets (*on/off device data* [8]).

Baseline, Assets, Data Source and Physical Process. The yellow colored entities are instances of the dark blue ones (types) and are populated or initiated during the strategic preparation. In the following, we explain the entities in detail.

- **Baseline**: The baseline lists all available data sources, since the forensic baseline includes the assessment of these [7,13,18]. Therefore, the baseline indicates the supposed state of the ICS, such as installed programs or archived projecting files, available assets and devices, etc.
- **Asset**: An asset can be connected with other assets, which is indicated by the *connectedWith* relation. Each asset can be affected by different MITRE TTPs to limit the scope of data that needs to be identified. The assets also include the *criticality* attribute to prioritize identification. Additionally, it is documented whether the asset is a third-party asset, as these must be assessed separately due to their different capabilities in comparison with the main vendor system.

- **Data Source**: A data source is an instance of a data type. It can contain further data sources (of different types) which is indicated over the *containedIn* relation. This allows a mapping to identify which additional data a data type or its instance can be examined for (such as a file from a harddrive image). It is determined whether the data source is human-readable or binary (and therefore requires specific examination tools), along with other forensically relevant attributes such as *volatility* and the timestamp format.
- **Physical Process**: The *operatedBy* relation indicates the responsible asset of a monitoring and controlling a physical process. As the impact of an attack on the physical processes must be assessed [16], we relate the physical process to the data sources that contain information about it. This means that this entity includes the physical component (e.g., circuit breaker), plant site, and function (*plant site area*) in connection with the ICS assets that operate and monitor them.

The introduced relations allow for a systematic identification and representation of the ICS to determine how required data (data types) are actually available, together with their relevant attributes. Therefore, once the ER is initiated, TADFICS indicates where the data reside and what forensic-relevant characteristics it possesses (e.g. volatility, format, properties). This facilitates the adaptation of the model to the unique characteristics and actual assets of an ICS, which is recommended for ICS forensics [9]. This approach bridges theoretically required data with actual available ICS data, taking vendor-specific dependencies into account.

Forensic Tools and Their Capabilities to Acquire or Examine Forensic Data to Provide Artefacts. The entities in light blue must be assessed after the assets and data sources have been identified. They are populated once the actual ICS data have been identified during strategic preparation and allow for the determination of forensic capabilities. The green entities, as *acquiredData* and *artefact* are initiated and populated only during the acquisition and examination.

- **forensicTool**: This entity includes all tools capable of collecting and examining data, such as official forensic tools, diagnostic tools, and vendor-specific software that can read or export ICS specific data. This approach is common in ICS forensics, as vendor tools are often the only way to acquire and read specific ICS data due to propertiary and safety constraints [9].
- **acquisitionCapability**: This specifies the data types each tool is capable of acquiring, allowing one to assess how which data can be acquired. Alongside the supported data type, the output format is determined. In addition, it includes attributes known from IT forensics and are also applicable to ICS. This includes attributes like *live capability, impact, remote capability*.
- **examinationCapability**: Examination capabilities define which tools can examine acquired data to identify evidence or artefacts. According to our TADFICS or its relational model, each examination tool receives an input (consisting of a *data type* and *format*) and provides an output. The output can

be a further data type with a new format (as human-readable). An analysis tool can thus extract an artefact from the acquired data.

- **Acquired data**: This entity includes all data acquired during a forensic investigation and includes which tool was used, while also specifying its original data source.
- **Artefact**: An artefact is derived by examining previously acquired data and provides potential evidence for an existing attack or MITRE TTP. For example, a related log entry within the acquired alarms/events could serve as such artefact by indicating an attacker's action or impact. The tool used to acquire or gather (examine) the artefact are also specified here, along with other forensically relevant attributes such as the timestamp or *event information*.

These relationships allow for the identification and indication of how specific data can be acquired and examined together with resulting evidence with respect to the MITRE TTPs. This enables forensic investigations to determine which ICS data is available, along with possible methods and tools for acquisition and examination. Once the model is initiated, flexible queries can be created to provide guidance and answers to forensic questions (e.g. which data should be acquired how) during an ICS forensic investigation.

5 Initializing TADFICS for the Strategic Preparation of a Real World ICS

In the strategic preparation phase, all available forensic data and acquisition capabilities are identified [4]. We apply TADFICS to prepare an existing ICS for forensics, to trace an unknown attack afterward. Using a real DCS as a testbed ensures realistic constraints and compliance with ICS standards, covering typical ICS environments. As the DCS had not previously been evaluated from a forensic perspective, this also allows for a realistic evaluation. We outline how TADFICS is utilized, initiated, and populated during strategic preparation, including an introduction of the testbed or DCS used.

5.1 Proceedings of the Strategic Preparation

Here, we describe our general approach for the strategic preparation.

1. **Creation of a database**: We create a database based on the entity relation model of TADFICS. This enables dynamically querying data once the tables or entities have been populated.
2. **Identifying critical components**: In the next step, we identify all existing critical assets that correspond to the Purdue model to be assessed. We identify these by the asset types provided by TADFICS.
3. **Analysis of available data sources**: We identify data sources using manuals and reverse engineering techniques to search and find the data types of Table 1. The identified data is then examined for known formats and forensic attributes (e.g., human-readable or binary) as defined by TADFICS. We also identify the software installed by the vendor.

4. **Analysis of available forensic functions**: In a last step, we analyze how the identified data types in the ICS can be acquired and examined by which existing tools.

5.2 Productive ABB 800xA DCS Used as Testbed for the Strategic Preparation and Evaluation

As testbed for the application of TADFICS we use a productive DCS of an energy supplier based on the ABB 800xA suite. The DCS consists of several local field sites (*plant sites*) divided into functional areas (*plant site areas*). Proprietary TCP/IP protocols are used for data exchange between all components. The architecture of 800xA in scope is shown in Fig. 3. The PLCs are located within the *operating network* (O-net), while the IT components reside in the *Human System Interface* (HSI) network.

ABB 800xA Components. The DCS is based on the ABB 800xA system which is widely used in different domains such as substations/power distribution, power generation, mining and batch processes [2,3]. In the following, we describe which 800xA components correspond to which Purdue components.

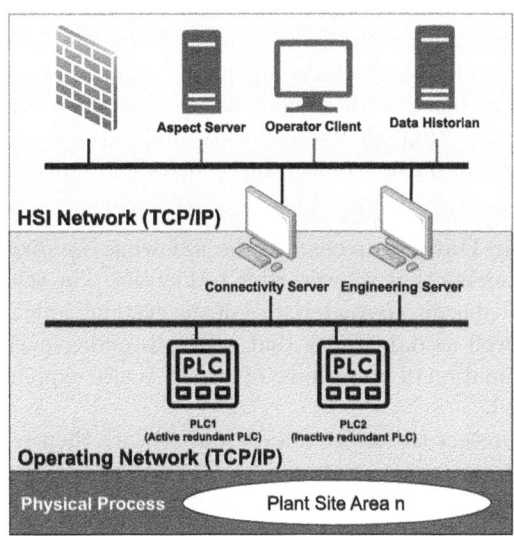

Fig. 3. ABB 800xA components in scope of the application and evaluation.

– **Aspect Server:** The aspect server corresponds to the *Control Server* as the configuration and all faceplates regarding the PCS are stored here. The Aspect Server comes with an own project planning software and is required for the HMIs. All IT components base on Windows.

- **Connectivity Server:** This server corresponds to the *Data Gateway* as it exchanges the data between the two networks (e.g. HMI to PLC).
- **Operator Client:** This client is an IT machine that runs only the 800xA HMI software. It is connected to both the Aspect- and the Connectivity Server while they supervise the plant areas or field sites.
- **EWS Server:** This corresponds to the EWS and contains the engineering software to program the PLCs, including diagnostic tools.
- **ABB legacy PLCs:** The L1/2 consists of legacy PLCs which also use the TCP/IP protocols mentioned above to exchange data. They only support the standardized programming language *Sequential Function Chart* (SFC).

The DG is connected to multiple redundant PLCs, which monitor one or multiple *plant site areas*. The areas are organized according to the functions of the physical processes of the ICS, such as an area *self-consumption control*, comprising circuit breakers and transformers. These in turn are monitored by a corresponding HMI in the control room. All components are available in multiple instances, both for redundancy reasons and to support the different plant sites and areas. The time of the components are synchronized by GPS clock modules of the 800xA system.

Resulting Constraints of the Productive Environment. Due to the real ICS environment, several constraints arise. Many forensic tools are not supported due to lack of compatibility with legacy systems. For safety and stability reasons, nothing must be installed on the L3 components. In addition, portable tools and other forensic actions must be thoroughly assessed for their impact before being used. This also means that all forensic tools and actions must not affect the ability of the control room to monitor and control ICS, affecting safety.

Assets and Their Data Sources. In the following, we discuss selected data sources with their assets that we were able to identify. The selection is based on the uniqueness and specific characteristics of the system, which were determined by our model, as well as data types that relate to multiple MITRE ATT&CK TTPs. The determination of uniqueness of an ICS is also explicitly recommended for ICS forensics [9].

In Table 3, we present the selected data sources with their relevant attributes. The first three data sources correspond to IT forensic data types and apply to all L3 assets of our DCS [4,9]. We use classes to indicate the data's volatility and retention period. The latter indicates how long the data can be acquired. As timestamps are crucial for forensics and a further challenge in ICS, we also determine to which extent and how these are available for the data sources including the tools.

- **Control Server**: In addition to examining the manuals, we partially reverse-engineered the ABB software by monitoring accessed files. This revealed the project database and its storage location (ID 5) as well as statically stored alarms/events of a plant site (ID 7). Various configuration data such as alarm

Table 3. Selected data sources of the DCS on the initiated TADFICS model.

id	sourceName	Data Category	Data Type	onAsset	dataVolatility	retPeriod	binary	baseli.	Format
1	RAM image	Raw	RAM image	L3	volatile	immediate	yes	partly	*.raw
2	Hard drive image	Raw	Disk image	L3	volatile	long-term	yes	yes	*.raw
3	Drive C:	Det. a. data	Filesystem	L3	static	long-term	no	yes	NTFS
5	MainDb.afwdb	User	Project Files	CS	static	long-term	yes	yes	*.afwdb
6	Alarm Configuration	Configuration	Alarm settings	CS	static	short-term	no	NA	unknown
7	alarms/events	Physical process	Alarms/Events	CS	semi-dynamic	long-term	yes	NA	*.lgd
8	Config.mdf	Det. a. data	Operational Database	DG	semi-dynamic	long-term	yes	yes	*.mdf
9	Composer database	User	Project files	EWS	static	long-term	yes	yes	*.bo*
10	project interactions	Session	Audit log	EWS	semi-dynamic	long-term	no	yes	*.rep
11	Code generation files	user	user application code	EWS	semi-dynamic	long-term	no	no	*.obl
12	Programminfo	User	user application code	PLC1	long-term	long-term	no	yes	unknown
13	Measured values	Diagnostics	indicated live tags	PLC1	volatile	immediate	no	no	unknown
14	Error buffer	Diagnostics	Diagnostic buffer	PLC1	semi-dynamic	long-term	no	yes	unknown

settings, are stored in this database, while its readable contents are generated dynamically in the ABB software. The project database cannot be directly acquired during operation due to active access of the OT software.

– **EWS**: Using the same approach, we identified the engineering database (ID 9) storing all O-net related configuration. Additionally, we were able to determine the path in which the generated user application code is stored. This code is saved in the form of a .txt file and contains human-readable instructions instead of SFC. Furthermore, we also identified data types known from IT forensics, such as network configuration files where all managed PLCs are registered.

– **PLC**: The NIST OT DFIR guide excludes postmortem examination as dismantling of the device in production is excluded [13]. This also applies to our DCS used as testbed so we could only use the diagnostics tool to connect with the PLC and query all available data (as user code) why the format is unknown.

For all L3 components, we identified the OT related software processes such as alarm/event-, PLC connection handling, HMI GUI process, next to the other data types of our model. Regarding timestamps, alarms and events are recorded in UTC, including only the event time—not when messages were sent or received.

Forensic Tools. In a last step we determine the forensic capabilities. For this purpose, we examine established tools of IT forensics that are compatible with the data types of our data sources. In addition, we review preinstalled 800xA tools to determine which data types they can acquire or examine. This primarily concerns diagnostic tools, which is common practice in ICS environments and often the only way to acquire system internal data [11, 29].

Acquisition Capabilities. Regarding the acquisition, we identified four different main default tools capable of acquiring many of the data sources related to ICS and IT data types.

- **System Checker Tool**: Queries ICS node status of L3 components, configurations, and user/role information essential for forensics [4,18].
- **System Information Tool**: Collects L3 component data including error messages, port bindings, and OT software files checksums. Latter is essential as well for integrity or detecting changed files [5].
- **Diagnostic Log Collector**: Gathers comprehensive data (software, DLLs, logs, processes etc.) and HMI alarms/events, limited to L3 components.
- **PLC analyzer**: Queries PLC data remotely or via local serial interface. The latter is a useful capability for data acquisition during network compromises or unavailability.

Other components, such as the data historian, have their own software capable of exporting specific types such as alarms and events to *Excel*. Each export function can therefore serve as acquisition function as well. Since the IT data is already covered by existing IT tools, we exclude them here. This includes, for example, tools for acquiring disk images.

Examination Capabilities. We initially assess standard forensic tools like *Volatility*, *Autopsy*, and *Wireshark* for IT based ICS related data. *Volatility* can analyze a given RAM image for various data types such as process activity, while Autopsy can examine a file system from an HDD image for, e.g. vendor project files. Since these tools are well-known in established IT forensics, they are not described here. The following tools of the DCS are useful for ICS-specific data, as they are the only way to read or examine those. The first two tools are based on default tools, whereas the third one is a forensic tool, especially for databases.

- **Plant Explorer**: This is the project planning software running on the control server and the only means to export and read project data (ID 5 of Table 3).
- **ABB EWS tool**: The EWS tool is used to administer and configure the PLCs. Due to the proprietary format of the engineering database, only this tool can be used to read acquired project or engineering data. The EWS software can read and export project data related to the PLCs.
- **MDF Viewer**: Regarding OT, multiple SQL databases of the ABB software were identified which is common for ICS [23] and can be read by MDF Viewer. This applies to the *operational databases* and contains the configuration of the system (ID 8). The examination tool runs on the FWS.

Other data types of IT components are already covered by IT forensics tools. Particularly for log files, there are various tools such as Splunk and Excel that allow for their examination regardless of their IT or OT context.

During the strategic preparation most of the data types related data sources were identified, though some had unclear contents. E.g. we identified temporary binary files being created during opening faceplates on the HMI but couldn't interpret them further or determine what data types they contain. Other data types were only partially human readable, for instance variable names in the propertiary TCP/IP protocols could be read, but not their corresponding values.

Furthermore, by utilizing TADFICS we identified ways to acquire data when direct methods are not feasible. For example, the project database cannot be directly acquired during operation because it is accessed by the OT software. However, based on our initiated model, we determined that it is possible to acquire the disk or even RAM image during operation and extract the project database with an IT examination tool from these.

6 Evaluating TADFICS by Tracing an Attack

To evaluate TADFICS further, our productive DCS is attacked by an authorized adversary, while we use TADFICS to trace the incident and execute the other forensic phases. Due to the extent, we include in this work only the first iteration of the investigation.

The Attack. Prior to the attack, we are only aware of an estimated timeframe, but not which components are going to be attacked or how while the DCS is idle. The control room or operators are only informed about unscheduled maintenance tests and asked to report anything unusual. After some time, we receive a call reporting that the HMI monitoring *Plant Site Area 1* temporarily stopped displaying process values while no commands could be executed. The call marks the initial trigger for our forensic investigation.

6.1 Using TADFICS for Executing a Forensic Investigation

In the operator alarms/events, we can see the corresponding DG reporting a connection loss to PLC1 followed by an error trail of several other errors. This is concluded by a *Return-to-Normal (RTN)* event of the system. In the following text, we refer to the HMI for Plant Site Area 1 as HMI1, the active PLC as PLC1, and its redundant (inactive) PLC as PLC2 (see Fig. 3).

Table 4. Queried table with selected data of affected assets mapped to potential acquisition tools based on our data model.

ID	Asset	Data Category	Data Type	sourceName	Volatility	retPeriod	remote	Acquisition Tools	Typ.	Impact
1	DH	Physical process	Alarms/Events	Values over time	Semi-dynamic	archival	no	*Event Explorer*	OT	Low
2	DH	Physical process	Alarms/Events	Site Alarms/events	Semi-dynamic	archival	no	*Event Explorer*	OT	Low
3	DG	Raw	RAM image	RAM image	Volatile	Immediate	no	*RAM capturer*	IT	Low
4	DG	Raw	Disk image	HDD image	Static	Long-term	no	*FTK Imager*	IT	Low
5	DG	Details about data	Filesystem	System C:	Static	Long-term	no	*FTK Imager*	IT	Low
6	DG	Diagnostics	Error logs	Error logs	Semi-dynamic	Long-term	yes	*Diagnostic Log Collector*	OT	Medium
7	DG	Session	Log	History files	Semi-dynamic	Short-term	yes	*System Information Tool*	OT	Low
8	DG	Communication	Connected hosts	PCS connections	Volatile	Immediate	yes	*System Information Tool*	OT	Low
9	DG	Communication	Connected hosts	Port binding DG	Volatile	Immediate	no	*Windows cmd (netstat)*	IT	Low
10	DG	Communication	Connection status	Port binding DG	Volatile	Immediate	yes	*System Information Tool*	IT	Low
11	DG	Process	Process activity	Process operations	Volatile	Immediate	no	*ProcMon*	IT	Medium
12	DG	Process	Process activity	Process activity	Volatile	Immediate	no	*Process Explorer*	IT	Low
13	PLC1/2	Hardware	Operating mode	Controller status	Volatile	Immediate	both	*PLC Analyzer*	OT	Low
14	PLC1/2	Communication	Connected devices	Participantslist	Semi-dynamic	Immediate	both	*PLC Analyzer*	OT	Low
15	PLC1/2	Diagnostics	Diagnostic buffer	Error buffer	Semi-dynamic	Long-term	both	*PLC Analyzer*	OT	Low
16	PLC1/2	Diagnostics	Utilization	CPU utilization	Volatile	Immediate	both	*PLC Analyzer*	OT	Low
17	CS	Physical process	Alarms/Events	*.lgd files	Dynamic	Short-term	no	*FTK Imager*	IT	Low

Operational Preparation. We use TADFICS and its initiated data model to query all data available from affected assets to create a list of data to be acquired. Based on the indicated error messages we narrow the data down on potential MITRE TTPs such as *Block Command message, Block Reporting Message, Service Stop* and *Denial of Service*. Table 4 shows the resulting data that can be acquired or is in scope, considering Off-Device data of other (unaffected) assets. Therefore, the data historian is included, as it stores all alarms/events of the whole DCS while we prioritize all volatile data types.

Data Acquisition. In Table 5, we present the collected data based on our model. The *originalDataSourceID* is the foreign key for the data sources table. We summarize the data for all L3 components and include in the query the asset from which the tool was executed as required by forensics for traceability reasons [4]. First, we acquire the status of all L3 components to identify or confirm affected components and ICS state, followed by alarms and events. Using the diagnostic tools, we collect the diagnostic buffer of the PLCs, but also diagnostic events of the other HSI's network components. The *functionId* indicates which acquisition capability or tool was applied.

Table 5. Acquired data which is now located on the forensic workstation (FW).

ID	originalDataSourceID	ofAsset	onAsset	acquisitionCapabiltiy	format	execOn
1	Nodes Status	L3	FW	System Checker Tool	*.txt	CS
2	Alarms/events	DH	FW	Event Explorer	*.xls	DH
3	Alarms/events	HMI1	FW	Diagnostic Log Collector	*.txt	DH
4	RAM image	DG	FW	Magnet RAM capture tool	*.raw	GS
5	Log files	L3	FW	System Information Tool	*.txt	CS
6	Exceptions logs	L3	FW	System Information Tool	*.txt	CS
7	Port bindings	L3	FW	System Information Tool	*.txt	CS
8	Log files	L3	FW	System Checker Tool	*.txt	CS
9	Controller status	L1/2	EWS	Vendor PLC Analyzer	*.txt	EWS
10	Bus participants	L1/2	EWS	Vendor PLC Analyzer	*.txt	EWS
11	Error buffer	L1/2	EWS	Vendor PLC Analyzer	*.txt	EWS
12	Traffic capture	L3	FW	tcpdump	*.pcap	FW
13	Traffic capture	L1/2	FW	tcpdump	*.pcap	FW

Examination of the Acquired Data and Resulting Artefacts. Once data acquisition is complete, the examination phase begins by searching the acquired data for evidence or artefact using the examination tools. We include the *format* to determine which examination tool is compatible and if it is human-readable (so no further examination tools might be required). Table 6 summarizes the examined artefacts and the potential MITRE TTPs they provide proof for.

- **Alarms/events**: In the alarms/events of the DCS, there are indications of a *DoS* and *Service Stop* attack, as the connection to PLC1 is lost. The alarms/events also reveal specific error messages related to PLC1. The critical alarms trail is concluded by by completion of a redundancy takeover or by the successful initiation of the redundant PLC2. Furthermore, the event trail is concluded by an *Return to Normal (RTN)* event.
- **PLC error logs**: We identified two distinct error messages that repeat for a period of time. Among them, the message *ETH0 network buffer overflow* and *CPU error* indicate a potential DoS attack as well. By reviewing all supported error messages from the PLC manual, a *Service Stop* on the PLC can be ruled out, as crashes or termination of PLC processes would create a specific error message.
- **Diagnostic data of L3 components**: Examination of the acquired ICS status data indicates that all 800xA components run normally. This speaks against a *Service Stop* attack, including the lack of exception logs (as a crashed process) during the specified time window. Additionally, the process data collected via the diagnostic tool indicates that all supposed processes are running.
- **RAM image of DG**: The latter conclusion is further supported by the examination of the acquired RAM image where we extracted all OT related process data. Here, also, no terminated software processes were identified, reinforcing the exclusion of a *Service Stop* attack.
- **Traffic Capture**: Here, we examine the network traffic, particularly the connections to and from the affected assets. We observe multiple connection attempts directed towards PLC1 that consist exclusively of SYN requests. This pattern is indicative of a SYN flood attack targeting PLC1, providing direct evidence of a (DoS) incident.

Table 6. Artefacts or examined data types to trace the attack based on our data model.

ID	forensicArtefact	onAsset	examCapability	examinedFrom	Event/action	Potentialy proving MITRE TTPs
1	DG connection loss to PLC	FW	Excel	Alarms/Events	Connection failure	*Block Reporting Message Denial of Service Alarm Suppression*
2	Connection loss to active PLC	FW	Volatility	RAM image	Comm. failure	*Same as ID 1 + Service Stop*
3	Error message of PLC	FW	Excel	Alarms/Events	PLC interface buffer full	*Block Reporting Message Denial of Service Alarm Suppression*
4	PLC interface errors	FW	PLC analyzer	Analyzer-outputfile	Comm. disruption	Same as ID 1
5	Inactive PLC switching to active	FW	Excel	Alarms/Events	Redundancy takeover	*None*
6	DG connecting to active PLC	FW	Excel	Alarms/Events	Redundancy takeover	*None*
7	Connection to (new) active PLC	FW	Volatility	RAM image	Redundancy takeover	*None*
8	Port binding to (new) active PLC	FW	System Information tool	Port bindning DG	Redundancy takeover	*None*
9	Connection to (new) active PLC	FW	Volatility	RAM image	Redundancy takeover	*None*
10	HMI Alarms/Events	FW	System Checker Tool	Alarms/events txt	error messages	*Same as ID 1*
11	SYN ACK requests	FW	Wireshark	Traffic capture	Incomplete requests	*Denial of Service*
12	ICS status in txt	FW	Excel	Alarms/Events	All L3 components online	*None*

The examination revealed several artefacts and initial hints of a DoS attack. Due to the loss of connection to PLC1, no data from Plant Site Area 1 could be exchanged with the HMI in the control room. This serves as evidence or an artefact for both *Block Reporting/Command Message* and *Alarm Suppression* until the RTN event or activation of the redundant PLC2.

In a following analysis phase the resulting artefacts would be analyzed to prove correlations including a cross-validation. e.g., comparing connection data from RAM, traffic, and alarms/events and statistical analysis. We examined that the system performed a redundancy takeover, restoring control and monitoring capabilities regarding the impact of the attack.

6.2   Advantages and Disadvantages of TADFICS

We have applied our model to enable forensic readiness and to prove an attack within a productive real-world DCS. In the following, we discuss the advantages and disadvantages observed during the strategic preparation and evaluation, in regards to ICS forensic challenges.

Advantages. First, we explain how TADFICS has particularly contributed to ICS forensics based on our use case.

– **General application**: Through the general (data) types provided by TADFICS, generalizable knowledge could be applied to an actual DCS. This helped address heterogeneity, as TADFICS enabled to systematically identify the vendor-specific implementation data of required forensics data.
– **Useful Attributes**: In conjunction with heterogeneity, the attributes that need to be assessed also proved to be helpful. This allowed to minimize the scope of whats needed to be assessed. This also helped during decision taking within a forensic investigation, such as which data to acquire how.
– **Relational Representation Useful**: The established relationships proved to be helpful, particularly in relation to forensic capabilities and live forensics. Our model, TADFICS, was used to query various forensic-relevant data for guidance. During the evaluation, it became possible to identify alternative ways to acquire specific data. This assisted in our investigation as we could asses different data sources with data of the same context (e.g. connection data acquired by the diagnostic tool and connection data extracted from the RAM image).
– **Threat-Awareness**: Our model was also able to narrow down data based on its reference to the MITRE TTPs. This approach also allowed for the identification of potential attacks making TADFICS threat-aware.

Disadvantages. In the following, we describe the issues that arose during the strategic preparation and execution of the investigation.

- **Extensive initial population/mapping**: The mapping of data types to specific ICS data was extensive, as these needed to be identified often without any documentation. In many cases, manual searches or basic reverse engineering was required to identify the data types.
- **Extent of components**: Although the primary components could be quickly identified through the specified asset types provided by TADFICS, the same does not apply to smaller, distinct devices such as smart sensors or external third-party devices. While TADFICS can model these theoretically, full ICS coverage is infeasible due to their amount.
- **Granularity of the data**: In some cases during the strategic preparation, TADFICS was not precise enough as some data is only partially human readable. Certain actual data may also be associated with MITRE TTPs that are additional or different from those provided by TADFICS. E.g. the ABB PLCs provide extensive error messages that can provide information into various attacks. However, this does not apply to the acquisition or examination phase, as such details or deviations are considered by attributes of the *artefact* as seen in the evaluation.

We could use TADFICs to find answers to the forensic questions of what happened, when, where, and why, as shown in our evaluation. Thus, TADFICS identifies and represents forensically relevant data, supporting forensic investigations and readiness within ICS systems. Comparing the CS' alarms/events with the transmitted events allows to derive when an event was send, partially restoring missing timestamps.

7   Future Work

Future work includes the analysis phase of the attack, which is beyond the scope of this paper, as TADFICS primarily focuses on modeling forensic data and the capabilities of ICS environments. However, the resulting artefacts can be further used for the analysis. In addition, we plan to integrate the TADFICS data model into a procedural ICS forensics framework. Further part of our future work also involves executing further attack scenarios to enhance and optimize TADFICS.

8   Conclusion

TADFICS can assist the phases of a forensic investigation by providing a foundation and relationships to represent actual data of an ICS in a forensic-useful way. It combined artefact knowledge from IT and OT forensics, making it compatible to both domains while specific attacks can be traced. Initiating the model, especially identifying the data sources, requires significant effort, and there is no general approach due to vendor-specific differences. Once filled, the model simplifies determining which existing data are available and how it can be acquired or examined, allowing for the creation of mapping tables via database queries, which support the forensic phases of acquisition and examination. As such, it can be utilized by practitioners or extended by researchers, including the development of forensic procedures.

References

1. Enterprise-control system integration – Part 1: Models and terminology (2013)
2. ABB: System 800xA Solutions Handbook (2013). https://library.e.abb.com/public/e2c8177d884cef5bc1257b4e004c577f/3BSE069330_C_en_System_800xA_Solutions_Handbook.pdf
3. ABB: Process control solutions for electrical and thermal energy supply chain (2025). https://new.abb.com/control-systems/industry-specific-solutions/power-energy-utilities. Accessed 29 Apr 2025
4. BSI: Leitfaden it-forensik. Tech. rep. (2011)
5. Casey, E.: Digital Evidence and Computer Crime - Forensic Science, Computers and the Internet, 3rd edn. (2011)
6. Commission, I.E.: IEC 62682: Management of Alarm Systems for the Process Industries. International Electrotechnical Commission, Geneva, Switzerland (2014)
7. Cook, M., Marnerides, A., Johnson, C., Pezaros, D.: A survey on industrial control system digital forensics: challenges, advances and future directions. IEEE Commun. Surv. Tutorials **25**(3), 1705–1747 (2023)
8. Cook, M., Stavrou, I., Dimmock, S., Johnson, C.: Introducing a forensics data type taxonomy of acquirable artefacts from PLCS, pp. 1–8 (06 2020)
9. Cornelius, E., Fabro, M.: Recommended practice: Creating cyber forensics plans for control systems (2008)
10. Cybersecurity and infrastructure security agency: safety system targeted malware Hatman. Tech. rep, Virginia, USA (2019)
11. Eden, P., Blyth, A., Burnap, P., CHERDANTSEVA, Y., Jones, K., Soulsby, H., Stoddart, K.: Forensic readiness for SCADA/ICS incident response (2016)
12. Emake, E., Adeyanju, I., Uzedhe, G.: Industrial control systems (ICS): cyber-attacks & security optimization. Int. J. Comput. Eng. Inf. Technol. **12**, 31–41 (2020)
13. Eran Salfati, M.P.: Nistir 8428. Digital forensics and incident response (DFIR) framework for operation technology (OT). Tech. rep., Gaithersburg, MD, USA (2022)
14. Programmable controllers - Part 3: Programming languages. Standard, International Electrotechnical Commission, Geneva, CH (2000)
15. Network access for IEC 60860-5-101 using standard transport profiles. Standard, International Electrotechnical Commission, Geneva, CH (2006)
16. Ike, M., Phan, K., Sadoski, K., Valme, R., Lee, W.: SCAPHY: detecting modern ICS attacks by correlating behaviors in SCADA and physical (2022)
17. Karagiozidis, A.: ERD ICS forensic data model (2025). https://git.new/3YPk5cL
18. Kent, K., Chevalier, S., Grance, T., Dang, H.: SP 800-86. guide to integrating forensic techniques into incident response. Tech. rep., MD, USA (2006)
19. Kleinmann, A., Amichay, O., Wool, A., Tenenbaum, D., Bar, O., Lev, L.: Stealthy deception attacks against SCADA systems (2017)
20. Marcella, A.J.: Cyber Forensics: Examining Emerging and Hybrid Technologies, 5, vol. 4, chap. 6, pp. 211–267. CRC PRess, Boca Raton, USA, 1 edn. (2021)
21. MITRE: MITRE ATT&CK for industrial control systems (2020). https://attack.mitre.org/tactics/ics/
22. MITRE: MITRE ATT&CK for industrial control systems (2023). https://attack.mitre.org/software/S1072/
23. de Oliveira, V., Pessoa, M., Junqueira, F., Miyagi, P.: SQL and NOSQL databases in the context of industry 4.0 (2021)

24. Lee, R.M., Assante, M.J., Conway, T.: Analysis of the cyber attack on the Ukrainian power grid. Tech. rep, EISA Center (2016)
25. Shahbi, F., Gardiner, J., Adepu, S., Rashid, A.: A digital forensic taxonomy for programmable logic controller data artefacts, pp. 320–328 (2023)
26. Stouffer, K.A., et al.: Guide to OT security (2023)
27. Taveras, P.: Scada live forensics: real time data acquisition process to detect, prevent or evaluate critical situations (2013)
28. Tyson Maculay, B.S.: Cybersecurity for Industrial Control Systems, chap. 1, pp. 17–82. CRC, Boca Raton, USA (2011)
29. Van Vliet, P., Kechadi, M.-T., Le-Khac, N.-A.: Forensics in Industrial Control System: A Case Study. In: Bécue, A., Cuppens-Boulahia, N., Cuppens, F., Katsikas, S., Lambrinoudakis, C. (eds.) CyberICS/WOS-CPS -2015. LNCS, vol. 9588, pp. 147–156. Springer, Cham (2016). https://doi.org/10.1007/978-3-319-40385-4_10

A Robust Hybrid Framework Combining Deductive Temporal Logic and Machine Learning for Fault and Cyber-Attack Detection in the Tennessee Eastman Process

Hoda Mehrpouyan(✉)(iD)

Boise State University, Boise ID 83725, USA
hodamehrpouyan@boisestate.edu

Abstract. Industrial control systems (ICS) face both physical faults and stealthy cyber-attacks, yet existing detection methods rarely address both threats comprehensively. Model-based monitors—such as temporal-logic rules—provide interpretable alarms but falter in high-dimensional settings and against novel anomalies, while data-driven approaches—like Random Forest classifiers or autoencoders—adapt to complex patterns but often obscure decision rationale and miss unseen threats such as replay attacks.

Alarms are fused using a graded, source-attributed strategy, and a class-balanced Random Forest learns nonlinear fusion, outperforming simple logical-OR baselines. On the Tennessee Eastman Process benchmark, our framework delivers near-perfect F_1 scores on process faults ($F_1 \approx 0.99$) with only seven false alarms over 24h, and boosts replay-attack detection from $F_1 < 0.10$ to 0.70 (precision 0.64, recall 0.78, AUC 0.99). These results demonstrate that combining symbolic logic, statistical learning, and temporal similarity detection yields a scalable, interpretable, and resilient solution for comprehensive ICS monitoring.

Keywords: Industrial Control Systems · Hybrid Anomaly Detection · Deductive Temporal Logic (DTL)

1 Introduction

As industrial control systems grow in scale, complexity, and connectivity, ensuring safe and reliable operation becomes ever more challenging [1,18,19]. Faults in process equipment or cyber-attacks on sensor and actuator signals can lead to hazardous conditions, environmental damage, and costly downtime [2,14,16]. Yet the sheer volume of real-time data generated by modern plants makes manual diagnosis impractical.

© The Author(s), under exclusive license to Springer Nature Switzerland AG 2025
B. Coppens et al. (Eds.): ARES 2025 Workshops, LNCS 15994, pp. 172–190, 2025.
https://doi.org/10.1007/978-3-032-00630-1_10

Model-based monitors—built on first-principles process models or simple threshold rules—offer interpretable alarms but often fail to generalize to high-dimensional, nonlinear dynamics [9]. Machine learning (ML) classifiers, in contrast, excel at recognizing complex patterns in large datasets, but their black-box nature can obscure why an alarm was raised, and they may overlook novel anomalies not represented in the training set [4].

In this work, we make the following contributions: 1- We introduce a three-source hybrid detector that fuses Deductive Temporal Logic, ML, and a novel replay-detector to cover faults and stealthy attacks in ICS. We formally define a rolling-window cosine similarity replay detector and analyze its sensitivity versus window size, threshold, and false-alarm trade-offs. 2- We demonstrate that simple DTL+ML (logical-OR) fusion still misses replay ($F1 < 0.1$), while our class-balanced Random Forest fusion achieves $F_1=0.70$ (AUC$\approx$0.99) on the Tennessee Eastman benchmark. 3-We stratify alarms by source (DTL, ML, Replay) to deliver transparent, graded alerts that operators can trust and act upon. Our hybrid framework combines: 1- **DTL** for interpretable, persistence-based rules, 2- a supervised **ML** classifier (Random Forest) for statistical anomalies, 3- a **Replay Detector** using rolling-window cosine similarity to catch time-duplicated signals.

We evaluate our approach on the Tennessee Eastman Process (TEP) [6] benchmark under three process faults and three synthetic cyber-attack types: bias injection, stealthy drift, and replay. Unlike prior DTL+ML hybrids, we explicitly address replay attacks—adding a memory-based module and a non-linear fusion layer—to fill the blind spot of both logic and autoencoder-only approaches. Our results show that the hybrid system improves overall precision and recall compared to standalone DTL or ML methods. It also enhances interpretability and robustness, particularly in challenging scenarios where traditional detectors fail. These findings suggest that integrating symbolic logic, statistical learning, and temporal similarity detection offers a scalable and resilient foundation for future ICS monitoring systems.

The rest of the paper is organized as follows. Section 2 reviews related work in model-based, machine-learning, and hybrid approaches for fault and anomaly detection in industrial control systems, with a focus on replay-attack methods. Section 3 presents the architecture of the proposed three-source hybrid framework, detailing the DTL logic, the supervised ML classifier, the rolling-window replay detector, and the fusion strategy. Section 4 describes our simulation environment, dataset preparation, feature engineering, and experimental setup on the Tennessee Eastman Process benchmark. Section 5 reports detection results:

- 5.1 Fault detection performance for DTL, ML, and simple logical-OR fusion,
- 5.2 Replay-attack detection with standalone DTL and LSTM,
- 5.3 RF-fusion performance including confusion matrix, feature importance, and decision-boundary analysis,
- 5.4 Ablation studies and ROC/PR curves that quantify threshold trade-offs.

Finally, Sect. 6 discusses the implications for operator trust and practical deployment, and Sect. 7 concludes with future work directions.

2 Background

Model-based techniques—such as observers, Kalman filters, or analytical redundancy relations—offer strong interpretability and robustness to noise but often suffer from scalability issues in large, nonlinear, or evolving systems [9,18]. In contrast, machine learning (ML) and deep learning methods have demonstrated high detection accuracy in complex environments by modeling intricate patterns in high-dimensional sensor data [4,7]. However, their black-box nature and susceptibility to distributional shifts and adversarial manipulation limit their standalone applicability in safety-critical domains.

More sophisticated hybrid detectors use STL in conjunction with deep learning or genetic programming. For example, Indri et al. [8] use a one-shot learning strategy to evolve ensembles of STL formulas for anomaly detection in cyber-physical systems, highlighting the promise of symbolic learning for interpretable alarms. In another direction, TeLEx by Jha et al. [10] infers STL formulas from positive examples using a "tightness" metric to guide specification learning.

Recent advances in Explainable Artificial Intelligence (XAI) seek to address the black-box nature of machine learning models, particularly in high-stakes domains such as manufacturing, energy, and critical infrastructure. In industrial fault detection, explainability is not just desirable—it is essential for operational trust, regulatory compliance, and human-in-the-loop decision-making.

Several works have explored model-agnostic XAI tools like SHAP (SHapley Additive exPlanations) and LIME (Local Interpretable Model-agnostic Explanations) to interpret predictions from classifiers in predictive maintenance and process monitoring tasks [12,15,17]. While these methods can reveal feature importance and local decision boundaries, they often lack the temporal context necessary for reasoning about system dynamics over time.

While several hybrid detection frameworks have explored the integration of Signal Temporal Logic (STL) with machine learning models [3,5,8], most focus on symbolic rule learning or temporal pattern classification. Recent work using causal graph neural networks [11] and attention mechanisms [13] improves structure-aware reasoning, but does not directly address temporally repeated attacks like replay scenarios. To the best of our knowledge, **our approach is the first to combine DTL, ML, and a temporal similarity module into a unified alarm system**, offering explicit replay detection alongside symbolic and statistical monitoring. This fusion not only improves detection coverage but also supports modular, interpretable alarms for operator-facing deployment.

3 Methodology

The workflow comprises the following stages: 1- *Simulation & Dataset Generation:* We use the pyTEP interface to simulate 72 h of the Tennessee Eastman Process and inject anomalies—process faults, bias/drift attacks, and replay attacks—beginning at step 8 h. 2- *Feature Extraction:* From each trace, we extract raw sensor readings and their first-order derivatives at one-minute intervals to capture both level and dynamic behavior. 3- *Parallel Detectors:* 1- **DTL**

Monitor: Applies interpretable persistence rules on signal derivatives to catch abrupt or sustained deviations. 2- **ML Classifier:** A Random Forest trained on labeled data identifies statistical anomalies in the feature space.3- **Replay Detector:** Computes cosine similarity between a sliding window and a delayed reference window to flag time-duplicated (replayed) segments. 4- *Hybrid Fusion:* The three binary alarm streams are merged either by logical-OR (baseline) or via a non-linear RF fusion model, which combines all features and raises graded alerts. The RF fusion variant achieves an F_1 of 0.70 on replay attacks, dramatically improving over logical-OR ($F_1 < 0.10$). 5- *Evaluation:* We assess performance with F_1 scores per scenario, ROC/AUC analysis for threshold trade-offs, and confusion matrices to report absolute counts of true/false positives and negatives.

Industrial control systems demand both high reliability and strong interpretability across a range of failure modes—from abrupt process faults to stealthy cyber-attacks. No single detector can satisfy these requirements:

- **DTL Monitors** provide transparent, rule-based alarms on persistent derivative violations but miss smooth, low-amplitude drifts and replayed data.
- **ML Classifiers** learn complex statistical patterns, capturing gradual or subtle anomalies, yet they act as black boxes and may overlook novel or untrained attack types.
- **Replay Detectors** based on temporal similarity specifically target time-duplicated signal segments, a blind spot for both logic rules and autoencoder reconstructions.

By combining these three sources—each addressing a distinct detection challenge—into a graded fusion layer, our framework achieves: (1) near-perfect recall on physical faults, (2) robust detection of distributional shifts and low-amplitude drifts, and (3) timely identification of replay attacks, all while preserving alarm interpretability and minimizing false positives.

Detection Logic: Mathematical Formulation

1. Derivative Computation

For any monitored process variable $x(t)$, we compute its discrete-time derivative:

$$\dot{x}(t) = \frac{x(t) - x(t-1)}{\Delta t}$$

2. Deductive Temporal Logic (DTL) Rule

A DTL-based alarm is raised if the magnitude of the derivative exceeds a threshold δ for w consecutive time steps:

$$\text{DTL\_alarm}(t) = \begin{cases} 1, & \text{if } \forall i \in [0, w-1], \ |\dot{x}(t-i)| > \delta \\ 0, & \text{otherwise} \end{cases}$$

To increase robustness, DTL alarms from multiple signals are combined:

$$\text{DTL\_fused}(t) = \bigvee_{j=1}^{n} \text{DTL}_j(t)$$

3. Machine Learning Classifier

A supervised classifier (Random Forest) predicts the likelihood of an anomaly at each time step based on input features $\mathbf{x}_t$:

$$p(t) = \text{RF}(\mathbf{x}_t), \quad p(t) \in [0, 1]$$

An ML-based alarm is triggered when $p(t)$ exceeds a classification threshold τ:

$$\text{ML\_alarm}(t) = \begin{cases} 1, & \text{if } p(t) \geq \tau \\ 0, & \text{otherwise} \end{cases}$$

4. Hybrid Fusion Logic

The hybrid alarm system triggers an alarm if either ML or DTL fires:

$$\text{Hybrid\_alarm}(t) = \text{ML\_alarm}(t) \vee \text{DTL\_fused}(t)$$

5. Fault-Specific DTL Monitoring

The following table lists fault types and the primary signals monitored using DTL logic (Table 1).

Table 1. DTL rules for process fault detection.

Fault ID	Description	DTL Signal Rule
Fault 1	A/C feed ratio change	$|\dot{x}_{\text{Feed}}(t)| > \delta$
Fault 2	Product separator pressure loss	$|\dot{x}_{\text{P\_Sep}}(t)| > \delta$
Fault 4	Reactor cooling failure	$|\dot{x}_{\text{Temp}}(t)| > \delta$

6. Attack-Specific Detection Behavior

The system responds to cyber-attacks as follows:

- **Bias Attack**: Sharp jump in value.

$$|\dot{x}(t)| > \delta \quad \text{after injection}$$

– **Stealth Drift Attack**: Gradual rise or fall.

$$|\dot{x}(t)| > \delta \quad \text{persistently over window } w$$

– **Replay Attack**: Copies past data; derivative remains low.

$$\dot{x}(t) \approx 0 \Rightarrow \text{No DTL alarm}$$

7. Replay Detection

To detect replay attacks—where previously observed signal sequences are maliciously replayed—we implement a memory-based similarity detector. For each monitored signal $x(t)$, we define a sliding window of length k, and compute the cosine similarity between the current segment and a reference segment from the past:

$$\text{sim}(t) = \frac{\langle x(t:t+k), x(t-\Delta:t-\Delta+k)\rangle}{\|x(t:t+k)\| \cdot \|x(t-\Delta:t-\Delta+k)\|}$$

An alarm is raised if $\text{sim}(t)$ exceeds a threshold γ for w consecutive time steps. The parameters k (window size), Δ (reference offset), and γ (similarity threshold) are chosen empirically. **Sensitivity analysis.** We found that smaller window sizes ($k < 30$ samples) were prone to false positives on periodic fluctuations, while larger windows ($k > 100$) introduced latency. A mid-range value ($k = 60$, corresponding to 1 h at 1-min sampling) provided a good trade-off between accuracy and response time. The similarity threshold γ was set between 0.95 and 0.98 to avoid spurious matches (Table 2).

Table 2. Threshold values used in DTL and ML alarm generation.

Parameter	Description	Typical Value
δ	Derivative threshold for DTL	0.005 to 0.01
w	Temporal window for DTL rule	2 to 3 steps
τ	ML classification threshold	0.5

4   Implementation

We use the `pyTEP` Python interface to simulate the Tennessee Eastman Process at 1-minute resolution over 72 h. Three classes of scenarios are generated: 1- **Normal Operation:** No faults or attacks, establishing baseline behavior. 2- **Process Faults (IDs 1, 2, 4):** Standard TEP disturbances introduced at the 8-hour mark and run for the remaining 64 h. 3- **Cyber-Attack Scenarios:** Synthetic manipulations from hour 8 onward: a- *Bias Injection:* Constant offset added to selected sensors. b- *Replay Attack:* A 60-sample segment replayed from historical data. c- *Stealth Drift:* Low-amplitude linear drift applied to multiple sensors.

4.1   Data Preparation

Each simulation produces a time-series labeled with

$$\text{label}(t) = \begin{cases} 0, & \text{normal,} \\ 1, & \text{fault or attack.} \end{cases}$$

We split the full dataset into:1- **Training Set (70%):** Normal runs, faults 1, 2, 4, and all synthetic attacks. 2- **Test Set (30%):** Independently generated scenarios, including new attack variants for generalization.

Features include raw sensor readings and their discrete derivatives for the key process variables.

4.2   Hybrid Detection Pipeline

The algorithm above outlines the procedure for evaluating hybrid DTL+ML detection performance across individual fault scenarios in the Tennessee Eastman Process (TEP). For each scenario, the system first computes discrete signal derivatives from selected process variables known to exhibit fault-sensitive behavior, such as reactor temperature, pressure, and feed rates. A Random Forest classifier is trained on labeled data to predict fault likelihoods, while DTL rules monitor derivative values over a fixed persistence window to flag persistent deviations. During evaluation, both DTL and ML outputs are combined into a hybrid logic that triggers alarms when either model detects an anomaly. F1 scores are then computed per fault type to assess the detection capability of each component and the hybrid system. This breakdown reveals which faults are best captured by rule-based logic versus learned statistical patterns, and where fusion enhances reliability or robustness in the presence of noisy or ambiguous conditions. The algorithm describes the process used to evaluate the performance of a hybrid detection framework that combines Deductive Temporal Logic (DTL) with machine learning (ML) for cyber-attack detection in industrial control systems. The method begins by labeling and merging time-series data from normal operation and various synthetic attack types (bias, replay, and stealth). Derivative features are computed for key process variables to enable rule-based monitoring of persistent signal deviations using DTL. Simultaneously, a Random Forest classifier is trained on labeled feature data to model statistical patterns. During evaluation, DTL, ML, and a hybrid fusion model are applied to the test data. F1 scores are computed separately for each attack type to highlight detection performance across different threat classes. This per-attack-type breakdown allows us to assess which detection method performs best under varying adversarial conditions and to identify cases—such as replay attacks—where new defenses may be required.

4.3   Feature Selection and Engineering

To enable effective detection of process anomalies and cyber-attacks, we selected a subset of key process variables from the Tennessee Eastman Process (TEP)

Algorithm 1: Per-Fault-Type Detection using Hybrid DTL and ML

Input: Time series datasets: $df_{normal}, df_{fault1}, df_{fault2}, \ldots$
Monitored variables: $\mathcal{V}$
DTL threshold δ, window size w, ML probability threshold τ
Output: F1-scores for each fault type using DTL, ML, and Hybrid detection

1 **Label and Merge Data:**
2 Assign label $= 0$ for df_{normal}, label $= 1$ for all faults;
3 Assign fault_type $\in \{fault1, fault2, \ldots\}$;
4 Concatenate all datasets into df_{all};

5 **Compute Derivatives:**
6 foreach $v \in \mathcal{V}$ do
7 | $\dot{v}(t) \leftarrow v(t) - v(t-1)$;
8 | Append $\dot{v}(t)$ to df_{all};

9 **Train/Test Split:**
10 Split $(X, y, \text{fault\_type}) \leftarrow df_{all}$ into training and test sets;

11 **Train Random Forest:**
12 Fit RF $\leftarrow$ RandomForestClassifier(X_{train}, y_{train});
13 Predict $p(t) \leftarrow$ RF.predict_proba(X_{test});

14 **Compute DTL Alarms:**
15 foreach $\dot{v} \in \{\dot{v}_1, \dot{v}_2, \ldots\}$ do
16 | $a_{\mathrm{DTL},v}(t) \leftarrow 1$ if $\forall i \in [0, w), |\dot{v}(t-i)| > \delta$;

17 $a_{\mathrm{DTL}}(t) \leftarrow \bigvee_v a_{\mathrm{DTL},v}(t)$;

18 **Compute ML and Hybrid Alarms:**
19 $a_{\mathrm{ML}}(t) \leftarrow 1$ if $p(t) \geq \tau$, else 0;
20 $a_{\mathrm{Hybrid}}(t) \leftarrow a_{\mathrm{DTL}}(t) \vee a_{\mathrm{ML}}(t)$;

21 **Per-Fault Evaluation:**
22 foreach $fault\_type \in \{fault1, fault2, \ldots\}$ do
23 | Select indices $\mathcal{I}_{type}$ where fault_type $=$ type;
24 | Compute F1-scores:
25 | $F1_{\mathrm{DTL}} \leftarrow$ F1($y[\mathcal{I}_{type}], a_{\mathrm{DTL}}[\mathcal{I}_{type}]$);
26 | $F1_{\mathrm{ML}} \leftarrow$ F1($y[\mathcal{I}_{type}], a_{\mathrm{ML}}[\mathcal{I}_{type}]$);
27 | $F1_{\mathrm{Hybrid}} \leftarrow$ F1($y[\mathcal{I}_{type}], a_{\mathrm{Hybrid}}[\mathcal{I}_{type}]$);
28 | Append scores to results table;

29 **return** *F1-score table*

---

simulation. Based on prior studies and physical relevance, we identified four critical signals: Reactor Temperature, Reactor Pressure, Reactor Feed Rate, and Product Separator Pressure. These variables were chosen because they exhibit measurable deviations in response to common process faults and sensor/actuator manipulation attacks.

For each of these signals, we extracted both the raw time-series values and their first-order discrete derivatives, computed as the difference between consecutive samples at one-minute resolution. The derivative terms capture the dynamic behavior of the system and are particularly useful for the DTL component, which operates by detecting persistent deviations in signal slopes. These same derivative features also enhance the discriminative capacity of the Random Forest classifier by embedding short-term temporal trends into the feature space.

In total, the feature vector for each time step consists of eight features: four raw values and four derivative signals. No additional preprocessing or normal-

---

Algorithm 2: Per-Attack-Type Detection using Hybrid DTL and ML

Input: Time series datasets: $df_{normal}, df_{bias}, df_{replay}, df_{stealth}$
Monitored variables: $\mathcal{V}$
DTL threshold δ, window size w, ML threshold τ
Output: F1-scores for each attack type using DTL, ML, and Hybrid detection

1 **Label and Merge Data:**
2 Assign label $= 0$ for df_{normal}, label $= 1$ for all attacks;
3 Assign attack_type $\in \{bias, replay, stealth, normal\}$;
4 Concatenate all datasets into df_{all};

5 **Compute Derivatives:**
6 **foreach** $v \in \mathcal{V}$ **do**
7 $\quad \dot{v}(t) \leftarrow v(t) - v(t-1)$;
8 $\quad$ Append $\dot{v}(t)$ to df_{all};

9 **Train/Test Split:**
10 Split $(X, y, attack\_type) \leftarrow df_{all}$ into train and test sets;

11 **Train Random Forest:**
12 Fit RF $\leftarrow$ RandomForestClassifier(X_{train}, y_{train});
13 Predict $p(t) \leftarrow$ RF.predict_proba(X_{test});

14 **Compute DTL Alarms:**
15 **foreach** $\dot{v} \in \{\dot{v}_1, \dot{v}_2, \dots\}$ **do**
16 $\quad a_{DTL,v}(t) \leftarrow 1$ if $\forall i \in [0, w)$, $|\dot{v}(t-i)| > \delta$;

17 $a_{DTL}(t) \leftarrow \bigvee_v a_{DTL,v}(t)$;
18 **Compute ML and Hybrid Alarms:**
19 $a_{ML}(t) \leftarrow 1$ if $p(t) \geq \tau$, else 0;
20 $a_{Hybrid}(t) \leftarrow a_{DTL}(t) \vee a_{ML}(t)$;

21 **Per-Attack Evaluation:**
22 **foreach** $attack\_type \in \{bias, replay, stealth\}$ **do**
23 $\quad$ Select indices $\mathcal{I}_{type}$ where attack_type = type;
24 $\quad$ Compute F1-scores:
25 $\quad\quad F1_{DTL} \leftarrow F1(y[\mathcal{I}_{type}], a_{DTL}[\mathcal{I}_{type}])$;
26 $\quad\quad F1_{ML} \leftarrow F1(y[\mathcal{I}_{type}], a_{ML}[\mathcal{I}_{type}])$;
27 $\quad\quad F1_{Hybrid} \leftarrow F1(y[\mathcal{I}_{type}], a_{Hybrid}[\mathcal{I}_{type}])$;
28 $\quad$ Append results to table;

29 **return** *F1-score table*

---

ization was applied, as both the logic rules and the tree-based ML model are inherently scale-invariant. This consistent feature representation enables parallel evaluation of DTL rules and ML predictions, and supports the fusion logic used to generate hybrid graded alarms.

5   Results

5.1   Fault Detection Result

To evaluate the performance of our hybrid detection system under known process fault conditions, we measured F1 scores for DTL-only, ML-only, and hybrid configurations across three benchmark fault types in the Tennessee Eastman Process. As shown in Fig. 1, DTL achieved near-perfect F1 scores across all faults (≥ 0.998), outperforming the Random Forest classifier slightly, particularly on Faults 2 and 3. The hybrid system matched or exceeded both, reaching an F1

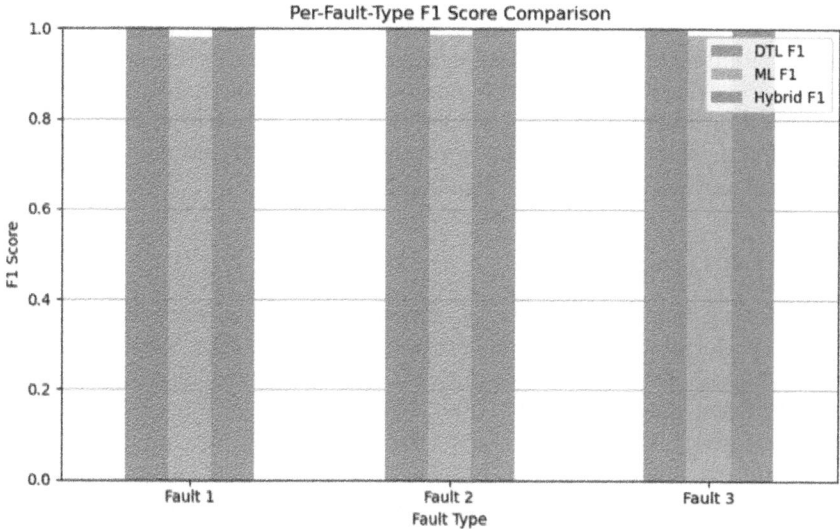

Fig. 1. F1 score comparison Per Fault detection using DTL-only, ML-only, and hybrid (DTL versus ML) configurations.

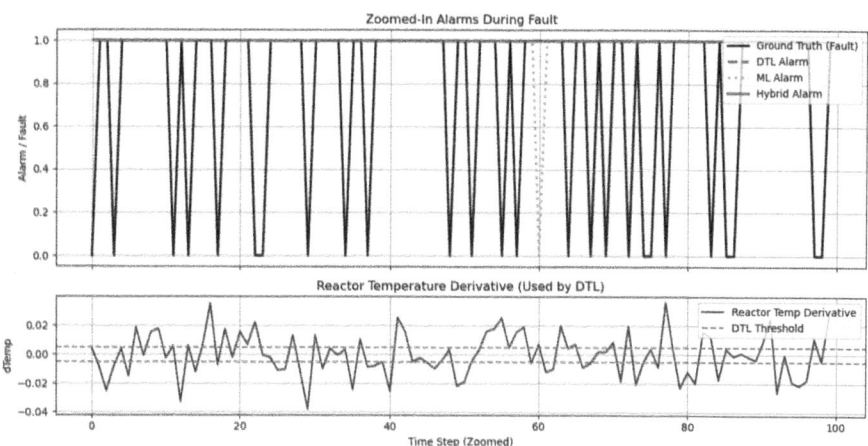

Fig. 2. Zoomed-in view of DTL, ML, and Hybrid alarms (top) and the corresponding derivative of the reactor temperature signal (bottom). The DTL monitor activates when the absolute derivative crosses a predefined threshold (gray dashed lines). While ML raises a brief alarm later in the sequence, DTL consistently detects persistent changes from the start. The hybrid alarm inherits DTL's early warning, highlighting its role in robust temporal anomaly detection (Color figure online).

of 1.00 in all cases. These results suggest that DTL rules over signal derivatives are highly effective in detecting persistent, physical process anomalies, and that fusing them with ML increases robustness while maintaining interpretability.

A side-by-side comparison of alarm behaviors reveals a fundamental contrast in the capabilities of DTL and ML across different anomaly types. In the fault detection scenario (Fig. 2), the DTL monitor responds consistently and early due to sustained derivative violations, while ML triggers only a brief delayed alarm. This highlights the robustness and interpretability of DTL in detecting process faults characterized by persistent signal shifts.

5.2   Attack Detection

Our per-attack-type analysis, Fig. 3, revealed that while both DTL and ML detectors perform well on certain classes of cyber-attacks, each has specific strengths and limitations. For bias injection attacks, the machine learning model achieved perfect detection ($F_1 = 1.00$), likely due to the consistent and easily separable signal shifts. DTL also detected these effectively, but hybrid fusion did not improve beyond the DTL baseline. In the case of stealthy drift attacks, ML slightly out performed DTL ($F_1 = 0.89$ versus 0.79), though both were effective, suggesting that persistent low-amplitude anomalies can be captured well by derivative-based logic as well as by learned patterns. However, both methods struggled with replay attacks ($F1 \approx 0.08$), reflecting a shared weakness in detecting temporally duplicated, distribution-conforming data. This finding underscores the need for additional mechanisms such as memory-based detectors, temporal pattern matching, or sequence modeling to improve detection in these scenarios.

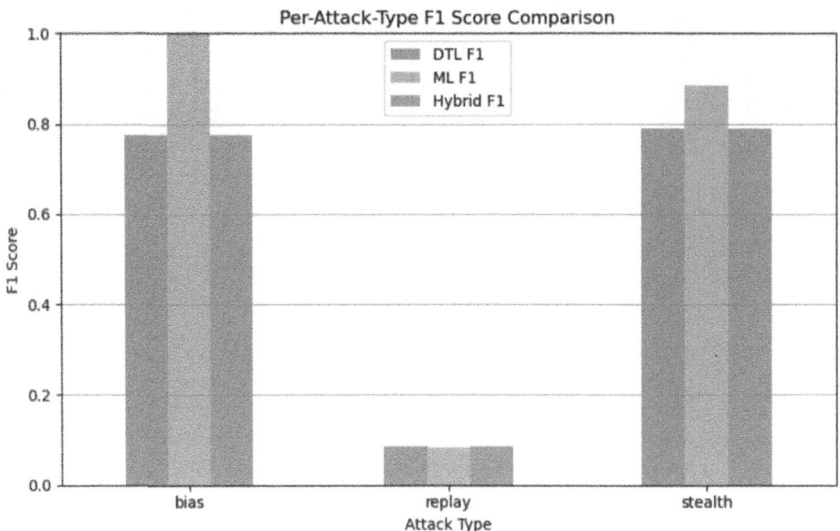

Fig. 3. F_1 score comparison Per Attack detection using DTL-only, ML-only, and hybrid (DTL versus ML) configurations.

6   Discussion

As demonstrated in our evaluation, replay attacks—which replicate valid historical data to evade detection—remain a significant challenge for both the DTL monitor and the Random Forest classifier. These attacks do not produce large signal derivatives or violate learned statistical distributions, making them inherently stealthy.

Table 3. Replay-attack detection performance of various methods on the Tennessee Eastman benchmark.

Detector	Precision	Recall	F_1-Score
DTL-Only	0.042	1.00	0.080
LSTM-Only	0.000	0.00	0.000
Hybrid (DTL + LSTM)	0.049	1.00	0.094
Logistic-Regression Fusion	0.000	0.00	0.000
Random-Forest Fusion (manual oversample)	0.636	0.778	0.700

Table 3 compares five replay-attack detectors on the Tennessee Eastman benchmark, reporting precision, recall and F_1-score for each. Below we briefly summarize each method and discuss its behavior: **DTL-Only**: The Deductive Temporal Logic monitor flags replay when a high cosine-similarity of a sliding window against a historic window coincides with very low within-window variance. Because replay segments are almost identical to past data, DTL achieves perfect recall (1.00) but at the cost of many false alarms—yielding a low precision (0.042) and $F_1 \approx 0.08$. **LSTM-Only**: Here we train an LSTM autoencoder on normal and fault data and raise an alarm if the reconstruction error exceeds the 95th percentile. Since replayed data lies on the learned data manifold, the autoencoder reconstructs it well, resulting in zero detections (precision = 0, recall = 0, $F_1 = 0$). **Hybrid (DTL + LSTM)**: A simple logical–OR fusion of the DTL and LSTM alarms inherits DTL's perfect recall but only marginally increases precision to 0.049 ($F_1 \approx 0.094$). The LSTM adds no new positive hits, since it remains blind to replay. **Logistic-Regression Fusion**: We trained a logistic regression on three features—LSTM reconstruction error, cosine similarity, and window variance—with class weighting. Because these features overlap almost completely for replay vs. normal, the model defaults to negative and fails to detect any replays (precision = recall = $F_1 = 0$). **Random-Forest Fusion (manual oversample)**: To overcome severe class imbalance, we up-sampled the few replay examples and trained a balanced-weight Random Forest on the same three features. This non-linear model achieves a much stronger trade-off (precision $\approx$ 0.636, recall $\approx$ 0.778, $F_1 = 0.70$), demonstrating the benefit of both oversampling and non-linear decision boundaries in capturing the subtle distinctions of replay attacks.

In summary, while pure logic-based monitoring (DTL) guarantees that no replay is missed, it suffers from a high false-alarm rate. Black-box LSTM reconstruction alone fails to detect replay. Simple fusion does little to improve performance. Only by introducing class-balanced, non-linear learning (Random Forest with oversampling) do we achieve a practical trade-off between precision and recall, boosting overall F_1 from below 0.10 to 0.70.

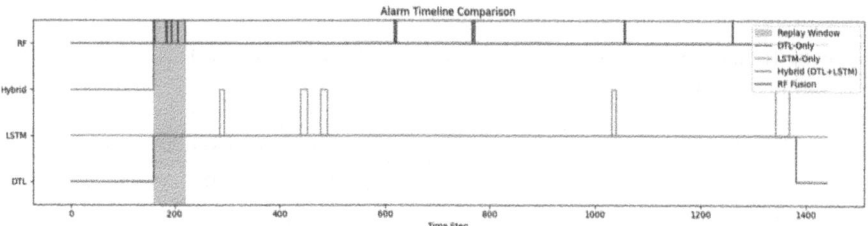

Fig. 4. The Alarm-timeline Comparison).

Figure 4 shows a time-series view of four detectors firing binary alarms (y = DTL, LSTM, Hybrid = DTL versus LSTM, and RF-fusion) overlaid on the true replay-attack interval (shaded). Several things stand out: 1-DTL-Only (blue): Spots the entire replay window (recall = 1.0), since the cosine-similarity rule immediately flags the repeated segment. Triggers a few spurious alarms at the very end (false positives), explaining its low precision (0.04). 2- LSTM-Only (orange): Fires only two small bursts—neither of which overlaps the true replay— so it misses the attack entirely (recall = 0). Demonstrates that reconstruction error alone cannot distinguish replayed data from normal operation. 3- Hybrid (DTL versus LSTM) (green): Exactly matches DTL-Only, because the LSTM component never adds any new true positives. Inherits DTL's perfect recall and poor precision. RF-Fusion (red): Learns a non-linear decision boundary over [error, cosine, variance], aided by manual oversampling. Fires multiple alarms tightly around the replay window (true positives) and only a handful of isolated false positives. This behavior matches its much higher F_1 (0.70) and AUC (0.99).

Figure 5 presents the CDFs of our three key features, highlighting why each standalone detector performs as it does:

- **Reconstruction Error (Left).** Replay windows cluster at lower error values (around 0.021–0.027), well below the 95th-percentile threshold (≈ 0.0337) used by the LSTM-only detector. Consequently, the autoencoder never flags replay as anomalous (recall = 0), since its learned manifold reproduces replay data too accurately.
- **Cosine Similarity (Middle).** Replay segments exhibit very high similarity (≈ 0.92–0.94) to their historic counterparts, whereas normal windows span a broader, lower range (≈ 0.87–0.94). A DTL threshold of 0.98 would indeed capture all replay (recall = 1.0), but many normal windows also exceed 0.98, producing a flurry of false positives (precision ≈ 0.04).

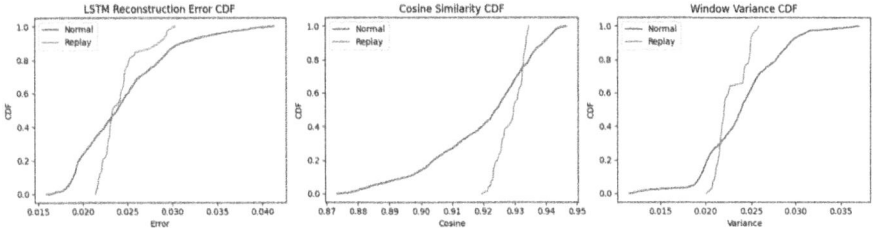

Fig. 5. Empirical cumulative distribution functions (CDFs) of the three core replay-detection features, for normal operation (blue) and replay segments (orange). Left: LSTM reconstruction error. Middle: rolling-window cosine similarity. Right: window variance. (Color figure online)

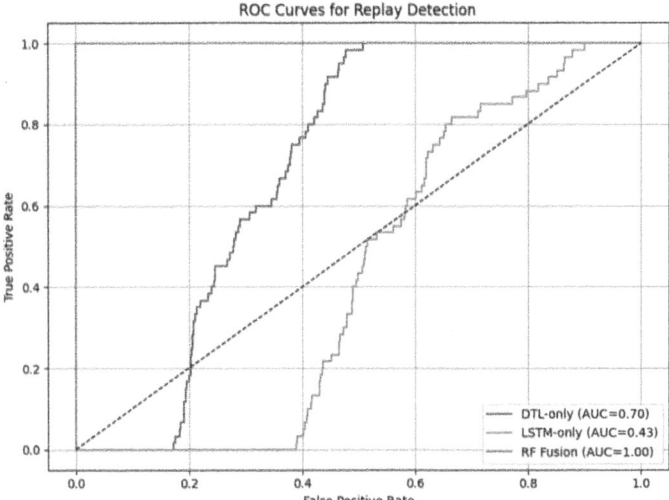

Fig. 6. Receiver-Operating-Characteristic (ROC) curves for replay-attack detection. Blue: DTL-Only (AUC=0.70); Orange: LSTM-Only (AUC=0.43); Green: RF-Fusion (AUC≈1.00). The near-unit AUC of the RF-fusion confirms its superior ability to trade off false positives and true positives. (Color figure online)

- **Window Variance (Right).** Replay windows have lower within-window variance (≈0.020–0.024) than most normal windows (≈0.022–0.036). While variance alone separates the classes better than reconstruction error, its overlap still leads to misclassifications if used in isolation.

  Together, these distributions explain:

1. *DTL-only* leverages cosine similarity to guarantee no misses, but suffers low precision due to overlap in normal data.
2. *LSTM-only* cannot distinguish replay from normal, as reconstruction error remains low on replay.

Table 4. Confusion matrix for Random-Forest fusion on replay detection (test set).

True \ Predicted	Normal	Replay
Normal	342 (TN)	7 (FP)
Replay	5 (FN)	13 (TP)

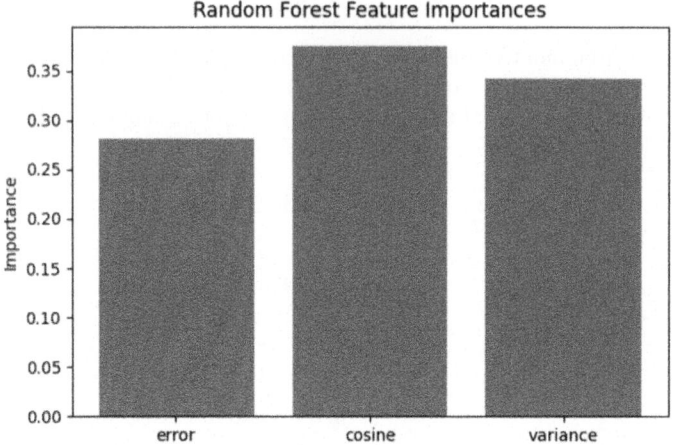

Fig. 7. Relative feature importances from the Random-Forest fusion model on replay-attack detection. Cosine similarity contributes the most ($\approx$0.37), followed by window variance ($\approx$0.34) and LSTM reconstruction error ($\approx$0.28).

3. *Logistic-fusion* fails because the three feature distributions overlap heavily, preventing a single linear decision boundary from isolating the replay cluster.
4. *RF-fusion*, by contrast, can learn non-linear splits across these three feature dimensions—effectively combining a moderate cosine cutoff, a variance threshold, and an error check—to concentrate alarms almost exclusively within the replay region (see Figure 4), yielding $F_1 = 0.70$ and AUC ≈ 0.99.

Figure 6 plots ROC curves for three detectors. The DTL-only monitor (blue) achieves AUC $= 0.70$ by varying its cosine-similarity threshold, demonstrating moderate separability but high false-alarm risk. The LSTM autoencoder (orange) attains AUC $= 0.43$, barely better than chance—reconstruction-error alone cannot distinguish replayed from normal data. Our Random-Forest fusion (green) achieves near-perfect AUC ($\approx$1.00), reflecting its ability to combine non-linear splits on reconstruction error, cosine similarity, and variance features to isolate the replay segment with both high true-positive rate and low false-positive rate. Table 4 quantifies RF-fusion's performance: out of 355 total replay examples in the test partition, only 5 were missed, and 7 normal windows were falsely flagged as replay, yielding a strong F1 of 0.70. Figure 7 quantifies each feature's contribution to the final RF decision. The high importance of cosine similarity confirms that DTL's rolling-window similarity is the strongest single indicator of

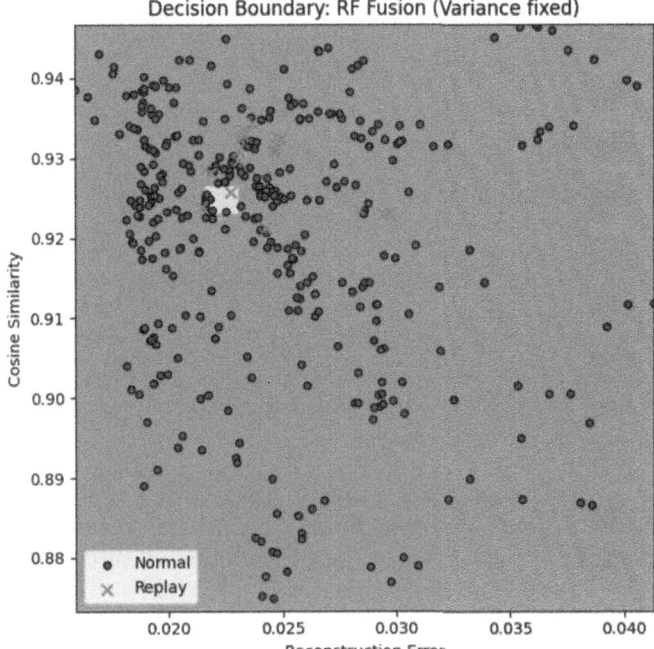

Fig. 8. Decision boundary of the Random-Forest fusion model in the space of LSTM reconstruction error and rolling-window cosine similarity (variance held at its median). Replay segments (orange ×) lie in the low-error/high-similarity region, which the RF non-linear classifier (light orange) successfully isolates from normal operation (blue •). (Color figure online)

replay, while window variance and reconstruction error provide complementary fine-tuning to suppress false positives and capture edge cases.

Figure 8 shows the decision regions learned by the Random-Forest fusion model in the 2D space of reconstruction error vs. cosine similarity (with variance fixed at its median). Replay points (orange ×) cluster tightly in the upper-left corner—low error but high similarity—while normal points (blue circles) spread out over a wider range. The non-linear RF boundary (light orange region) cleanly isolates most of the replay examples with only a handful of normal-point misclassifications, illustrating how the fusion leverages both features simultaneously.

7 Conclusion and Future Work

We have presented a novel three-source hybrid detection framework for industrial control systems that combines:

- **Deductive Temporal Logic (DTL)**, which provides interpretable, rule-based monitoring of persistent derivative deviations;

- **Supervised Machine Learning (Random Forest)**, which captures complex statistical anomalies in raw and derivative features;
- **Memory-based Replay Detection**, which uses rolling-window cosine similarity to flag time-duplicated signal segments invisible to both logic and reconstruction-error methods.

By fusing these complementary detectors—first via a simple logical-OR baseline and then via a learned class-balanced RF classifier—we achieve:

- Near-perfect $F_1 \approx 0.99$ on standard Tennessee Eastman process faults using DTL+ML;
- Dramatic improvement on replay attacks, from $F_1 < 0.10$ (logical-OR) to $F_1 \approx 0.70$ (RF-fusion, precision $\approx 0.64, recall \approx 0.78, AUC \approx 0.99$);
- Graded, source-attributed alarms that enhance operator trust and situational awareness with minimal false positives (seven over 24h).

These results demonstrate that explicitly integrating a memory-based replay detector—and leveraging non-linear fusion—fills a critical blind spot in prior DTL+ML hybrids. Our graded-alarm design retains full interpretability while delivering high coverage across both physical faults and stealthy cyber-attacks.

Future work will explore: (1) sequence-model extensions (e.g. attention-based temporal networks) to further improve replay and causality-breaking attack detection; (2) real-time, edge-deployable implementations with latency and resource profiling; and (3) generalization to multi-rate, heterogeneous sensor networks and longer-horizon dependencies in large-scale cyber-physical systems.

Acknowledgment. We would like to thank the National Science Foundation: Computer and Information Science and Engineering (CISE), award number 1846493 of the Secure and Trustworthy Cyberspace (SaTC) program: Formal TOols foR SafEty aNd. Security of Industrial Control Systems (FORENSICS).

References

1. Agbo, C., Mehrpouyan, H.: Conflict analysis and resolution of safety and security boundary conditions for industrial control systems. In: 2022 6th International Conference on System Reliability and Safety (ICSRS), pp. 145–156 (2022). https://doi.org/10.1109/ICSRS56243.2022.10067393
2. Agbo, C., Mehrpouyan, H.: Achieving cyber-informed engineering through Bayesian belief network and sensitivity analysis. In: 2023 10th International Conference on Dependable Systems and Their Applications (DSA), pp. 260–271 (2023). https://doi.org/10.1109/DSA59317.2023.00039
3. Bartocci, E., Deshmukh, J., Donzé, A., Fainekos, G., Maler, O., Ničković, D., Sankaranarayanan, S.: Specification-Based Monitoring of Cyber-Physical Systems: A Survey on Theory, Tools and Applications, pp. 135–175. Springer International Publishing, Cham (2018). https://doi.org/10.1007/978-3-319-75632-5_5

4. Chandola, V., Banerjee, A., Kumar, V.: Anomaly detection: a survey. ACM Comput. Surv. **41**(3) (2009).https://doi.org/10.1145/1541880.1541882
5. Chen, G., Liu, M., Kong, Z.: Temporal-logic-based semantic fault diagnosis with time-series data from industrial internet of things. IEEE Trans. Industr. Electron. **68**(5), 4393–4403 (2021). https://doi.org/10.1109/TIE.2020.2984976
6. Downs, J., Vogel, E.: A plant-wide industrial process control problem. Comput. Chem. Eng. **17**(3), 245–255 (1993). https://doi.org/10.1016/0098-1354(93)80018-I, https://www.sciencedirect.com/science/article/pii/009813549380018I, industrial challenge problems in process control
7. Fan, J., Wang, W., Zhang, H.: Autoencoder based high-dimensional data fault detection system. In: 2017 IEEE 15th International Conference on Industrial Informatics (INDIN), pp. 1001–1006 (2017). https://doi.org/10.1109/INDIN.2017.8104910
8. Indri, P., Bartoli, A., Medvet, E., Nenzi, L.: One-shot learning of ensembles of temporal logic formulas for anomaly detection in cyber-physical systems. In: Medvet, E., Pappa, G., Xue, B. (eds.) Genetic Programming, pp. 34–50. Springer International Publishing, Cham (2022). https://doi.org/10.1007/978-3-031-02056-8_3
9. Isermann, R.: Model-based fault-detection and diagnosis – Status and applications. Ann. Rev. Control **29**(1), 71–85 (2005). https://doi.org/10.1016/j.arcontrol.2004.12.002, https://www.sciencedirect.com/science/article/pii/S1367578805000052
10. Jha, S., Tiwari, A., Seshia, S.A., Sahai, T., Shankar, N.: Telex: learning signal temporal logic from positive examples using tightness metric. Formal Methods Syst. Des. **54**(3), 364–387 (2019). https://doi.org/10.1007/s10703-019-00332-1
11. Liu, R., Zhang, Q., Lin, D., Zhang, W., Ding, S.X.: Causal intervention graph neural network for fault diagnosis of complex industrial processes. Reliab. Eng. Syst. Saf. **251**, 110328 (2024). https://doi.org/10.1016/j.ress.2024.110328, https://www.sciencedirect.com/science/article/pii/S0951832024004009
12. Lundberg, S.M., Lee, S.I.: A unified approach to interpreting model predictions. In: Guyon, I., Luxburg, U.V., Bengio, S., Wallach, H., Fergus, R., Vishwanathan, S., Garnett, R. (eds.) Advances in Neural Information Processing Systems, vol. 30. Curran Associates, Inc. (2017). https://doi.org/10.5555/3295222.3295230
13. Luo, J., Jin, Z., Jin, H., Li, Q., Ji, X., Dai, Y.: Causal temporal graph attention network for fault diagnosis of chemical processes. Chin. J. Chem. Eng. **70**, 20–32 (2024). https://doi.org/10.1016/j.cjche.2024.01.019, https://www.sciencedirect.com/science/article/pii/S1004954124000636
14. Mitchell, R., Chen, I.R.: A survey of intrusion detection techniques for cyber-physical systems. ACM Comput. Surv. **46**(4) (2014). https://doi.org/10.1145/2542049, https://doi.org/10.1145/2542049
15. Molnar, C.: Interpretable machine learning: a guide for making black box models explainable. Leanpub (2020). https://christophm.github.io/interpretable-ml-book/
16. O'Toole, S., Mehrpouyan, H.: Towards cyber-physical representation and cyber-resilience against attack and failure within a hydraulic network simulation toolkit. In: 2024 IEEE Security and Privacy Workshops (SPW), pp. 246–252 (2024). https://doi.org/10.1109/SPW63631.2024.00029
17. Ribeiro, M.T., Singh, S., Guestrin, C.: "why should i trust you?": explaining the predictions of any classifier. In: Proceedings of the 22nd ACM SIGKDD International Conference on Knowledge Discovery and Data Mining, pp. 1135–1144. KDD '16, Association for Computing Machinery, New York, NY, USA (2016). https://doi.org/10.1145/2939672.2939778, https://doi.org/10.1145/2939672.2939778

18. Venkatasubramanian, V., Rengaswamy, R., Yin, K., Kavuri, S.N.: A review of process fault detection and diagnosis: part I: quantitative modelbased methods. Comput. Chem. Eng. **27**(3), 293–311 (2003). https://doi.org/10.1016/S0098-1354(02)00160-6, https://www.sciencedirect.com/science/article/pii/S0098135402001606
19. Xu, L.D., He, W., Li, S.: Internet of things in industries: a survey. IEEE Trans. Industr. Inf. **10**(4), 2233–2243 (2014). https://doi.org/10.1109/TII.2014.2300753

KIDS: Intrusion Detection for Industrial Control Systems

Nowshaba Jeelani Wani[(⊠)], Dirk Pesch, and Utz Roedig

School of Computer Science and IT, University College Cork, Cork, Ireland
nowshabawani@umail.ucc.ie, {d.pesch,u.roedig}@cs.ucc.ie

Abstract. The convergence of Information Technology (IT) and Operational Technology (OT) has significantly increased the vulnerability of Industrial Control Systems (ICS). Prolonged undetected intrusions and the frequent exploitation of zero-day vulnerabilities have made ICS highly susceptible to cyberattacks, resulting in data loss and physical damage. Despite growing threats, majority of Intrusion Detection Systems (IDS) ignore the significance of process-based data and equipment such as Programmable Logic Controllers (PLCs) and focus on the management components of ICS, which are essentially an IT system. Many suggested IDS are also only effective with known attacks and fail to detect zero-day exploits. The lack of a unified IDS across IT and OT, applicable irrespective of protocols employed or hardware heterogeneity, is another significant gap in this field. This paper presents Kestrel-Based Intrusion Detection System (KIDS), a query-based, process-aware framework tailored for OT. Built on the Kestrel threat hunting language, KIDS combines process monitoring with traditional threat intelligence to detect sophisticated attacks across all layers of ICS. By abstracting system components and complexities into unified query interfaces, KIDS enables holistic visibility, from management systems to PLCs, and supports scalable, cross-platform threat detection adaptable to evolving industrial threats.

Keywords: Industrial control systems · Intrusion detection systems · Operational technologies · Threat hunting · Security

1 Introduction

Industrial control systems are increasingly targeted by sophisticated cyber attacks, often resulting in operational disruptions, data breaches, or physical damage. Incidents such as Stuxnet [10], the Ukrainian power plant attack [14] have demonstrated how vulnerable critical infrastructure can be when targeted through both traditional and novel attack vectors. A significant contributor to this risk is the convergence of Information Technology (IT) and Operational Technology (OT), as industries integrate networked and remote capabilities into systems originally designed to be air-gaped and standalone.

B. Coppens et al. (Eds.): ARES 2025 Workshops, LNCS 15994, pp. 191–208, 2025.
https://doi.org/10.1007/978-3-032-00630-1_11

The exposure of OT components such as PLCs, sensors and actuators, to external networks introduces a threat surface that conventional security tools, particularly network based intrusion detection systems are ill equipped to handle. These IDS solutions, often implemented and manged by IT teams, typically focus on network traffic and management interfaces such as Human Machine Interface (HMI) and Data Historians. As a result, they largely overlook operational context and the behavior of underlying physical processes which are critical to understanding threats specific to ICS.

Moreover, traditional IDS models are heavily reliant on predefined rules or known attack signatures, limiting their effectiveness again zero-day threats, Advanced Persistent Threats (APTs) or attacks that subtly manipulate physical processes. Sophisticated adversaries can compromise ICS not just by exploiting software vulnerabilities but by introducing malicious control logic or altering operational thresholds, techniques that evade detection by systems blind to process dynamics.

To address these shortcomings, we propose KIDS, a Kestrel based IDS tailored for Industrial Internet of Things (IIoT). KIDS is a process aware detection framework that bridges the IT and OT divide by enabling security analysts to issue unified queries across network level and process level data. Built on the open source Kestrel [15] threat hunting language. KIDS introduces a flexible mechanism, to hunt for indicators of compromise across ICS layers, from Programmable Logic Controller (PLC) variables to network authentication logs. Additionally, once a hunt script is tuned for a particular scenario, it can be automated to run periodically as required, making KIDS a fully automated and customizable IDS to fit varying needs of unique ICS setups.

The key motivation for using Kestrel is that it already provides reusable and structured threat hunting queries for the IT domain and offers a high degree of flexibility. KIDS extends this capability by incorporating Kestrel in a high level IDS framework for threat hunting across IT and OT, using metadata about ICS processes (e.g. critical variables, process IDs), enabling the corelation of behavioral anomalies with security events. This integration allows for proactive identification of stealthy threats that target control logic, manipulate sensor data or induce subtle deviations in physical behavior; attack strategies that are commonly invisible to the traditional IDS.

The appendix of this paper demonstrates how a typical kestrel script is adapted to hunt lateral movement attacks using Windows Management Instrumentation (WMI), showcasing the language's flexibility. This serves as a foundation for expanding the same approach to ICS environments through KIDS, where process integrity, control state deviations and contextual metadata become central to intrusion detection.

In summary, our work contributes a scalable, extensible and vendor neutral threat detection framework for ICS providing the following:

– An extension of kestrel for ICS threat hunting includes OT data sources such as PLCs and Historians.

- A unified query abstraction that enables correlation of IT and OT events in a single hunt.
- A metadata driven approach that contextualizes process variables and operational behavior.
- An evaluation using a testbed implementation of KIDS and MITRE ATT&CK framework for ICS, demonstrating KIDS ability to detect complex attack chains.

By introducing operational semantics into threat hunting, KIDS enhances visibility, reduces false positives and provides a unified tool for securing ICS environments.

2 Background

2.1 Examples of ICS Breaches

Recent years have witnessed several attacks on ICS, but only a few were sophisticated enough to cause any physical damage. Among them, Stuxnet [7] remains the most complex. It exploited multiple zero-day vulnerabilities to alter centrifuge operation logic on the PLCs. The payload included a PLC rootkit recorded previous input and output values, mask anomalous behavior, allowing the malware to evade detection and ultimately damage the centrifuges [10].

A separate attack on a German steel mill caused critical control failures. The safe shutdown sequence, including the blow-down process, may have been bypassed, resulting in an uncontrolled furnace state. While there were no injuries, the incident led to significant physical damage [13]. Another major incident occurred in Ukrainian (2016), where attackers remotely accessed the HMI to disable switch-gears on the grid, log out operators, change passwords, wipe disks, and overwrite firmware, rendering the hardware inoperable. This caused outages for roughly 230,000 inhabitants for 1–6 h [14].

More recently, UK's Sellafield nuclear site was reportedly breached by sleeper malware, detected as early as 2015. The malware is suspected to have compromised activities such as handling radioactive waste, monitoring leaks without detection [1]. These incidents underline how attackers often infiltrate systems months before executing the payload, highlighting the need for timely detection to prevent damage.

2.2 Intrusion Detection and Threat Hunting

Intrusion detection involves monitoring networks and systems for signs of malicious activity, serving as a critical defense mechanism against cyber threats and enabled using intrusion detection systems. These help detect unauthorized access, policy violations, data breaches, and other types of threats. Depending on deployment and methodology, IDS can be host-based, network-based, or hybrid, and may use signature, anomaly, or behavior-based detection techniques. Despite their utility, IDS often struggle with high false positives, limited detection of zero-day threats, and rigidity. These limitations can be mitigated by incorporating proactive strategies such as threat hunting [17,20]. It involves actively searching for threats that evade conventional defense, using tools like Security Information and Event Management (SIEM), Event Detection and Response (EDR), threat intelligence, manual analysis. Integrating threat hunting into an IDS can enhance detection of stealthy threats, improve situational awareness, and strengthen overall security posture.

2.3   Threat Hunting with Kestrel

Threat hunting typically relies on tools such as Osquery, YARA, Zeek, Snort, and Wireshark, as well as languages such as SQL, YARA rule language and Powershell. However, threat hunters often face repetitive tasks such as creating scripts for varying Tactics, Techniques and Procedures (TTP), data sources, and environments, alongside handling complex data processing, handling threat intelligence, analytics setup, and hypothesis development. These efforts must often be repeated across diverse contexts, making the process tedious and inefficient. To address this, IBM introduced Kestrel [16], an open source threat hunting language. Kestrel enables reusable, composable hunt scripts and supports built-in and custom analytics (e.g., suspicious scores via Docker-based modules). It integrates with various EDRs, SIEMs, and other monitoring tools. Kestrel introduces entity-based reasoning, which essentially means building a hypothesis focused around entities (system, network, device) and what to hunt rather than how to hunt. It also supports forking and merging of hunts for ease of composability. An example Kestrel script for detecting lateral movement via Windows Management Infrastructure (WMI) on Windows systems is available online [4], demonstrating its utility for expressing complex threat hunting logic in reusable form.

3   Related Work

Numerous solutions have been developed to secure cyberspace such as IDSs. Khraisat et al. [12] review various methods and datasets for intrusion detection. They discuss the strengths and limitations of signature-based, anomaly-based, and behavior-based systems, along with evaluation techniques such as statistics-based methods. Several commonly used datasets for evaluating IDSs are also reviewed. Their work highlights general approaches in cyber intrusion detection but does not consider the unique needs of ICS environments, as proposed in our work.

Wang [20] reviews threat hunting literature and implementation methods, showing machine learning-based implementations to detect threats are the most popular. He also compares different threat hunting methods, such as intel-driven, observed data-driven, and TTP-driven approaches. Aldauiji et al. [3], review different threat-hunting models for detecting ransomware. They propose combining practical approaches with various models to detect unknown ransomware effectively. They also review the currently available ransomware datasets used in research. Both studies address proactive approaches but are focused on generic IT systems, and do not integrate operational intricacy or process control into detection.

Authors Jadidi and Lu [11] propose a unified threat-hunting framework for IT and ICS. This Threat Hunting Framework (ICS-THF) targets early identification of threats. It consists of three stages: threat hunting triggers, threat hunting, and cyber threat intelligence. The trigger stage detects events or external cues to initiate hunting. The hunting stage combines the MITRE ATT&CK Matrix and Diamond model to form and validate hypothesis and predict adversary behavior. The final stage identifies Indicators of Compromise (IoC) for future use as threat intelligence. While this work is one of the few to bridge IT and ICS, it does not incorporate process-level metadata into the IDS framework to provide operational context, which is unique to KIDS.

In a study, Ajmal et al. [2], use threat hunting in conjunction with cyber deception and kill chain to detect attacks, including unknown adversaries. They introduce a decoy farm to lure attackers to a non-critical, deceptive setup within the ICS environment. Evaluation was conducted using several attacks on an emulated Supervisory Control and Data Acquisition (SCADA) network, compared with reactive approaches such as Zeek Bro, firewall (Palo Alto), and Windows Defender. The final results show that the threat-hunting approach is 60% faster and can detect known and unknown attacks. While the work emphasizes proactive detection and performance improvements, it does not address process-aware security or interpret ICS data in threat detection.

Bibi et al. [9] proposes a threat intelligence and detection method using convolutional neural networks Long Short Term Memory 2 Dimensional (LSTM2D). It is described as self-sufficient and self-optimizing, overcoming limitations of other models and dynamically detecting sophisticated threats in IIoT. They evaluated the model on a dataset with 21 million attack patterns and vector instances, showing high detection accuracy with a trade-off in speed. In contrast, our work does not rely on deep learning but leverages flexible scripting, annotated process metadata, offering interoperability and integration of control systems in the detection process.

Given the heterogeneous nature of ICS devices, securing diverse data is complex. Yazdinejad et al. [21] introduce an ensemble deep learning model with Long Short Term Memory (LSTM) and auto-encoder to identify unknown threats. The LSTM model learns the standard patterns of behavior while the autoencoder reduces data dimensionality. The model accounts for dataset imbalance using balanced subsets. Evaluated on Gas Pipeline (GP) and Secure Water Treatment (SWaT) datasets, it achieved 99.3% and 99.7% accuracy, respectively. Unlike our framework, this model does not enable correlation across systems, nor does it integrate control-specific annotations.

Arafune et al. [6], discuss an automated method of extracting threat intelligence, along with generating and validating hypotheses for threat hunting. The work uses MITRE's ATT&CK framework for threat intelligence. It also leverages open-source tools such as Elasticsearch, Conpot, Metasploit, Web Single Page Application and a machine learning analyzer. The paper highlights the need for more research in automating threat hunting in ICS networks. Unlike other solutions that are cloud-based, expensive, and prone to human errors, this solution is central and open-source. The authors demonstrate that the solution can identify network attacks and alert a threat hunter with a hypothesis generated based on TTPs from ICS MITRE ATT&CK. They also employ a machine learning classifier to automatically predict future actions of the attack. This work emphasizes automation and hypothesis generation, whereas, KIDS focuses on context aware detections that can identify violations of physical process constraints.

Bhardwaj and Goundar [8] propose a framework for effectively implementing cybersecurity threat Hunting. The framework aims to empower organizations with the tools and methodologies to enhance their threat-hunting capabilities. Additionally, the proposed framework is compared against existing security operations using 20 key Threat Hunting metrics. Their approach, while methodical, focuses on aspects of threat hunting programs rather than ICS specific adaptations.

IIoT systems rely on many edge devices, including sensors, controllers, and robots, for various tasks such as data collection, transmission, storage, and processing. However, any malicious or abnormal behavior exhibited by these devices can compromise the security of the entire IIoT network. Additionally, such devices can serve as entry points for malicious software to infiltrate the network. To address these concerns, Yazdinejad et al. [22] proposes a parallel ensemble model for threat hunting that focuses on detecting anomalies in the behavior of IIoT edge devices. The model is designed to be flexible and can utilize multiple state-of-the-art classifiers as essential learners. It efficiently classifies multi-class anomalies using Multi-class AdaBoost and majority voting techniques. Experimental evaluations on a dataset comprising standard records from multiple sources and multi-class anomalies demonstrate that the proposed model outperforms existing approaches in accuracy, F1 score, recall, and precision. Our framework differs by focusing on control systems, operational context and integration of OT and IT data sources via Kestrel.

As evident from the works discussed in this section, the current scope of study in this field focuses on the management and network level of the ICS, completely neglecting the lower-level vulnerabilities, such as on the PLC level. There needs to be a standard solution that dives into the granular specific and can detect threats across the entire ICS setup. The approach proposed in this paper overcomes this gap and looks at the vulnerabilities throughout the ICS systems, including lower-levels.

4   KIDS: Kestrel-Based Intrusion Detection System

Classic IDS are traditionally deployed as dedicated network monitoring systems for traffic within an organization's IT infrastructure. They analyze network communications and raise alerts when they detect anomalies, either known attack signatures or deviations from the baseline behaviors. Such IDS solutions are typically operated by the IT departments, tasked with maintaining enterprise security. This approach is effective in conventional IT environments, where attackers use a standard sets of exploits.

However, as discussed, this standard approach has its limitations when applied to a hybrid IT/OT setup. First, traditional IDS solutions offer little to no visibility into the OT domain. They primarily observe IT-layer components, such as servers, authentication systems and management interfaces, while remaining blind to the underlying industrial processes. This invisibility is reinforced by organizational silos, while IT manages the IDS, OT systems are designed and maintained by process engineers, with minimal coordination between the two groups. Second, industrial environments are inherently heterogeneous. They encompass a wide range of devices, vendors, and protocols, resulting in a far broader and more complex attack surface than typically seen in pure IT environments. Consequently, an effective IDS in this setting must be tailored to the specific operational context of the facility and the latest threat landscape. KIDS addresses the two aforementioned shortcomings for effectively implementing an IDS in a hybrid IT/OT.

Improved IDS Visibility: Kestrel provides abstractions and interfaces defined for IT environments, for manual threat hunting. It enables security analysts to gather security relevant information via queries across diverse systems using standardized abstractions. For example, analysts can issue requests to gather relevant data, such as "Were there any user logins between 2am and 5am?" or "Which systems executed a large number of processes between 2am and 5am?". These queries are modular, composable and reusable. Combining the two examples, we can now search for unusual timed logins together with unusual activity which may reveal an ongoing attack. We can also use these refined hunt scripts in an automated context and run it periodically, essentially forming an IDS. We extended the Kestrel framework to form KIDS to provide interfaces for OT infrastructure components. With that, you may now extend the example and include queries such as "Were any critical process variables outside their safe operating bounds?". Now, it is possible to see if there were unusual logins linked to unusual system activity and unusual behavior in the physical process. This of course requires an understanding of what critical variables are and what bounds may be. We envision that these contextual annotations are provided by process engineers designing automation. This approach provides a defined process to bridge the communication gap between OT engineers and IT staff safeguarding the infrastructure.

Improved IDS Customization: As outlined, it is possible with KIDS to compose hunt scripts and customize them to look for different security aspects in a combined IT/OT infrastructure. As production environments vary vastly it is necessary to adapt the IDS. For example, what is considered normal in an automotive factory might be considered anomalous in power plant. The Kestrel abstraction provides a scripting interface that abstracts from the underlying heterogeneous infrastructure. Adaptation to a use case is possible without interacting with individual OT components (once a KIDS abstraction is available for a component).

In the following sections, we provide more detail on KIDS and show how it can be used in specific contexts. We describe examples of specific KIDS/Kestrel syntax used to implement queries such as "Were there any user logins between 2am and 5am?". Figure 1 presents a high-level overview of the KIDS framework architecture and its core design elements.

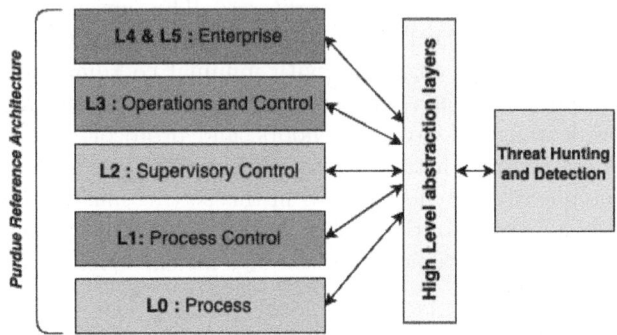

Fig. 1. KIDS, high-level view of the framework.

4.1 Testbed Environment

To demonstrate the KIDS implementation a small scale but comprehensive testbed was constructed, emulating a modern manufacturing factory. We also use this testbed to evaluate KIDS in a realistic setting. This testbed captures key architectural components typically present in industrial environments:

– **Control System:** The control logic is executed by OpenPLC [5], deployed on a raspberrypi 5. This simulated PLC drives a six servo-based robotic arm, simulating tasks like material handling or assembly.
– **Engineering workstations:** A windows Virtual Machine (VM) serves as the primary engineering interface for developing, compiling and uploading PLC programs via OpenPLC editor.
– **Human-Machine interface:** Two HMIs are used; OpenPLC built-in web interface and ScadaBR [18] on a windows VM is used for real time monitoring and manual control.
– **Data Historians:**
  • *SQLite:* serves as the Historian for process variables (e.g., servo motor angles, alarm status).
  • *MySQL:* Captures IT centric security events, such as SSH login attempts and system access logs.

All components communicate over a secure LAN, closely mirroring the communication patterns in actual factory floor systems. Figure 2 shows a reference ICS architecture [19] and Fig. 3 our physical testbed implementation.

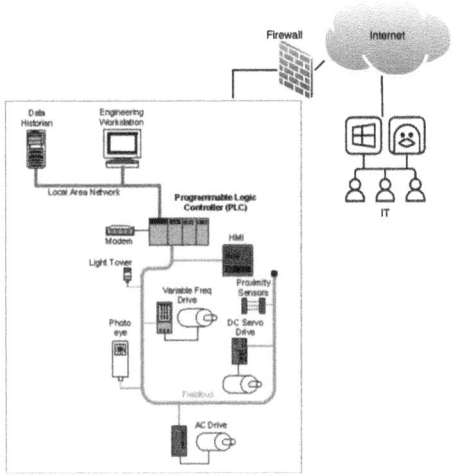

Fig. 2. Reference PLC control system from NIST 800-82.

4.2   KIDS Implementation in the Testbed

The core design philosophy of KIDS revolves around a unified query interface. It allows analysts to issue a single, abstracted command to retrieve data from various sources, whether it's firewall logs from SIEM or process variable readings from a PLC. This capability is built on top of the Kestrel threat hunting language, an open source tool that enables structured, reusable threat hunting scripts.

Key innovations in KIDS include: First, **process-aware querying** enables operational data such as servo motor angles or alarm states can be analyzed with the same ease as traditional log files. Second, **contextual annotation** enriches ICS process variables with metadata including threshold values, process IDs to aid interpretation, even for security analysts without domain expertise in ICS. Third, **cross-domain correlation** is made possible by linking events across IT and OT domains; for example, KIDS can relate a failed SSH login attempt to anomalous PLC behavior within the same analytical framework.

To address the challenge of heterogeneity in ICS, KIDS uses *custom data source interfaces* that standardize diverse inputs into a consistent schema (Structured Threat Information Expression (STIX)). These interfaces translate operational data and control logic annotations into structured threat intelligence, supporting rich correlation and automated detection across systems. The implementation of KIDS in the testbed involve several components working in unison to provide complete threat visibility. The design consists of a set of customizable modules that allow KIDS to access, interpret and correlate process-level data from industrial environments in the same way Kestrel language typically does with conventional IT data:

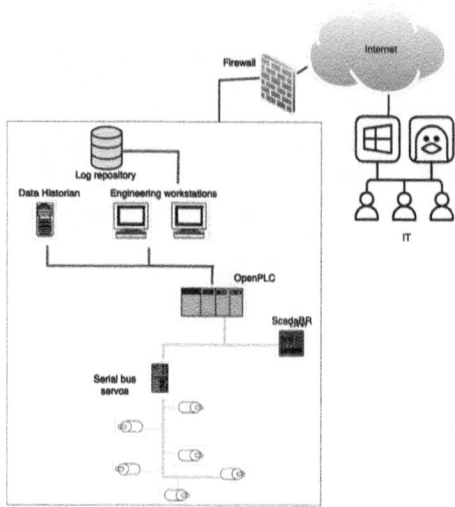

Fig. 3. Testbed implementation with Raspberry Pi and robotic arm.

1. Custom Data Source Interfaces: A fundamental concept that makes Kestrel structured, reusable and flexible are the Kestrel "interfaces", which connect the hunting logic to a data source. Interfaces in Kestrel decouple the "what" and "where" of the hunted data from "how" to query it. Each interface id registered with a unique URI-like schema prefix (e.g., stixshifter://, kestrel://, or custom interfaces like plc://) that tells Kestrel how to fetch, translate and transform data from the associated backend (such as EDRs, SIEM). These interfaces are enabled by underlying plug-ins that translate Kestrel commands (like GET) into backend native queries (e.g., MySQL), transform retrieved data into STIX objects and then return results into Kestrel's in-memory data store (firepit). The Kestrel language currently provides support for numerous standard interfaces such as:

STIX-Shifter Data Source Interface (stixshifter://) for numerous commercial and open-source EDRs, log repositories such as IBM QRadar, Elastic Search and so on.

STIX bundle Data Source Interface (file:///, https://, http://) for canned STIX bundle data.

Analytics interfaces such as Python Analytics Interface (python://) and Docker Analytics Interface (docker://).

To adapt Kestrel to ICS environments, we develop custom data source interfaces tailored for such systems:

plc://data: connects to the SQLite historian.

plc://openplc: retrieves runtime data from OpenPLC in near real-time.

plc://metadata: loads the contextual YAML annotations provided by the automation engineers.

stixshifter://mysql: pulls authorization and security events from MySQL.

These custom interfaces follow the same principles as standard Kestrel interfaces but are adapted to industrial systems and data formats. they enable Kestrel to ingest and normalize data from both OT and IT data sources into STIX format, facilitating correlation and analysis within Kestrel's in-memory environment.

2. Annotated Process Metadata: In ICS, security tools lack process context and domain semantics. This leads to blind spots, where even a valid Modbus command can produce dangerous states if not interpreted in relation to the underlying industrial processes. Annotated metadata bridges this gap, allowing Kestrel to understand what constitutes unsafe or unexpected process behavior. These Annotations serve as a structured medium through which automation engineers convey industrial semantics, such as which variables are critical, which processes are active on which PLC and what operational states and thresholds should not be violated. this improves detection accuracy and reduces false positives.

Automation engineers encode these annotations in a YAML file that defines but is not limited to:

- PLC IDs and their associated processes.
- Definitions of critical variables (e.g., angle, voltage, pressure, Revolutions per minute (RPM)).
- Safe operating thresholds.

This metadata is loaded into KIDS and enables process-aware detections. For example:

```
GET x-openplc-int FROM plc://plcdata WHERE name = 'angle'
```

can retrieve the current value of the process variable "angle". KIDS uses the annotated limits to flag anomalies where thresholds are exceeded, regardless of whether the triggering action appears legitimate.

3. Scripted Threat Hunting and Process-aware Correlation: Using KIDS, analysts construct modular threat hunts using Kestrel's primitives: "GET" for data retrieval, "JOIN" for correlation, and "DISP" for visualization. These operations allow complex hunts to be executed across multiple data layers. A typical hunt script may proceed as follows:

1. Query plc://plcdata for abnormal process variable values.
2. Retrieve login events from stixshifter://mysql.
3. Use "JOIN" to correlate anomalies in process telemetry with unauthorized user activity.

This approach enables detection of overlaps between suspicious IT actions and OT anomalies. Analysts can explore relationships between entities without requiring deep domain expertise in control systems. Figure 4 shows how Kestrel is

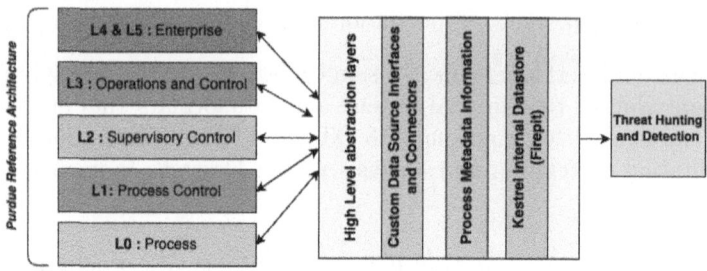

Fig. 4. KIDS implementation with Kestrel and custom data source interfaces.

integrated in KIDS framework to enable detection. Data from SQLite, OpenPLC, YAML annotations and MySQL are routed via interfaces into Kestrel's memory, where hunt logic processes them.

By combining process metadata with real-time telemetry, KIDS provides a rich, multilayered view into ICS security, empowering both IT and OT teams to detect and respond to threats collaboratively.

5   Evaluation

Evaluating an IDS for industrial environments poses unique challenges. Unlike IT security systems, where large scale benchmarks, public datasets and competitive baselines exists, evaluating a threat hunting based IDS, especially the ones targeting control layer anomalies requires carefully curated testbeds and contextual simulations. Furthermore, our proposed system, KIDS, is designed to focus on detecting nuanced, process level deviations that cannot be fully assessed using packet traces or standard SIEM logs alone. In this work, we evaluate KIDS through:

- **Controlled Testbed Attacks:** Simulating real-world ICS threats in our lab testbed and assessing KIDS detection capabilities.
- **MITRE ATT&CK for ICS:** Using MITRE ATT&CK navigator to benchmark which attack techniques can be recognized by KIDS in general.

This allows us to ground our results in both practical and theoretical frameworks. The evaluation focuses primarily on detecting *operational level attacks* (e.g., unauthorized process changes, sensor spoofing), as traditional network-based detection (e.g., lateral movement) is already well-handled by Kestrel's available connectors for various EDRs and SIEMs and log analytics platforms. Thus, we emphasize gaps left by traditional IDS and demonstrate how KIDS extends coverage into physical process domain strengthened further by the default capabilities of Kestrel.

5.1   Evaluation in the Testbed

We base our evaluation on the testbed described in Sect. 4, where a raspber-rypi controlled robotic arm performs repetitive tasks simulating a manufacturing/assembly line. Critical variables such as servo motor angles and LED alarms are annotated by the automation engineer using YAML metadata file. These annotations expose what the process engineer considers safety-critical or indicative of abnormal process behavior. KIDS interfaces with the Historian (SQLite), OpenPLC runtime and metadata files using custom interfaces (see Sect. 4). A baseline KIDS hunt script is constructed, querying and joining OT and IT records. Once tuned manually, these scripts can be automated to run periodically as an automated IDS. We emulated threats such as:

1. **Unauthorized Modbus commands to change process setpoints:** The attacker compromises a remote engineering workstation and sends a legitimate looking Modbus read and write commands directly to the robotic arm, altering the target angle to an unsafe value (e.g., 140°C when the safe limit is 120). Traditional IDS tools observe no anomaly because the packets are valid and authenticated. KIDS, however, correlates the timing of this Modbus access with a recent login and observes the arm's angle exceeding its annotated safety threshold.
   The hunt script flags this as a potential process violation. Kestrel's "GET" retrieves both login and PLC variables, and "JOIN" correlates the two based on timestamps. The use of process-aware context enabled by annotated process metadata makes its evident that although the access was technically legitimate, the result was an unsafe operational state.
2. **Injection of new PLC logic via valid but unauthorized users:** An attacker uploads new operating logic to the PLC via OpenPLC's web interface using a stolen engineer credential. The uploaded program includes a subroutine that overrides safe limits under certain conditions. KIDS detects this configuration drift by querying the process metadata and comparing it to the new events. This inconsistency would go unnoticed in traditional tools. Instead of using complex and explicit process signatures or rules written for each logic variation, KIDS simply highlights this deviation from expected process variable behavior.
3. **Suppression of alarm triggered by crossing the operational thresholds:** The attacker modifies the LED alarm output variable to remain inactive, even when the critical thresholds are crossed. During testing, angle values breach thresholds, but the alarm is not triggered. Using historical trends from SQLite Historian and variable thresholds from process metadata, KIDS identifies abnormal suppression of the LED alarms system in response to out-of-bounds values. This form of suppression can also mimic hardware fault rather than an attack, which can be dangerous. KIDS correlation reveals contradiction between expected and observed process behavior.

The above mentioned attack strategies mimic techniques employed in sophisticated ICS attacks like *Stuxnet, Industroyer* and *PLC-Blaster*. They highlight

KIDS's unique strength in process-aware security monitoring and detecting subtle manipulations that blend in at the protocol level but disrupt operations.

5.2   Evaluation Using the MITRE ATT&CK for ICS

The MITRE ATT&CK framework for ICS is a structured knowledge base of known adversarial behaviors. It catalogs tactics and techniques that adversaries use across the kill chain, from initial access to impact, within ICS contexts. By evaluating KIDS against MITRE ATT&CK for ICS, we aim to assess how well our proposed system covers known tactics used in real-world intrusions. Since Kestrel already provides robust integration with many IT security tools, our evaluation is centered on process level impact and operational disruptions; areas often invisible to security solutions.

To perform this evaluation, we first simulated representative techniques of attacks such as Stuxnet, Industroyer and PLC-Blaster within our testbed, as described in the Sect. 5.1. Then using the ATT&CK Navigator tool, we mapped:

1. The techniques employed during these simulated attacks, colored in red (Industroyer), yellow (Stuxnet), blue (PLC-Blaster) and orange (techniques used two or more attacks)).
2. The techniques KIDS was able to detect (highlighted in green).

Fig. 5 presents a view of the techniques employed by major ICS malware campaigns such as Stuxnet (e.g., T0832 - Manipulation of Control, T0812 - Logic Injection), Industroyer (e.g., T0810 - Alarm Suppression, T0855 - System Firmware) and PLC-Blaster (e.g., T0803 - Unauthorized Change). These techniques are color-coded for clarity as described above. This visualization reflects the diversity of tactics employed across phases such as Execution, Inhibit Response Function and Impact. It also highlights the complexity of multi-phase attack chains used to compromise both IT and OT.

Figure 6 provides a view of the techniques described above, that might be detected by classic IDS such as Snort. This alongside the figure below, shows that many techniques on the operational side are undetectable. KIDS paired with a classic IDS covers most techniques and provides a holistic security view.

Figure 7 illustrates the techniques successfully detected by KIDS, represented in green. This figure demonstrates that KIDS focuses on detection in latter stages of attack chain involving operational changes, such as Manipulation of control (T0831), unauthorized command message (T0855), service stop (T0881) and so on.

KIDS demonstrated coverage of multiple high-impact OT specific techniques that are typically missed by traditional IDS solutions. the green highlights in Fig. 7 illustrate that KIDS successfully detected process-layer manipulation, even when no conventional network anomaly was visible. For example, KIDS detected malicious logic injection by recognizing changes to the process outputs that diverged from annotated process metadata, and flagged Alarm suppression by correlating lack of alarms with breached thresholds. This section demonstrates

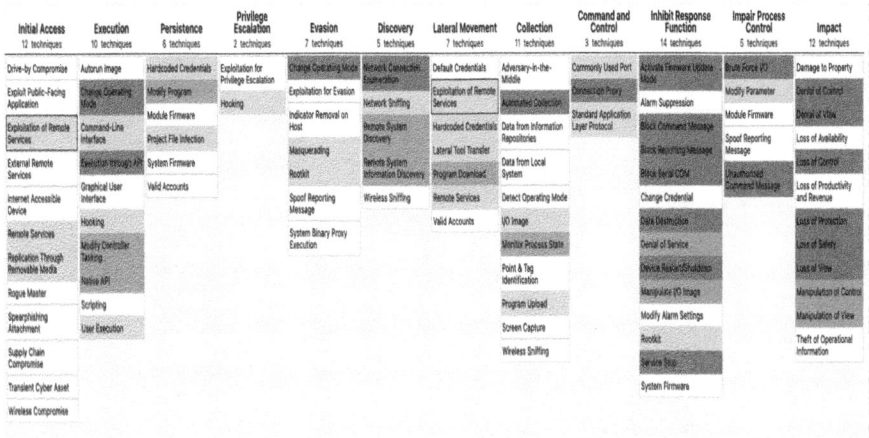

Fig. 5. MITRE ATT&CK Navigator for ICS: ■ Industroyer, ▦ Stuxnet, ■ PLC-Blaster, ▦ Used by multiple attacks.

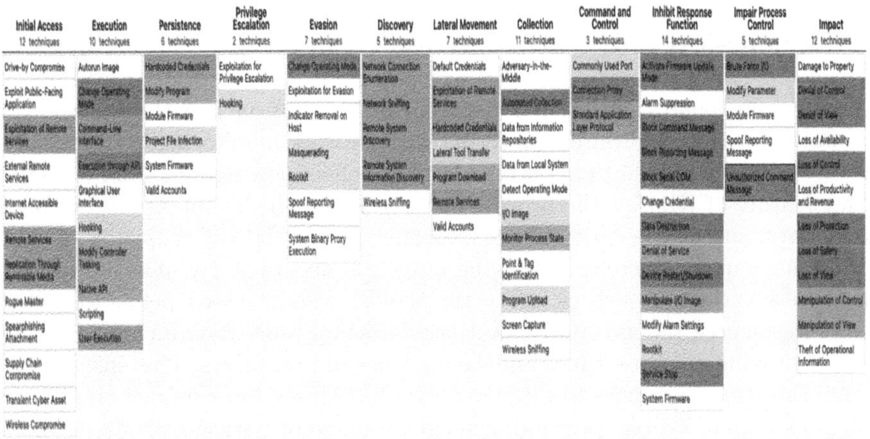

Fig. 6. MITRE ATT&CK Navigator: Techniques from known attacks that might be detected by classic IDS like Snort.

how KIDS covers techniques that directly affect the physical systems. These are often not detectable by IT focused tools alone, reinforcing the value of process-aware detection, as employed by KIDS.

By using MITRE ATT&CK for ICS as a benchmark, we confirm that KIDS fills a critical gap in the detection landscape, bridging the blind spot between IT centric defenses and OT operational realities.

Initial Access 12 techniques	Execution 10 techniques	Persistence 6 techniques	Privilege Escalation 2 techniques	Evasion 7 techniques	Discovery 5 techniques	Lateral Movement 7 techniques	Collection 11 techniques	Command and Control 3 techniques	Inhibit Response Function 14 techniques	Impair Process Control 5 techniques	Impact 12 techniques
Drive-by Compromise	Autorun Image	Hardcoded Credentials	Exploitation for Privilege Escalation	Change Operating Mode	Network Connection Enumeration	Default Credentials	Adversary-in-the-Middle	Commonly Used Port	Activate Firmware Update Mode	Brute Force I/O	Damage to Property
Exploit Public-Facing Application	Change Operating Mode	Modify Program	Hooking	Exploitation for Evasion	Network Sniffing	Exploitation of Remote Services	Automated Collection	Connection Proxy	Alarm Suppression	Modify Parameter	Denial of Control
Exploitation of Remote Services	Command-Line Interface	Module Firmware		Indicator Removal on Host	Remote System Discovery	Hardcoded Credentials	Data from Information Repositories	Standard Application Layer Protocol	Block Command Message	Module Firmware	Denial of View
External Remote Services	Execution through API	Project File Infection		Masquerading	Remote System Information Discovery	Lateral Tool Transfer	Data from Local System		Block Reporting Message	Spoof Reporting Message	Loss of Availability
Internet Accessible Device	Graphical User Interface	System Firmware		Rootkit	Wireless Sniffing	Program Download	Detect Operating Mode		Block Serial COM	Unauthorized Command Message	Loss of Control
Remote Services	Hooking	Valid Accounts		Spoof Reporting Message		Remote Services	I/O Image		Change Credential		Loss of Productivity and Revenue
Replication Through Removable Media	Modify Controller Tasking			System Binary Proxy Execution		Valid Accounts	Monitor Process State		Data Destruction		Loss of Protection
Rogue Master	Native API						Point & Tag Identification		Denial of Service		Loss of Safety
Spearphishing Attachment	Scripting						Program Upload		Device Restart/Shutdown		Loss of View
Supply Chain Compromise	User Execution						Screen Capture		Manipulate I/O Image		Manipulation of Control
Transient Cyber Asset							Wireless Sniffing		Modify Alarm Settings		Manipulation of View
Wireless Compromise									Rootkit		Theft of Operational Information
									Service Stop		
									System Firmware		

Fig. 7. MITRE ATT&CK Navigator: Techniques from known attacks detected by KIDS.

6   Conclusion and Future Work

This work demonstrates that KIDS significantly enhances ICS threat detection by integrating process aware monitoring with network monitoring. KIDS ensures the adversarial actions at operational level are effectively exposed and detected. A key feature of KIDS is the process metadata file, which contextualizes operational data, enabling security teams to better understand the criticality of operational maneuvers, thereby improving detection accuracy. By annotating critical process variables, such as safety thresholds, system interdependence, KIDS allows for focused precise control over the detection process, reducing false positives improving response times and saving time and resources. This ensures that even if the attacker bypass traditional network defenses, their impact on physical processes remain visible, preventing silent sabotage of critical operations.

One of the fundamental challenges in ICS security is that evasion techniques have significantly evolved in IT environments due to the advancements in technology. However, in OT environments, evasion methods remain relatively stagnant, primarily because control systems are inherently constrained in their execution capabilities. Attackers operating at the control layers do not have access to the same flexibilities provided by sophisticated IT systems. This imbalance creates a unique opportunity for ICS security, while advanced IT solutions struggle to detect advanced evasive threats, process aware monitoring at OT control layers offers more stable and predictable deception landscape. KIDS leverages this advantage by focusing on process integrity, ensuring that even well disguised cyberthreats can be hunted.

The future work aims to further enhance KIDS by automating threat hunting by using automating tools to run the scripts periodically as and when required to make KIDS more flexible. Furthermore, we also aim to integrate Artificial

Intelligence (AI) generated threat hunting hypothesis and hunting scripts using deep learning models. This will enable adaptive and user friendly interface which will eliminate the resource intensive nature of producing scripts manually for hunting threats. This will also add better scope for qualitative analysis of KIDS in future. By bridging IT-OT security gaps, automating threat hunting and detecting in future and leveraging the advances in AI such as Large language Models (LLMs), KIDS aims to set a better standard for industrial cybersecurity ensuring sophisticated adversaries do not remain undetected within such setups including critical infrastructures.

Acknowledgements. This publication has emanated from research conducted with the financial support of Taighde Éireann – Research Ireland under Grant number 18/CRT/6222. For the purpose of Open Access, the author has applied a CC BY public copyright licence to any Author Accepted Manuscript version arising from this submission.

References

1. Sellafield nuclear site hacked by groups linked to Russia and china (2023). https://www.theguardian.com/business/2023/dec/04/sellafield-nuclear-site-hacked-groups-russia-china

2. Ajmal, A.B., Alam, M., Khaliq, A.A., Khan, S., Qadir, Z., Mahmud, M.: Last line of defense: reliability through inducing cyber threat hunting with deception in SCADA networks. IEEE Access **9**, 126789–126800 (2021). https://doi.org/10.1109/ACCESS.2021.3111420

3. Aldauiji, F., Batarfi, O., Bayousef, M.: Utilizing cyber threat hunting techniques to find ransomware attacks: a survey of the state of the art. IEEE Access **10**, 61695–61706 (2022). https://doi.org/10.1109/ACCESS.2022.3181278

4. Alliance, O.C.: Lateral movement via WMI Huntbook. https://github.com/opencybersecurityalliance/kestrel-huntbook/blob/main/huntbooks/Lateral%20Movement%20via%20WMI.ipynb (2022). open Cybersecurity Alliance GitHub Repository

5. Alves, T.R., Buratto, M., De Souza, F.M., Rodrigues, T.V.: OpenPLC: an open source alternative to automation. In: IEEE Global Humanitarian Technology Conference (GHTC 2014), pp. 585–589. IEEE (2014)

6. Arafune, M., Rajalakshmi, S., Jaldon, L., Jadidi, Z., Pal, S., Foo, E., Venkatachalam, N.: Design and development of automated threat hunting in industrial control systems. In: 2022 IEEE International Conference on Pervasive Computing and Communications Workshops and other Affiliated Events (PerCom Workshops), pp. 618–623 (2022). https://doi.org/10.1109/PerComWorkshops53856.2022.9767375

7. Baezner, M., Robin, P.: Stuxnet. Tech. rep, ETH Zurich (2017)

8. Bhardwaj, A., Goundar, S.: A framework for effective threat hunting. Netw. Secur. **2019**(6), 15–19 (2019). https://doi.org/10.1016/S1353-4858(19)30074-1

9. Bibi, I., Akhunzada, A., Kumar, N.: Deep AI-powered cyber threat analysis in IIoT. IEEE Internet Things J. **10**(9), 7749–7760 (2023). https://doi.org/10.1109/JIOT.2022.3229722

10. Farwell, J.P., Rohozinski, R.: Stuxnet and the future of cyber war. Survival **53**(1), 23–40 (2011)

11. Jadidi, Z., Lu, Y.: A threat hunting framework for industrial control systems. IEEE Access **9**, 164118–164130 (2021). https://doi.org/10.1109/ACCESS.2021.3133260

12. Khraisat, A., Gondal, I., Vamplew, P., Kamruzzaman, J.: Survey of intrusion detection systems: techniques, datasets and challenges. Cybersecurity **2**(1), 1–22 (2019). https://doi.org/10.1186/s42400-019-0038-7

13. Lee, R.M., Assante, M.J., Conway, T.: German steel mill cyber attack. Ind. Control Syst. **30**(62), 1–15 (2014)

14. Lehman, G.: Cyber-attack against Ukrainian power plants

15. Open Cyber Security Alliance: Kestrel threat hunting language documentation. https://kestrel.readthedocs.io/en/stable/index.html (2024). Accessed 11 May 2025

16. Research, I.: The thrill of cyber threat hunting with kestrel. https://research.ibm.com/blog/kestrel-cyber-threat-hunting (2021). Accessed 05 Oct 2023

17. Shu, X., et al.: Threat intelligence computing. In: Proceedings of the 2018 ACM SIGSAC Conference on Computer and Communications Security, pp. 1883–1898. CCS '18, Association for Computing Machinery, New York, NY, USA (2018). https://doi.org/10.1145/3243734.3243829

18. da Silva, J.P.S., Cunha, E.N.: Supervisory system for Hydraulic distribution apparatus SCADABR application. In: 2017 IEEE First Summer School on Smart Cities (S3C), pp. 161–164. IEEE (2017)

19. Stouffer, K., Falco, J., Scarfone, K.: Guide to industrial control systems (ICS) security. Tech. Rep. NIST Special Publication 800-82 Revision 2, National Institute of Standards and Technology (NIST) (2015). https://doi.org/10.6028/NIST.SP.800-82r2, https://nvlpubs.nist.gov/nistpubs/SpecialPublications/NIST.SP.800-82r2.pdf

20. Wang, Z.: A systematic literature review on cyber threat hunting (2022)

21. Yazdinejad, A., Kazemi, M., Parizi, R., Dehghantanha, A., Karimipour, H.: An ensemble deep learning model for cyber threat hunting in industrial Internet of Things. Digital Commun. Netw. **9** (2022). https://doi.org/10.1016/j.dcan.2022.09.008

22. Yazdinejad, A., Zolfaghari, B., Dehghantanha, A., Karimipour, H., Srivastava, G., Parizi, R.M.: Accurate threat hunting in industrial Internet of Things edge devices. Digital Commun. Netw. (2022). https://doi.org/10.1016/j.dcan.2022.09.010, https://www.sciencedirect.com/science/article/pii/S2352864822001857

Proceedings of the First Workshop on Sustainable Security and Awareness For Next Generation Infrastructures (SAFER 2025)

SAFER 2025 Preface

The Workshop on Sustainable Security and Awareness For Next Generation Infrastructures (SAFER) was held at Ghent University, Ghent, Belgium, on August 11–14, 2025, in conjunction with the 20th International Conference on Availability, Reliability and Security (ARES).

Cybersecurity poses a significant and ongoing challenge in our increasingly interconnected world, particularly in light of the rapid advancements in the Internet of Things and artificial intelligence. While substantial research is dedicated to enhancing security measures, with many promising developments, the primary focus often remains limited to improving security systems, disregarding their impact on the surrounding environment. This perspective can overlook broader considerations, such as Environmental, Social, and Governance (ESG) factors. For example, the energy requirements of data centers that manage advanced encryption systems or support large-scale neural network training contribute substantially to carbon emissions. The implementation of robust cybersecurity measures can incur significant costs, which may disproportionately affect small and medium-sized enterprises, thereby exacerbating existing inequalities. Socially, security systems—particularly those that incorporate surveillance—can infringe upon individual privacy and diminish public trust. From a governance perspective, emphasizing security without sufficient protections for civil liberties can result in potential abuses of power. These challenges highlight the pressing need to reconsider cybersecurity within a broader context. A more sustainable approach must encompass not only technological resilience but also environmental responsibility, social equity, privacy protection, and ethical governance.

This workshop served as a venue to facilitate the dissemination of research and unite interdisciplinary academics and practitioners at the intersection of cybersecurity and its impact on ESG factors. Authors were asked to submit manuscripts with a maximum length of 18 pages for a double-blind peer review process. We received 10 submissions and we completed the revision process thanks to our Program Committee, composed of 21 experts, and 9 additional reviewers. In the end, each paper was revised by at least three reviewers, and, based on the feedback, we accepted 4 papers for the oral presentation at the workshop (with an acceptance rate of 40%).

We would like to express our gratitude to the authors for submitting their outstanding work, to our reviewers for their prompt and thorough evaluations, and to all our attendees. We sincerely hope that the collaborative efforts to organize this workshop will have a positive impact on cybersecurity worldwide.

August 2025

Daniele Canavese
Mohamed Ali Kandi
Leonardo Regano

SAFER 2025 Organization

Workshop Chairs

Daniele Canavese — IRIT-CNRS, France
Mohamed Ali Kandi — IRIT-University of Toulouse, France
Leonardo Regano — University of Cagliari, Italy

Program Committee

Cataldo Basile — Politecnico di Torino, Italy
Laurent Bobelin — INSA Centre Val de Loire, France
Luca Caviglione — CNR-IMATI, Italy
Paolo Falcarin — Ca' Foscari University of Venice, Italy
Davide Ferraris — University of Málaga, Spain
Giorgio Giacinto — University of Cagliari, Italy
Marko Hölbl — University of Maribor, Slovenia
Youcef Imine — University Polytechnic Hauts-De-France, France
Romain Laborde — IRIT-University of Toulouse, France
Abir Laraba — IRIT-University of Toulouse, France
Davide Maiorca — University of Cagliari, Italy
Luca Mannella — Politecnico di Torino, Italy
Marco Martalò — University of Cagliari, Italy
Antonio Muñoz — University of Málaga, Spain
Francesco Pagano — Università di Verona, Italy
Matteo Repetto — CNR-IMATI, Italy
Rubén Ríos — University of Málaga, Spain
Arianna Rossi — Sant'Anna School of Advanced Studies, Italy
Alessandro Sanna — University of Cagliari, Italy
Fulvio Valenza — Politecnico di Torino, Italy
Ahmad Samer Wazan — Zayed University, UAE

Additional Reviewers

Purbasha Chowdhury
Nicola Deidda
Jonathan Gobbo
Luca Minnei
Lorenzo Pisu

Louis Sahi
Silvia Lucia Sanna
Silvia Sisinni
Mohamed Yacine Touahria Miliani

Effects of the Cyber Resilience Act (CRA) on Industrial Equipment Manufacturing Companies

Roosa Risto[(✉)][iD], Mohit Sethi[iD], and Mika Katara[iD]

KONE Corporation, Espoo, Finland
{roosa.risto,mohit.sethi,mika.katara}@kone.com

Abstract. The Cyber Resilience Act (CRA) is a new European Union (EU) regulation aimed at enhancing the security of digital products and services by requiring them to meet stringent cybersecurity requirements. To understand the practical implications of CRA for industrial equipment manufacturing companies, a survey was conducted to identify key challenges. The results revealed significant hurdles, including the implementation of secure development lifecycle practices, managing vulnerability notifications within strict timelines, and addressing gaps in cybersecurity expertise. Based on these findings, the paper offers targeted recommendations in key focus areas such as vulnerability management and tooling improvements to support industrial equipment manufacturers in preparing for CRA compliance.

Keywords: CRA · Regulation · Challenges · Survey · IEC-62443 · Standards

1 Introduction

Motivated by the growing number of cyberattacks targeting connected devices and the lack of consistent baseline cybersecurity practices among manufacturers, the European Union (EU) Cyber Resilience Act (CRA) [4] sets common security requirements for all products with digital elements within the EU. This broad scope intentionally covers all software and hardware products, as well as their remote data processing solutions, with exceptions for medical devices, aeronautical equipment, etc. which are already subject to similar existing EU regulations. The primary goal of CRA is to enhance cybersecurity across the European Union by ensuring that products with digital elements are designed, developed, and maintained with robust security measures. While the act imposes requirements on many stakeholders, a significant portion of these requirements are directed towards manufacturers. The requirements for manufacturers can broadly be classified into software development lifecycle (SDL) process requirements, technical requirements, vulnerability management and notification requirements, and preparation of technical and user documentation.

B. Coppens et al. (Eds.): ARES 2025 Workshops, LNCS 15994, pp. 213–229, 2025.
https://doi.org/10.1007/978-3-032-00630-1_12

The **SDL and technical** requirements outlined in Annex I Part I of the act require manufacturers to perform a risk assessment and subsequently ensure an appropriate level of cybersecurity throughout the design, development, and production process based on the risk assessment. SDL practices must ensure that the products are free of known exploitable vulnerabilities, configured securely by default, and support timely security updates, including automatic updates with opt-out options. Additional technical measures include protecting data confidentiality, integrity, and availability through mechanisms like encryption and access controls, minimizing attack surfaces, implementing resilience against denial-of-service attacks, and data minimization. Furthermore, technical measures must also ensure logging of security-relevant activity, possibility of secure data removal, and mitigation of negative impact on other devices or networks.

Annex I Part II of the CRA sets forth **vulnerability management** requirements, obligating manufacturers to identify and document components and vulnerabilities in their products, including the creation of a software bill of materials (SBOM) in a standard, machine-readable format. Manufacturers are also required to address and remediate vulnerabilities promptly, providing security updates as necessary. When releasing a security update, the manufacturers must publicly disclose details about the fixed vulnerabilities, such as impacts, severity, and remediation steps. Lastly, manufacturers must perform regular testing to identify new vulnerabilities.

CRA specifies **vulnerability notification** practices in articles 14 and 15, mandating manufacturers to inform the European Union Agency for Cybersecurity (ENISA) and national computer security incident response teams (CSIRTs) within 24 h of identifying actively exploited vulnerabilities or severe cyber incidents. The initial notification is followed by a detailed report within 72 h, and a final report within 14 days for actively exploited vulnerabilities and within one month for other incidents. Manufacturers are also encouraged to voluntarily report near misses or incidents impacting the security of their products.

User documentation requirements listed in Annex II of CRA expect manufacturers to provide documentation containing, among other things, contact details for reporting vulnerabilities, the name and type information for uniquely identifying the product, information on the intended purpose of the product, detailed guidance on secure commissioning, update installation, and decommissioning, the type and duration of technical security support, and optionally, access to the product SBOM.

Requirements in Annex VII of CRA instruct that **technical documentation** must include a general description of the product, its intended purpose, relevant software versions, and, for hardware products, visual representations like photographs or diagrams of external and internal interfaces. Additionally, the technical documentation should detail the cybersecurity risk assessments performed, the SDL practices followed, the system architecture designed and developed, a list of applicable standards with which the product is compliant, as well as test reports verifying conformity with the technical requirements in those standards, and potentially the product SBOM.

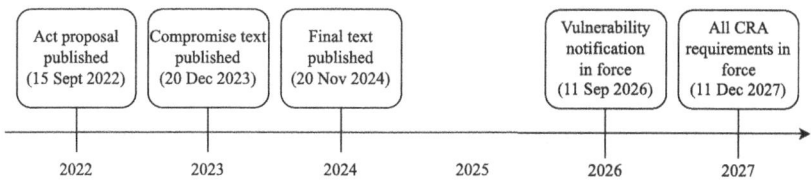

Fig. 1. CRA timeline

Figure 1 shows the timeline for when different CRA requirements come into force. The final CRA text was published on 20 November 2024, implying that the transition period for vulnerability notification responsibilities will end on 11 September 2026, and all CRA requirements will become mandatory from 11 December 2027.

Non-compliance with the CRA can have serious consequences for manufacturers, including restricted market access, mandatory product recalls, or financial penalties. Given the extensive regulatory obligations and the relatively short timeline for full compliance, we conducted a survey to identify the specific challenges faced by industrial equipment manufacturing companies. These companies typically have well-established engineering practices, large development organizations, and structured product lifecycle processes already in place. However, their products often include deeply embedded digital elements integrated into complex, safety-critical, bespoke system installations, such as cranes and mining equipment. In such contexts, supporting requirements like automatic security updates and configuration changes are non-trivial. Additionally, organizational inertia and the need to coordinate changes across multiple product lines, regulatory environments, and customer expectations can make the adoption of CRA particularly challenging. Our goal was to identify concrete pain points and offer targeted recommendations to aid in their preparation for compliance.

The rest of this paper is organized as follows. Section 2 reviews prior work on the challenges associated with CRA implementation. Section 3 examines the IEC 62443 series of standards and discusses how they align with CRA requirements. The study design, including participant background and familiarity, is described in Sect. 4. Section 5 presents the key challenges identified by the surveyed industrial equipment manufacturers. In Sect. 6, we provide targeted recommendations to address the challenges identified. Finally, Sect. 7 concludes the paper and summarizes the main findings.

2   Previous Work on CRA Challenges

Szedlak et al. [19] examine the awareness and preparedness of Small and Medium-sized Enterprises (SMEs) for CRA. Their findings reveal significant disparities in CRA awareness and readiness, with only 12.3% of SMEs being aware of the CRA compared to 83.5% of very large enterprises.

Thiel [20] in his article discusses challenges in CRA compliance, particularly ensuring third-party components being integrated into products also meet CRA standards. He also highlights the issue of lacking in-house cybersecurity expertise, which may necessitate the need for external support.

The European Cyber Security Organisation (ECSO) conducted an online survey to identify potential challenges linked to the implementation of CRA [7]. The survey participants included a subset of ECSO members, primarily security service providers and manufacturers of digital devices, along with other public and private organizations. The survey revealed several key challenges, including the lack of clarity with product categories, the proposed timeline for implementation, and the need for clear guidelines on conducting risk and conformity assessments. Respondents emphasized the necessity for harmonized standards and methodologies at the EU level, as well as the importance of guidelines, templates, and training to facilitate CRA implementation.

A joint letter by experts published by the Center for Cybersecurity Policy and Law [5] raised concerns about the CRA's vulnerability disclosure requirements, including risks of misuse by governments, potential compromise of the vulnerability database by malicious actors, and discouraging effect on collaboration among manufacturers and researchers. The letter emphasizes the need for a risk-based approach, considering factors such as the severity of the vulnerability, the availability of mitigations, the potential impact on users, and the likelihood of broader exploitation.

A blog post by the Open Source Initiative [17] captures feedback on the draft text of CRA from various organizations in the open source community, highlighting concerns such as the unclear scope of exemptions for open source software, the risk of imposing disproportionate regulatory burdens on non-commercial contributors, and potential disruption to collaborative development models.

Schoo [18] in his paper examines some of the challenges from the Cyber Resilience Act (CRA). Among other things, he highlights the need for establishing uniform cybersecurity standards across the European Union and the necessity for a significant increase in the number of conformity assessment bodies to effectively manage and enforce these standards.

While previous work highlighted several challenges associated with CRA, our survey focuses on investigating the specific challenges that CRA poses for industrial equipment manufacturing companies. By identifying these challenges, we aim to provide an understanding of how CRA impacts industrial equipment manufacturers and offer insights into effective strategies in key focus areas for seamless CRA compliance.

3   CRA and IEC 62443

CRA [4] in Annex VIII offers four conformity assessment options, including internal control, where manufacturers self-declare conformity, and EU-type examination, where a notified body verifies conformity before issuing a certificate. Harmonized standards play a pivotal role in all assessment options. As noted in recital 79 of the act, harmonized standards translating CRA's requirements into detailed technical specifications, offer manufacturers clear and actionable compliance guidelines. Recital 81 further underscores that products with digital elements certified or declared in conformity with harmonized standards will benefit from a presumption of conformity, streamlining the compliance process.

The IEC 62443 series of standards provides a comprehensive framework for securing industrial automation and control systems (IACS) against cybersecurity threats. This series of standards is likely to form the basis for any harmonized standard used for CRA compliance by industrial equipment manufacturing companies. This is also evident from the ECSO survey on CRA challenges [7], which noted IEC 62443 as one of the most quoted standards by survey participants. While CENELEC, the European electrotechnical standards body, and specialized industrial equipment manufacturers may develop other harmonized standards, they will still reuse the IEC 62443 series as the building block. For example, the ISO 8102-20 [16] standard for elevators is based on IEC 62443.

The IEC 62443 standard series is structured into multiple parts, addressing different aspects of security, from general concepts and policies to technical requirements and processes. Among these, the parts relevant for CRA requirements include IEC 62443-4-1 [12], which outlines secure product development lifecycle (SDL) requirements for vendors; IEC 62443-4-2 [14], which specifies technical security requirements for IACS components, such as controllers and software applications; and IEC 62443-3-2 [15], which focuses on security risk assessment and system design. The relevance of these standards for CRA compliance is also captured in the standard mapping report prepared by the European Union Agency for Cybersecurity (ENISA) [8].

In our survey, a major component of the questions focused on the IEC 62443-4-1 secure development lifecycle (SDL) process requirements relevant to CRA compliance. Organizations that have already adopted IEC 62443 practices are generally well positioned to meet many of the CRA's expectations, especially in areas related to secure development, risk-based design, and technical protections for the confidentiality and integrity of transmitted and stored data. Many of the participating companies were indeed applying IEC 62443 development practices internally. However, CRA introduces additional requirements not fully covered by the current IEC 62443 series. These include fixed timelines for vulnerability notification, mandatory public disclosure under specific conditions, and more detailed user documentation expectations. Therefore, in addition to questions on SDL process challenges, our survey also explored participants' views on meeting CRA's vulnerability notification obligations and user documentation requirements, which extend beyond what is explicitly addressed in IEC 62443. To deliver CRA-compliant products by December 2027, manufacturers will need to develop and integrate these additional capabilities into their existing processes.

4   Study Design

Between June and August 2024, we conducted a survey to gather insights into the compliance challenges faced by industrial equipment manufacturing companies. The survey utilized a detailed online questionnaire comprising 44 questions that covered various aspects of CRA and IEC 62443-4-1 compliance. The questionnaire included both multiple-choice and freeform questions, focusing on topics such as the role of EU standards within the organization, familiarity with IEC 62443 and CRA, existing secure software development lifecycle (SDL) practices, whether companies already follow IEC 62443-4-1, perceived difficulty in implementing specific practices, challenges in meeting CRA requirements such as vulnerability management and notification, expected role and budget changes, and anticipated compliance timelines.

Participants completed the questionnaire during one-hour video meetings, where they could provide additional feedback using the think-aloud protocol. This approach helped capture verbal comments that might otherwise have been missed, especially in response to the freeform qualitative questions. All meetings were hosted by the same author, and the questionnaire was shared with participants prior to the video call. Each session concluded with an open-ended discussion to gather broader feedback on challenges and potential solutions. Participants were free to refer to the IEC 62443 standard and the CRA text while answering the questions. If they asked for clarification about the meaning of specific requirements or practices, the facilitator provided contextual explanations and examples to ensure a shared understanding.

A total of 12 companies participated in the survey. This group included seven large companies (with over 500 employees) that manufacture industrial equipment such as cranes, elevators, and machinery for the shipping and mining industries. The remaining five companies were consultancies or partner organizations providing software and support services to the large industrial equipment manufacturers we surveyed. For each company, we ensured that the survey was answered by a senior technical cybersecurity manager who had a comprehensive understanding of both the organizational perspective and the technical challenges. Only one response per company was allowed, although multiple cybersecurity experts from the organization could join the calls. In fact, for two of the 12 companies, more than one expert participated in answering the questions. All participating companies had a sizable portion of their revenues in Europe, which motivated their interest in maintaining compliance in the region.

The survey responses were analyzed using a qualitative coding approach commonly used in exploratory user studies. One of the authors reviewed the meeting recordings and annotated relevant open-ended comments that were not captured in the survey form. These responses were then coded thematically to identify recurring topics and pain points. Both text-based and spoken responses were included in the frequency analysis to determine how often specific concerns or challenges were mentioned across participants. Observed patterns and consistent themes were synthesized to form the basis for the practical recommendations presented later in the paper.

During the survey, we used the CRA text from December 2023 [6]. Participants were aware that the final text would be published in the first half of 2024, with a 21-month transition period for notification responsibilities ending in 2026, and a 36-month period for other responsibilities ending in 2027. Given that these expected timelines were similar to the final dates, it is unlikely that the survey responses were significantly affected.

Baseline Understanding. Before delving into questions about compliance challenges, we wanted to gauge the familiarity of the participants with the IEC 62443-4-1 standard and the relatively new CRA regulation. As shown in Fig. 2, most participants were familiar with both IEC 62443-4-1 and CRA, with 75% (9 out of 12) companies being quite or very familiar. Given that the IEC 62443 series of standards has been around for several years, it is not surprising that participants were more familiar with it compared to CRA. While participants demonstrated familiarity with both the standard and the regulation, they were allowed and encouraged to consult the official text during the survey and if any participant had questions about specific requirements, we provided assistance by referring to the relevant sections in the text.

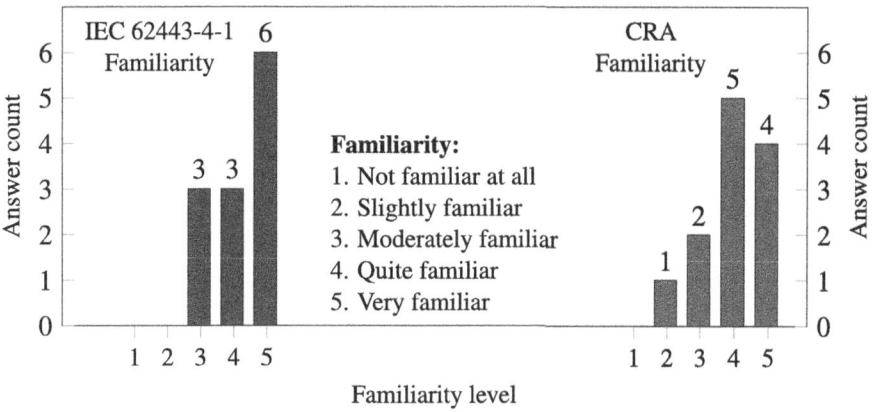

Fig. 2. Participant familiarity with IEC 62443-4-1 and CRA.

IEC 62443-4-1 includes different levels of maturity: Maturity Level 1 (Initial), Maturity Level 2 (Managed), Maturity Level 3 (Defined/Practiced), and Maturity Level 4 (Improving). All of the industrial equipment manufacturing companies interviewed had already established an internal SDL compliant with IEC 62443-4-1, and a few of them had reached Maturity Level 3, meaning they were actively practicing the SDL. Several manufacturers had even undergone third-party audits and obtained certifications. Naturally, the consulting and partner companies followed the SDL practices of the equipment manufacturing companies they worked with to ensure their customers remained compliant but were not developing their own SDL.

Limitations. We recruited survey participants based on their involvement in a joint research project focused on automating compliance with the IEC 62443 series of standards. Additional participants were invited through recommendations from those already involved. All participating companies were predominantly based in Northern Europe, which may limit the generalizability of the findings to all industrial manufacturers subject to the CRA. Although some participants were international, with products sold outside the EU and not subject to CRA, the challenges faced by manufacturers outside the EU but selling products in the EU may differ. Another limitation is the small sample size of 12 companies, which makes it inappropriate to draw statistically significant conclusions. This limitation highlights the qualitative nature of our study, which is primarily descriptive and exploratory rather than statistically validated. Nonetheless, the findings provide valuable insights into the challenges faced by industrial equipment manufacturers. Since the focus was on identifying challenges specific to industrial equipment manufacturers, the recommendations may not apply to manufacturers of other products, such as consumer electronics.

5   Challenges

IEC 62443-4-1 organizes the SDL requirements into eight distinct practices, covering various aspects of the development lifecycle, which are listed in Table 1. The survey asked participants to select any practice that they found challenging to incorporate into their SDL. Participants were free to choose multiple practices when selecting those they found difficult. The survey responses for the practices that participants found challenging to implement are illustrated in Fig. 3.

Table 1. IEC 62443-4-1 practices

Practice 1	Security management
Practice 2	Specification of security requirements
Practice 3	Secure by design
Practice 4	Secure implementation
Practice 5	Security verification and validation testing
Practice 6	Management of security-related issues
Practice 7	Security update management
Practice 8	Security guidelines

As shown in Fig. 3, survey participants identified security management, secure by design, and security update management practices as the most challenging. Participants who selected a practice as difficult to implement had the opportunity to elaborate on their specific challenges through a freeform text question and verbal explanations during the meeting. Several recurring themes emerged from their responses.

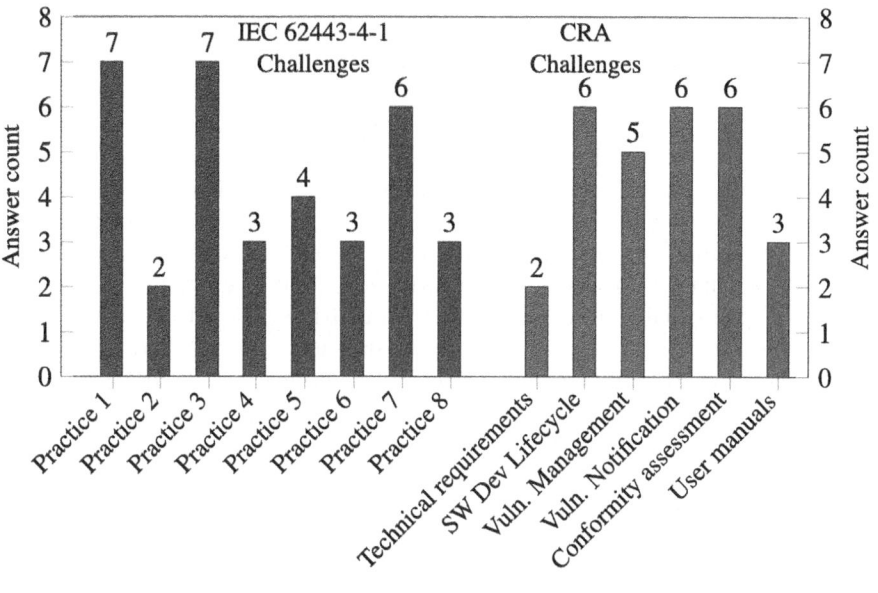

IEC 62443-4-1 and CRA components

Fig. 3. Challenges with IEC 62443-4-1 and CRA requirements.

After selecting the security management practice as a challenge, the participants voiced several concerns. This practice requires establishing a comprehensive SDL as part of the product development process and enforcing it across the organization for both existing and new projects makes it inherently complex. Another challenge highlighted was determining the applicability of specific requirements in the standard. For instance, participants noted difficulty in deciding when requirements, such as providing hardening guidelines, apply to their unique circumstances as industrial equipment manufacturers since often end users are not responsible for installation, hardening, or maintenance of industrial equipment on their own. Another significant issue was identifying and allocating responsibilities, as organizational structures often do not align with the process structures outlined in the standard. This misalignment necessitates negotiating additional responsibilities for teams and securing management buy-in at various levels. Communication gaps between management, developers, and cybersecurity teams were also frequently mentioned. Upper management often lacks sufficient understanding of cybersecurity requirements, while cybersecurity specialists sometimes struggle to effectively convey challenges and issues to leadership, leaving participants uncertain about how to address these communication barriers. Additionally, the practice mandates ensuring adequate security expertise and it was seen as a challenge, with participants citing a perceived shortage of qualified cybersecurity professionals. A perhaps subtle challenge that might have been missed is also the difficulty in evaluating whether personnel assigned to roles have the appropriate cybersecurity skills. Interestingly, participants did not report difficulties with the more technical controls within the security management practice 1, such as SM-6 (file integrity) or SM-8 (controls for private keys), suggesting that technical controls are generally perceived as less challenging compared to organizational and procedural aspects.

Participants identified a lack of cybersecurity-educated or experienced experts as a key challenge with the secure by design practice 3. They noted the difficulty of finding seasoned professionals who possess a broad understanding of defense-in-depth practices, such as least privilege, audit logging, and secure boot, while also being capable of collaborating with multiple product teams. Additionally, these experts must be able to dedicate sufficient time to thoroughly document design reviews and assessments, further complicating the implementation of this practice.

Security update management practice evoked conversation on several challenges that survey participants face when aiming to comply. This is understandable, as many industrial equipment manufacturers rely on embedded software packages that are delivered as complete images, unlike desktop software libraries where individual patches can be built, delivered, and applied to address specific vulnerabilities. Furthermore, industrial equipment often has intermittent or no connectivity, making it difficult to meet timely update requirements. While the standard acknowledges that the availability and safety properties of industrial equipment take precedence over addressing theoretical vulnerabilities, participants still found compliance with the update management practice challenging. Finally, the end users of industrial equipment are often not qualified to access or apply updates. This creates a disconnect between the standard's requirements for security-update documentation and the practical realities of end-user capabilities.

Challenges in CRA Implementation

When exploring challenges with CRA compliance, we categorized the act's requirements into technical requirements, secure development lifecycle (SDL) requirements, vulnerability management, vulnerability notification, conformity assessment, and user manuals. Technical documentation, including risk assessments and interface descriptions, was not queried as a separate category but was considered part of a mature SDL. Participants were allowed to select multiple answers to indicate the areas they found challenging. The responses for each category of requirements are summarized in Fig. 3.

The CRA requirement text *"Products with digital elements shall be designed, developed, and produced in such a way that they ensure an appropriate level of cybersecurity based on the risks"* implies the need for a mature secure software development lifecycle (SDL). Many survey participants found this challenging, echoing the difficulties observed with the IEC 62443-4-1 requirements discussed earlier. Establishing and enforcing an SDL across an organization is a substantial undertaking.

Participants were also uncertain whether their vulnerability management processes and tools were sufficiently mature to meet CRA expectations. Several respondents highlighted challenges such as generating accurate and up-to-date SBOMs, running and integrating appropriate vulnerability scanning tools, and effectively triaging and prioritizing vulnerabilities. Even when vulnerabilities are identified, issuing timely patches can be difficult in practice, particularly in industrial settings where the update cycles are inherently slower due to end-user demands for high availability and minimal downtime. These operational realities were identified as barriers to fulfilling CRA's requirements for timely remediation and clear vulnerability reporting.

Similarly, vulnerability notification requirements were also highlighted as a significant challenge, as many participants had little prior experience with such practices. The CRA deadline of notifying within 24 h of an actively exploited vulnerability was perceived as stringent. Some participants even expressed doubts about their ability to detect actively exploited vulnerabilities promptly.

Conformity assessment was another major area of concern. Participants were unsure whether their products required external assessment by a notified body or if internal self-declaration would suffice based on their product type. Even when self-declaration was deemed acceptable, participants questioned whether their quality teams, which currently oversee self-declaration and CE marking, were adequately equipped to evaluate compliance with the cybersecurity requirements of the CRA. In addition, it was not clear to participants whether sector-specific standards based on IEC 62443 would be sufficient for demonstrating conformity under the CRA. For example, the maritime sector has adopted the International Association of Classification Societies (IACS) Unified Requirements UR E26 [9] and UR E27 [10], which apply to new ships contracted from 1 January 2024 and draw on IEC 62443. However, it was unclear to participants whether compliance with or certification against these standards will fully meet all CRA requirements or be sufficient for self-declaration or assessment by a notified body.

Cost Impact and Organizational Changes. When asked about the estimated cost impacts of CRA compliance, as shown in Fig. 4, 50% of participants expect costs to remain under 20%, 25% anticipate costs to increase by 20–40%, and, surprisingly, 25% foresee no cost impact at all. The question asked participants to estimate how much additional cost CRA compliance would introduce relative to their current product development budgets, including expenses related to personnel, tooling, and process adjustments. Similarly, when participants were asked about potential changes in employee roles, also shown in Fig. 4, the majority (50%) expect roles to remain unchanged after the CRA comes into force, while 33.3% anticipate role changes, and 16.7% remain uncertain. These findings suggest that CRA may not significantly impact employee roles or organizational costs. This could indicate that manufacturers are either reasonably prepared or have resigned themselves to achieving compliance using their existing resources without expecting additional budget or support for structural changes.

Transition Period. The questionnaire included a freeform question about whether the CRA transition period of 21 months for vulnerability notification

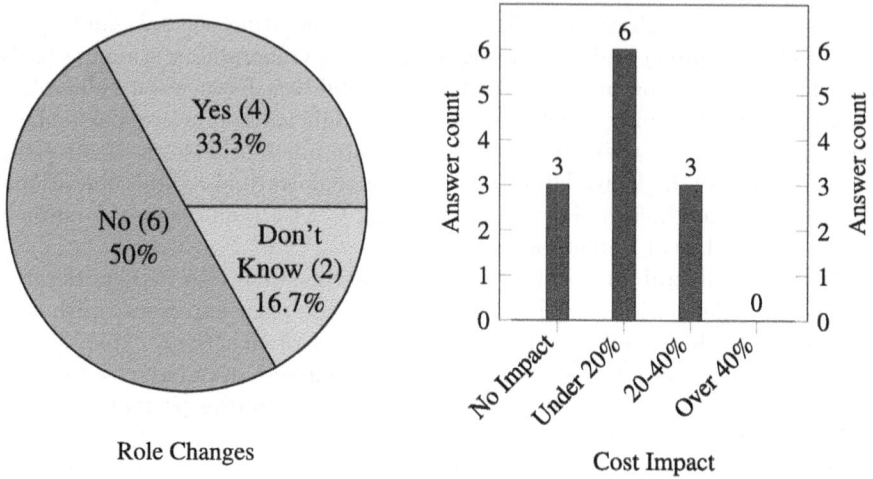

Fig. 4. Anticipated Role Changes and Cost Impact of CRA.

requirements and 36 months for all other requirements is reasonable. The general consensus was that the transition period is reasonable, though some participants expressed concerns about uncertainty surrounding conformity assessment requirements. Additionally, some acknowledged that a longer transition period might not necessarily make compliance easier, as it could simply encourage companies to delay action until the last minute. One participant noted that while the transition period might seem reasonable on paper, it could prove insufficient without strong leadership commitment to the significant organizational changes required.

Use of Open-Source Software. To investigate any specific concerns related to open-source software, we included the following question in the survey: *"What impacts do you see on the use of open-source software in your products that need to comply with the CRA?"* Participants acknowledged that complying with the CRA would make the use of open-source software more complex. They emphasized the need for accurate SBOM tracking tools to detect and document all open-source components comprehensively. Additionally, participants highlighted the need for more rigorous vetting processes to ensure components are actively maintained and the necessity of establishing reliable channels for receiving vulnerability information.

Role of CRA in Improving Security Posture. When asked about their overall impressions of how significantly the CRA is expected to enhance the cybersecurity of their products, participants provided varied responses. While the majority leaned toward the belief that the act would improve the security posture of their products, a few participants expressed skepticism, with some stating they did not anticipate any tangible improvements. This suggests that while many manufacturers recognize the potential benefits of the CRA, not all perceive it as a guaranteed driver of enhanced cybersecurity. Some may regard the act as more of a regulatory burden than a practical means to improve product security.

6   Tackling CRA Challenges

As is evident from the survey results, industrial equipment manufacturers anticipate several challenges in preparing for CRA compliance. This section focuses on the main areas where participants discussed practical difficulties and explores recommendations that emerged during the survey conversations to help address these challenges.

Cybersecurity Experts. Several survey participants identified the shortage of qualified cybersecurity professionals as a critical challenge, particularly in the context of implementing IEC 62443-4-1 practices related to security management and secure-by-design principles. Article 10 of the CRA [4] acknowledges this issue but stops short of mandating specific actions. Instead, it encourages EU member states, ENISA, and the European Cybersecurity Competence Centre to develop *"organizational and technological tools to ensure sufficient availability of skilled professionals."* Addressing this shortage requires broad, long-term planning. However, in the interim, industrial equipment manufacturers must prioritize internal training, upskilling, and adopting a shift-left strategy. This approach integrates security responsibilities across all teams, rather than confining them to a dedicated cybersecurity team.

Communication. Survey participants highlighted several communication challenges at various levels, including the need for clear and effective communication between the cybersecurity team and leadership to convey the CRA's extensive requirements, the number of affected products, required investment, management commitment, and the short transition timeline. Additionally, challenges arise between the cybersecurity team, which is well-versed in the SDL and technical requirements, and the quality team, which oversees self-declaration and CE labeling. The quality team will need to collaborate with cybersecurity to verify CRA compliance and ensure technical documentation is complete before signing a self-declaration. Lastly, participants raised concerns about communication with external authorities, such as ENISA and national CSIRTs, when making vulnerability notifications.

To address communication challenges, it is essential to establish regular cross-departmental meetings involving the cybersecurity team, company leadership, and the quality team. These meetings should ensure alignment on CRA requirements, investment needs, and clearly define the roles and responsibilities of each organizational unit in achieving CRA compliance. Additionally, setting clear next steps and timelines will help streamline the process and foster effective collaboration. Training sessions and workshops tailored for the quality team can further build a shared understanding of CRA requirements. Establishing dedicated communication channels and implementing feedback mechanisms will also help mitigate anticipated communication challenges. Adopting a shift-left strategy will integrate security considerations early in the development process, ensuring that security becomes a shared responsibility across all teams. To address communication challenges related to vulnerability notifications, ENISA and national CSIRTs should prioritize developing a unified Coordinated Vulnerability Disclosure (CVD) ecosystem with clear communication practices and automated tools for streamlined disclosures.

Tooling. To encourage discussion, not only on the challenges but also on potential techniques to overcome them, our survey included an optional freeform question: *What kind of tooling would help your organization in fulfilling the CRA requirements and realizing its full benefits?* Participants had many suggestions, which we synthesized into four tooling categories, along with specific recommendations that refine their preliminary thoughts.

Several participants expressed a desire for advanced, cost-efficient *DevSecOps* tools that support the entire development lifecycle, from threat modeling to requirements tracking, source code scanning, and penetration testing. While many tools are already available for such tasks, organizations should first study their existing development pipelines and understand how new projects and features are introduced and specified. It is crucial to ensure that the chosen DevSecOps tools can integrate seamlessly with these development pipelines. If the development pipelines do not align with modern DevSecOps principles, companies should reconsider and modify them accordingly.

The importance of *vulnerability management* tools was a recurring theme among participants. Many recognized the value of standard SBOM formats like CycloneDX [2] and tools for tracking vulnerabilities based on SBOM data. While vulnerability management tools are necessary and readily available, companies should also prepare for centrally aggregating vulnerabilities from multiple sources and constructing a hierarchy of vulnerabilities that accurately reflects the composition of their product components. Adopting a vulnerability risk scoring methodology grounded in Common Vulnerability Scoring System (CVSS) is essential too. To reduce noise from false positives or low-impact vulnerabilities, organizations should consider advanced risk-rating methods, including AI-driven analysis if necessary.

Governance Risk and Compliance (GRC) tools were also mentioned by a couple of participants. While GRC tools can be helpful, the primary goal for industrial equipment manufacturing companies should be setting a company-wide Cybersecurity Management System (CSMS) aligned with IEC 62443 if it hasn't already been done. Once the CSMS is developed, it needs to be put into practice, and GRC tools can help operationalize and monitor its implementation. However, ensuring that all the policies in the CSMS are understood by employees and effectively applied across the organization is a significant challenge that cannot be solved by GRC tools alone.

Participants also emphasized the necessity of *incident response and workflow automation* tools to comply with CRA notification responsibilities. For this, ENISA and national CSIRTs should develop a unified CVD policy that supports the use of protocols such as Structured Threat Information eXpression (STIX) [3] to automate the exchange of threat and vulnerability information and standard vulnerability reporting formats like the Common Vulnerability Reporting Framework (CVRF) [1]. Concurrently, organizations should prepare templates for initial, detailed, and final reports to streamline the notification process if and when an actively exploited vulnerability is discovered.

As a general recommendation for selecting tools to ensure CRA compliance, organizations should thoroughly evaluate the application programming interface (API) and integration support of each tool before adoption. This evaluation is crucial for building an end-to-end automated pipeline that spans from threat modeling to continuous penetration testing. Additionally, selecting tools with flexible licensing models that can scale with project needs is essential. Prior to making a commitment, organizations should pilot and verify that tools conform to organizational workflows. Lastly, engaging with peers at industry forums to share experiences and adopt best practices based on insights of others can enhance tool selection and implementation.

Vulnerability Management and Notification Practices. In addition to tooling, manufacturers should develop and document internal vulnerability management processes that clearly define roles, responsibilities, and workflows from detection to resolution. These should cover vulnerability identification using scanning tools, risk triage to assess severity and impact, and escalation procedures for critical or high-priority findings. The process must also include handling false positives, assigning remediation tasks, and coordinating actions across relevant teams such as product owners, security engineers, and operations. It should define criteria for when public vulnerability notification is required under CRA, and assign roles to ensure timely and accurate reporting to authorities such as ENISA or national CSIRTs. The process should also account for compensating controls when immediate fixes are not feasible, and include steps for planning, approving, and deploying fixes through the organization's existing change management procedures. It must also support verification of fixes, handle residual risk through formal exception workflows, and be overseen by a central governance structure that regularly reviews critical findings and notification decisions. Where available, manufacturers are encouraged to base their process on harmonized standards that are intended to demonstrate CRA compliance within their sector. In the absence of such a standard, ISO/IEC 29147 [11] and ISO/IEC 30111 [13] can serve as useful inputs for designing an effective internal process.

7 Conclusion

We conducted a survey of industrial equipment manufacturing companies to explore the challenges they anticipate as they prepare for CRA compliance. The survey revealed several key concerns, including the tight timelines for vulnerability notifications, the requirement to support timely automatic security updates with opt-out options, the need for updated user manuals, the complexities associated with using open-source software, and uncertainty around conformity assessment procedures and the applicability of sector-specific standards. Through freeform discussions during the survey, participants shared ideas for addressing these challenges, which we have synthesized into practical recommendations across several focus areas. These include improving internal vulnerability management processes and notification readiness, enhancing communication between cybersecurity, quality, and leadership teams, addressing gaps in cybersecurity expertise through training and shift-left strategies, integrating supportive tooling into development workflows, and ensuring that conformity assessment processes are well understood and documented. While organizations already following IEC 62443 are better prepared, CRA introduces additional obligations, particularly in the areas of documentation, vulnerability notification, and timely update readiness, that must be addressed now to ensure compliance by December 2027. The findings and recommendations presented in this paper offer practical guidance to help industrial equipment manufacturers and other organizations facing similar challenges prepare effectively for CRA compliance.

Acknowledgements. The authors gratefully acknowledge the partial funding provided by the Business Finland Veturi project *CybersecuriTy Assurance for IEC62443 Based Environments (CTAC)*. We extend our sincere thanks to all the members of the CTAC project for their invaluable contributions. Additionally, we would like to express our gratitude to the participants of the study for their insightful feedback on CRA and the challenges it presents.

References

1. CVRF 1.1. https://github.com/CVRF/cvrf1.1
2. CycloneDX bill of materials standard. https://cyclonedx.org/
3. STIX documentation. https://oasis-open.github.io/cti-documentation/stix/intro.html
4. Cyber resilience act (2024). https://eur-lex.europa.eu/legal-content/EN/TXT/?uri=OJ:L_202402847#d1e47-71-1. Official Journal of the European Union, L 284/7
5. Center for Cybersecurity Policy and Law: Joint letter of experts on the EU cyber resilience act and vulnerability disclosure (2023). https://www.centerforcybersecuritypolicy.org/insights-and-research/joint-letter-of-experts-on-cra-and-vulnerability-disclosure
6. Council of the European Union: Regulation of the European parliament and of the council on horizontal cybersecurity requirements for products with digital elements

and amending regulation (EU) 2019/1020 (2023). https://data.consilium.europa.eu/doc/document/ST-17000-2023-INIT/EN/pdf

7. European Cyber Security Organisation (ECSO): Challenges of the industry to implement the CRA. Tech. rep. (2024). https://ecs-org.eu/ecso-uploads/2024/03/ECSO_Survey_CRA_2024.pdf
8. European Union Agency for Cybersecurity (ENISA): Cyber resilience act requirements standards mapping (2024). https://www.enisa.europa.eu/sites/default/files/2024-11/Cyber%20Resilience%20Act%20Requirements%20Standards%20Mapping%20-%20final_with_identifiers_0.pdf
9. International Association of Classification Societies (IACS): UR E26: Cyber resilience of ships (2023)
10. International Association of Classification Societies (IACS): UR E27: Cyber resilience of on-board systems and equipment (2023)
11. International Electrotechnical Commission (IEC): ISO/IEC 29147 vulnerability disclosure (2018)
12. International Electrotechnical Commission (IEC): Security for industrial automation and control systems – Part 4-1: Secure product development lifecycle requirements (2018)
13. International Electrotechnical Commission (IEC): ISO/IEC 30111 vulnerability handling processes (2019)
14. International Electrotechnical Commission (IEC): Security for industrial automation and control systems – Part 4-2: Technical security requirements for IACS components (2019)
15. International Electrotechnical Commission (IEC): Security for industrial automation and control systems – Part 3-2: Security risk assessment and system design (2020)
16. International Organization for Standardization (ISO): Lifts for the transport of persons and goods – Part 20: Cybersecurity requirements (2023)
17. Phipps, S.: The ultimate list of reactions to the cyber resilience act (2023). https://opensource.org/blog/the-ultimate-list-of-reactions-to-the-cyber-resilience-act
18. Schoo, P.: Navigating the CRA: A brief analysis of European cyber resilience act and resulting actions for product development. In: Proceedings of the 9th International Conference on Internet of Things, Big Data and Security (IoTBDS 2024), pp. 245–251. SCITEPRESS – Science and Technology Publications, Lda. (2024). https://doi.org/10.5220/0012690500003705
19. Szedlak, C., Reinemann, H., Hatzelmann, S.: Ensuring cybersecurity compliance: assessing SME awareness and preparedness for the cyber resilience act. In: 5th Asia Pacific Conference on Industrial Engineering and Operations Management. IEOM Society International, USA, Tokyo, Japan (2024). https://doi.org/10.46254/AP05.20240160
20. Thiel, M.: Challenges and opportunities of the EU cyber resilience act. Risk Management Magazine (2024). https://www.rmmagazine.com/articles/article/2024/08/08/challenges-and-opportunities-of-the-eu-cyber-resilience-act

Dynamic Access Policies for Energy Cost Management of Microservices

Thor Kristoffersen$^{(\boxtimes)}$ (iD)

Norwegian Computing Center, Gaustadalleen 23a, 0373 Oslo, Norway
thor@nr.no

Abstract. Data centers consume increasing amounts of electrical energy, driven by artificial intelligence services, and in many energy markets the price of electrical energy is highly volatile, leading to challenges with cost management. The direct energy costs of computational services offered by data centers are not transparent to their clients, providing neither easy means nor incentives for service clients to reduce operational costs. As a possible contribution to solutions, this paper demonstrates a simple system that can be implemented as an application-level proxy that balances the priority of service requests against real-time energy costs, for example by limiting low-priority traffic during periods of higher prices or by deferring it to periods of lower prices. The principle of operation is similar to rate limiting, and the rate limiting function is precisely governed by formal access policies, consisting of a mathematical function that combines dynamic variables from internal and external sources. To manage energy costs, access policies are designed so that decisions depend on the real-time price of energy, which is obtained from an external source. A proof-of-concept system was developed, and simulations show that even straightforward dynamic access policies can be effective in managing energy costs.

1 Introduction

The worldwide electricity consumption of data centers, excluding data networks and crypto mining, was estimated to be 240–340 terawatt-hours in 2022, accounting for 1–1.3% of global electricity consumption, and the demand is anticipated to increase significantly by the end of the decade, to a large extent driven by artificial intelligence (AI) and machine learning (ML) services [1].

AI and ML services consume energy in two phases, first during the training phase and then during the inference phase. The training phase is energy consuming due to factors such as the complexity of the models, the volume of data required for training, and the duration of the phase. The inference phase is generally less energy consuming, but since the energy consumed for inferences is proportional to the number of requests, the total energy costs for this phase may also become significant when there are many clients that make requests over long periods of time [15]. There are also some other common tasks, like customizing large language models (LLMs), retrieval-augmented generation (RAG), and fine-tuning, which generally consume more energy than inference [25].

B. Coppens et al. (Eds.): ARES 2025 Workshops, LNCS 15994, pp. 230–247, 2025.
https://doi.org/10.1007/978-3-032-00630-1_13

When such computationally intensive microservices are integrated in distributed systems, the cost structure of agreements will normally reflect the energy usage over time, but not rapid or unexpected variations in energy costs, so clients do not have the means or incentives to limit energy usage. There is, however, an emerging trend called metered billing or smart metering, in which data centers track power usage and bill customers for consumed energy [13]. This provides improved transparency and an incentive to limit costs, but no effective means to do so.

The solution proposed here focuses on limiting energy costs while at the same time ensuring fairness in the prioritization of clients. The approach is similar to rate limiting or throttling; the novel element is that it depends on a factor that is entirely external to the computer system, namely the real-time price of energy.

Combined with metered billing, this solution enables service operators to include formal policies as part of contractual agreements, making management of operational energy costs transparent to their clients in real time. This would give the clients a proactive role, effectively transferring the responsibility and the cost savings of energy management to the client side.

1.1 Related Work

One way to optimize or reduce the energy consumption of a system is through the use of energy-aware scheduling algorithms, which can be applied at different levels, from dynamic voltage and frequency scaling of processors to task scheduling in cloud computing. These algorithms can be either static, relying on prior knowledge of system characteristics, or dynamic, making real-time decisions based on the current state of the system. At the lowest level, Ramesh and Sentilles proposed a taxonomy for low-power, embedded IoT applications [20]. At the other end of the scale, Buyya et al. proposed a general architecture for energy-efficient management of cloud computing and data centers [5]. Whereas the commonly employed techniques entail some form of task scheduling in time and space, some of the more drastic approaches proposed work by switching equipment on or off according to needs, such as the so-called *green policies* proposed by Orgerie et al. [16].

Energy-aware scheduling has also been applied at the microservice level; a recent example was demonstrated by Rao and Li [21]. A comprehensive review of energy-aware scheduling techniques in the cloud was done by Medara and Singh [12]. Common to these techniques are two things: first, they manage energy consumption by employing various advanced optimization algorithms, and second, the goals of each such algorithm embody a policy that is centralized for the cloud provider.

Most of the work done in the area of energy-aware scheduling has focused on energy management *per se*, but Qureshi et al. also discussed the idea of reducing energy *costs* by using routing schemes to distribute workloads across data centers in order to deal with rapidly varying energy prices in different geographical regions [19]. This idea was also the focus of the work of Sripavithra and Kirubanand, who proposed a task scheduling algorithm that operates under user-specified budget constraints, incorporating real-time spot pricing of electrical energy [24].

One general technique used for capacity management in computer systems is *rate limiting*, which is used to control the rate at which requests are processed by a system [11]. Rate limiting can be applied both at the network layer and at the application layer. At the network layer it can limit the flow rate of packets, and at the application layer it can limit the flow rate of Application Program Interface (API) calls, for example.

It is also possible to improve rate limiting by means of adaptive algorithms. For example, by employing machine learning algorithms to analyze historical user interactions and predict future behavior, a system can dynamically adjust rate limits based on the predicted demand [23].

A variant of rate limiting that is sometimes employed at the application layer is *throttling*, which does not put a hard limit on requests by denying them but rather delays their execution, thus smoothing out bursts of requests and providing a more graceful degradation of service.

A related concept is *admission control*, which refers to a set of techniques used at the network layer to determine if a new traffic flow can be admitted to the network [10]. When a connection request is made, the network will determine if this is to be accepted or rejected based on the current network resource usage, the priority of the connection, and policies set by network administrators. Accurately estimating system capacity and resource availability is critical for effective admission control. In dynamic environments with fluctuating loads, admission control mechanisms need to adapt quickly to changing conditions.

A governing method that is often combined with these techniques is service level tiering, which is often used in business environments to differentiate the level of service provided to customers based on various factors such as the customer's subscription level, payment plan, or volume of business [28]. Each tier has clearly defined service levels, and higher tiers often receive more favorable terms.

1.2   Contributions

The contributions of this paper are the following:

1. A rate-limiting algorithm implemented purely at the application level and customizable on a per-customer basis, enabling the governing policy to be exposed to, and potentially also modified by, data center customers.
2. A general method for governing this rate-limiting algorithm through *dynamic policies*, that is, formal policies whose key variables are obtained from external, dynamic real-time information.
3. The specific application of this algorithm for the purpose of energy cost management of computationally intensive microservices through the design of dynamic policies that incorporate information on energy prices as well as the specific energy characteristics of the target services.

2   Approach

This section presents a computational and mathematical model of the system as well as a the design and implementation of a proof-of-concept system able to simulate different scenarios.

2.1   Access Decision Function

Since rate limiting works essentially by granting or denying access, it is functionally similar to access control, so it is reasonable to adopt the conceptual model of access control defined in the Security Frameworks for Open Systems [7]. This model involves an Access Decision Function (ADF), which makes decisions on whether to grant or deny access, and an Access Enforcement Function (AEF), whose purpose is to enforce those decisions. Service access requests contain various metadata items that are considered Access Decision Information (ADI), that is, information relevant in the context of access control decisions. Other information sources for access control decisions include access control policy rules, retained ADI, and contextual information. What is important here is the ADF and the information sources that it bases its decisions on, specifically, a dynamic access control policy, retained ADI from earlier requests, contextual information obtained from a pricing API, and contextual information obtained from an energy estimation API. It should be noted that microservices will typically employ traditional access control mechanisms based on credentials, address ranges, domain names, and so on. These need to be applied at an earlier stage and are not discussed here since the concern is only with decisions and enforcement of access for the purpose of rate limiting energy usage.

The ADI includes the following metadata items:

- the identity of the client,
- the group memberships of the client, such as its subscription class,
- the access time,
- the API function accessed, as identified by its endpoint, and
- the arguments supplied to the API function.

The retained ADI may include the original ADI plus other metadata items stored by the ADF, including access decisions made.

The pricing model provides the ADF with the real-time price of electrical energy for the data center that hosts the services. The computational resources model provides the ADF with estimates of the energy required to complete a given request based on information about the characteristics of the API function and the arguments provided to it. The retained ADI provides the ADF with a persistent storage of ADI received in requests, which it can retrieve at a later point in time and use, for example, as a basis for assessing the frequency of requests from any given client. The dynamic access policy provides the ADF with a set of rules that it can use to make decisions based on all the other information.

Several freely available APIs exist that provide real-time energy prices in the European Union, for example, the European Network of Transmission System Operators for Electricity (ENTSO-E) Transparency Platform API [2].

The energy estimation API can be implemented as additional endpoints on the pertinent service. For a given endpoint and parameter set, the service should return a real number representing the estimated energy required to carry out the request. It is then the responsibility of the implementing party to implement this API in addition to the API itself.

2.2 Policy Specification

In order to describe the ADF and the ADI, nomenclature for the following elements is needed (with units in brackets):

- P: A price [EUR].
- P_U: A unit price [EUR/kWh].
- H: A history of all granted accesses.
- s: A subscriber, that is, a microservice API client with an agreement.
- c: A subscription class.
- t: Time since epoch [s].
- f: An API function consisting of a method (like GET, POST, PUT) and an endpoint.
- a: A set of arguments to an API function (in the URL or in the request body).
- p: A policy function, which determines the outcome of access decisions.

Three primitive information functions are needed:

- $\mathrm{Upr}(t)$: The unit price of electrical energy at time t.
- $\mathrm{Eng}(f, a)$: The estimated energy consumption of API function f called with arguments a.
- $\mathrm{Cls}(s)$: The subscription class of s.

The implementation of these functions is opaque to the ADF, and the values of both $\mathrm{Upr}(t)$ and $\mathrm{Eng}(f, a)$ are obtained from sources external to the system.

The ADI is a tuple, (t, s, f, a), where t is the time of the access, s is the subscriber, f is the API function to be executed, and a is the set of arguments to be supplied to f. Based on the ADI in a given request, the ADF can calculate the price of executing it. The price, P, of executing a function, f, with a set of arguments, a, at a particular time, t, is given by the utility function $\mathrm{Prc}(t, f, a)$, which is defined as

$$\mathrm{Prc}(t, f, a) \overset{\mathrm{def}}{=} \mathrm{Upr}(t) \cdot \mathrm{Eng}(f, a) \tag{1}$$

If an access is granted, the tuple (t, s, P) is added to the history, H, which is part of the retained ADI.

The aggregated energy price of all granted accesses by subscriber s over the history between t_1 and t_2 is given by the primitive function Hst, which is defined as

$$\mathrm{Hst}(s, t_1, t_2) \overset{\mathrm{def}}{=} \sum_i P_i \ \mathrm{for}(t_i, s, P_i) \in H \wedge t_1 \le t_i \le t_2 \tag{2}$$

An energy access policy for the ADF, $p(t, s, f, a)$, can then be defined as a disjunction of logical expressions:

$$p(t, s, f, a) \stackrel{\text{def}}{=} \bigvee_i \text{Cls}(s) = c_i \wedge \alpha_i \tag{3}$$

where each α_i is a term in t, s, f, and a. That is, for a subscriber of any given subscription class, c_i, access is granted only if the corresponding expression α_i is true. For example, assuming that there are three different subscription classes, the α_i clauses could be defined as follows:

$$\alpha_1 \stackrel{\text{def}}{=} \text{true}$$
$$\alpha_2 \stackrel{\text{def}}{=} (\text{Prc}(t, f, a) + \text{Hst}(s, t - 20, t)) \leq 10 \tag{4}$$
$$\alpha_3 \stackrel{\text{def}}{=} (\text{Prc}(t, f, a) + \text{Hst}(s, t - 60, t)) \leq 5$$

The first rule says that requests from subscribers of class c_1 are always granted. The second rule says that for subscribers of class c_2, the combined energy consumption of the current API call and the granted calls over the last 20 s must not exceed 10 kWh. The third rule says that for subscribers of class c_3, the combined energy consumption of the current API call and the granted calls over the last 60 s must not exceed 5 kWh.

Substituting the α clauses in Eq. (4) for α_i in Eq. (3), the full definition of the policy function then becomes

$$\begin{aligned} p(t, s, f, a) \stackrel{\text{def}}{=} \\ \text{Cls}(s) = c_1 \\ \vee\, \text{Cls}(s) = c_2 \wedge (\text{Prc}(t, f, a) + \text{Hst}(s, t - 20, t)) \leq 10 \\ \vee\, \text{Cls}(s) = c_3 \wedge (\text{Prc}(t, f, a) + \text{Hst}(s, t - 60, t)) \leq 5 \end{aligned} \tag{5}$$

The policy format in Eq. (3) is a convenient template since it assigns a sub-policy to each subscription class, c_i, through the α_i clauses, but in principle a policy can be written in any format as long as it is a Boolean function.

2.3   Implementation

As a proof of concept of the previous section, a simple system was implemented in order to run simulations of policies under specific loads. The system components and the essential control flows are shown in Fig. 1.

The rate limiting is performed by a proxy that sits in front of the target service, acting as an interceptor of access requests. The request is processed by the AEF, which sends a decision request to the ADF. The ADF makes its decision based on all the information sources discussed in Sect. 2, specifically, ADI from the request, retained ADI stored as a history of granted requests, the dynamic access policy, and information retrieved from the Energy Estimation API and the Pricing API. The Energy Estimation API is co-located with the target API, whereas the Pricing API can be any of the freely available APIs in the European

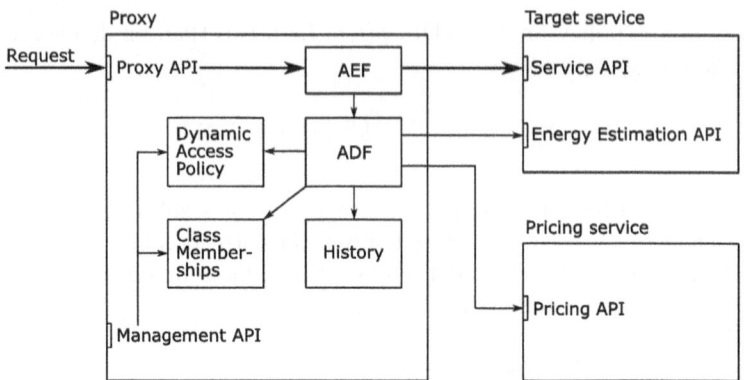

Fig. 1. System components and control flows

energy marketplace. If the ADF grants the request, the AEF will forward it to the target API. If the ADF denies the request, the service must indicate to the client that a given request has been declined due to energy constraints as opposed to lacking privileges, and the client must also be able to understand this distinction. The error mode is indicated with an agreed-upon (Hypertext Transfer Protocol) HTTP response code, and the appropriate response code in case of a declined request for the purposes of rate limiting would seem to be 429 ("Too Many Requests"). This response code indicates to the client that it has temporarily exceeded the acceptable request rate and therefore needs to wait before making another request. If the client keeps repeating the request at a regular rate, a rate-limiting action is achieved.

The proxy also includes a management interface that enables administrators to update the dynamic access policy, which is represented by the function p, and the subscription class of clients, which is represented by the function Cls.

The ADF algorithm, shown in Algorithm 1, is quite trivial since most of the work is done by the policy function, p. The initialization function, init, is called at start-up in order to initialize the history, H, to an empty list. The access decision function, ADF, is a Boolean function that returns true if and only if access is granted. The access decision, D, is a result of evaluating the policy function with the arguments to the ADF function. If the access decision is true, the estimated price of the request is calculated by calling the Prc function, which in turn calls the Upr and Eng functions in order to retrieve the required information from the external APIs, and then a triple containing the time, the subscriber id, and the estimated price is appended to the history, H. Finally, the access decision, D, is returned as the value of the ADF function call.

3   Results

This section presents the results of a series of simulations of policies, showing their performance under varying prices. For brevity and clarity, the policies are

Algorithm 1. Access Decision Function algorithm

---

function init()
$H \leftarrow []$

function ADF(t, s, f, a)
$D \leftarrow p(t, s, f, a)$
if D **then**
$\quad P \leftarrow$ Prc(t, f, a)
$\quad H \leftarrow$ append$(H, [t, s, P])$
end if
return D

---

shown in the standard mathematical form exemplified in Eq. (4) rather than the JSON encoding implemented in the proof-of-concept system.

3.1 A Basic Policy Example

The first simulation tests the performance of the basic policy given in Sect. 2.2:

$$
\begin{aligned}
\alpha_1 &\overset{\text{def}}{=} \text{true} \\
\alpha_2 &\overset{\text{def}}{=} (\text{Prc}(t, f, a) + \text{Hst}(s, t - 20, t)) \leq 10 \\
\alpha_3 &\overset{\text{def}}{=} (\text{Prc}(t, f, a) + \text{Hst}(s, t - 60, t)) \leq 5
\end{aligned} \tag{6}
$$

Figure 2 shows a simulation of three clients, one from each subscriber class, under this access policy. At five-second intervals, each client performs the same function call with the same parameters, at an estimated energy cost of 6 kWh. In this simulation, the unit price of energy starts out at 0.5 EUR/kWh, then rises to 1.0 EUR/kWh at the 40-second mark, and then falls to 0.1 EUR/kWh at the 90-second mark. As the policy specifies, all accesses done by the client in class c_1 are granted.

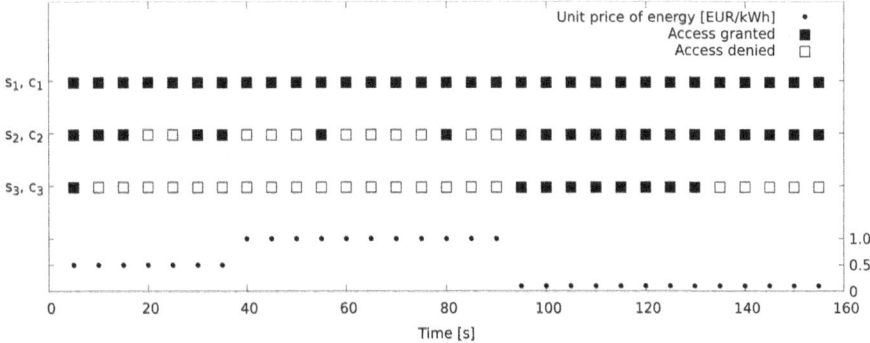

Fig. 2. Simulation of basic policy, different classes

For the client in class c_2, some accesses are granted and some are denied. Even after the unit price of energy is doubled, it retains some level of service. When the unit price of energy drops to a tenth of this level, all accesses are granted.

The client in class c_3 gets only minimal service when the unit price of energy is 0.5. When the price doubles, it gets no service at all. When the unit price of energy drops to a tenth, it gets a higher level of service, but there are still some accesses that are denied. The costs of accesses are shown in Table 1a. In the absence of rate limiting controlled by dynamic access policies, all three subscribers would effectively be in class c_1, giving a combined energy cost of 284.4, whereas with rate limiting the combined energy cost is 137.4, a 51.7 % cost reduction.

3.2   Automatic Tuning of Policy Parameters

Although the policies suggested above are quite simple, the simulations show that even simple policies can be effective for reducing energy consumption while still maintaining a service level commensurate with subscription class. In a production system, one would employ policies tuned for specific subscriber schemes. One way to do this type of tuning is through the use of ML techniques. Provided that one designs simple policies, such as the ones suggested here, the problem of tuning the constants becomes very similar to a classical problem in control systems, namely that of tuning a proportional-integrative-derivative (PID) controller for a particular performance under a given type of load. A PID controller is a highly useful mechanism for controlling industrial processes, yet it is very simple, characterized by only three parameters [27]. Traditionally, the parameters were often tuned using manual methods based on heuristics, but contemporary tuning methods include ML-based approaches, such as regression models [14] and reinforcement learning [8]. Thus, the complexities of finding the optimal set of parameters can be left to opaque ML algorithms, and when these parameters have been found and configured, the PID controller offers full transparency of operation due to its simplicity.

Analogously, based on a simple energy consumption policy definition, like the one given in Eq. (6) above, the numeric constants can be replaced with parameters K_1 to K_4 as follows:

$$\alpha_1 \stackrel{\text{def}}{=} \text{true}$$
$$\alpha_2 \stackrel{\text{def}}{=} (\text{Prc}(t, f, a) + \text{Hst}(s, t - K_1, t)) \leq K_2 \qquad (7)$$
$$\alpha_3 \stackrel{\text{def}}{=} (\text{Prc}(t, f, a) + \text{Hst}(s, t - K_3, t)) \leq K_4$$

Then an ML-based approach can be applied to find the optimal set of parameters for a desired energy consumption performance under a typical load determined by access patterns and variations in the unit price.

As an experiment, automatic tuning of the parameterized policy above was tested using the NLopt library for nonlinear optimization [9] with the Constrained Optimization By Linear Approximations (COBYLA) algorithm [17].

The goal function was defined so that compared to the numbers in Table 1a the cost of c_2 should be reduced to 30.0, while the cost of c_3 should remain at 7.8. The optimization was then carried out with the constants in Eq. (6) as a starting point, that is, $K_1 = 20$, $K_2 = 10$, $K_3 = 60$, and $K_4 = 5$. The optimization algorithm found $K_1 = 34.25$, while the other parameters were unchanged. The results of running the simulation with the updated value of K_1 is shown in Fig. 3. The energy costs are now as shown in Table 1b. The advantage of tuning a simple energy policy is that performance characteristics can be changed according to circumstances, yet the policy remains simple and transparent for service users and other stakeholders.

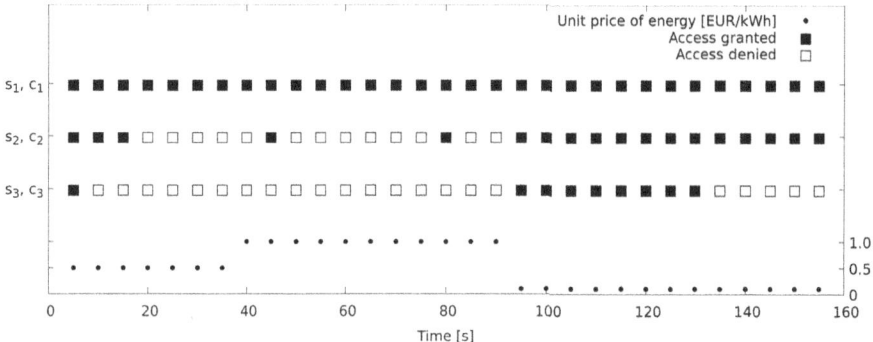

Fig. 3. Simulation of basic policy with tuned parameters

3.3 A Policy Utilizing Future Information

Although the prices of electrical energy in the European market can fluctuate considerably, in practice they are not actually determined in real time; they are typically known 24 h in advance. This makes it possible to implement a refinement of the policy, adapting it to the prices in the near future. If it is known that the price will soon drop significantly, the policy should be more restrictive with granting access to lower-priority subscribers, thus delaying most of the energy consumption until the price has dropped. On the other hand, if it is known that the price will rise significantly, it should be more liberal in granting access to lower-priority subscribers, thus consuming most of the energy while the price is still low. This can be done simply by modifying the threshold values in Eq. (6) as follows:

$$
\begin{aligned}
\alpha_1 &\overset{\text{def}}{=} \text{true} \\
\alpha_2 &\overset{\text{def}}{=} (\text{Prc}(t, f, a) + \text{Hst}(s, t - 20, t)) \leq r \cdot 10 \\
\alpha_3 &\overset{\text{def}}{=} (\text{Prc}(t, f, a) + \text{Hst}(s, t - 60, t)) \leq r \cdot 5
\end{aligned}
\tag{8}
$$

Setting $r > 1$ will result in more access requests being granted, and setting $r < 1$ will result in fewer being granted. A suitable definition of r can then be given that considers the change in the unit price over the next 60 s:

$$r \stackrel{\text{def}}{=} 1 + \text{Upr}(t + 60) - \text{Upr}(t) \qquad (9)$$

Thus, a positive change will yield $r > 1$, which will scale up the threshold values, a negative change will yield $r < 1$, which will scale down the threshold values, and if there is no change, then $r = 1$, in which case the default thresholds apply. The results of re-running the simulation with the modified policy is shown in Fig. 4. Comparing this with Fig. 2, the main effect of this simple modification is to grant the first six access requests in class c_2 early, before the unit price of energy doubles, and during the more expensive interval no requests are granted, bringing the total cost down. The costs of accesses are shown in Table 1c. The cost for c_2 is down by 9, but for c_3 it is up by 3, so the total reduction is 6, yielding a 4.4 % reduction in energy costs compared to the basic policy.

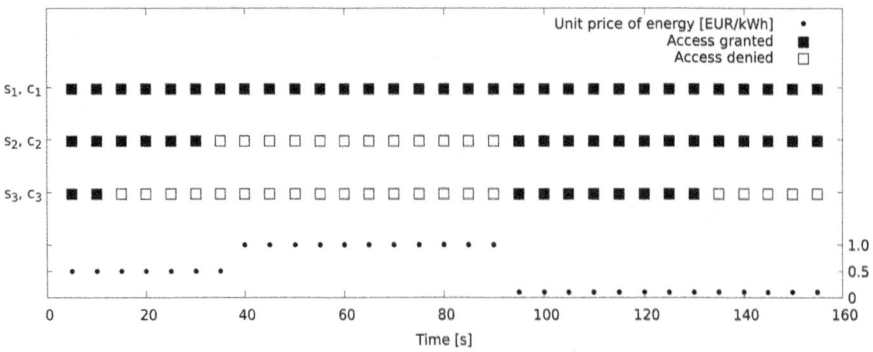

Fig. 4. Simulation of policy utilizing future price information

3.4   Policies that Utilize Collective Information

In the policies described so far, access decisions for any given subscriber are based solely on the actions of that particular subscriber. By adding more primitive functions based on the one defined in Eq. (2), it is possible to achieve integration of information across subscribers of the same class or of all subscribers. The following primitive function aggregates the price of accesses in the given subscription class and timeframe:

$$\text{Chs}(c, t_1, t_2) \stackrel{\text{def}}{=} \sum_i P_i \text{ for } (t_i, s_i, P_i) \in H \wedge t_1 \leq t_i \leq t_2 \wedge \text{Cls}(s_i) = c \qquad (10)$$

In the following policy, the sub-policies for classes c_1 and c_2 use the same constants, but the former applies the individual version of the history function, while the latter applies the collective version to subscription class c_2:

$$\alpha_1 \stackrel{\text{def}}{=} (\text{Prc}(t, f, a) + \text{Hst}(s, t - 10, t)) \leq 10$$
$$\alpha_2 \stackrel{\text{def}}{=} (\text{Prc}(t, f, a) + \text{Chs}(c_2, t - 10, t)) \leq 10 \tag{11}$$

Figure 5 shows a simulation of one subscriber in class c_1 and two in class c_2. The energy costs are as shown in Table 1d. The access requests from both subscribers in class c_2 count toward the same aggregated value, so the combined energy costs are brought down. As is evident from the simulation, the internal order of requests from the clients in class c_2 matters. In the simulation, requests are performed in the order from top to bottom, so granting a given request from subscriber s_2 will sometimes lead to denying the subsequent request from s_3 since the former request exceeds the threshold.

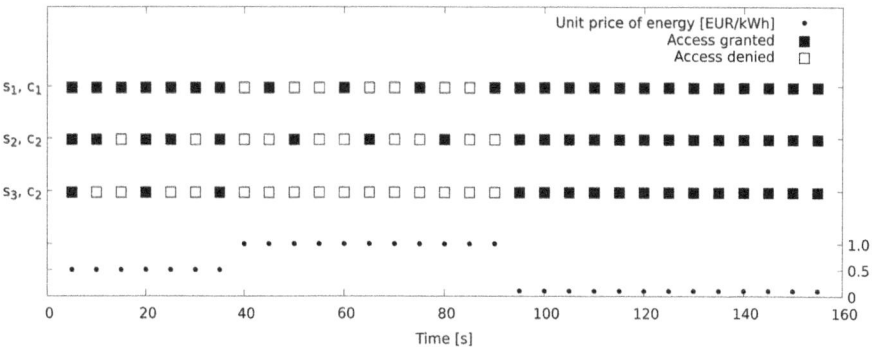

Fig. 5. Simulation of policy utilizing history of given class

The idea of collective policies can be carried one step further. The following primitive function aggregates the total price of *all* accesses in all subscription classes in the given timeframe:

$$\text{Ths}(t_1, t_2) \stackrel{\text{def}}{=} \sum_i P_i \text{ for}(t_i, s_i, P_i) \in H \wedge t_1 \leq t_i \leq t_2 \tag{12}$$

The following policy is similar to the one defined in Eq. (10), except that the Chs function has been replaced with Ths:

$$\alpha_1 \stackrel{\text{def}}{=} (\text{Prc}(t, f, a) + \text{Hst}(s, t - 10, t)) \leq 10$$
$$\alpha_2 \stackrel{\text{def}}{=} (\text{Prc}(t, f, a) + \text{Ths}(t - 10, t)) \leq 10 \tag{13}$$

Figure 6 shows a simulation of one subscriber in class c_1 and two in class c_2. The energy costs are as shown in Table 1e. For requests from s_1 only the history of c_1 is considered, so it gets the same service as in the previous simulation run. On the other hand, for requests from s_2 and s_3, the history of all classes combined is considered, so these two quickly lose service until the price drops to 0.1 EUR/kWh.

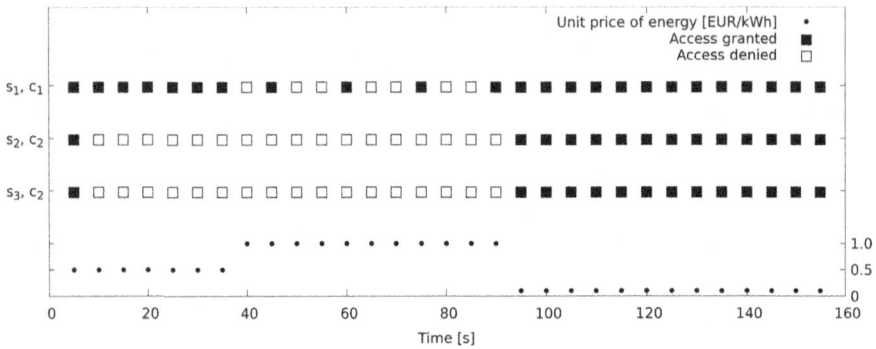

Fig. 6. Simulation of policy utilizing history of all classes

4   Discussion

Since the approach proposed here makes no attempt to optimize the workflow of tasks, it is clearly a simpler mechanism than the scheduling algorithms described in the literature. In the context of the taxonomy for resource scheduling techiques proposed by Sana and Li [22], the approach covers three different areas:

- *Cost-aware scheduling based on user expenses*, since it considers the calculated cumulative price of accesses.
- *Energy-aware scheduling*, since it considers the amount of energy as determined by the energy estimation function.
- *SLA-aware scheduling*, since its operation is dictated by a formal policy, which can be included in an SLA.

The proposed solution can be implemented as a Representational State Transfer (REST) proxy at the application level. The policy language consists of a basic set four variables and seven primitive functions in addition to mathematical and logical functions. Based on this language it is possible, as shown in Sect. 3, to formulate clear policies with a range of different effects, and an optimal set of parameters for a typical load and desired cost profile can then be found using automatic optimization algorithms. The system does not limit the complexity of the access policies employed. However, straightforward policies with a small set of parameters offer better transparency for stakeholders than complex policies.

Table 1. Summary of costs under different policies

Policy	Subscriber	Class	Cost [EUR]
a. Basic with different classes	s_1	c_1	94.8
	s_2	c_2	34.8
	s_3	c_3	7.8
	Total		137.4
b. Basic with tuned parameters	s_1	c_1	94.8
	s_2	c_2	28.8
	s_3	c_3	7.8
	Total		131.4
c. Utilizing future prices	s_1	c_1	94.8
	s_2	c_2	25.8
	s_3	c_3	10.8
	Total		131.4
d. Utilizing history of given class	s_1	c_1	52.8
	s_2	c_2	40.8
	s_3	c_2	16.8
	Total		110.4
e. Utilizing history of all classes	s_1	c_1	52.8
	s_2	c_2	10.8
	s_3	c_2	10.8
	Total		74.4

Some cloud providers offer frameworks for REST proxies governed by formal policies for the purposes of decoupling, security, monitoring, as well as rate limiting [3], so most of the required infrastructure is already in place. Since the solution works entirely at the application level, it can be applied on a per-service basis, and customized policies can be developed individually for each service. By exposing the management of the policies and the costs incurred by the respective subscription classes to data center customers, they can actively develop and fine-tune their own policies in order to find the right balance between performance and cost. This could also be combined with metered billing.

The proposed access decision function has two important dependencies that have to be provided by external means: the unit price function, $\text{Upr}(t)$, and the energy estimation function, $\text{Eng}(f, a)$. The unit price function is trivial to integrate into the ADF, since several providers make this information freely available through open APIs. Implementing the energy estimation function, on the other hand, is associated with some practical challenges. The function should be able to provide an accurate estimate of the required energy for any function call, so it is necessary to create a model of the energy consumption that takes into account any variation in energy caused by variation in the arguments. In general, the energy consumption of a given function call can be found by integrating its power consumption over time, so the problem is reduced to finding the power consumption. There are principally two techniques for doing this: direct measurement and modeling, although hybrid approaches are often used in practice. For direct measurement of power consumption, Tiwari et al. give a comprehensive overview of techniques [26]. Measuring the exact energy consumption incurred by individual service requests can be complex due to factors like hardware differences, operating system overhead, and the nature of the tasks being performed. For modeling, many approaches have been suggested, including those of Balsini et al. [4] and Fischer et al. [6]. For direct measurement, Qiao et al. proposed a software-based energy accounting framework for Linux called Wattmeter, which measures per-process energy consumption with low overhead [18]. The energy estimation function should be provided via a REST API, and implementing and providing it should be the responsibility of the implementers of the corresponding microservice. A potential secondary effect of requiring an energy estimation API is that over time it could lead to increased awareness of energy consumption, incentivizing providers of computationally intensive services to focus on energy efficiency, in much the same way that publication of fuel consumption data has incentivized car manufacturers to compete in creating ever more energy-efficient cars.

The system requires some flexibility with respect to latency on the part of the client, so it will not be an adequate solution for latency-critical clients, but such clients can be accommodated by assigning them to a subscriber class without rate limiting, such as c_1 in the policy example provided in Eq. (4). On the other hand, many AI and ML services, such as customization of LLMs, RAG, and fine-tuning of models are not usually latency-critical. Clients of such services need to be aware that they are dealing with a dynamic access policy system. In particular, each client must understand the HTTP response code that indicates that a given function call has been declined due to energy constraints, as discussed in Sect. 2. In this case it may simply retry calling the function at a predefined interval until it succeeds.

The functionality of the system can be extended by considering not only the time of the access request but also the location. It is possible to imagine a scenario where multiple service instances are running in geographical regions where energy prices tend to vary independently of one another. For example, Norway is divided into five energy zones, and the prices in these zones can sometimes differ by more than an order of magnitude. Provided that an operator has data centers in several zones, significant cost savings are possible by executing computations in the zone where the cost is the lowest at any given time. A simple technical solution would be to use HTTP response code 307 (Temporary Redirect).

Several other extensions of the system are possible. The suggested set of primitive functions is quite simple, and as was demonstrated in Sect. 3.4, it is possible to extend this set by adding functions that offer more advanced analytical capabilities. It would also be trivial to include other types of external data from other open APIs. For example, some of the APIs that offer electrical energy prices also offer the emissions intensity of that energy, so this could be added as another primitive function in the policy language. Then it would be possible to formulate policies that focus on reducing emissions.

5   Conclusions

The proposed energy management approach can be implemented straightforwardly as a proxy, and in container-based environments like Kubernetes, it can also be realized as a container. Dynamic policies can be included in SLAs and tailored by data center customers to their individual needs, similarly to what is already the case for other types of customer-defined policies for data centers. In the policy language it is possible to express clear and understandable policies that are nevertheless effective at managing energy costs. Through the use of parameterization, dynamic policies can be tuned according to high-level goals using ML algorithms or other optimization techniques. Policies can be employed to limit power consumption in general through a throttling action on requests. Using future pricing information, it is possible to achieve a scheduling effect that advances or delays operations in relation to transients of expensive energy. Finally, policies can be used to establish effective price quotas for given subscription classes, for example, for the purpose of reducing energy costs due to non-essential operations. A drawback of the approach is that the power consumption of each target service needs to be characterized accurately and provided via the energy estimation API, but technical frameworks for doing this exist.

Acknowledgements. The work in this paper was carried out and funded as part of the FAME project of the European Union's Horizon research and innovation programme under Grant Agreement no. 101092639. Many thanks to Sandeep Pirbhulal, who provided valuable feedback and suggestions.

Disclosure of Interests. The author declares no conflicts of interest.

References

1. World Energy Outlook 2024. Tech. rep., International Energy Agency (2024). https://www.iea.org/reports/world-energy-outlook-2024
2. ENTSO-E: Transparency Platform Restful API (2025). https://documenter. getpostman.com/view/7009892/2s93JtP3F6
3. Apigee: Build RESTful APIs. https://docs.apigee.com/
4. Balsini, A., Pannocchi, L., Cucinotta, T.: Modeling and simulation of power consumption and execution times for real-time tasks on embedded heterogeneous architectures. ACM SIGBED Rev. **16**(3), 51–56 (2019). https://doi.org/10.1145/ 3373400.3373408
5. Buyya, R., Beloglazov, A., Abawajy, J.: Energy-Efficient Management of Data Center Resources for Cloud Computing: A Vision, Architectural Elements, and Open Challenges (2010). https://doi.org/10.48550/ARXIV.1006.0308

6. Fischer, B., Cech, C., Muhr, H.: Power modeling and analysis in early design phases. In: Design, Automation & Test in Europe Conference & Exhibition (DATE), 2014, pp. 1–6. IEEE Conference Publications, Dresden, Germany (2014). https://doi.org/10.7873/DATE.2014.210

7. ISO/IEC 10181-3:1996 | ITU-T Recommendation X.812: Information technology – Open Systems Interconnection – Security frameworks for open systems: Access control framework

8. Jesawada, H., Yerudkar, A., Del Vecchio, C., Singh, N.: A Model-Based Reinforcement Learning Approach for PID Design (2022). https://doi.org/10.48550/ARXIV.2206.03567

9. Johnson, S.G.: The NLopt nonlinear-optimization package. https://github.com/stevengj/nlopt (2007)

10. Knightly, E., Shroff, N.: Admission control for statistical QoS: theory and practice. IEEE Netw. **13**(2), 20–29 (1999). https://doi.org/10.1109/65.768485

11. Kurose, J.F., Ross, K.: Computer Networking: A Top-Down Approach, Global Edition. Pearson Higher Ed (2021). ISBN: 978-1-292-40551-3

12. Medara, R., Singh, R.S.: A review on energy-aware scheduling techniques for workflows in IaaS clouds. Wireless Pers. Commun. **125**(2), 1545–1584 (2022). https://doi.org/10.1007/s11277-022-09621-1

13. Narayan, A., Rao, S., Ranjan, G., Dheenadayalan, K.: Smart metering of cloud services. In: 2012 IEEE International Systems Conference SysCon 2012, pp. 1–7. IEEE, Vancouver, BC, Canada (2012). https://doi.org/10.1109/SysCon.2012.6189462

14. Niembro-Ceceña, J., Gómez-Loenzo, R., Rodríguez-Reséndiz, J., Rodríguez-Abreo, O., Odry, A.: Auto-regression model-based off-line PID controller tuning: an adaptive strategy for DC motor control. Micromachines **13**(8), 1264 (2022). https://doi.org/10.3390/mi13081264

15. Ning, Z., Vandersteegen, M., Beeck, K.V., Goedemé, T., Vandewalle, P.: Power consumption benchmark for embedded AI inference. In: International Conferences on Applied Computing 2024. Zagreb, Croatia (2024)

16. Orgerie, A.C., Lefèvre, L., Gelas, J.P.: Save watts in your grid: green strategies for energy-aware framework in large scale distributed systems. In: 2008 14th IEEE International Conference on Parallel and Distributed Systems, pp. 171–178. IEEE, Melbourne, Australia (2008). https://doi.org/10.1109/ICPADS.2008.97

17. Powell, M.J.D.: A direct search optimization method that models the objective and constraint functions by linear interpolation. In: Gomez, S., Hennart, J.P. (eds.) Advances in Optimization and Numerical Analysis, Mathematics and Its Applications, vol. 275, pp. 51–67. Springer (1994). https://doi.org/10.1007/978-94-015-8330-5_4

18. Qiao, F., Fang, Y., Cidon, A.: Energy-aware process scheduling in Linux. SIGENERGY Energy Inform. Rev. **4**(5), 91–97 (2024). https://doi.org/10.1145/3727200.3727214

19. Qureshi, A., Weber, R., Balakrishnan, H., Guttag, J., Maggs, B.: Cutting the electric bill for internet-scale systems. In: Proceedings of the ACM SIGCOMM 2009 Conference on Data Communication, pp. 123–134. ACM, Barcelona Spain (2009). https://doi.org/10.1145/1592568.1592584

20. Ramesh, U.B.K., Sentilles, S., Crnkovic, I.: Energy management in embedded systems: towards a taxonomy. In: 2012 First International Workshop on Green and Sustainable Software (GREENS), pp. 41–44. IEEE, Zurich, Switzerland (2012). https://doi.org/10.1109/GREENS.2012.6224254

21. Rao, W., Li, H.: Energy-aware scheduling algorithm for microservices in Kubernetes clouds. J. Grid Comput. **23**(1), 2 (2025). https://doi.org/10.1007/s10723-024-09788-w
22. Sana, M.U., Li, Z.: Efficiency aware scheduling techniques in cloud computing: a descriptive literature review. PeerJ Comput. Sci. **7**, e509 (2021). https://doi.org/10.7717/peerj-cs.509
23. Shah, S., Khan, B.: Dynamic rate limiting in microservices: a user behavior aware approach. Int. J. Res. Anal. Rev. **8**(1), 221–233 (2021)
24. Sripavithra, C., Kirubanand, Dr.V.B.: An energy-aware dynamic scheduling algorithm for optimizing workflows under budget-constraints. J. Internet Serv. Inf. Secur. **15**(1), 182–199 (2025). https://doi.org/10.58346/JISIS.2025.I1.012
25. Strubell, E., Ganesh, A., McCallum, A.: Energy and policy considerations for deep learning in NLP. In: Proceedings of the 57th Annual Meeting of the Association for Computational Linguistics, pp. 3645–3650. Association for Computational Linguistics, Florence, Italy (2019). https://doi.org/10.18653/v1/P19-1355
26. Tiwari, V., Malik, S., Wolfe, A.: Power analysis of embedded software: a first step towards software power minimization. IEEE Trans. Very Large Scale Integration (VLSI) Syst. **2**(4) (1994). https://doi.org/10.1109/92.335012
27. Wang, L.: PID Control System Design and Automatic Tuning Using MATLAB/Simulink. Wiley, IEEE Press, Hoboken, NJ (2020). 978-1-119-46934-6
28. Wieder, P., Butler, J.M., Theilmann, W., Yahyapour, R. (eds.): Service Level Agreements for Cloud Computing. Springer, New York (2011). 978-1-4614-1613-5

Are Trees Really Green? A Detection Approach of IoT Malware Attacks

Silvia Lucia Sanna[1]([✉])(iD), Diego Soi[1](iD), Davide Maiorca[1](iD),
and Giorgio Giacinto[1,2](iD)

[1] Dip. Ingegneria Elettrica ed Elettronica, Università degli Studi di Cagliari,
Cagliari, Italy
{silvial.sanna,diego.soi,davide.maiorca,giogio.giacinto}@unica.it
[2] CINI, Consorzio Interuniversitario Nazionale per l'Informatica, Roma, Italy

Abstract. Nowadays, the Internet of Things (IoT) is widely employed, and its usage is growing exponentially because it facilitates remote monitoring, predictive maintenance, and data-driven decision making, especially in the healthcare and industrial sectors. However, IoT devices remain vulnerable due to their resource constraints and difficulty in applying security patches. Consequently, various cybersecurity attacks are reported daily, such as Denial of Service, particularly in IoT-driven solutions.

Most attack detection methodologies are based on Machine Learning (ML) techniques, which can detect attack patterns. However, the focus is more on identification rather than on considering the impact of ML algorithms on computational resources.

This paper proposes a *green* methodology to identify IoT malware networking attacks based on flow privacy-preserving statistical features. In particular, the hyperparameters of three tree-based models – Decision Trees, Random Forest, and Extra-Trees – are optimized based on energy consumption and test-time performance in terms of Matthew's Correlation Coefficient.

Our results show that models maintain high performance and detection accuracy while consistently reducing power usage in terms of watthours (Wh). This suggests that on-premise ML-based Intrusion Detection Systems are suitable for IoT and other resource-constrained devices.

Keywords: Green ML · IoT · Malware Traffic · Network Analysis

1 Introduction

Nowadays, Internet of Things (IoT) devices and their interconnections are becoming exponentially important in everyday life, from industry [32] to houses, vehicles, and smart cities of interconnected systems [20]. Such devices have low capabilities in terms of energy and computational resources compared to desktop and server computers. They are often employed to measure specific data,

---

S. L. Sanna and D. Soi—Equal Contribution.

i.e., *sensors*, and control mechanical systems or forces, i.e., *actuators*. With the advent of Artificial Intelligence (AI), these devices are becoming more intelligent and capable of making decisions independently [2].

Over the years, IoT devices and interconnected networks have been found to be susceptible to various vulnerabilities [21], which have allowed several types of cybersecurity attacks, such as data exfiltration, Denial of Service (DoS), and its Distributed variant (DDoS). Most of the time, these attacks are perpetrated by malware specifically designed for IoT systems, which are generally equipped with limited operating systems (OS) based on the Linux kernel, such as `Miraii` [1], and `Torii` [30], and `Hide&Seek` [7]. Detecting the presence of malware in an IoT environment is crucial as a first step to counteract a large number of cyber-attacks, given the growing importance of IoT devices, their security disadvantages [25], and the limited resources they are provided with.

In this work, we focused on three detection strategies based on network communications made by IoT devices, which normally communicate with remote servers for data exchange. When malware takes control over the expected operability, the packet transmissions change, and attack patterns can be identified to detect anomalous behavior. These systems, called Intrusion Detection Systems (IDS), are generally deployed on-premise in ad-hoc devices, i.e., firewalls or routers, which work as access points for the IoT devices, or they are host-based, running directly on the device under analysis. However, these systems are typically resource-consuming, especially if they rely on Machine Learning (ML) algorithms [12], which require significant computational power and memory, making them unsuitable for deployment on resource-constrained devices.

To the best of our knowledge, few works at the state of the art focus on *Green Machine Learning* for network security applications [16,27], that is, optimizing the underlying ML model to find a balance between drained energy and performance. Indeed, a green ML strategy is necessary mainly for two aspects. First, maintaining high detection performance while reducing consumed energy allows the deployment of IDS on-premise directly in IoT devices. Second, the longer an attack remains undetected, the greater the energy consumption will be due to malware operation and legitimate activities the IoT device may perform. As a consequence, the operability lifecycle of the device diminishes, causing the so-called *e-waste* [22] of electronics. Therefore, reducing the size of detection algorithms and the consumed energy would increase the device's life. Additionally, reducing the overall energy consumed is fundamental to decreasing the equivalent carbon footprint, helping to combat climate change.

In this paper, we employed a dataset of common network cyberattacks in different IoT scenarios [26] (e.g., DoS and port-scanning) to identify post-mortem anomalies based on network features. We optimized the hyperparameters of three tree-based ML algorithms to minimize energy consumption during the testing phase while maximizing performance. We demonstrate that accuracy is not significantly affected by lower power usage. Our approach can be seen as an adaptive, energy-efficient IDS designed for network traffic detection.

To this end, we sketch two modes of operation:

a) *non-green*, i.e., the training phase, in which the ML algorithm is optimized on a server, enabling fast learning and handling large training datasets, while still prioritizing power usage reduction during testing;

b) *green* mode during runtime in resource-constrained devices, triggering alerts when an anomaly is detected as in the testing phase.

In this way, the algorithm is trained with large datasets to account for most learning patterns, while the algorithm running on-premise lowers power consumption, maintaining similar accuracy.

In summary, *i*) we developed a detection methodology based on networking post-mortem features, optimizing the ML algorithms for energy consumption in terms of μWh and performance during the testing phase; *ii*) we selected only statistical features per flow without considering the body of the packets, i.e., a *privacy-preserving* approach; *iii*) we compared different ML algorithms to understand which is the most *green* during the testing phase; and *iv*) we defined the importance of false negative flows not detected by the system.

The rest of the paper is organized as follows. Section 2 reviews the literature on detecting malware networking communication and the energy consumption of ML systems, and Sect. 3 describes the dataset, features, and employed algorithms. Section 4 discusses the results of the classification with respect to the performance and energy consumption of the models. Finally, Sect. 5 discusses the limitations of the approach and future works.

2   Related Works

This section reviews recent works on current advancements in energy estimation with respect to AI technologies in Sect. 2.1, and the state-of-the-art regarding the detection of IoT malware through traffic patterns in Sect. 2.2.

2.1   Energy Consumption Measurement

Advancements in computer science technology powered by Cloud Computing and AI have substantially increased the demand for energy resources. This rise in energy consumption affects the feasibility of implementing cybersecurity solutions in battery-powered systems like IoT and mobile environments, while also contributing to CO_2 emissions, exacerbating environmental challenges such as climate change. Thus, the reduction of software energy consumption is becoming an interesting topic for the research community [9,33,34]. A recent survey [13] reviewed two techniques for estimating the energy consumption of algorithms to better design software: *i*) *hardware-level* to compute the energy efficiency of hardware components (i.e., CPU, RAM, and I/O peripherals); *ii*) *software-level* through simulation or real-time estimation at the instruction level to trace the consumed energy by performance counter profiling or instruction-set simulation.

Among the most recent approaches, Budennyy et al. proposed Eco2AI [6], a framework that measures energy consumption in terms of Joules or KWh, focusing on CPU, GPU, and RAM real-time evaluation. `PyJoule`[1] employs the `Intel RAPL` (Running Average Power Limit) technology to estimate the power consumption of CPU, RAM and integrated GPU. Additionally, Antony et al. proposed `Carbon Tracker`, a tool to track the energy and carbon footprint of ML models. The authors evaluated the tool's efficiency by comparing the estimations with the actual measurements done in monitoring 1 training epoch for two models, i.e., CNN and Autoencoders, with errors between 5% and 19%. Due to its efficiency and attested good results, in this work we based the optimization of detection algorithms on the measurements done by `Carbon Tracker` as explained in Sect. 3.

Other works, besides measuring the energy efficiency of neural network models and their training, suggest ways to reduce consumption. Tipp et al. [28] suggest, among other methods, reducing idle time when accessing memory to eliminate excess energy due to idle power drawn and reducing memory access by using specialized hardware to hold larger parameters in cache.

2.2 Detection of IoT Malware Traffic

The rapid evolution of IoT devices has attracted malware authors interested in exploiting security vulnerabilities through malicious software, whose aim is generally to gain unauthorized privileges in the network to which IoT devices are connected, like in the case of `Mirai` [1] and `SILEX` [23] attacks. For this reason, one of the main approaches to identify this kind of malicious activity is to leverage the network patterns they generate.

One of the first works was published by Bilge et al. [5] in 2012, whose main goal was to propose invariant network features without considering the application protocols due to differences in each client/server communication. In particular, they selected flow size-based, client access pattern-based features, and temporal ones to characterize the variability of client flow volume as a function of time. Recently, Davanian et al. [11] proposed a methodology to identify live C&C servers with zero-priori knowledge to separate the C2-bound traffic from other traffic accurately. Their methodology is based on a SYN-DATA-aware approach, depending on the number of SYN flags and the data exchanged. Moreover, they focus on a grammar-based representation of the traffic, considered as a dialog, to create a fingerprint-aware identification method. Barradas et al. [4] adapted the existing methodologies for C&C traffic with TLS 1.3 protocol, which improves the TCP handshake protocol. They employed features related to the packet sizes, discarding all timing features since they are affected by the distance between client and server, as well as by network conditions.

Other works, have addressed the multi-classification problem to identify several kinds of attacks in IoT networks, e.g., Denial of Service (DoS), and Port Scanning with several Machine Learning algorithms [10,18] by considering both temporal and content-based features reaching accuracies in the order of 90%.

---

[1] https://github.com/powerapi-ng/pyJoules.

Despite the importance of in-edge attack identification [15,17], and its efficient resource management, few existing works addresses the usage of green machine learning algorithms for network security applications [16,27]. The current proposed approaches (e.g., TinyML[2] techniques) reduce the size of learning algorithms to be suitable for IoT devices, selecting one method over the other without a real optimization step based on the power usage.

3   Methodology

This section introduces the proposed methodology to optimize ML models based on both energy consumption and performance, as depicted in Fig. 1. Specifically, Sect. 3.1 describes the employed dataset, Sect. 3.2 discusses the extracted features, and Sect. 3.3 introduces the model training approach with the optimization strategy.

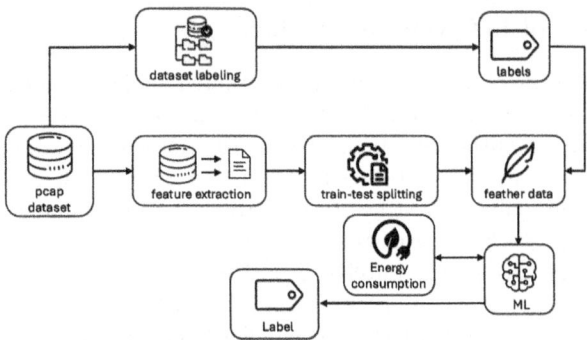

Fig. 1. Training workflow with the basic blocks of the methodology: dataset labeling, feature extraction, training, and energy-based optimization.

3.1   Dataset

To evaluate the approach, we used the Aposemat IoT-23 dataset [26] by Garcia et al., a freely available labeled dataset of multiple PCAP network capture files. The dataset contains benign and malicious traffic involving a variety of IoT sources (e.g., smart hubs, smart lights, door lock devices) and malware.

The NFStream[3] tool was employed to analyze the PCAP files, obtain the label of the flows, and extract several meaningful statistical features, computed when a flow is closed, (i.e., utilizing the totality of a connection), since our approach is tailored to *post-mortem* traffic analysis. To identify each flow in

---

[2] https://github.com/mit-han-lab/tinyml.
[3] https://www.nfstream.org/.

the PCAP, we employed the five-tuple (source IP address, source IP port, destination IP address, destination IP port, timestamp) to match the identifiers of the original dataset in the file labels. The dataset was originally labeled by the authors Garcia et al. using the network traffic analyzer Zeek[4]. Moreover, to remove noise, we dropped the flows with multiple contrasting labels (e.g., a flow belonging both to a Mirai and Kenjiro botnet), or with no existing match in the Zeek results.

Table 1 shows the list of flow counts per class. Our processed dataset contains malicious traffic from seven malware tools: Kenjiro, Mirai, Hakai, IRCBOT, Hajime, Hide&Seek, and Muhstick, which represent the majority of malware found in real-world scenarios [31]. As noticeable, the majority of malware samples belong to the port-scan attack and the dataset is unbalanced in the malware/benign flows ratio. However, as it will be detailed in Section 4.4, we reduced it by removing this class of attack, making the dataset nearly balanced and obtaining better results.

Table 1. Flow count grouped by class and attack types, i.e., port scan, C&C and DoS attacks.

CLASS	FAMILY	FLOWS
Malicious	IRCBOT – port scan	3627968
	Kenjiro – port scan	3525075
	Mirai – port scan	3236207
	Hajime – port scan	506947
	Hide and Seek – port scan	9558
	Muhstik – port scan	3671
	Mirai – C&C	559
	Hakai – C&C	103
	Kenjiro – DoS	776087
	Mirai – DoS	18344
	Muhstik – DoS	298
Benign	-	1532194

3.2 Extracted Features

NFStream was also employed to extract various statistical features, listed in Table 2 for each correctly labeled flow. These features were chosen since using statistics computed per flow in combination with Machine Learning techniques

---

[4] https://zeek.org/.

to identify attacks is a time-proven approach in the scientific literature [3,8]. Specifically, we computed each feature for three representations: *i*) *bidirectional*, which includes packets exchanged in both directions of the communication, i.e., source and destination; *ii*) *source-to-destination*, where features are calculated solely on packets sent from the source to the destination; and *iii*) *destination-to-source*, which focuses on packets flowing in the reverse direction. We purposely omitted the IP addresses and ports from the list of features for training and testing our models since these values are either meaningless or easy to spoof and especially to train a more generic model adaptable to every situation, while preserving privacy.

Table 2. Statistical features employed in our methodology. Each statistic has been computed for the bidirectional, source-to-destination, and destination-to-source communications.

FEATURE	UNIT
protocol	
IP version	
flow duration	ms
maximum packet inter-arrival time	
minimum packet inter-arrival time	
mean packet inter-arrival time	
standard deviation packet inter-arrival time	
transmitted bytes	bytes
maximum packet size	
minimum packet size	
mean packet size	
standard deviation packet size	
transmitted packets	packets
TCP packets with ACK set	packets
TCP packets with CWR set	
TCP packets with ECE set	
TCP packets with FIN set	
TCP packets with PSH set	
TCP packets with RST set	
TCP packets with SYN set	
TCP packets with URG set	

Our statistics are based solely on packet timings, and they are computed only by analyzing the IP and TCP headers, which identify a flow in a communication. Moreover, the IP payload is not processed, and, therefore, this approach allows us to be encryption-agnostic with two main advantages. First, our methodology works equally well when the IP payload is encrypted (e.g., with a TLS or DTLS connection). Second, our approach safeguards the users' privacy since the content of the IP packets is never inspected.

Once we built our dataset, we randomly split it into a training and a test set following an 80–20 ratio.

3.3   Model Training

In our experiments, we tested three of the most employed Machine Learning algorithms for network security applications [3,8] using the well-known Python package `scikit-learn`[5]. In particular, the models are tree-based techniques: *i*) a *decision tree*, or single-tree [24], which is a hierarchical model that recursively splits data based on feature conditions to make predictions. Internal nodes represent decisions, and leaf nodes represent outcomes; a *ii*) *random forest* [19] that is an ensemble of multiple decision trees that usually shows improved accuracy over a single tree by carefully deciding how to split the nodes; and *iii*) *extra-trees* (Extremely Randomized Trees) [14], which are also ensembles of trees, but they split the nodes randomly.

For each algorithm, we leveraged `optuna`[6], a well-known hyperparameter optimization framework that helps to automate parameter search, to train four versions of each model given a function to optimize:

- a *default* model, that is, the model trained with the default hyperparameters of `scikit-learn`;
- a *max green* model, that is, the optimized model with the lowest energy consumption at testing time;
- a *max MCC* model, that is, the optimized model with the highest MCC (Matthew's Correlation Coefficient[7]);
- a *balanced* model, that is, the model obtained with a multi-objective optimization to maximize the MCC and minimize the energy consumption. Due to how `optuna` works, we might encounter multiple optimal models. As specified later in Sect. 4.3, we selected the best model as the one that is geometrically closest to the point $(0, 1)$ in the Pareto front, where the first value is the power consumption and the second is the MCC. In other words, a model offering good discriminating capabilities and power saving without sacrificing too much of the two metrics.

To compute consumed energy, we employed **Carbon Tracker** which is, as outlined in Secion 2.1, the best tool at the state of the art able to estimate the actual power usage.

Model optimization was performed based on energy consumption and performance during the testing phase. That is because the ultimate goal is to lower resources for the running algorithm on-premises while the training is performed

---

[5] https://scikit-learn.org/.

[6] https://optuna.org/.

[7] https://scikit-learn.org/stable/modules/generated/sklearn.metrics. matthews_corrcoef.html.

on the server to account for large datasets. Additionally, due to class imbalance, model performance is computed with the Matthew's Correlation Coefficient that considers all four values of the confusion matrix, i.e., True Positives (TP), True Negatives (TN), False Positives (FP), and False Negatives (FN).

Table 3. Specifics of our experimental setup.

CPU	Intel® Core^{TM} i9-11950H CPU @ 2.60GHz
RAM	32 GiB
OS	Debian GNU/Linux
kernel	6.2.10
Python	3.13.1
scikit-learn	1.6.1
optuna	4.2.0
CarbonTracker	2.0.1

4   Results

This Section discusses the results we obtained. In particular, Sect. 4.1 outlines the experimental setup we employed, Sect. 4.2 gives an overview of the obtained general results, Sect. 4.3 concerns the hyperparameter tuning results, and Sect. 4.4 examines the False Negative samples.

4.1   Experimental Setup

The experiments were conducted on a machine equipped with the specifications in Table 3. In this preliminary work, we employed a server machine for both the training and testing phases. First, the server is used in the training for large-scale datasets, which need many resources in terms of memory (RAM), CPU/GPU usage, storage capabilities, and battery life that IoT devices do not support. We preferred to use the server even in the testing phase to ensure reproducibility, precise power measurement, and full control of the experimental setup. As there is a wide variety of different IoT devices and some of them have proprietary systems, achieving large reproducibility, adaptability, and comparison of the results on different systems is difficult because of the different available environments.

In fact, as mentioned in Sect. 4.2, the consumed energy remains low (in the order of μWh), which is in line with the constrained resources of IoT devices [2]. Therefore, while the experiments were conducted on a server, the methodology remains compatible with resource-constrained environments.

Moreover, the measurement of consumption in the server is extremely useful when measuring the consumption of the algorithms for the retraining phase,

Table 4. Hyperparameter chosen by `optuna` for each model.

TYPE	VERSION	HYPERPARAMETER		
		MAX_DEPTH	MIN_LEAF	MIN_SPLIT
single-tree	default	∞	1	2
	max green	1	3	9
	max MCC	14	5	29
	balanced	13	5	13

(a) Hyperparameters for single-tree classifiers.

TYPE	VERSION	HYPERPARAMETER				
		MAX_DEPTH	MIN_LEAF	MIN_SPLIT	MAX_FEAT	ESTIM.
random forest	default	∞	1	2	sqrt	100
	max green	71	7	29	14	10
	max MCC	11	6	17	11	133
	balanced	17	6	20	7	18

(b) Hyperparameters for random forest classifiers.

TYPE	VERSION	HYPERPARAMETER				
		MAX_DEPTH	MIN_LEAF	MIN_SPLIT	MAX_FEAT	ESTIM.
extra trees	default	∞	1	2	sqrt	100
	max green	169	6	18	6	10
	max MCC	18	2	20	23	205
	balanced	14	2	18	24	204

(c) Hyperparameters for extra-trees classifiers.

essential when considering time and space drift. In fact, the retraining phase also affects an economic aspect, i.e., running the algorithm again on new samples and testing its performance, produces more energy consumption that we claim must be regulated by a green ML model. All the energy consumption measurement has obviously an economic effect that for companies must be considered appropriately, also depending on the adopted algorithm and the amount of data.

4.2 Overview

Tables 4 and 5 report the selected hyperparameters by `optuna` for each of the trained models, and the average energy consumption per testing sample and model performance in terms of Matthews' Correlation Coefficient (MCC), balanced accuracy, and F1-score to account for class imbalance in the dataset. These scores are chosen to consider both the dataset imbalance and the need to keep false negatives low to avoid malicious flows going undetected.

Table 5. Performance statistics of our classifiers. In particular, for each model, performance is shown in terms of average μWh per test sample, Matthews' Correlation Coefficient (MCC), Balanced Accuracy, and F1-score.

TYPE	VERSION	μWH	MCC	B. ACC.	F1
single-tree	default	19.35	0.52	94.70	75.46
	max green	6.50	0.23	89.05	6.42
	max MCC	8.13	0.60	95.35	76.11
	balanced	7.93	0.60	95.32	72.10
random forest	default	299.83	0.52	94.68	75.76
	max green	22.72	0.58	95.24	76.70
	max MCC	124.90	0.61	95.33	73.85
	balanced	28.70	0.61	95.33	74.20
extra-trees	default	284.45	0.526	94.69	75.64
	max green	22.04	0.57	95.09	72.26
	max MCC	213.38	0.61	95.33	74.38
	balanced	49.68	0.60	95.24	74.08

Interestingly, the default models offer strong discriminating power, reaching about 99% balanced accuracy and 76% F1-score. However, they are always the most energy-hungry, consuming about 13 times more μWh than their max green counterparts. This is consistent with the default hyperparameters (see Table 4) in scikit-learn, which were chosen to offer good performance in multiple scenarios, completely ignoring power consumption.

As expected, the max green models are the most eco-friendly. However, this version of the single-tree has poor performance with 6% of F1-score and 0.239 of MCC. This suggests that the green model has a weak correlation between its prediction and the label class. These relatively poor results may be caused by optuna selecting a max depth of 1 (see Table 4a), meaning that the model makes a single split based on one feature, oversimplifying the classification. Instead, the other versions of the single-tree seem to be the most efficient and high-performing, even with respect to the other models, i.e., random-forest and extra-trees, which still offer good performance statistics but are highly resource-demanding due to the ensemble nature of these classifiers, which aggregate multiple weak learners, requiring more CPU and memory. Despite the balanced single-tree model has achieved the best performance in terms of MCC and F1-score, while keeping low energy consumption, False Negatives remain high. The reason for these poor results, as discussed in Sect. 4.4, is the presence of port scanning attacks that have similar features with respect to the legitimate flows, causing an overlap with the normal network activity. Indeed, typically, attackers try to mimic normal traffic by using common ports and protocols, and distributing the scanning by different IP addresses.

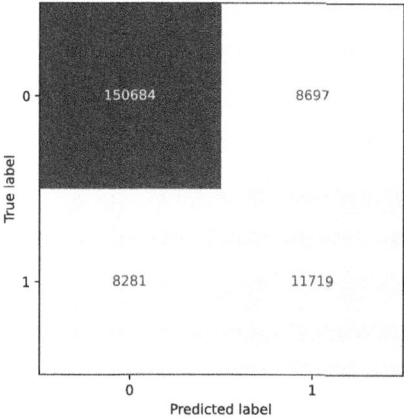

(a) Simplified Confusion Matrix of the balanced single-tree model.

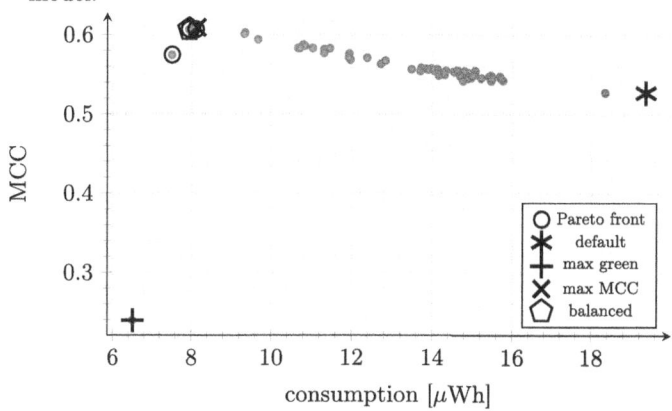

(b) Pareto front for the single-tree models. The x-axis shows the mean energy consumption in terms of μWh, and the y-axis is the MCC score.

Fig. 2. Confusion Matrix and Pareto front for the single-tree models showing classification accuracy and the performance in relation to the consumed energy.

4.3   Optimization of the Balanced Models

This section discusses the hyperparameter tuning process of the balanced version of the selected models. For each optimization, we asked optuna to perform 64 iterations, i.e., the best number of iterations to achieve good optimization. The optimizations aimed to maximize the MCC and minimize the energy footprint during the inference phase. In particular, we refer only to the single-tree model, which was found to be the most efficient and to have the highest performance as outlined in Sect. 4.2. Similar considerations can be made for the other models.

The Pareto front in Fig. 2b helps in understanding how optuna selects the best models. It shows all the single-tree models tested by optuna in a scatter plot, where the points represent the Pareto front, the x-axis is the mean energy consumption per sample, and the y-axis represents the performance in terms of MCC. A solution is considered Pareto-optimal if no other configuration performs better in both objectives simultaneously [29]. Points on the front are non-dominated, meaning improving one metric would negatively impact the other. For example, increasing the MCC beyond a certain point may require a model that consumes significantly more energy, while reducing energy usage might come at the cost of lower classification accuracy. This provides a valuable decision boundary, allowing model selection based on application-specific priorities, such as maximizing accuracy, minimizing energy usage, or achieving a balanced compromise.

The default model (black star) presents high energy consumption (∼19 μWh) with moderate MCC (∼0.53) and, as noticeable even from Table 5, it is not efficient but is a reference point for suboptimal optimizations of the model. The max green (green cross) has the lowest consumption (∼7 μWh), but low MCC (∼0.4), i.e., it is optimized only for energy consumption, suitable only if energy minimization is the priority, and accuracy is less critical. Conversely, the max MCC (red cross) is appropriate when maximizing the performance is critical, even though the consumed energy is not as low as for the green model (∼8 μWh). Finally, the balanced model (blue pentagon) is similar to the max MCC version with similar consumed energy and performance. Indeed, they both remain eco-friendly, maintaining the generalization capability. This means that both max MCC and balanced variants are suitable for running on an IoT device.

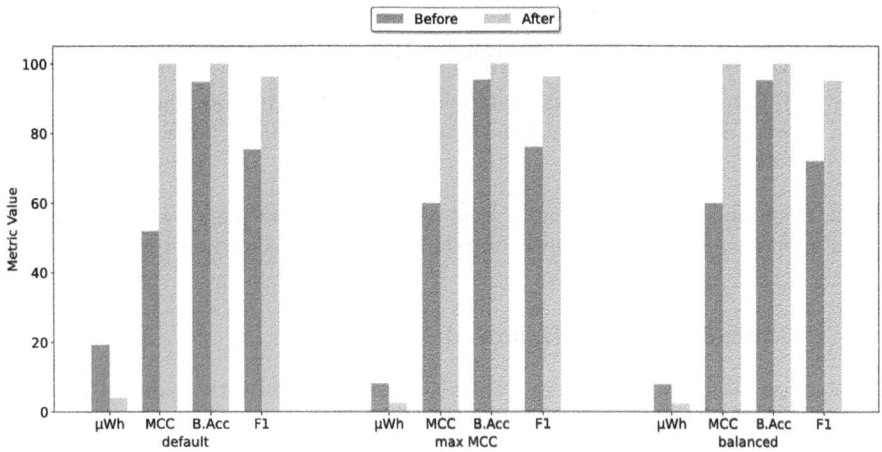

Fig. 3. Comparison between performance of the optimized single-tree models (i.e., default, max MCC, and balanced) before (left bars) and after (right bars) port-scanning attack removal. MCC is multiplied by 100 to be suitable for the graph.

4.4   Error Analysis

As outlined in Sects. 4.2 and 4.3, single-tree model variants are the most efficient both in terms of performance and energy consumption. In particular, the
balanced model, even though similar to the max MCC version, requires fewer
resources and achieves comparable MCC. Figure 2a shows the model confusion
matrix, depicting that legitimate samples are well recognized, while it fails to
clearly recognize a good portion of malicious flows—over 40% of actual true positives are misclassified. Therefore, even though MCC is good, i.e., greater than
0, it is not good enough to be comparable with other works at the state-of-the-
art [11] and requires attention due to the criticality of the application.

Analyzing the dataset and the corresponding features, we found that the
models failed to recognize port-scan attacks whose flows are similar to legitimate ones. Therefore, we conducted a study of methodology performance while
removing port-scan attacks from the dataset in Table 1, training only the single-
tree model, which was the best performing of the three selected algorithms. We
did not optimize the hyperparameters to achieve optimal energy consumption,
as we expected it to have low accuracy.

Figure 3 shows a comparison of single-tree model performance before and
after the removal of port-scan attacks. As noticeable, MCC, Balanced Accuracy
and F1 score increased after removing port-scan attacks while the average consumed μWh reduced. The latter is expected because the less are the flows, the
less complex the model is and therefore less resources are employed.

As before, we analyze the Pareto front in Fig. 4. It includes many points
tightly clustered around low consumption ($\sim$2.3âĂŞ2.6 μWh) with near-perfect
MCC, suggesting that it is possible to reduce energy without compromising the
performance. For example, the max MCC (red cross) offers the absolute best
MCC performance (1.0) but at a slightly higher energy cost, while the balanced
model (blue pentagon) lies on the Pareto front, delivering strong performance

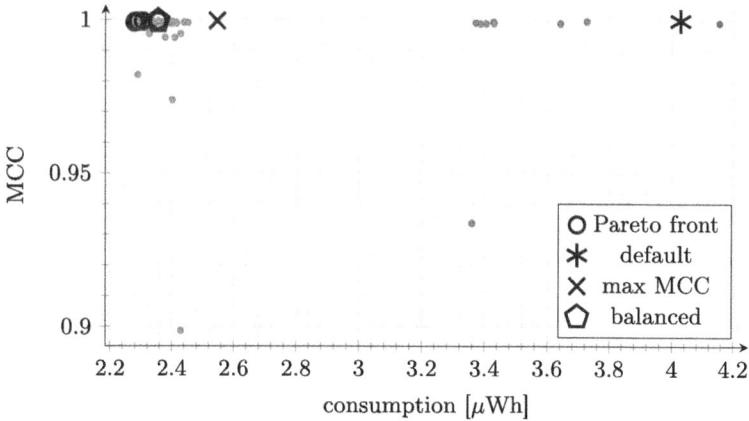

Fig. 4. Pareto front for the single tree model after removing port-scanning flows.

(0.995) with modest energy use (2.35 μWh). On the contrary, the default model (black star), despite achieving a high MCC (0.9997), is inefficient because it consumes significantly more energy than necessary, i.e., $\sim 50\%$ more than the other two versions, for comparable accuracy, as discussed in Sects. 4.2 and 4.3.

5   Conclusion

In this work, we tested the energy efficiency of tree-based Machine Learning algorithms trained to detect malicious network traffic generated by common IoT malware. The methodology is based on flow statistical features to preserve the privacy of legitimate communications. Additionally, we developed an optimization strategy with `optuna` and `Carbon Tracker` based on testing phase performance, considering both power consumption in Wh and MCC, while the training stage does not take power limitations into consideration. The reason is twofold. First, the trained detection algorithms can run on-premises, ideally on constrained IoT devices. Second, reducing the energy impact of the testing stage counteracts energy waste, increases the device operability lifecycle, and reduces the carbon footprint, having effects also on the companies' economy aspect.

We tested the methodology on a dataset consisting of three IoT attacks, reaching interesting results. Indeed, the models maintain high performance while keeping low energy consumption. The balanced version of the models, i.e., models trained to balance both MCC and μWh, attained about 0.60 MCC and a reduction of $60 - 90\%$ in consumed resources compared to the models trained with the default hyperparameters. These results suggest that ML-based IDS systems are suitable for running on-premise devices. Additionally, we studied the model errors and found that the dataset has biases with respect to port-scanning attacks, which have similar features to legitimate traffic flows.

However, the proposed approach still has some limitations. It is tested on only one dataset, limiting generalizability with respect to different network topologies and attacks. Additionally, the experimental setup lacks a constrained device to run the trained model to compute energy efficiency. Indeed, the optimization of the hyperparameters with respect to the testing phase results is done on the same server where the models are trained. However, results show that the consumed energy is suitable for constrained devices. Despite the results showing that the consumed energy is suitable for constrained devices, the feasibility of the approach on them is only theoretical. Therefore, we plan in the future to test the approach on constrained devices such as smartphones or IoT systems to reveal unforeseen challenges on deployment.

In the future, we plan to improve our methodology with live analysis to test energy efficiency and inspect incoming network streaming. Additionally, we will test the approach with Deep Learning algorithms, which are more energy-demanding than the tree-based algorithms we selected. Indeed, the usage of a Deep Learning algorithm may be necessary to increase the identification capability, while keeping a low energy consumption on constrained devices.

Acknowledgements. This work was carried out while Silvia Lucia Sanna was enrolled in the Italian National Doctorate on Artificial Intelligence run by Sapienza University of Rome in collaboration with the University of Cagliari.

References

1. What is the Mirai botnet? (2025). https://www.cloudflare.com/it-it/learning/ddos/glossary/mirai-botnet/
2. Atzori, L., Iera, A., Morabito, G.: The Internet of Things: a survey. Comput. Netw. **54**(15), 2787–2805 (2010). https://doi.org/10.1016/j.comnet.2010.05.010
3. Bader, O., Lichy, A., Hajaj, C., Dubin, R., Dvir, A.: MalDIST: from encrypted traffic classification to malware traffic detection and classification. In: 2022 IEEE 19th Annual Consumer Communications and Networking Conference (CCNC), pp. 527–533 (2022). https://doi.org/10.1109/CCNC49033.2022.9700625
4. Barradas, D., Novo, C., Portela, B., Romeiro, S., Santos, N.: Extending c2 traffic detection methodologies: from TLS 1.2 to TLS 1.3-enabled malware. In: Proceedings of the 27th International Symposium on Research in Attacks, Intrusions and Defenses. RAID '24, Association for Computing Machinery, New York, (2024). https://doi.org/10.1145/3678890.3678921
5. Bilge, L., Balzarotti, D., Robertson, W., Kirda, E., Kruegel, C.: Disclosure: detecting botnet command and control servers through large-scale netflow analysis. In: Proceedings of the 28th Annual Computer Security Applications Conference, pp. 129–138. ACSAC '12, Association for Computing Machinery, New York (2012). https://doi.org/10.1145/2420950.2420969
6. Budennyy, S., et al.: eco2AI: carbon emissions tracking of machine learning models as the first step towards sustainable AI. Dokl. Math. (2022). https://doi.org/10.1134/S1064562422060230
7. Business, T.: 'Hide'n seek' botnet uses peer-to-peer infrastructure to compromise IoT devices (2018). https://www.trendmicro.com/vinfo/us/security/news/internet-of-things/-hide-n-seek-botnet-uses-peer-to-peer-infrastructure-to-compromise-iot-devices
8. Canavese, D., Regano, L., Basile, C., Ciravegna, G., Lioy, A.: Encryption-agnostic classifiers of traffic originators and their application to anomaly detection. Comput. Electr. Eng. **97**, 107621 (2022). https://doi.org/10.1016/j.compeleceng.2021.107621
9. Candelieri, A., Ponti, A., Archetti, F.: Fair and green hyperparameter optimization via multi-objective and multiple information source Bayesian optimization. Mach. Learn. **113** (2024). https://doi.org/10.1007/s10994-024-06515-0
10. Churcher, A., et al.: An experimental analysis of attack classification using machine learning in IoT networks. Sensors **21**(2) (2021). https://doi.org/10.3390/s21020446
11. Davanian, A., Faloutsos, M., Lindorfer, M.: C2miner: Tricking IoT malware into revealing live command and control servers. In: Proceedings of the 19th ACM Asia Conference on Computer and Communications Security. ASIA CCS '24, Association for Computing Machinery, New York (2024). https://doi.org/10.1145/3634737.3644992
12. García-Martín, E., Lavesson, N., Grahn, H., Casalicchio, E., Boeva, V.: How to measure energy consumption in machine learning algorithms. In: ECML PKDD 2018 Workshops, pp. 243–255. Springer International Publishing, Cham (2019). https://doi.org/10.1007/978-3-030-13453-2_20

13. García-Martín, E., Rodrigues, C.F., Riley, G., Grahn, H.: Estimation of energy consumption in machine learning. J. Parallel Distrib. Comput. **134**, 75–88 (2019). https://doi.org/10.1016/j.jpdc.2019.07.007

14. Geurst, P., Ernst, D., Wehenkel, L.: Extremely randomized trees. Mach. Learn. **63** (2006). https://doi.org/10.1007/s10994-006-6226-1

15. Huong, T.T., et al.: LocKedge: low-complexity cyberattack detection in IoT edge computing. IEEE Access **9**, 29696–29710 (2021). https://doi.org/10.1109/ACCESS.2021.3058528

16. Ioannou, I., et al.: GEMLIDS-MIOT: a green effective machine learning intrusion detection system based on federated learning for medical IoT network security hardening. Comput. Commun. **218** (2024).https://doi.org/10.1016/j.comcom.2024.02.023

17. Jia, Y., Zhong, F., Alrawais, A., Gong, B., Cheng, X.: FlowGuard: an intelligent edge defense mechanism against IoT DDoS attacks. IEEE Internet Things J. **7**(10), 9552–9562 (2020). https://doi.org/10.1109/JIOT.2020.2993782

18. Kumar, R., Swarnkar, M., Singal, G., Kumar, N.: IoT network traffic classification using machine learning algorithms: an experimental analysis. IEEE Internet Things J. **9**(2), 989–1008 (2022). https://doi.org/10.1109/JIOT.2021.3121517

19. Liu, Y., Wang, Y., Zhang, J.: New machine learning algorithm: random forest. In: Liu, B., Ma, M., Chang, J. (eds.) ICICA 2012. LNCS, vol. 7473, pp. 246–252. Springer, Heidelberg (2012). https://doi.org/10.1007/978-3-642-34062-8_32

20. Keertikumar, M., Shubham, M., Banakar, R.: Evolution of IoT in smart vehicles: an overview. In: 2015 International Conference on Green Computing and Internet of Things (ICGCIoT), pp. 804–809 (2015). https://doi.org/10.1109/ICGCIoT.2015.7380573

21. Meneghello, F., Calore, M., Zucchetto, D., Polese, M., Zanella, A.: IoT: internet of threats? A survey of practical security vulnerabilities in real IoT devices. IEEE Internet Things J. **6**(5), 8182–8201 (2019). https://doi.org/10.1109/JIOT.2019.2935189

22. Modarress, F.B., Ansari, A., Al, A.: Threats of Internet-of-Thing on environmental sustainability by e-waste. Sustainability (2022). https://doi.org/10.3390/su141610161

23. Mukhtar, B.I., Elsayed, M.S., Jurcut, A.D., Azer, M.A.: IoT vulnerabilities and attacks: silex malware case study. Symmetry **15**(11) (2023).https://doi.org/10.3390/sym15111978

24. Navada, A., Ansari, A.N., Patil, S., Sonkamble, B.A.: Overview of use of decision tree algorithms in machine learning. In: 2011 IEEE Control and System Graduate Research Colloquium, pp. 37–42 (2011). https://doi.org/10.1109/ICSGRC.2011.5991826

25. Schiller, E., et al.: Landscape of IoT security. Comput. Sci. Rev. **44**, 100467 (2022). https://doi.org/10.1016/j.cosrev.2022.100467

26. Garcia, S., Agustin Parmisano, M.J.E.: IoT-23: a labeled dataset with malicious and benign IoT network traffic https://doi.org/10.5281/zenodo.4743746

27. Tekin, N., Acar, A., Aris, A., Uluagac, A.S., Gungor, V.C.: Energy consumption of on-device machine learning models for IoT intrusion detection. Internet Things **21**, 100670 (2023). https://doi.org/10.1016/j.iot.2022.100670

28. Tripp, C.E., et al.: Measuring the energy consumption and efficiency of deep neural networks: an empirical analysis and design recommendations (2024). https://doi.org/10.48550/arXiv.2403.08151

29. Tušar, T., Filipič, B.: Visualization of pareto front approximations in evolutionary multiobjective optimization: a critical review and the prosection method. IEEE Trans. Evol. Comput. **19**(2), 225–245 (2015). https://doi.org/10.1109/TEVC.2014.2313407

30. Vijayan, J.: 'torii' breaks new ground for IoT malware (2018). https://www.darkreading.com/cyberattacks-data-breaches/-torii-breaks-new-ground-for-iot-malware

31. Wang, H.: An evolutionary study of IoT malware. IEEE Internet Things J. **8**(20), 15422–15440 (2021). https://doi.org/10.1109/JIOT.2021.3063840

32. Xu, L.D., He, W., Li, S.: Internet of things in industries: a survey. IEEE Trans. Industr. Inf. **10**(4), 2233–2243 (2014). https://doi.org/10.1109/TII.2014.2300753

33. Yarally, T., Cruz, L., Feitosa, D., Sallou, J., van Deursen, A.: Uncovering energy-efficient practices in deep learning training: preliminary steps towards green AI. In: 2023 IEEE/ACM 2nd International Conference on AI Engineering – Software Engineering for AI (CAIN), pp. 25–36 (2023). https://doi.org/10.1109/CAIN58948.2023.00012

34. Yokoyama, A.M., Ferro, M., Schulze, B.: A multi-objective hyperparameter optimization for machine learning using genetic algorithms: A green AI centric approach. In: Bicharra Garcia, A.C., Ferro, M., Rodríguez Ribón, J.C. (eds.) Advances in Artificial Intelligence – IBERAMIA 2022. Springer International Publishing (2022). https://doi.org/10.1007/978-3-031-22419-5_12

Towards A Capability Model of Kubernetes Runtime Security Enforcement Mechanisms

Francesco Settanni$^{(\boxtimes)}$, Giuseppe Lisena , and Cataldo Basile

Politecnico di Torino, Torino, Italy
{francesco.settanni,giuseppe.lisena,cataldo.basile}@polito.it

Abstract. The shift toward cloud-native and microservice-based architectures has made Kubernetes the de facto platform for managing containerized applications. However, its limited native support for security features has led to the proliferation of diverse enforcement mechanisms, such as Cilium, Calico, Tetragon, and KubeArmor. These tools vary in capabilities and configuration, complicating the establishment of an effective security posture. This work proposes a conceptual model that abstracts runtime security enforcement across these tools, enabling intent-based security policy design and automation. We present a model-driven approach to bridge high-level security requirements with low-level enforcement configurations. Our approach facilitates cloud portability, simplifies policy refinement, and enhances security consistency for heterogeneous environments. Validation across real-world microservice architectures and security policy catalogs demonstrates its practicality and effectiveness.

Keywords: Kubernetes · security enforcement · cloud security · network policy · Cilium · Calico · Tetragon · KubeArmor

1 Introduction

The approach to security in modern network environments and infrastructures is a continuously evolving discipline. With the advent of cloud-native architectures and increasingly distributed hybrid and multi-cloud environments, new paradigms have been devised to counteract emerging attack methodologies and risks inherent to these architectures. Pursuing zero-trust capabilities in such environments has driven significant innovation in technologies and approaches for enforcing security, particularly since traditional perimeter-based defenses are ill-suited to their highly distributed nature. This shift has necessitated relocating security policy enforcement closer to the core operational units. Trust zones are no longer bastion-based but revolve around the smallest software units in which microservices are deployed, namely, the pods [11].

B. Coppens et al. (Eds.): ARES 2025 Workshops, LNCS 15994, pp. 266–284, 2025.
https://doi.org/10.1007/978-3-032-00630-1_15

Kubernetes (K8s) has emerged as one of the most widely used microservice orchestrators. It effectively manages the dynamic nature of microservice-based cloud architectures, ensuring agility and scalability in complex deployments.

While K8s is valued for its ability to manage software resources effectively, it also introduces significant challenges for developers and engineers. Many aspects of K8s environments remain the responsibility of end users, necessitating the design and deployment of extension mechanisms on top of vanilla installations. Although these mechanisms provide useful features, they often introduce additional complexities exacerbated by the myriad of overlapping solutions, each with its own unique characteristics.

This is particularly evident in runtime security enforcement, with the market not yet mature and the adoption of effective solutions stalling. K8s provides limited native support for security enforcement at runtime, especially regarding network security. Specifically, it declares the APIs for basic network restriction functionalities but leaves their implementation to the underlying network infrastructure provider. As a result, a diverse ecosystem of tools, such as CNI (Container Network Interface) plugins, operators, and other extension mechanisms, has emerged. These tools work in conjunction with K8s orchestrator to enforce security policies effectively.

Despite the availability of such tools, integrating them with K8s often presents challenges. These tools must be tailored to the underlying Kubernetes infrastructure or cloud provider and validated against the specific features required by the deployed services. This is particularly crucial in telco scenarios, where fine-grained control over the network stack is often necessary [13].

These tools often provide varying functionalities and levels of configurability for the aspects they cover, such as network-based isolation. These differences arise from the enforcement mechanisms, which may not support comprehensive or fine-grained control mechanisms or require deep expertise to configure effectively. As a result, security intents may be implemented inconsistently, making it difficult to maintain a coherent and unified security posture across diverse environments.

The persistent complexity of cloud-native systems emerges as a primary challenge across all stages of adoption, underscoring the growing intricacy of managing increasingly integral and distributed architectures [5]. As organizations expand their reliance on cloud infrastructures, regulatory compliance becomes progressively demanding. This is due not only to the inherently dynamic nature of these environments but also to a shift in security responsibility, from predominantly technical controls to broader organizational governance. Compliance efforts are increasingly assessed against established frameworks, with particular emphasis on zero-trust principles, which are both widely recommended and, in some cases, mandated by contemporary standards [11]. Furthermore, the exposure to security incidents in cloud contexts is increasingly important. This vulnerability is largely attributed to the transient and rapidly changing nature of cloud components, which can hinder the enforcement of uniform security policies and create exploitable inconsistencies [5].

The goal of our research is to provide an actionable model of the security capabilities of the enforcement mechanisms available in K8s through the available tools and CNI plugins. This model must also abstract the configuration details exposed by the enforcement mechanisms. Such modelling would facilitate the adoption of the automatic enforcement of high-level security intents in cloud environments, as it would provide transparent access to security functionality agnostic of the enforcement mechanisms available.

Towards this goal, this paper presents the systematization of concepts related to runtime security enforcement in K8s-orchestrated environments. We introduce a conceptual framework that formally models the commonalities and differences among widely used and emerging security tools. The contributions of our research are:

1. an analysis of the runtime security enforcement capabilities in K8s and a *formal model* capturing the findings. To the best of our knowledge, this is the first attempt to systematize runtime security enforcement in K8s;
2. an *analyzer*, that, from an input K8s cluster, provides an abstract representation of the security requirements implemented. This analyzer also reports the full list of tools available in the K8s ecosystem among the ones we modelled, that are able to enforce them;
3. a *translator* that generates the low-level configuration for a target security tool from an abstract representation of the desired security requirements.

We then demonstrate how this conceptualization enables the automation of security management tasks, particularly in policy translation and intent-based security management. First, our approach facilitates service migration between cloud providers, even when each relies on a different subset of security mechanisms to enforce security policies. Second, we propose a method for generating security configurations for microservice architectures based on high-level security requirements, leveraging cloud-native enforcement mechanisms.

The rest of the paper is organized as follows. Section 2 provides background on K8s security enforcement and related research. Section 3 summarizes the analysis we conducted on K8s security mechanisms and our conceptualization approach. Section 4 and 5 present the model architecture, the components, and workflow our PoC implements. Section 6 explains the validation we performed to assess the effectiveness of our proposal and the performance penalties it adds. Section 7 draws conclusions and provides hints for future works.

2   Background and Related Works

In cloud-native environments, K8s is the de facto orchestrator to deploy and manage the life cycle of microservices. Several managed cloud solutions build upon vanilla K8s, particularly those offered by major cloud providers, by extending its functionalities or supplying the underlying network plumbing to the K8s cluster. K8s, in fact, on its own, lacks basic networking functionalities, which are instead implemented via CNI plugins, hereafter referred to simply as plugins. Plugins are one of several extension mechanisms offering additional or advanced functionalities. Plugins, in particular, provide pod connectivity, injecting network interfaces into the pods' namespaces and configuring them. The K8s network architecture follows a novel paradigm to guarantee interconnection among pods and services across namespaces and nodes [8].

CNI plugins are also modular, in that they can be used in conjunction, resulting in hybrid solutions where each plugin provides specific functionalities. A well-known example was Canal, which combined two plugins: Calico for enabling network policies and Flannel for basic connectivity. This possibility has, however, been deprecated in the last versions of Flannel. At the same time, a community project[1] with goals set among several K8s SIG working groups (Special Interest Groups) has introduced a basic network policy implementation based on netfilter, albeit still in development and not appropriate for production use. We anticipate that this implementation will target scenarios where the plugin in use lacks network policy enforcement capabilities, such as Flannel.

Performance comparison of plugins has been proposed by Qi et al. [10], attributing the observed differences to network stack interactions and proposing other useful technical considerations to select one plugin over another.

Additional ways to extend the API-enabled infrastructure provided by K8s include *controllers*, *operators*, and *service meshes*. Each extends the platform's capabilities to address specific needs beyond standard features, such as pod connectivity across nodes and channel protection.

These mechanisms introduce new resources implemented according to the Custom Resource Definition (CRD) specification, which enables the extension of the K8s declarative API. Operators continuously reconcile the current state with the desired state of these resources by taking appropriate actions [2,15]. Operators and controllers are mainly for resource management and orchestration without a clear focus on security. They have been hence excluded from our model.

Service meshes provide functionality by attaching an additional software layer to pods, abstracting certain tasks away from the core application logic. This is typically achieved by deploying a proxy container alongside each pod exposing a service, using the sidecar pattern. The proxy extends the service's functionality without requiring modifications to the application itself.

Service meshes primarily focus on application-level features such as authentication and authorization, service discovery, traffic management (e.g., load balancing), and observability across services. When it comes to security functionalities, service meshes present severe limitations from an infrastructure layer perspective, as they are designed to manage application services rather than individual pod entities. In fact, service meshes typically operate on top of the network infrastructure provided by the cluster's CNI plugin. As a result, they follow and are constrained by the network rules enforced by that plugin. Even if Layer 7 authorization policies are configured through the service mesh, they will have no effect if the underlying CNI network policies are not aligned.

---

[1] https://github.com/kubernetes-sigs/kube-network-policies.

For these reasons, service meshes have not been explicitly included in our model, they are only considered when they are used by the tools in the scope of our analysis as a way to implement layer 7 features (as it will be explained in Sect. 3.

This shift in networking design inherently introduces new security risks and needs. Some derive from microservice architectures' highly distributed nature, and others stem from K8s one. Several studies have explored the security implications, challenges, and potential mitigations in K8s-orchestrated environments. A primary focus has been on the security of the orchestrator infrastructure, as it serves as the central component overseeing the life cycle of managed resources. More recently, the security of the services deployed has also been investigated [4,17]. While the security issues plaguing microservice architecture are investigated, laying the groundwork for the definition of appropriate threat models and their mitigative measures, the ways to enact them are only covered iteratively. Nam et al. [9] propose a network stack specifically designed to address fundamental issues in cloud-native network architectures. Their work, along with other related studies, builds upon a substantial body of research in traditional and software-defined networking. They often focus on proposing frameworks for optimized performance from a networking standpoint or target specific categories of security issues and attacks, with mitigative approaches suited specifically for those. Other research has focused on comparing prominent open-source security tools based on their technical implementation [16], but still, they are mainly concerned with performance evaluation, particularly on their observability and monitoring functionality, rather than assessing the actual features exposed by the tools and their capabilities. Our work instead focuses on systematizing the latter.

The growing adoption of eBPF in the last few years, initially for observability and later for enforcement, highlights the increasing interest in leveraging kernel-level mechanisms to provide native security enforcement within K8s environments. Alongside eBPF, Linux Security Modules (LSM), far predating K8s, originally designed to integrate Mandatory Access Control (MAC) capabilities within the Linux kernel, have seen similar interest. Despite the strengths of these solutions, they are often challenging to configure, given their low-level nature.

Many solutions have been proposed recently to leverage the ePBF capabilities available in recent versions of the Linux kernel. Notable examples include KubeArmor and Tetragon, which are standalone security tools providing observability and runtime enforcement functionalities such as file access control, process execution permissions, and network-based access control and isolation. They gained traction within the cloud-native community as they coupled several novel capabilities with an ease of use, serving as an extension mechanism for K8s. Similarly, plugins have expanded their scope, introducing network security functionalities. Cilium and Calico have notably expanded upon the standard K8s network policy specification by increasing rule granularity and enabling control over additional resources.

3   K8s Runtime Security Enforcement Analysis

Enabling automated management of security within K8s environments requires the ability to accurately describe the features that each (SM) can provide and the precision in enforcing them into the operational environment. Moreover, it requires expressing authorization rules to allow their correct configuration.

The abstract model we have built conceptualizes the capabilities and behavior of the SMs based on a thorough analysis of the current solutions and their limitations, features, and granularity.

We analyzed and modeled five SMs, selected based on their feature sets and adoption: *Calico* (v3.28.1), *Cilium* (1.16.5), *KubeArmor* (v1.4.9), *Tetragon* (v1.3.0), and the vanilla K8s network policies model (v1.25.0). The latter is not a standalone SM, but rather represents the default policy specification interface exposed by K8s. It offers a more limited subset of features compared to the other SMs, and requires a dedicated enforcement backend, e.g., a SM, to implement the rules defined using its specification language. Most plugin SMs support the standard K8s network policy API alongside their proprietary extensions, to maintain compatibility. This is true both for Calico and Cilium. Despite its limitations, it remains the official mechanism for specifying network policies in K8s and defines a baseline security model that has been adopted by several other SM.

As previously noted, Flannel, despite its popularity due to being bundled with many lightweight K8s clusters, does not support network policies and was therefore excluded from the analysis. However, complementary enforcement solutions, such as the one previously mentioned, currently being developed within the scope of various K8s SIGs, adhere to the vanilla K8s specification, thereby highlighting its continued relevance as the canonical policy definition model in K8s.

Cilium is built around eBPF. Using it, both the `CiliumNetworkPolicy` and vanilla K8s `NetworkPolicy` rules are enforced by injecting eBPF bytecode directly into the kernel. Layer 7 network policies, however, are enforced via the Envoy proxy, a node-local instance through which traffic is proxied to enforce Layer 7 policies.

Calico operates using either the standard Linux data plane, i.e., by translating network policies into *iptables* rules, or with eBPF, injecting eBPF bytecode similarly to Cilium. Calico is offered in three distinct versions: Open-Source, Cloud, and Enterprise. Our analysis considered only the free version, but feature support, particularly for advanced features, varies between versions. In particular, Layer 7 policies differ in availability and enforcement approach, which will be briefly discussed later in this section.

Tetragon and KubeArmor can enforce restrictions on processes, file access, and network operations by regulating the system-level behavior within pods. KubeArmor relies on Linux Security Modules (LSMs), such as AppArmor and BPF-LSM. The latter is a recently introduced kernel capability that integrates eBPF with LSM hooks. Tetragon, on the other hand, relies entirely on eBPF with a custom implementation for kernel-level enforcement.

Our analysis categorized the analyzed features according to the three main operational defensive techniques in the *Isolate* tactic of the MITRE D3FEND framework [6] (v1.0.0): *Network Isolation, Access Policy Administration,* and *Execution Isolation.* Figure 1 summarizes the main analysis findings. These concepts are the basic elements of the model presented in Sect. 4.

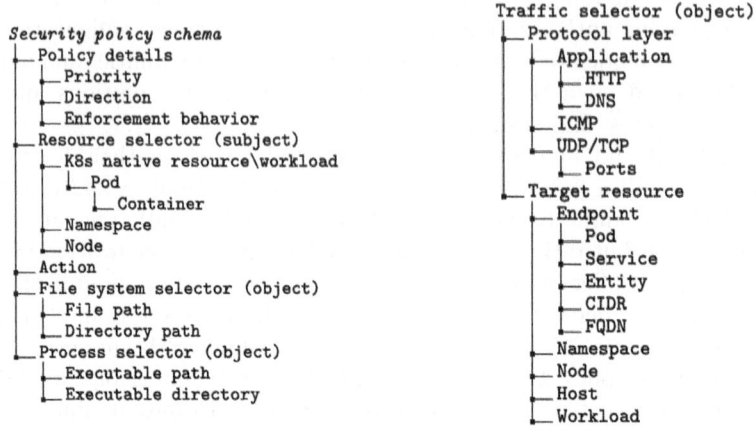

Fig. 1. Summary of the main policy concepts

3.1   Network Isolation Capabilities

The network-based capabilities are the richest and most complex provided by the SMs we analyzed. They are composed of different elements. The *resource selector* selects the entity, typically pods, that is targeted by the policy, that is, the entity for which network restrictions are defined. Then, the *object selector* identifies the traffic targeted by the policy action with a list of rules selecting the other end of the communication channel, the type, and details of the selected traffic. The *resource selector* identifies the entity to be protected, typically pods. The *object selector* then identifies the traffic targeted by the policy action through a set of rules that specify the other end of the communication channel, the traffic type, and other details of the selected traffic. This element is where most of the specification's granularity resides.

Then, the *action element* specifies what happens on the pinpointed objects of the identified resource, such as denying or logging the communication. Other traffic concepts are used to configure SMs, such as the communication direction and fundamental policy enforcement behaviors, such as policy resolution strategies and allow-deny listing behavior.

The most widely used plugins are currently also the most feature-rich SMs. Network policies enforced by plugins typically use an allow-list approach to implement restrictions. By default, each pod can communicate with any other pod without restriction. As soon as a network policy selects a pod, only the selected traffic, in that specific direction, will be allowed. This is typically referred to as the "default-deny" behavior. Vanilla K8s network policies, together with plugin network policy specifications, adhere to it.

KubeArmor and Tetragon also provide network restrictions, albeit with significantly looser granularity and reduced functionality. The former enforces network policies at the container level by configuring the behavior of system calls for network operations (e.g., `bind()`, `listen()`, `accept()`, and `connect()`). For Cilium, we considered only the `CiliumNetworkPolicy` resource and left the `ClusterWide` to future work. The same applies to Calico's managed resources capabilities. Tetragon has similar functionalities but doesn't offer a high-level interface, requiring individual rules for the system calls involved in the target network operation. Moreover we haven't considered cross-cluster policies, that require the Cluster Mesh functionality, both in Cilium and Calico, the latter limited to the enterprise version. The other two SMs do not support multi-cluster functionalities.

The following paragraphs summarize some of the main findings concerning the network isolation capabilities we modeled.

Priority. Cilium network policies have only two priority levels, whereas deny policies take precedence over allow ones. In Calico, the priority can be set freely with an integer instead. The resulting behavior in the network for a specific traffic *event* is derived from the union of all deny and allow policies, with their respective precedence order. The vanilla K8s specification instead lacks an explicit priority field, thus, their effect is determined by the union of all policies selecting a specific pod.

Selector Mechanisms. In K8s, given the ephemeral nature of pods, the resource and traffic selection in policies typically use labels instead of IP addresses to cope with IP address changes. Hereafter, when we refer to pod selection, we mean the case in which a policy targets a pod, i.e., when the policy includes that specific pod in its subject or resource selector field. Entities external to the cluster can be referenced by traditional identifiers such as IP addresses or Fully Qualified Domain Names (FQDNs). Both analyzed plugins support this, while KubeArmor does not support specifying the destination endpoint. Vanilla K8s policies only support K8s-native `LabelSelector` for traffic endpoint selection. However, Calico support for DNS-based policy through FQDN selectors for the destination endpoint is limited to the enterprise versions. Whereas Calico has a single selector supporting multiple entities, Cilium uses multiple sub-selectors, each used for different types of entities. Both plugins also support non-K8s-native entities, typically relevant in managed environments. For example, Cilium's entity selector allows the specification of network infrastructure components such as the K8s API server, health endpoints, and external networks. A current limitation in our mapping concerns application-layer capabilities, which are currently limited to HTTP and DNS. However, Cilium supports additional protocols via the Envoy proxy, such as gRPC and Kafka (the latter currently in beta). Furthermore, Cilium provides a framework to extend its capabilities by supporting additional

Layer 7 protocols, including custom ones, through Envoy, by allowing the definition and implementation of the appropriate custom parsing logic. This feature remains in beta at the time of writing, but significant community contributions are expected to expand support for more Layer 7 protocols in the future.

Protocol Support. The main distinction at the network level lies between plugins and standalone tools. Plugins provide higher-level protocol support at Layer 7 (L7), whereas tools like KubeArmor and Tetragon do not. Specifically, these tools do not natively support the definition of application-layer policies, such as those targeting specific HTTP methods, paths, or headers, as they operate at lower levels of the network stack (i.e., L3/L4 and system call level). For example, KubeArmor supports rules for TCP, UDP, and ICMP traffic. Both Cilium and Calico support L3/L4 network policies. However, in terms of L7 protocols, Cilium is more advanced, as previously noted. It supports multiple application-layer protocols and allows for extensibility. Cilium also supports L7 DNS policies, which define rules for DNS queries themselves. These are distinct rules from the ones using fully qualified domain names (FQDNs) merely as selectors in L3/L4 policies. Vanilla K8s policies support TCP, UDP, and SCTP. Calico's support for L7 policies merits further discussion. Our analysis reveals that the technical implementation differs between the open-source version and other editions. In the open-source version, L7 policy enforcement requires deploying the Istio service mesh within the cluster. In this configuration, each pod is paired with an Envoy sidecar proxy, through which traffic is tunneled and policy enforcement is enabled. In contrast, other Calico versions appear to use an internal implementation for L7 policy support, similar to Cilium. In the first case, the policy capabilities are tied to those offered by Istio, whereas in the latter, a proprietary specification is provided. We hypothesize that these architectural differences may also result in significant performance variations. However, to the best of our research, no detailed performance comparisons have been presented in the literature.

Granularity of Rules. With KubeArmor, fine-grained rules at the process level can be enforced, enabling network restrictions targeting singular executables specified in the policy, which is a unique feature among the SMs we analyzed. But, on the other hand, its functionalities are particularly limited regarding the traffic selection as it does not allow specifying ports but only protocol specification. Similarly, Tetragon allows defining low-level rules targeting even specific system calls being used. We found these functionalities only in these standalone tools, as plugins typically expose higher-level APIs, hence with a higher-level interface.

Enforcement Behavior and Supported Actions. An important feature recently introduced in both Cilium and Calico is the use of deny rules. These rules allow for expressing policies with a deny-listing behavior rather than the default allow-listing approach. However, there are differences between the two plugins. In Calico, the action field within each rule specifies whether traffic should be allowed or denied, regardless of the policy's direction. In contrast, Cilium uses direction-specific fields, `ingressDeny` and `egressDeny`, to specify dedicated deny rules to block traffic explicitly. Additionally, deny rules in Cilium do not support L7 rules, and also the use of FQDN entity selectors in the traffic selector of L3/L4 policy rules. Importantly, we note that plugins follow an allow-list model that triggers default-deny behavior as soon as a policy selects a pod, even when using deny policies. This means that once a deny rule selects a pod in a given direction and specifies that certain traffic is forbidden, all other traffic is also denied and dropped by default, unless it matches at least one allow rule. This behavior may be undesirable and can be avoided, for example, by accompanying deny rules with a global allow rule for each pod targeted by such policies. This approach effectively enables a deny-listing model for restricting network access. Vanilla K8s network policies, by contrast, do not support deny rules at all. In Cilium, alternatively, the allow-list behavior can be disabled via the *enableDefaultDeny* setting, which allows disabling it per direction. In that case, deny policies can be used without automatically dropping non-targeted traffic, eliminating the need to add a global allow rule alongside every deny rule within a pod policy. However, at the time of writing, *enableDefaultDeny* does not apply to L7 policies. Calico supports the `Log` action, disabling enforcement to monitor the selected traffic. This option is not supported at the same level in other SMs. For example, in Cilium, there's a global `Audit` option with similar behavior, but that can be enabled per cluster and directly on the CNI daemon. Once activated, the enforcement of the applied policies is turned off. KubeArmor supports both deny and allow listing with `Block` and `Allow`, and an audit mode with the `Audit` action.

3.2   File Access Restriction Capabilities

These capabilities are currently only supported by two of the SMs we analyzed, Tetragon and KubeArmor. The policy they support enables defining path-specific file access restrictions and pinpointing the protection of individual sensitive files, such as configuration files, certificates, or credentials. Directory-based controls enable broader protection across entire directory trees.

These restrictions can be applied at the pod level, ensuring that all processes run within their context comply with the policy or with higher precision for specific executables run within the pod. Both SMs support `Allow`, `Block`, and `Audit` actions. KubeArmor has native support for those actions.

With Tetragon, it is necessary to craft a low-level policy for handling syscalls instead. In particular, this can be done either by altering the return value of a function to prevent its execution or by sending signals, such as `SIGKILL`, to terminate processes that meet specific criteria. Depending on the desired behavior, a policy can use an override or signal action, which can also be combined. In our case, we mapped the generic `Deny` action as a combination of `SIGKILL` and `Override` of the return value with -1. The generic `Allow` and `Log` actions are mapped, respectively, to Tetragon's `NoPost` and `Post`.

3.3   Process Execution Restriction Capabilities

The process execution restriction capability modeling and its translation behavior follow the same pattern as the file restrictions, since they operate on file system elements. KubeArmor process restriction can be enforced by specifying the `Allow`, `Block`, or `Audit` action.

Tetragon process restriction follows the same pattern as the file access restriction capabilities in that the limits are enforced by manipulating the system calls used for the operation. Hence, we do not repeat the detailed explanation here. The only difference between process and file access restriction capabilities lies in the system calls targeted by the policies.

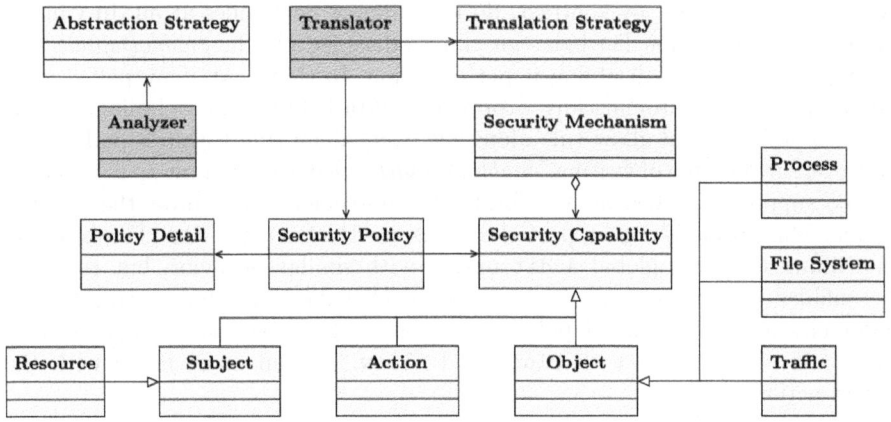

Fig. 2. Model architecture

4   The Model

The model categorizes the concepts to specify policies that drive the behavior of K8s SMs, as shown in Fig. 2. This abstract model systematizes the security features that can be enforced through the SMs we've analyzed and the rules they rely on to configure them.

A *Security Policy* refers to one or many *Security Capabilities* and additional *Enforcement Details* that better determine the way a policy will be evaluated and enforced [3].

The model design is based on a hierarchical scheme with high-level concepts representing the features provided by SMs, regardless of the configuration details required to implement them properly. Within each high-level concept, low-level characteristics are represented by subclassing the higher-level entity, further refining the feature with increasing levels of granularity. Security policies are statements expressed according to the *subject-action-object* authorization policy paradigm [14]. Hence, each security capability is categorized according to the *Subject*, *Object*, and *Action* classes. The subjects determine the K8s resources on which the policy applies, and objects clarify the entities on which the authorization action needs to be enforced. The objects identified by our analysis have been determined via subclassing using the *Traffic*, *File System* and *Process* classes. The two tasks, further described in Sect. 5, that the model allows to perform are represented in this model. Indeed, the model includes the *Analyzer (AZ)* and *Translator (TR)*, and their configuration details, i.e., the *Abstraction Strategy* and the *Translation Strategy*.

5   Implementation

We implemented a proof-of-concept for exploiting the security enforcement capabilities our model exposes with the *AZ* and the *TR*. Both tools have been developed as standalone Python modules.

The functional architecture of our tools is presented in Fig. 3. The *AZ* gathers all network policies applied within a K8s cluster using the K8s APIs. The collected information is represented as an instance of our Abstract Model. It includes the concrete values of the policy and the target SM.

The *TR* gets as input abstract policies. The administrator can manually write these policies, be the output of the *AZ*, or other tools. These functionalities allow our approach to be used seamlessly for intent-based security management workflows. The generic features the abstract policies describe are converted into SM-specific semantically-equivalent constructs.

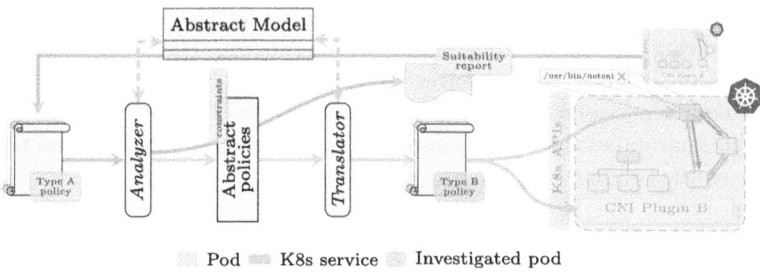

Pod ▨ K8s service ▨ Investigated pod

Fig. 3. Functional architecture and workflow

5.1   Analyzer

The *Analyzer (AZ)* component first parses the YAML content of each policy found in the target K8s system and verifies that the policy is syntactically and semantically correct. This step requires checking the presence of given keys and values in the data structure and their positioning.

Then, policies are compared against a predefined set of security concepts with rule-matching. This step transforms enforcement-specific configurations into high-level, SM-agnostic logical rule statements and constitutes the Abstraction Strategy details. It decomposes policy attributes according to their SM-specific patterns, normalizes identifiers, and applies a set of transformation functions that remove direct dependencies on SM-specific constructs while preserving semantics, breaking it down into the key components (i.e., `subjects`, `actions`, `object`, and `enforcement constraints`).

The *AZ* returns two outputs: a *suitability report*, which includes the list of SMs able to enforce that input policy and the list of unsupported or missing features or concepts, and an abstract policy, representing the high-level description of the input policy, conveying the generic features and its related security requirements, stripped of their original SM language syntax and semantic specifics. The suitability report also includes the features in the input policy that are not yet represented in the model, as is the case with Cilium's `authorization` feature.

5.2 Translator

The *Translator (TR)* component receives abstract policies as input, e.g., the data structure produced by the *AZ*, which contains generic features as defined by the abstract model, the concrete values of the policy, and the target SM. The translation engine then processes these features by routing their data to the appropriate converter classes, reported in the Translation Strategy class details. These classes inherit the hierarchical structure of the abstract model, as they are bound to each generic feature and provide the necessary conversion functions for each composing element.

For example, the `Traffic selector` will invoke the function of the `Pod` entity, following the chain from `Endpoint selector`. These functions handle the conversion from generic features to SM-specific constructs while ensuring semantic equivalence across different implementations of the same isolation capability. This guarantees that the converted policy maintains the same enforcement behavior as the original.

For instance, the *TR* component manages the differences in enforcement behavior arising from the different implementations of deny policies in Calico and Cilium. A simple abstract deny-policy for specific traffic will be translated in Cilium to a policy with the default-deny behavior disabled and a deny direction selector. At the same time, in Calico, it will be converted into an allow policy that grants full access, combined with a deny policy that is assigned a higher priority. In the current PoC, the generated policies are stored in the file system, but future work will integrate them with the K8s APIs.

6   Validation and Discussion

We evaluated the effectiveness of our framework in three use cases. The first two are based on widely used microservice architectures, selected after reviewing several publicly available solutions. Aderaldo et al. [1] proposed a benchmark for such architectures. However, many of these have since been abandoned or are no longer actively maintained. Ultimately, we based our validation on the Google Online-Boutique demo, one of the most up-to-date and comprehensive solutions used for evaluation of enterprise cloud solutions, and Sock Shop, which serve as the first and second use case scenarios, respectively.

These architectures are frequently used in research as experimental environments and have been employed in prior studies on policy-based access control and network isolation in K8s environments [7]. Regardless of the specific services exposed, i.e., online shops, they exemplify complex, distributed, real-world microservice applications. They consist of multiple interconnected services that necessitate network-level segmentation, and spanning a variety of frameworks and programming languages, reflecting heterogeneous conditions typical of cloud-native environments across IT domains. Online-Boutique has also been adopted for validating internal components of the iTrust6G EC-funded project's framework. In both scenarios, segmentation is applied at the pod level using the vanilla K8s specification, following an allow-listing approach.

In these scenarios, we simulated a cloud provider wanting to migrate from different SMs, as in Fig. 3. We prepared *ad hoc* K8s clusters with the target SMs, created with Minikube and hosted on an OpenStack infrastructure with Intel Xeon 32 vCPUs, Cascade Lake, 128 GB RAM.

For Boutique, the migration was from native K8s to Calico, and for Sock Shop to Cilium. The validation workflow employed the *AZ* and the *TR*. The network policies deployed in the original clusters were retrieved, selecting all NetworkPolicy resources, 14 for Boutique, and 13 for Sock Shop. Their correctness was verified, and an abstract representation was crafted according to the *Abstract model*, extracting all security features and then translating into the language of the SM in the target cluster. The *suitability report* by the *AZ* reported that both Cilium and Calico supported the origin network isolation prescriptions, whereas KubeArmor lacked sufficient granularity, as its system-based enforcement mode does not support specific ports at the transport layer, used in the original network policies. We report an example of translation performed by our tools in Fig. 4.

In the Cilium case, the selector mechanism was translated to the specific entity selector for the resource used in the origin policies endpointSelector, i.e., pods, based on the label filter. A deny-all default policy was present in both, even though Sock Shop used an early beta-version expression dating back to before the K8s NetworkPolicy specification was stabilized and nowadays deprecated. Hence, the *AZ* reported it as unsupported and discarded it in the translation process. Finding unsupported features or configurations may endanger the security, as for the Sock Shop cluster, given that the isolation would be missing, hence the importance of reporting the issue and the need for correct policy configurations due to the intrinsic difficulties in handling different SM formats.

```
apiVersion: cilium.io/v2              apiVersion:
kind: CiliumNetworkPolicy                 projectcalico.org/v3
metadata:                             kind: NetworkPolicy
  namespace: default                  metadata:
  ...                                   namespace: default
spec:                                   ...
  description: ...                     spec:
  endpointSelector:                     description: ...
    matchLabels: app: example-service   selector: app ==
  ingress:                                 'example-service'
  - {}                                  egress:
  egress:                               - action: Allow
  - toEndpoints:                          destination:
    - matchLabels: app: example-service     selector: app ==
    toPorts:                                   'example-service'
    - ports:                              ports:
      - port: "80"                        - 80
  - toEndpoints:                         - action: Allow
    - matchLabels:                         protocol: UDP
        io.kubernetes.pod.namespace:       destination:
          kube-system                        selector: k8s-app ==
        k8s-app: kube-dns                       'kube-dns'
    toPorts:                               namespaceSelector:
    - ports:                                 pod.namespace ==
      - port: "53" protocol: UDP               'kube-system'
      rules: dns:                         ports:
        - matchPattern: "*.google.com"    - 53
```

```
{"details": {"namespace": "default"},
"enforcement_behavior": "default-deny",
"resource_selector": {"type": "pod", "filter_labels":[{"app": [
  ↪ "example-service"]}]},
"rules": [{"direction": "Egress", "action": "allow", "traffic_selector": {
  "type": "pod", "proto": ["UDP"], "port": ["53"],
  "filter": {"type": "labels", "filters": [{"pod.namespace": [
  ↪ "kube-system"]}]},
  "payload_rule": {"proto": "DNS", "filter": {"header": {}, "payload": {
  ↪ "pattern": "*.google.com"}}}}
},{"direction": "Egress", "action": "allow", "traffic_selector": {
  "type": "pod", "proto": [], "port": ["80"],
  "filter": {"type": "labels", "filters": [{"pod.namespace": [
  ↪ "kube-system"]}]}}
}}]}
```

```
{{"sm_compatibility": {"Calico": {"policy_compatilibity": "partially⎵
  ↪ supported", "capabilities":
  [{"type": "enforcement_behavior", "id": "default-deny","unsupported": []},
   {"type": "policy_action","id": "action","unsupported": []},
   {"type": "resource_sel","capability": "entity-sel","sel":
    ↪ "labels","unsupported": []},
   {"rule": "2","type": "traffic_sel","capabilities": {"details": {"proto":
    ↪ {},"port":{},"unsupported":[]}, {"rule": 1, "unsupported": []}
   "entity_sel": {"sel_type": "labels","entity_type":
    ↪ "pod","unsupported":[]},
   "payload_rule": {"rule_type": "DNS","unsupported":["DNS"]}}}]},
"KubeArmor": {"policy_compatibility": "unsupported","capabilities":
  [{"type": "enforcement_behavior","capability":
    ↪ "default-deny","unsupported": ["default-deny"]},
   {"type": "policy_action","capability": "action","unsupported": []},
   {"type": "resource_sel","capability": "entity-sel", "selector":
    ↪ "labels","unsupported": []}, {"rule": 1, "unsupported": [
    ↪ "port", "entity_type", "sel_type"]}
   {"rule": 2, "type": "traffic_sel","capabilities": {"details": {
    ↪ "proto": {},"port": {}, "unsupported": ["port"]},
   "entity_sel": {"sel_type": "labels","entity_type":
    ↪ "pod","unsupported":["entity_type", "sel_type"]},
   "payload_rule": {"rule_type":
    ↪ "DNS","unsupported":["rule_type"]}}}}]}},{"..."}}}
```

Fig. 4. Policy translation at the top, security requirements of abstract policy and suitability report excerpts, redacted for brevity, in the middle, and at the bottom, respectively.

Aside from this, the *TR* correctly handled the resource selector, using labels for selecting the specific pod resources and the traffic selector, which in both Boutique and Sock Shop were specified at the transport layer using ports, protocol, and the traffic direction. Once generated, we manually pushed them into the destination clusters and verified the correctness of the pods' connection restrictions as per the policy specified with the *netcat* utility. For this purpose, we attached a "sidecar" ephemeral container with the utility pre-installed to the pods investigated, as many of the pods' containers did not expose a shell. As expected, a major isolation gap was found in Sock Shop, as the missing global ingress isolation policy caused all incoming traffic to pods other than the directions filtered by the policies to be permitted.

As the third and last use case, we tested the use of our tools to implement an intent-based workflow, i.e., to refine high-level requirements into network security configurations ready to use for target K8s networks. The high-level requirements were imported, through the *AZ*, from a catalog of existing K8s system- and network-based hardening requirements for specific services or infrastructures,

For this last scenario, we considered the open-source catalogue of hardening rules publicly maintained and curated by AccuKnox[2], designed for common cloud-native and 5G telco infrastructures and services. The catalogue includes both system-level and network-level isolation rules. Among its recommendations are numerous controls and related rules mapped to widely adopted compliance frameworks, such as NIST SP 800âĂŞ53, CIS Benchmarks, and STIG, as well as mitigations aligned with common adversary techniques identified in the MITRE ATT&CK framework. Many of these rules provide technical guidance and implementation benchmarks that play a central role in governance processes aimed at achieving a security baseline, particularly within organizations adopting structured methodologies like the Risk Management Framework (RMF).

We fed each hardening requirement into the *AZ*. Our tool showed the mechanisms supporting the concepts implied by the recommendations and identified any missing ones when applicable. In particular, it reported that the system-based recommendations for KubeArmor were only supported by one other SM, that is, Tetragon, while the network-based recommendations from Cilium were only partially supported by Calico, given the presence of certain selectors not available in it, and not by KubeArmor. Additionally, the suitability report issued when analyzing the group, highlighted the use of the `CiliumClusterWide` policy type that is not yet supported by our model, specifically the `NodeSelector`, together with Kyverno policies. Kyverno has not been covered in our research as it focuses on admission-time security enforcement, rather than on runtime enforcement, which is the focus of this research, and has been left to future work. In Fig. 4, we show an example with its abstract representation (bottom right), where the concepts and concrete constraints are reported. In particular, we note that starting from those high-level requirements, as per the original policy (left), a resulting Calico instance would be lossy since the layer 7 DNS capability, filtering DNS traffic based on their request, is not supported in Calico.

---

[2] https://github.com/kubearmor/policy-templates.

Finally, we measured the performance of analysis and translation for the two migration scenarios using the `timeit` utility. As expected, the footprint was minimal, measuring just under 0,147 ms and 0,132 ms on average, with a 2 μs standard deviation for the Boutique and Sock Shop migrations, respectively. The cluster network performance varies depending on the SMs, as some of them, i.e., plugins, also provide the underlying network connectivity, hence being the main element in determining the actual network performance. However, this variation is independent of the policy refinement and was not considered in our performance analysis. The same applies to the policy loading time to the K8s APIs and enforcement time. We refer to existing research for further insights into these aspects, such as [10].

7   Conclusions

In this paper, we investigated the landscape of K8s native runtime enforcement of security policies by analyzing the most widely used and promising solutions, comparing their features and functionalities, and providing a general overview that can help identify the most effective combination of enforcement mechanisms to achieve the desired security goals. This work is important to help automate tasks that are needed for compliance with governance standards, which are increasingly required to prove effectiveness in coping with the cybersecurity risks of emerging threats in cloud environments.

Furthermore, we introduced a model-driven approach to translating high-level abstract requirements into valid configurations for a set of SMs for K8s that resulted from the conceptualization effort. This has led to an abstract model of the capabilities exposed by various K8s security solutions. This abstraction streamlines management operations for K8s security policies by providing a higher-level representation that abstracts away the complexities from the configuration details.

We evaluated our approach using three use cases: two cloud-provider migrations involving real-world, complex microservice architectures, which required adapting security policies to different SMs, and the analysis of a public policy catalog for the security hardening of cloud-native environments, including common services and 5G architectures. Our goal is to integrate the runtime security enforcement abstraction capabilities into a cloud-native, intent-based framework developed in previous work [13], as well as into a playbook-based security orchestration platform to support the orchestration of security operations in K8s environments [12].

Acknowledgments. This work is supported by the Smart Networks and Services Joint Undertaking (SNS JU) under the European Union's Horizon Europe research and innovation programme under Grant Agreement No. 101139198, iTrust6G project. Views and opinions expressed are, however, those of the author(s) only and do not necessarily reflect those of the European Union or SNS-JU. Neither the European Union nor the granting authority can be held responsible for them.

References

1. Aderaldo, C.M., Mendonça, N.C., Pahl, C., Jamshidi, P.: Benchmark requirements for microservices architecture research. In: 2017 IEEE/ACM 1st International Workshop on Establishing the Community-Wide Infrastructure for Architecture-Based Software Engineering (ECASE), pp. 8–13 (2017). https://doi.org/10.1109/ECASE.2017.4
2. Attaoui, W., Sabir, E., Elbiaze, H., Guizani, M.: VNF and CNF placement in 5G: recent advances and future trends. IEEE Trans. Netw. Serv. Manage. **20**(4), 4698–4733 (2023). https://doi.org/10.1109/TNSM.2023.3264005
3. Clemm, A., Ciavaglia, L., Granville, L.Z., Tantsura, J.: Intent-Based Networking - Concepts and Definitions. RFC 9315 (2022). https://doi.org/10.17487/RFC9315
4. Haindl, P., Kochberger, P., Sveggen, M.: A systematic literature review of inter-service security threats and mitigation strategies in microservice architectures. IEEE Access **12**, 90252–90286 (2024). https://doi.org/10.1109/ACCESS.2024.3406500
5. Hendrick, S., Lawson, A., Sica, J.: 2024 Cloud Native Security Report. Tech. rep., The Linux Foundation (2024). https://doi.org/10.70828/MRCE5096, https://www.linuxfoundation.org/hubfs/Research%20Reports/lfr_cloudnative_security24_101424a.pdf
6. Kaloroumakis, P.E., Smith, M.J.: Toward a knowledge graph of cybersecurity countermeasures. The MITRE Corporation **11** (2021)
7. Li, X., Chen, Y., Lin, Z., Wang, X., Chen, J.H.: Automatic policy generation for Inter-Service access control of microservices. In: 30th USENIX Security Symposium (USENIX Security 21), pp. 3971–3988. USENIX Association (2021)
8. Minna, F., Blaise, A., Rebecchi, F., Chandrasekaran, B., Massacci, F.: Understanding the security implications of kubernetes networking. IEEE Secur. Priv. **19**(5), 46–56 (2021). https://doi.org/10.1109/MSEC.2021.3094726
9. Nam, J., et al.: BASTION: a security enforcement network stack for container networks. In: 2020 USENIX Annual Technical Conference (USENIX ATC 20), pp. 81–95. USENIX Association (2020)
10. Qi, S., Kulkarni, S.G., Ramakrishnan, K.K.: Understanding container network interface plugins: design considerations and performance. In: 2020 IEEE International Symposium on Local and Metropolitan Area Networks (LANMAN), pp. 1–6 (2020). https://doi.org/10.1109/LANMAN49260.2020.9153266
11. Rose, S., Borchert, O., Mitchell, S., Connelly, S.: Zero trust architecture (2020). https://doi.org/10.6028/NIST.SP.800-207, https://tsapps.nist.gov/publication/get_pdf.cfm?pub_id=930420
12. Settanni, F., Regano, L., Basile, C., Lioy, A.: A model for automated cybersecurity threat remediation and sharing. In: 2023 IEEE 9th International Conference on Network Softwarization (NetSoft), pp. 492–497 (2023). https://doi.org/10.1109/NetSoft57336.2023.10175486
13. Settanni, F., Zamponi, A., Basile, C.: Dynamic security provisioning for cloud-native networks: an intent-based approach. In: 2024 IEEE International Conference on Cyber Security and Resilience (CSR), pp. 321–328 (2024). https://doi.org/10.1109/CSR61664.2024.10679397
14. Snyder: formal models of capability-based protection systems. IEEE Trans. on Comput. **C-30**(3), 172–181 (1981). https://doi.org/10.1109/TC.1981.1675753
15. Vayghan, L.A., Saied, M.A., Toeroe, M., Khendek, F.: A Kubernetes controller for managing the availability of elastic microservice based stateful applications. J. of Syst. and Softw. **175**, 110924 (2021). https://doi.org/10.1016/j.jss.2021.110924

16. van Vugt, T.M., Malik, T.: A practical analysis of open-source security tools in microservice Kubernetes environments. In: 2023 Cyber Research Conference - Ireland (Cyber-RCI), pp. 1–8 (2023).https://doi.org/10.1109/Cyber-RCI59474.2023.10671405
17. Yarygina, T., Bagge, A.H.: Overcoming security challenges in microservice architectures. In: 2018 IEEE Symposium on Service-Oriented System Engineering (SOSE), pp. 11–20 (2018). https://doi.org/10.1109/SOSE.2018.00011

Proceedings of the Fourth Workshop on Cybersecurity in Industry 4.0 (SecIndustry 2025)

SecIndustry 2025 Preface

The fourth Industry 4.0 workshop (SecIndustry 2025) was a forum for researchers and practitioners focused on revolutionizing technology and rethinking value-added processes. It includes several critical infrastructures, which are needed to make the different technologies come together to create better products, more effective and efficient production processes. To enhance the security and resilience of Industry 4.0, it is critical to advance our understanding of adversary modelling, foster interdisciplinary collaboration, and refine simulation and testing methods to validate security models under realistic conditions. It is also important to look at the human side of security and privacy when doing digital transformation. Innovation to better understand fast learning, with the use of laboratories, catapult centres and learning factories, applied to real-life security problems, is essential. Using learning factories to simulate and test and set up laboratory production lines, simulating real production lines, gives unprecedented insights into various testing mechanisms and better understanding of the threats and vulnerabilities of Industry 4.0 production lines.

The key technologies that boost Industry 4.0 are the Internet of Things (IoT), Industrial Internet of Things (IIoT), Artificial Intelligence (AI), Cloud Computing, Machine Learning, Security, Big Data, Blockchain, Deep Learning, Digitalization, Digital Twins, Cyber-Physical Systems (CPS), Advanced Analytics, Robotics, and Cognitive Computing. These technologies can expand the attack surface of Industry 4.0. Furthermore, as information technology (IT) and operational technology (OT) become integrated, a new range of security issues can arise, necessitating the defense of both IT and OT. Addressing these security challenges of IT-OT integration is crucial for the implementation of Industry 4.0 technologies.

The workshop garnered the attention of research communities and fostered novel insights and advancements, with a specific focus on cybersecurity threats detection through AI tools for industrial sectors, security and safety for supply chain, digital twin-driven cyber-resilient supply chains, and emerging EU legislations for industry. The 4th Workshop on Cybersecurity in Industry 4.0 (SecIndustry 2025) was held in person. The workshop was organized in conjunction with the 20th International Conference on Availability, Reliability and Security (ARES 2025), Ghent, Belgium, August 11–14, 2025.

A total of eight submissions were received by the workshop, of which seven were subsequently sent for reviews and one desk rejected. As a result of an extensive peer-review process, four papers were selected to be presented at the workshop. The review process primarily emphasized the quality, scientific novelty, and applicability of the papers to safeguarding critical infrastructure and services. The acceptance rate stood at 50%. The accepted articles encompass a diverse range of techniques addressing, monitoring and predicting security threats using AI models in critical infrastructures, additive manufacturing process chains, emerging EU regulations and legislation for industrial sectors.

The workshop consisted of one keynote and technical presentations, with an attendance of approximately 30 individuals. The workshop showcased one significant and thought-provoking keynote on the topics of "Digital Twins for Enhancing Cybersecurity in Industry 4.0".

The workshop was supported by the Center for Research-based Innovation (SFI) Norwegian Centre for Cybersecurity in Critical Sectors (NORCICS) project and the International Alliance for Strengthening Cybersecurity and Privacy in Healthcare (CybAlliance) project. The organizers would like to thank these projects for supporting the SecIndustry 2025 workshop.

The organizers of the SecIndustry workshop would like to extend their heartfelt appreciation to the SecIndustry 2025 Program Committee for their meticulous and punctual review process, which played a crucial role in bringing the workshop to fruition. We would like to express our gratitude to Ghent University, Belgium for graciously hosting the workshop, and extend our appreciation to the ARES 2025 chairs for their invaluable assistance and support.

August 2025

Sandeep Pirbhulal
Habtamu Abie
Halvor Holtskog
Sokratis Katsikas

SecIndustry 2025 Organization

Workshop Chairs

Sandeep Pirbhulal	Norwegian Computing Center, Norway
Habtamu Abie	Norwegian Computing Center, Norway
Halvor Holtskog	Norwegian University of Science and Technology, Norway
Sokratis Katsikas	Norwegian University of Science and Technology, Norway

Program Committee

Cristina Alcaraz	University of Malaga, Spain
Manos Athanatos	Foundation for Research and Technology Hellas, Crete
Sabarathinam Chockalingam	Institute for Energy Technology, Norway
Hervé Debar	Télécom SudParis, France
Sabine Delaitre	BOSONIT, Spain
Vasileios Gkioulos	Norwegian University of Science and Technology, Norway
Ilias Gkotsis	Inlecom Innovation, Greece
Dieter Gollmann	Hamburg University of Technology, Germany
Siv Hilde Houmb	Norwegian University of Science and Technology, Norway
Martin Gilje Jaatun	University of Stavanger, Norway
Basel Katt	Norwegian University of Science and Technology, Norway
Maryline Laurent	Télécom SudParis, France
Wolfgang Leister	Norwegian Computing Center, Norway
Aida Omerovic	The Foundation for Industrial and Technical Research, Norway
Kai Rannenberg	Goethe University Frankfurt, Germany
Reijo Savola	University of Jyväskylä, Finland
Ankur Shukla	Institute for Energy Technology, Norway
Ali Hassan Sodhro	Kristianstad University, Sweden
Mohsen Toorani	University of South-Eastern Norway, Norway
Christos Xenakis	University of Piraeus, Greece
Shouhuai Xu	University of Colorado Colorado Springs, USA

A Method for Explainable Anomaly Detection in Substation Networks Through Deep Learning

Paul Tavolato[1], Oliver Eigner[2], Philipp Kreimel-Haindl[3], Antonella Santone[4], Fabio Martinelli[5], and Francesco Mercaldo[1,4(✉)]

[1] Faculty of Computer Science, University of Vienna, Vienna, Austria
{paul.tavolato,mercaldof67}@univie.ac.at
[2] Department of Computer Science and Security, St. Pölten University of Applied Sciences, Sankt Pölten, Austria
oliver.eigner@fhstp.ac.at
[3] OMV, Vienna, Austria
Philipp.KreimelHaindl@omv.com
[4] Department of Medicine and Health Sciences "V. Tiberio", University of Molise, Campobasso, Italy
{antonella.santone,francesco.mercaldo}@unimol.it
[5] Institute of High Performance Computing and Networking, National Research Council of Italy (CNR), Rende, Italy
fabio.martinelli@icar.cnr.it

Abstract. Electrical substations manage electrical energy, therefore a cyber-attack on these systems would cause significant damage to the population, but also to hospitals and all critical and non-critical infrastructures. In this paper we propose a method, based on deep learning, to identify anomalies in electrical substations. The proposed method directly analyzes network logs to highlight the possible presence of anomalies in the substation networks. In order to push the adoption of deep learning in real contexts, the proposed method also provides a kind of prediction explainability behind the classifier predictions, by highlighting the section of the network trace that has been detected as symptomatic of an anomaly from the deep learning classifier point of view.

Keywords: substation · SCADA · Modbus · anomaly · deep learning

1 Introduction and Related Work

Critical infrastructure is facing a significant threat, with cyber-attacks surging by 30% in a single year [9]. The energy, transportation, and telecommunications sectors have emerged as prime targets. This trend is unsurprising, as these industries, particularly in developed nations, have become increasingly reliant on digital technologies, which in turn expose new vulnerabilities to cyber-threats. According to a report by KnowBe4 security experts, published in August 2024[1],

---

[1] https://industrialcyber.co/critical-infrastructure/critical-infrastructure-faces-30-percent-surge-in-cyber-attacks-knowbe4-report-highlights/.

B. Coppens et al. (Eds.): ARES 2025 Workshops, LNCS 15994, pp. 289–303, 2025.
https://doi.org/10.1007/978-3-032-00630-1_16

such attacks can have devastating consequences for nations. As a result, geopolitical adversaries have leveraged these vulnerabilities, making cyber-attacks a potent addition to their arsenal of digital weaponry.

We are witnessing a continuous and escalating wave of cyber-attacks on critical infrastructure, posing a significant global threat with the potential to cause widespread social and economic disruption [2].

One of the most alarming scenarios would be a cyber-attack targeting the energy sector, which encompasses power generation, water treatment, electricity production, and other interconnected systems. Such an attack could plunge communities into chaos; for instance, during a time of war, a sudden power outage could critically disrupt the operations of hospitals, first responders, and military installations [14].

The frequency of attacks on critical infrastructure is escalating at an alarming rate. Between January 2023 and January 2024, over 420 million attacks were recorded, ranging in severity, according to Forescout Research – Vedere Labs[2]. This equates to 13 attacks per second, representing a 30% increase from 2022. These attacks have affected 163 countries, with the United States being the primary target, followed by the United Kingdom, Germany, India, and Japan. Moreover, Forescout Research from Vedere Labs researchers highlight also that on the other side, China hosts the highest concentration of threat actors targeting critical infrastructure, trailed by Russia and Iran.

As power systems evolved, substations expanded in size and became more widely distributed and thus more prone to cyber-attacks. The demand for transformer and switchyard substations far outpaced that for generator stations, necessitating a shift from manual to remote monitoring and control systems. Ensuring the high availability and continuous operation of electrical substations has always been a priority for electrical companies. Frequent faults lead to service interruptions for clients, which in turn result in revenue losses—an undesirable outcome for any company [1].

With the increasing availability of remote information, advanced supervisory systems were developed to assist operators in control centers. One such system, the Supervisory Control and Data Acquisition (SCADA) system, enables the collection of data from various systems such as Intelligent Electronic Devices (IEDs) and Remote Terminal Units (RTUs) within an electrical system using diverse standard communication protocols (IEC 60870-5-104, IEC 61850 or Modbus). SCADA systems not only facilitate the monitoring and control of these devices through advanced visualization technologies but can also automate supervision tasks based on predefined parameters and algorithms, significantly improving operational efficiency and decision-making [2].

A Human-Machine Interface (HMI) is implemented in each substation to provide operators with essential local control and monitoring capabilities. These interfaces are particularly important during critical activities such as configuration, commissioning, or maintenance of the substation, ensuring efficient and reliable management of operations on-site.

---

[2] https://www.forescout.com/research-labs/.

At the dawn of the digital era, each manufacturer adopted its own methods for interpreting and implementing various components of intelligent systems. This diversity in approaches resulted in a lack of interoperability and created dependency on specific vendors. To address these challenges, the Modbus protocol was developed. Initially designed for use with Programmable Logic Controllers (PLCs), Modbus has since become a widely accepted standard communication protocol for facilitating communication between industrial electronic devices across various buses and networks.

The aim of the Modbus protocol is to facilitate communication between Intelligent Electronic Devices (IEDs) and SCADA Human-Machine Interfaces (HMIs). The logic of an IED is designed to periodically change voltage values either randomly or in response to requests received from the SCADA HMI. Meanwhile, the logic of the SCADA HMI involves adjusting the tap-changes based on the values received from the IED and opening or closing circuits in response to overvoltage or undervoltage conditions [7].

For these reasons, in this paper we propose a method aimed to detect anomalies in substation networks. We consider deep learning, in particular we resort to convolutional neural networks (CNN) to discriminate between anomalous and legitimate network traces. As demonstrated in literature, CNN showed interesting performances when trained with datasets composed by images [4,5,11,15], for this reason we provide a way to generate an image from network traces stored in PCAP file.

Moreover, considering that one of the limits that prevent the adoption of deep learning in the real-world is its obscurity behind the decision related to a certain prediction (at least from the final user point of view), in this paper we take into account a way to provide prediction explainability i.e., a kind of explanation aimed to understand the area of the images under analysis (obtained from the network trace) that from the model point of view are responsible for a certain prediction. In this way, by exploiting the proposed method, a network trace is classified, for instance, as anomalous, and we provide, into the image representing the network trace, the areas of the image that, from the network point of view, as responsible for the anomalous prediction of the trace under analysis.

Anomaly detection in substation networks is vital for ensuring the safety and reliability of power grids. This is the reason why several studies have explored machine learning techniques for this purpose, focusing on various modeling approaches and the accuracy of predictions.

For instance, researchers in [14] introduce a Deep Neural Network (DNN)-based Intrusion Detection System (IDS) to detect malicious Generic Object-Oriented Substation Event (GOOSE) communications over process and station bus networks. The study focuses on classification accuracy but does not address the explainability of the model's predictions.

Valdes and colleagues [17] apply unsupervised machine learning to detect anomalies in electrical substations by inferring physical invariants from data.

While the approach is innovative, it does not provide mechanisms for interpreting the model's decisions, which is crucial for practical deployment.

Most and colleagues [13] consider the non-negative tensor decomposition to identify anomalies in SCADA systems, which are integral to substation operations. The method focuses on statistical behavior analysis but does not emphasize the explainability of the detection process

Authors in [10] introduce a Deep Neural Network model that incorporates the graph structure of communication networks to improve interpretability. The approach provides a hierarchical set of features, enabling analysis at different levels of granularity, and offers self-supervised training without requiring labeled data.

In contrast to the current state-of-the-art in the context of anomaly detection in substation networks, the proposed method integrates four different Class Activation Mapping (CAM) techniques to provide an interpretable framework for deep learning-based anomaly detection in substation networks. Specifically, it utilizes Grad-CAM, Grad-CAM++, Score-CAM, and Score-CAM Fast to visually highlight the regions in the input data that the model deems most relevant for its predictions. Grad-CAM, in particular, generates heatmaps by leveraging the gradients of the target class concerning the final convolutional layer, offering insight into the most influential areas of the network trace images. This approach enhances explainability, allowing operators to understand why a network trace is classified as anomalous, thereby improving trust and facilitating real-world deployment of deep learning models in substation management. Thus, the key distinction of the proposed approach lies in its focus on improving model interpretability, a crucial factor that can facilitate the broader adoption of deep learning solutions in the industry.

The paper proceeds as follows: in the next section we present the proposed method for explainable anomaly detection in substation networks, in Sect. 3 we discuss the experimental analysis results, aimed to demonstrate the effectiveness of the proposed method and, finally, conclusion and future research plans are drawn in the last section.

2   The Method

In this section we present the proposed method for explainable anomaly detection in substation networks, which workflow is shown in Fig. 1.

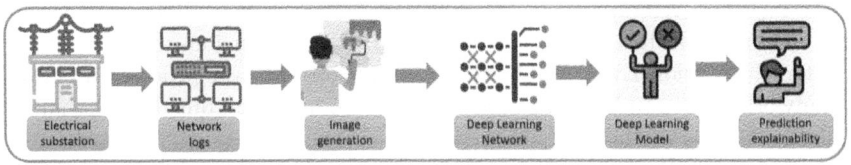

Fig. 1. The workflow of the proposed method.

The proposed method for identifying anomalies in an electrical substation involves several steps, each designed to process and analyze data effectively to detect potential attacks i.e., anomalies. The proposed method, as shown in Fig. 1, begins with the collection of network logs from the electrical substation. These logs are generated by the various systems and devices operating within the substation and capture essential information about their activities, interactions, and overall performance.

Once the network logs are collected, they undergo an image generation process.

To convert a network trace in PCAP format into an image, we used a script developed by the authors using the Python programming language.

For each PCAP file, the script reads the binary data and processes it into a numerical format using NumPy. The data is then reshaped to match the specified dimensions of the output image (that is fixed to 100×100). If the binary data size is smaller than required, the script pads it with zeros, and if it is larger, it truncates the data. The generated images are composed by three channels i.e., the images are in RGB. The resulting image is saved as a PNG file.

The generated images are then input into a deep learning network, as shown in Fig. 1. We exploited several networks, with the aim to find the best one in distinguishing normal behavior from anomalous events. The training phase involves exposing the model to a labeled dataset that includes examples of both normal and anomalous scenarios. By learning from these traces, labelled as attack or benign (we consider a binary classification), the deep learning networks leverage their multi-layered architecture to extract high-level, abstract features from the input images, making it highly effective for anomaly detection tasks.

As shown in Fig. 1, the last step of the proposed method incorporates a prediction explainability component to enhance trust in the model decisions.

Explainability techniques, such as saliency maps or feature importance visualization, are employed to provide insights into the specific factors or patterns that influenced the predictions of the model. This step is essential for making the anomaly detection process interpretable to human operators and stakeholders, enabling them to understand the reasoning behind the outputs of the model. By offering clear explanations for its decisions, the proposed method supports better decision-making and fosters confidence in its deployment within real-world substation environments.

In particular, for prediction explainability we exploit for different Class Activation Mapping (CAM) techniques: Gradient-weighted Class Activation Mapping (Grad-CAM) [16], Grad-CAM++ [6], Score-Weighted Class Activation Mapping (Score-CAM) [18], and Score-CAM Fast [8]. CAMs help in visualizing which parts of an input image contribute most to the model's decision, providing insights into the decision-making process. In the context of substation networks, where a PCAP trace is converted into an image for anomaly detection, we exploit these methods for understanding why certain network behaviors, captured in the form of visual data, are flagged as anomalous by the model.

Grad-CAM is a popular technique that uses the gradients of the target class with respect to the last convolutional layer in a CNN to generate a heatmap. This heatmap highlights the regions in the input image that had the most significant influence on the model's prediction. By backpropagating the gradients, Grad-CAM produces a visualization that shows the important areas in the image for the given prediction, allowing us to pinpoint anomalies in substation network data represented as images. In the case of PCAP traces converted into images, Grad-CAM helps in identifying specific network activities that may correspond to anomalies such as unusual traffic patterns or suspicious packets.

Grad-CAM++ improves upon Grad-CAM by addressing some of its limitations. While Grad-CAM uses the gradients to weight the feature maps, Grad-CAM++ employs a more refined approach by calculating the contribution of each feature map to the class prediction using second-order derivatives. This method enhances the localization accuracy of the important regions in the image, making it more sensitive to small and subtle changes in the network data. For anomaly detection in substation networks, Grad-CAM++ provides more detailed insights into which specific components of the network data, like a particular packet or traffic spike, contributed to the detection of an anomaly.

Score-CAM, on the other hand, takes a different approach by eliminating the dependence on gradients. Instead of using the gradient information, it computes the importance of each feature map by evaluating the class score directly, using the output score of the network when the feature maps are activated. The resulting heatmap highlights regions that most positively influence the prediction, but without the computational complexities and potential instabilities of gradient-based methods. Score-CAM provides a more robust and less noisy visualization of the areas relevant to the model's decision, which is particularly useful when the gradients are difficult to interpret or when the model's decision-making process is highly non-linear.

Score-CAM Fast is an optimized version of Score-CAM designed to be faster and more efficient, particularly when dealing with large datasets or high-resolution images. It accelerates the computation of the importance scores by reducing the number of forward passes required and utilizing faster approximations for the class score computation. In substation network anomaly detection, Score-CAM Fast can quickly identify the relevant features in the PCAP image, making it easier to deploy the technique in real-time monitoring systems where speed is crucial.

The main difference between these CAMs lies in the underlying approach for generating the heatmap. While Grad-CAM and Grad-CAM++ rely on gradient-based methods to compute the influence of each feature map, Score-CAM and Score-CAM Fast use the output score of the network, making them gradient-free. Additionally, Grad-CAM++ improves on Grad-CAM by refining the weight calculations using second-order derivatives, which increases its accuracy in capturing fine-grained details. Score-CAM and Score-CAM Fast are generally more robust in cases where gradient-based methods are unstable or difficult to compute, offering a cleaner and more interpretable visualization.

When applied to anomaly detection in substation networks, these techniques allow for better understanding and hence increase trust in the model's predictions. By converting PCAP traces into images and applying one of these CAMs, operators and engineers can visualize the specific network behaviors or irregularities that lead to the detection of anomalies, making it easier to identify the root causes of issues and improve the overall monitoring and maintenance of the system.

3   Experimental Analysis

With the aim to demonstrate the effectiveness of the proposed method we resort to the CIC Modbus 2023 dataset [3] freely available for research purposes[3]. The dataset comprises network captures and attack logs from a simulated substation network, divided into two categories: attack and the benign network traces.

The attack dataset contains network traffic captures that simulate various types of Modbus protocol attacks within a substation environment. These attacks include reconnaissance, query flooding, payload loading, delayed responses, modification of length parameters, false data injection, stacking Modbus frames, brute force writes, and baseline replays. These attack types are based on techniques from the MITRE ICS ATT&CK framework[4]. In contrast, the benign dataset consists of normal network traffic captures that represent legitimate Modbus communication within the substation network. The captures are divided into 100 MB files.

Table 1 shows the experimental analysis results. As shown from Table 1 we exploited several state-of-the-art models (i.e., MobileNet, EfficientNet, GoogleNet, Inception, ResNet50, VGG16 and VGG19) and a model developed by authors (i.e., STANDARD_CNN) [12].

The experimental results, shown in Table 1, are related to the performance of several deep learning models in detecting attacks within an electrical substation, evaluated across key metrics including loss, accuracy, precision, recall, F-measure, AUC, and execution time. As shown in Table 1, after 20 epochs, ResNet50 emerges as the best-performing model, achieving a high accuracy of 98.5%, accompanied by precision, recall, and F-measure values of 0.985 and the highest AUC of 0.998. This indicates its exceptional ability to distinguish between normal and anomalous behavior with minimal error. Despite its relatively high execution time of 19 min and 43 s, ResNet50 balances performance and computational efficiency effectively.

Inception and GoogleNet also perform well after 20 epochs, with Inception achieving an accuracy of 96.9% and an AUC of 0.967, while GoogleNet achieves a slightly lower accuracy of 96.8% but a higher AUC of 0.992. The execution times for these models are moderate, with Inception taking 23 min and 39 s and GoogleNet requiring 8 min and 50 s. MobileNet demonstrates good performance, achieving an accuracy of 93.8% and an AUC of 0.961, while maintaining

---

[3] https://www.unb.ca/cic/datasets/modbus-2023.html.
[4] https://attack.mitre.org/techniques/ics/.

Table 1. Experimental analysis results.

Model	Epoch	Loss	Accuracy	Precision	Recall	F-Measure	AUC	Execution time
MobileNet	20	0.368	0.938	0.938	0.938	0.938	0.961	0:23:54
EfficientNet	20	0.941	0.667	0.667	0.667	0.667	0.759	0:24:04
STANDARD_CNN	20	0.234	0.922	0.922	0.922	0.922	0.976	0:07:06
GoogleNet	20	0.105	0.968	0.968	0.968	0.968	0.992	0:08:50
Inception	20	0.348	0.969	0.969	0.969	0.969	0.967	0:23:39
ResNet50	20	0.0324	0.985	0.985	0.985	0.985	0.998	0:19:43
VGG16	20	0.678	0.584	0.584	0.584	0.584	0.584	0:24:25
VGG19	20	0.678	0.584	0.584	0.584	0.584	0.584	0:41:02
MobileNet	50	0.029	0.995	0.995	0.995	0.995	0.997	0:29:04
STANDARD_CNN	50	0.282	0.926	0.926	0.926	0.926	0.973	0:28:59
GoogleNet	50	0.0841	0.981	0.981	0.981	0.981	0.995	0:35:29
Inception	50	0.145	0.994	0.994	0.994	0.994	0.997	0:50:38
ResNet50	50	0.0761	0.985	0.985	0.985	0.985	0.992	0:40:23
VGG16	50	0.678	0.584	0.584	0.584	0.584	0.584	1:06:55
VGG19	50	0.678	0.584	0.584	0.584	0.584	0.584	0:55:21

a reasonable execution time of 23 min and 54 s. However, it does not match the top-performing models in accuracy.

STANDARD_CNN provides a competitive accuracy of 92.2% and an AUC of 0.976 while standing out as the fastest model, with an execution time of only 7 min and 6 s. This makes it a highly efficient option for scenarios where computational speed is a priority. On the other hand, EfficientNet underperforms significantly, with an accuracy of only 66.7% and an AUC of 0.759, indicating its limited ability to learn and detect anomalies. Similarly, VGG16 and VGG19 perform poorly across all metrics, with an accuracy of 58.4%, no improvement in AUC, and the longest execution times of 24 min and 25 s, and 41 min and 2 s, respectively, making them unsuitable for this task.

After 50 epochs, MobileNet exhibits the most significant improvement, achieving the highest accuracy of 99.5% with precision, recall, and F-measure values of 0.995, and an AUC of 0.997. This demonstrates its strong generalization capability and ability to converge effectively with extended training. The execution time increases slightly to 29 min and 4 s, which is reasonable given its superior performance. Inception also shows remarkable improvement after 50 epochs, achieving an accuracy of 99.4% with an AUC of 0.997. However, its execution time increases substantially to 50 min and 38 s, making it less efficient than MobileNet.

GoogleNet maintains excellent performance after 50 epochs, with an accuracy of 98.1%, precision, recall, and F-measure values of 0.981, and an AUC of 0.995. Its execution time of 35 min and 29 s remains moderate, striking a balance between accuracy and computational efficiency. ResNet50 retains its strong performance, achieving an accuracy of 98.5% and an AUC of 0.992, although its execution time increases to 40 min and 23 s, slightly reducing its efficiency advantage. STANDARD_CNN shows minor improvement, with an accuracy of 92.6%

and an AUC of 0.973, but its execution time increases significantly to 28 min and 59 s, diminishing its speed advantage.

EfficientNet, VGG16, and VGG19 continue to perform poorly even after 50 epochs, with no significant improvement in accuracy or other metrics. Efficient-Net maintains an accuracy of 66.7% and an AUC of 0.759, while both VGG16 and VGG19 remain stagnant at 58.4% accuracy and require excessive execution times of over 55 min.

Overall, MobileNet proves to be the most effective model, offering the best combination of accuracy, AUC, and reasonable execution time, particularly after 50 epochs. ResNet50 and GoogleNet also deliver strong performance, making them suitable alternatives depending on the specific application needs. In contrast, models such as EfficientNet, VGG16, and VGG19 are unsuitable due to their poor accuracy and high computational costs. These results highlight the importance of selecting models that balance predictive accuracy with computational efficiency for real-time anomaly detection in electrical substations.

Among the models evaluated, MobileNet emerged as the best-performing architecture, particularly when trained for 50 epochs, achieving the highest accuracy (0.995), precision, recall, and F-measure (0.995), along with a strong AUC (0.997). Its execution time of 29 min and 4 s remains reasonable, making it an efficient choice for real-time applications. The superior performance of MobileNet can be attributed to its lightweight architecture and depthwise separable convolutions, which optimize feature extraction while maintaining computational efficiency. Compared to ResNet50 and Inception, which also performed well, MobileNet provides a better trade-off between accuracy and execution time. In contrast, models such as VGG16 and VGG19 struggled due to their higher parameter count and lack of optimization for network trace images, leading to lower accuracy (0.584) and longer training times (55+ minutes). These results indicate that MobileNet is the most suitable model for real-time anomaly detection in substation networks, offering both high predictive accuracy and computational efficiency.

To better understand the MobileNet performance, in Fig. 2 we show the confusion matrix related to the MobileNet model trained for 50 epochs.

As shown from confusion matrix, shown in Fig. 2, all 405 images related to possible attacks, and therefore anomalies, were correctly classified by the model as such, relative to the images obtained from benign network traces, 290 were correctly classified as legitimate, while only 3 benign traces were incorrectly classified as attacks, thus confirming the effectiveness of the proposed MobileNet model trained for 50 epochs.

In the follow, by considering the model with the best performances (i.e., the MobileNet trained for 50 epochs), we provide examples of explainability by showing for example an image obtained from a network trace of the four CAMS i.e., Grad-CAM, Grad-CAM++, Score-CAM, and Score-CAM Fast, with the aim to understand the area of the images highlighted by each CAM and to understand if different CAMs highlight the same area of the image under analysis.

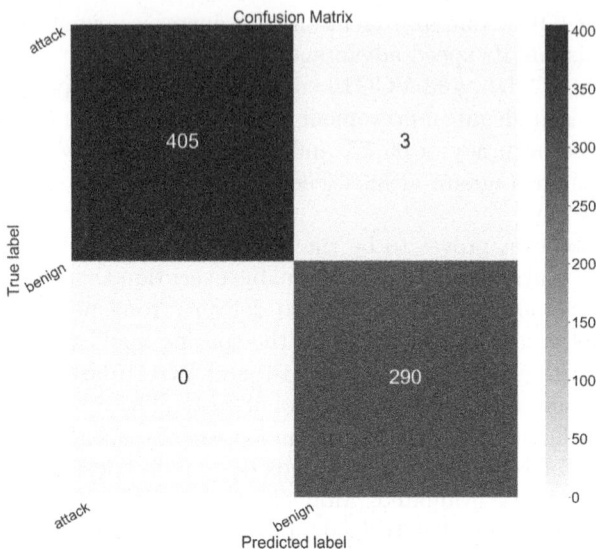

Fig. 2. The confusion matrix related to the MobileNet model trained for 50 epochs.

Figure 3 is related to an example of prediction explainability of an image obtained from a network trace related to an attack.

The provided figure demonstrates the application of different CAM techniques to an image derived from a PCAP file. Each row in the figure corresponds to a different CAM variant: Grad-CAM, Grad-CAM++, Score-CAM, and Score-CAM Fast, respectively, from top to bottom.

For each CAM, three images are displayed: the original image derived from the PCAP file, the heatmap generated by the specific CAM method, and the overlay of the original image with the heatmap. The heatmaps indicate the areas of the image that the model finds most relevant for its prediction. In the case shown in Fig. 3, the model predicts a potential "attack" with a confidence level of 100% across all CAM methods. The overlay images provide an intuitive visualization of these heatmaps, showing the correspondence between the original data and the model's regions of interest.

In the heatmaps, yellow regions represent areas of the image that are highly indicative of the prediction according to the model—these are the most critical areas for the classification. Green regions indicate areas of moderate importance, while violet regions correspond to parts of the image that are not considered significant by the model for making its prediction. This gradient of interest highlights how the model weighs different parts of the image when arriving at a decision.

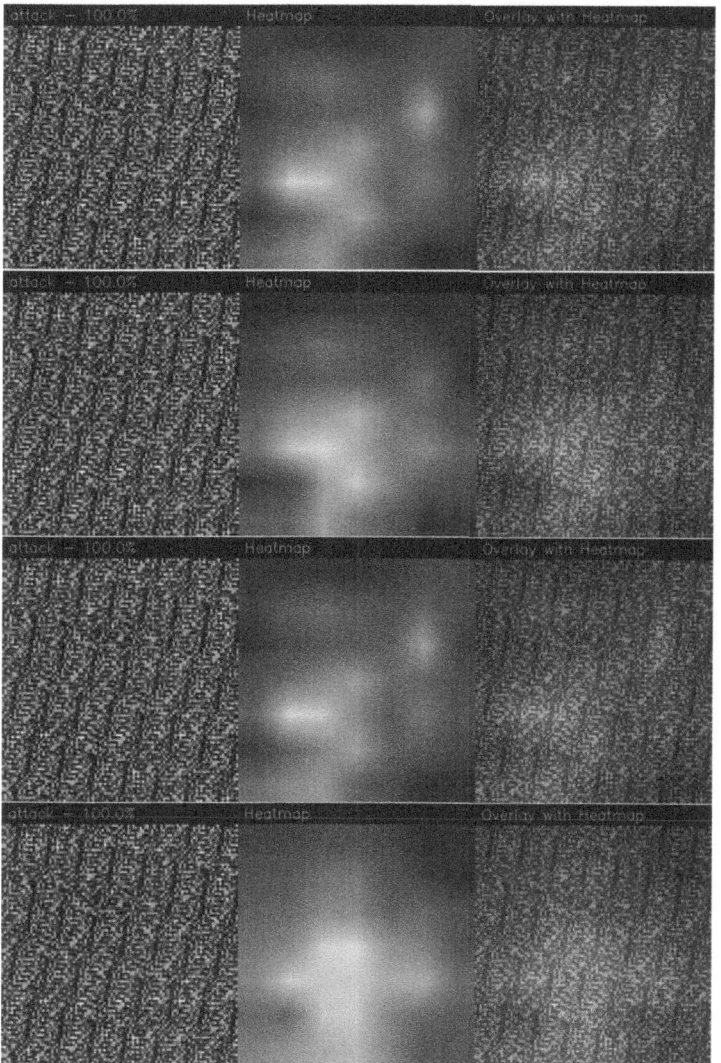

Fig. 3. An example of prediction explainability provided by the adoption of Grad-CAM, Grad-CAM++, Score-CAM, and Score-CAM Fast on an image obtained from a network trace related to an attack.

The comparison of heatmaps generated by the different CAM methods shows a high degree of consistency in identifying the same regions of the image as significant for classification. This coherence across methods, despite differences in their underlying mechanisms, reinforces the reliability of the CAMs in highlighting relevant areas. Grad-CAM and Grad-CAM++ use gradient-based approaches to produce heatmaps, while Score-CAM and Score-CAM Fast rely on activation maps combined with perturbation strategies to ensure robust saliency identification.

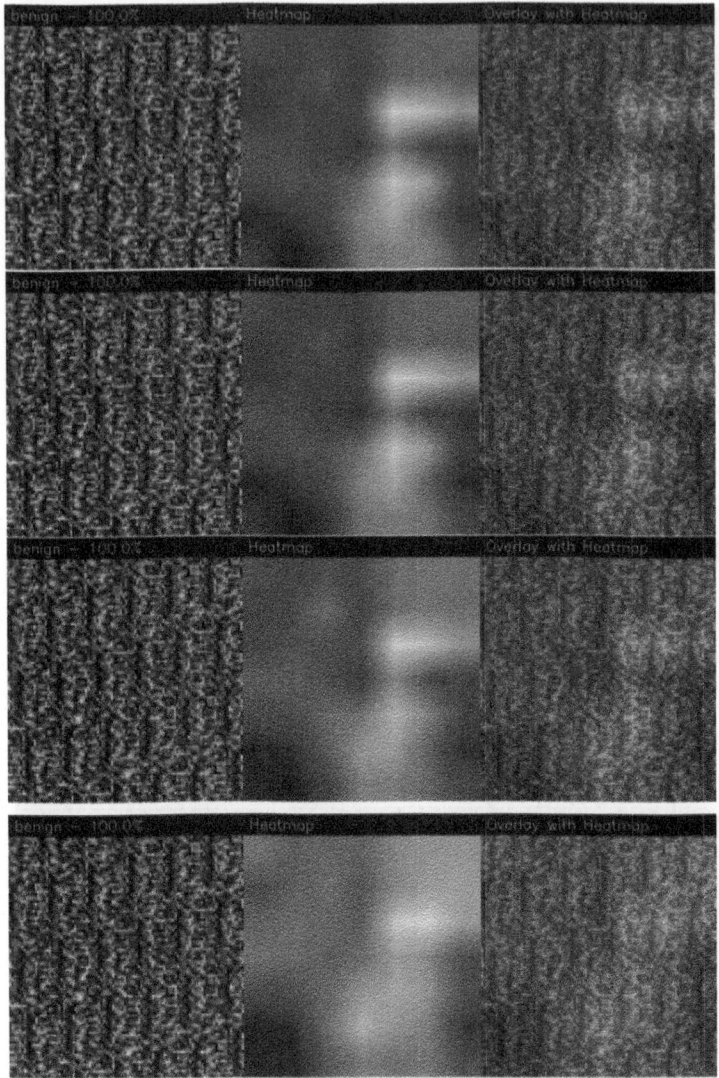

Fig. 4. An example of prediction explainability provided by the adoption of Grad-CAM, Grad-CAM++, Score-CAM, and Score-CAM Fast on an image obtained from a network trace related to a legitimate activity.

This use of CAMs not only supports the validation of the model's predictions but also provides a critical layer of explainability. By visualizing the specific regions that contribute most to the model's decision, stakeholders can interpret and trust the model's behavior more effectively. This explainability is particularly important in sensitive applications, such as anomaly detection in substation networks, where understanding the reasoning behind predictions is essential for ensuring the reliability of the system.

Figure 4 is related to an example of prediction explainability on an image obtained from a network trace related to a benign behaviour i.e., a legitimate trace.

Also in Fig. 4, the comparison of heatmaps produced by the various CAM methods reveals a strong consistency in identifying the same regions of the image as crucial for classification. This alignment across different CAMs, despite differences in their underlying mechanisms (described in the previous section), strengthens the dependability of the CAMs in pinpointing relevant areas. As a matter of fact, while Grad-CAM and Grad-CAM++ generate heatmaps through gradient-based techniques, Score-CAM and Score-CAM Fast rely on activation maps combined with perturbation strategies to ensure the robust identification of salient features inside the image obtained from the network trace under analysis.

4   Conclusion and Future Work

Considering the importance of electrical substations to be protected as critical infrastructures for a series of services that require a constant presence of electricity, in this paper we proposed a method to identify anomalies inside electrical substations. Different models have been considered, the best performances has been achieved by the MobileNet model, trained with 50 epochs, with an accuracy, a precision and a recall equal to 0.995. Furthermore, to highlight the areas of the network trace symptomatic of an attack, four different CAM algorithms have been considered, in order to provide insight into the model prediction. From the point of view of future works, we plan to design a method able to label a network trace with the specific attack, not only providing a (generic) binary classification. Furthermore, we plan to introduce object detection models, in order to try to obtain better performances in terms of accuracy and to provide a way to get back to the PCAP file from the selected areas of the image.

Acknowledgment. This work has been partially supported by EU DUCA, EU Cyber-SecPro, SYNAPSE, PTR 22-24 P2.01 (Cybersecurity) and SERICS (PE00000014) under the MUR National Recovery and Resilience Plan funded by the EU - NextGenerationEU projects, by MUR - REASONING: foRmal mEthods for computAtional analySis for diagnOsis and progNosis in imagING - PRIN, e-DAI (Digital ecosystem for integrated analysis of heterogeneous health data related to high-impact diseases: innovative model of care and research), Health Operational Plan, FSC 2014-2020, PRIN-MUR-Ministry of Health, Progetto MolisCTe, Ministero delle Imprese e del Made in Italy, Italy, CUP: D33B22000060001, FORESEEN: FORmal mEthodS for attack dEtEction in autonomous driviNg systems CUP N.P2022WYAEW and ALOHA: a framework for monitoring the physical and psychological health status of the Worker through Object detection and federated machine learning, Call for Collaborative Research BRiC -2024, INAIL.

References

1. Abasıkeleş-Turgut, I., Daş, R.: Anomaly and intrusion detection systems for smart grids. In: Cyber Security Solutions for Protecting and Building the Future Smart Grid, pp. 231–270. Elsevier (2025)
2. Alomari, M.A.: Security of smart grid: cybersecurity issues, potential cyberattacks, major incidents, and future directions. Energies **18**(1), 141 (2025)
3. Boakye-Boateng, K., Ghorbani, A.A., Lashkari, A.H.: Securing substations with trust, risk posture, and multi-agent systems: a comprehensive approach. In: 2023 20th Annual International Conference on Privacy, Security and Trust (PST), pp. 1–12. IEEE (2023)
4. Di Giammarco, M., et al.: A robust and explainable deep learning method for cervical cancer screening. In: International Conference on Applied Intelligence and Informatics, pp. 111–125. Springer (2023)
5. He, H., Yang, H., Mercaldo, F., Santone, A., Huang, P.: Isolation forest-voting fusion-multioutput: a stroke risk classification method based on the multidimensional output of abnormal sample detection. Comput. Methods Programs Biomed. **253**, 108255 (2024)
6. Jamil, M.S., Banik, S.P., Rahaman, G.A., Saha, S.: Advanced GradCAM++: improved visual explanations of CNN decisions in diabetic retinopathy. In: Computer Vision and Image Analysis for Industry 4.0, pp. 64–75. Chapman and Hall/CRC (2023)
7. Kreimel, P., Eigner, O., Mercaldo, F., Santone, A., Tavolato, P.: Anomaly detection in substation networks. J. Inf. Secur. Appl. **54**, 102527 (2020)
8. Li, J., Zhang, D., Meng, B., Li, Y., Luo, L.: FIMF score-CAM: fast score-cam based on local multi-feature integration for visual interpretation of CNNs. IET Image Proc. **17**(3), 761–772 (2023)
9. Maghami, M.R., Mutambara, A., Gomes, C.: Assessing cyber attack vulnerabilities of distributed generation in grid-connected systems, pp. 1–27. Environment, Development and Sustainability (2025)
10. Marino, D.L., Wickramasinghe, C.S., Rieger, C., Manic, M.: Self-supervised and interpretable anomaly detection using network transformers. arXiv preprint arXiv:2202.12997 (2022)
11. Martinelli, F., Mercaldo, F., Petrillo, L., Santone, A.: Security policy generation and verification through large language models: a proposal. In: Proceedings of the Fourteenth ACM Conference on Data and Application Security and Privacy, pp. 143–145 (2024)
12. Mercaldo, F., et al.: Diabetic retinopathy detection and diagnosis by means of robust and explainable convolutional neural networks. Neural Comput. Appl. **35**(23), 17429–17441 (2023)
13. Most, A.B., Eren, M.E., Alexandrov, B.S., Lawrence, N.: Electrical grid anomaly detection via tensor decomposition. In: MILCOM 2023-2023 IEEE Military Communications Conference (MILCOM), pp. 162–169. IEEE (2023)
14. Nhung-Nguyen, H., Girdhar, M., Kim, Y.H., Hong, J.: Machine-learning-based anomaly detection for goose in digital substations. Energies **17**(15), 3745 (2024)
15. Qu, Y., et al.: CGAM: an end-to-end causality graph attention mamba network for esophageal pathology grading. Biomed. Signal Process. Control **103**, 107452 (2025)
16. Selvaraju, R.R., et al.: Grad-CAM: visual explanations from deep networks via gradient-based localization. In: Proceedings of the IEEE International Conference on Computer Vision, pp. 618–626 (2017)

17. Valdes, A., Macwan, R., Backes, M.: Anomaly detection in electrical substation circuits via unsupervised machine learning. In: 2016 IEEE 17th International Conference on Information Reuse and Integration (IRI), pp. 500–505. IEEE (2016)
18. Wang, H., et al.: Score-CAM: score-weighted visual explanations for convolutional neural networks. In: Proceedings of the IEEE/CVF Conference on Computer Vision and Pattern Recognition Workshops, pp. 24–25 (2020)

Safety and Cybersecurity Under Emerging EU Legislation for Industry: A Use-Case Driven Perspective

Ndeye G. Ndiaye[1]([✉]), Karl Waedt[1], Nicolas Dejon[2], Chrystel Gaber[2],
Achilleas Marinakis[3], Christos A. Gizelis[3], Gürkan Gür[4], Marc Rennhard[4],
Oumayma Zeddini[1], Jean-Philippe Wary[2], Dominico Orlando[5],
Claire Loiseaux[6], Vangelis Photiou[7], Nikolaos Koulierakis[8],
and Vasiliki Danilatou[8]

[1] Framatome GmbH, Erlangen, Germany
{ndeye-gagnessiry.ndiaye,karl.waedt,oumayma.zeddini}@framatome.com
[2] Orange Research, Paris, France
[3] OTE Group of Companies, Maroussi, Greece
[4] Zurich University of Applied Sciences (ZHAW), Winterthur, Switzerland
{gueu,rema}@zhaw.ch
[5] CEFRIEL Politechnica di Milano, Milan, Italy
[6] Internet Of Trust (IOTR), Paris, France
[7] National Computer Security Incident Response Team of Cyprus, Nicosia, Cyprus
[8] Eunomia LTD, Dublin, Ireland

Abstract. In the era of Industry 4.0, the European Union's evolving regulatory landscape—comprising the European Cyber Resilience Act (EU CRA), the NIS2 Directives, and the European Artificial Intelligence Act (EU AI Act)—requires organizations to align technical, organizational, and risk governance practices across complex operational environments. However, this alignment is far from straightforward, particularly in sectors where safety-critical systems are also exposed to cyber threats, and where compliance must extend across diverse supply chains. In fact, the increasing convergence of functional safety and cybersecurity requirements introduces a significant challenge for industrial sectors operating under both domain-specific standards and emerging EU regulations. This paper examines the practical implications through three industrial use cases from the energy, telecommunications, and manufacturing sectors. Each use case highlights the interplay between vertical safety standards (e.g., IEC 61508, ISO 10218, ISO/TS 15066, SEVESO), cybersecurity frameworks (e.g., IEC 62443, PCI DSS), and EU-wide legislative requirements. The paper identifies cross-sector patterns and highlights the need for harmonized approaches to risk management and compliance in both the safety and cybersecurity domains. It contributes to a strong foundation to share practical challenges from real-world integration, which leans towards a novel, harmonized co-assurance and continuous certification framework.

Keywords: Industry 4.0 · Safety and Cybersecurity Convergence · EU Cybersecurity Framework · Verticals · Platform-oriented Protection Profile (PoPP)

B. Coppens et al. (Eds.): ARES 2025 Workshops, LNCS 15994, pp. 304–321, 2025.
https://doi.org/10.1007/978-3-032-00630-1_17

1   Introduction

As the Fourth Industrial Revolution continues to accelerate, the European Union (EU) is navigating a rapidly changing cybersecurity landscape, characterized by increasingly sophisticated threats. To address these challenges, the EU has resolved to expand its cybersecurity framework and strengthen its cybersecurity resilience across its member states, fostering trust and supporting innovation within Europe's digital environment. Following the adoption of the NIS Directive (2016/1148) [6] and the EU Cybersecurity Strategy (EU CSA) (2019/881) [4], key novel initiatives are the European Cyber Resilience Act (EU CRA) [8], the updated NIS2 Directives [9] and the EU AI Act. In 2024, the European Union Agency for Cybersecurity (ENISA) released its first-ever report on the state of cybersecurity in the EU, in accordance with Article 18 of Directive (EU) 2022/2555 (NIS2) [13]. The biennial report highlights the growing complexity of assessing cybersecurity risks, particularly due to evolving threats and the increasing frequency of supply chain attacks. It further highlights the significant efforts made by the EU to establish comprehensive cybersecurity frameworks across organizations, with a particular focus on critical infrastructure and national cybersecurity authorities. Furthermore, the report emphasizes that despite the formal alignment between member states, supported by national cybersecurity strategies (NCSS) aimed at promoting international collaboration and information sharing, adoption within heavy industries introduces open challenges in securing legacy systems and operational technology. As captured by the union-wide methodology presented to assess maturity and criticality of each NIS2 sector commencing with 10 pilot subsectors, these challenges are particularly acute in highly regulated industries (e.g., electricity, gas, health, rail, oil) where critical operations span both cyber and physical systems and safety is a paradigm to consider along with cybersecurity.

The domain of functional safety and cybersecurity individually brings their own significant complexity, with their distinct assurance levels, certification frameworks, and defense-in-depth architectures. In practice, vertical industries are required to conduct risk analyzes in both domains when adhering to industry-specific standards and horizontal regulations. Consequently, the overlap and often fragmented nature of EU legislation, combined with sector-specific cybersecurity and safety standards, creates a complex landscape. Effective planning and governance require a deep understanding of information security frameworks, regulatory obligations, and industry-specific standards, along with the capability to implement these in alignment with business objectives [28].

This paper explores pragmatically the aforementioned challenges through Industry 4.0 use cases in the sectors of energy (smart grids), manufacturing (robotics), and telecommunication (cloud providers). It focuses on how these entities manage cybersecurity vulnerabilities and safety hazards across their entire asset base within the evolving EU cybersecurity landscape. Building on these practical insights, the main contribution of the paper is twofold: (1) to demonstrate the complexity of siloed ecosystem of verticals and horizontals cybersecurity and safety requirements across operational environments; and (2) to systematically analyze the resulting regulatory and technical gaps between horizontal legislation and sector-specific standards, and reveal cross-sector patterns of compliance difficulties, (3) to propose a foundation for Platform-oriented Protection Profile approach capable of supporting adaptive and dynamic safety-cybersecurity risk management across diverse Industry 4.0 systems.

This paper is structured as follows. It first examines the convergence of safety and cybersecurity (Sect. 2) and reviews key EU regulations impacting industry (Sect. 3). It then analyzes industrial use cases across the energy, telecommunications, and manufacturing sectors to illustrate how safety, cybersecurity, and regulatory obligations intersect in practice (Sect. 4), discusses observed gaps, and proposes pathways toward more harmonized and dynamic assurance approaches (Sect. 5), and concludes with key findings and future directions where we introduce our main concept of Platform-oriented Protection Profile (Sect. 6).

2   Joint Consideration of Safety and Cybersecurity in Industry 4.0

The emergence of Industry 4.0 has led to a paradigm shift in industrial systems through the integration of cyber-physical systems, Industrial Internet of Things (IIoT), and cloud-connected platforms. Although these technologies offer significant benefits in terms of automation, data-driven decision making, and operational efficiency, they also blur the traditional boundaries between Information Technology (IT) and Operational Technology (OT). As a result, safety and cybersecurity can no longer be treated as separate disciplines [24].

2.1   Convergence of Domains and Technical Challenges

Safety encompasses different dimensions; however, in the context of Industry 4.0, references to "safety" will primarily concern functional safety. Functional safety was historically ensured through deterministic and fail-safe designs governed by standards such as IEC 61508 [20] or ISO 13849 [22] while cybersecurity was largely the concern of IT departments. A cybersecurity breach can now directly compromise the safe operation (functional safety) of Industry 4.0 systems [16]. For example, manipulated sensor values or unauthorized actuator control may lead to unsafe states or physical harm. Process safety, organizational safety, and physical safety may also be affected, but often as secondary consequences resulting from functional safety failures. Consequently, there is no safety without cybersecurity. The deeper we analyze our cybersecurity risks, the more underlying safety challenges we uncover.

This convergence demands a co-engineering approach, where safety and security requirements are jointly analyzed and implemented, which introduces several challenges [17]. Firstly, security-induced safety failures can occur when cyber-attacks disable or bypass safety mechanisms. Secondly, safety-induced security vulnerabilities may arise when predictable system behavior (e.g., a known fail-safe state) becomes exploitable by attackers. Moreover, there are often conflicting requirements, such as the need for real-time, deterministic communication in safety systems versus the added latency and complexity introduced by encryption or authentication mechanisms in cybersecurity.

2.2 Risk-Based Approaches

Both functional safety and cybersecurity rely on risk-based approaches. This means that each domain begins with a form of analysis, hazard analysis in the case of functional safety, and threat analysis for cybersecurity. These analyses are followed by risk estimation, risk evaluation, and the implementation of appropriate mitigation measures to reduce risk to an acceptable level. Although the underlying philosophy of risk reduction is common in both fields, the methodologies and timelines differ. Functional safety risk assessments typically occur at defined stages of the system lifecycle (i.e., during design, commissioning, and periodic re-certification), often driven by changes in the system or operational context. In contrast, cybersecurity risk assessments require more frequent dynamic reviews, often triggered by external events (e.g., new vulnerabilities, threat intelligence updates) or internal changes (e.g., system updates, new device connections). The rapidly evolving nature of cyber threats requires continuous monitoring and agile risk reassessment, which is less common in traditional safety engineering [1]. Despite these differences, both assessments serve as foundational activities within their respective lifecycles and are increasingly being integrated, especially in Industry 4.0 environments [28].

2.3 Integrated Risk Management Approach

Since cybersecurity can directly impact safety functions, it is imperative that security requirements are integrated throughout the entire lifecycle of industrial systems [25]. This integration was traditionally addressed by conducting joint hazard and threat analyses to identify how cyber vulnerabilities could potentially lead to hazardous scenarios that compromise safety. Defense-in-depth strategies [32], which combine traditional safety barriers with cybersecurity controls such as secure boot mechanisms, network segmentation, and intrusion detection systems, are fundamental in mitigating these risks [17]. These layered protections ensure that security mechanisms complement rather than conflict with safety systems, especially in complex, high-risk industrial domains.

Recent research has highlighted the need for more structured co-assurance methodologies that treat safety and cybersecurity as interdependent rather than siloed domains. Notably, compositional assurance approaches, such as those proposed by Rushby [29], emphasize modular reasoning and the ability to incrementally build assurance cases across components and layers of a system. These methods are increasingly being adopted in safety-critical sectors, including aviation and automotive, where integration of cross-domain risks is essential.

Several efforts have also explored how Model-Based Systems Engineering (MBSE) can facilitate this integration by providing traceable, tool-supported frameworks that align system functions with assurance requirements. For instance, Nguyen et al. [26] present a meta-model that co-engineers safety and security requirements from early design stages, improving traceability and reducing conflicting mitigations.

A practical step toward operationalizing the convergence of safety and cybersecurity is IEC TR 63069 [21], which offers guidance for the joint application of IEC 61508 (functional safety) and IEC 62443 (industrial cybersecurity) within Industrial Automation and Control Systems (IACS). While IEC 63069 establishes a common vocabulary and lifecycle alignment, its real-world applicability relies on how organizations contextualize its recommendations within existing engineering workflows and regulatory environments.

While foundational standards and frameworks are evolving to support co-assurance, significant research continues to refine the theoretical underpinnings (e.g., compositional arguments, integrated assurance cases) and practical enablers (e.g., MBSE tools, certification schemes) necessary for robust safety-security integration. However, existing co-assurance frameworks rarely incorporate regulatory dimensions, and thus lack provisions for lifecycle-spanning accountability, conformity evidence generation, or harmonized compliance mappings [32].

3   Overview of the EU Cybersecurity Framework

The EU has reinforced its cybersecurity framework through a series of recent legislative initiatives. Three key legislative instruments in evolution are the NIS 2 Directive [9], the Cyber Resilience Act [11], and the EU Artificial Intelligence Act [3]. Together, they mark a shift toward a horizontal risk-based regulatory approach. Unlike earlier frameworks such as NIS 1 [6], which were sector-specific and inconsistently applied, these new laws impose security obligations across sectors and scale requirements according to the risk profile of products, services, and entities. This reflects a broader commitment to cybersecurity-by-design and lifecycle risk management in the EU digital ecosystem.

3.1   NIS2: Organizational Cybersecurity Standards

Organizations falling under NIS2 [9] as essential or important entities are required to implement appropriate risk management measures. These include, but are not limited to, access control, incident detection and response, supply chain security, basic cyber hygiene practices, cybersecurity training, encryption, and vulnerability management. Organizations must report cybersecurity incidents to national authorities within strict time frames by providing a three-stage reporting of incidents referred to in the NIS2 [9] as early warning notification, interim notification, and final notification. Essential entities have a higher obligation to demonstrate compliance with the NIS2 Directives as they are subject to ex post and ex ante supervisory measures, whereas important entities are subjected only to ex post supervisory measures. Furthermore, an important element of the NIS2 Directive is that it recognizes the impact of the supply chain and therefore requires organizations to ensure supply chain security, extending obligations to third-party providers. NIS2 should have been transposed into national law in the 27 member states by October 2024, but so far only 15 of them have taken that action by April 2025. Each national law can set different deadlines for the months and years to come.

3.2 EU CRA: Security Requirements for Digital Products

The EU Cyber Resilience Act (CRA) [11] establishes horizontal cybersecurity rules for products with digital elements throughout Europe, aiming to protect consumers and businesses through mandatory security requirements. Products are classified into the default category, Class I, or Class II based on their criticality, i.e., their impact on essential services, public safety/national security, and/or their exposure to cyber risks based on their role in essential services, with increasing security obligations. Manufacturers must apply security-by-design and security-by-default principles, ensure secure updates, manage vulnerabilities, and maintain support for at least five years. They must also implement market surveillance, report incidents, and certify high-risk products (Class II). The CRA entered into force in 2024 with a transitional period of 36 months (i.e., vulnerability reporting begins mid-2026 and full compliance is required by mid-2027), thus complementing the NIS2 Directive [9] in strengthening Europe's cybersecurity framework.

3.3 EU Artificial Intelligence Act (EU AIA)

The EU Artificial Intelligence Act (EU AIA) [3] adopts a risk-based approach to regulate AI systems based on their potential impact on fundamental rights and safety. AI systems are classified into prohibited, high-risk, or low-risk categories, with high-risk systems subject to strict obligations on data quality, transparency, risk management, human oversight, technical robustness, and cybersecurity. Providers must ensure thorough security assessments and apply appropriate safeguards throughout the lifecycle of the AI system, integrating both traditional cybersecurity practices and AI-specific protections. The EU AI Act [3] is being implemented gradually from 2025 to 2027. The ban on activities with unacceptable risk has been operational since last February. Most of the obligations will be operational from August 2025, including those for general-purpose AIs and governance provisions. Furthermore, sanctions may also be imposed from August 2025 onward. The obligations for activities classified as high-risk will be operational from August 2026, with a further one-year extension for particular systems already regulated by other EU legislation.

3.4 Overview on Safety Considerations

CRA [11] and AIA [3] provide the most explicit legal recognition of how cybersecurity failures can impact safety. CRA (Recital 4, Articles 5 & 10) links cyber risks to potential safety consequences (via "reasonably foreseeable misuse"). AIA (Article 6, Annex III & VII) integrates safety into its high-risk AI classification, embedding it in conformity and risk management requirements. Although the joint consideration of cybersecurity and safety in the NIS2 Directive [9] is not systematic or operationalized (unlike what the CRA and AIA begin to approach), it is explicitly present and legally relevant in determining which entities are covered and why. In fact, the NIS2 Directive acknowledges that cybersecurity disruptions can affect safety (especially physical safety in essential services like energy, health, and water). However, it does not require entities to perform integrated cyber-physical functional safety and cybersecurity risk assessments.

In summary, recent and emerging regulatory frameworks reflect a growing consensus that cybersecurity is no longer sufficient alone in the context of connected industrial systems. Nevertheless, it creates practical confusion in implementation, as integrated risk management of safety and cybersecurity remains project-specific, especially for Industry 4.0 systems.

4 Industrial Use Cases and Sectoral Analysis

4.1 Methodology for Use Case Selection

Smart Energy Systems, Advanced Manufacturing Systems, and Digital Service providers were selected along with representative use cases due to their direct exposure to the EU's evolving regulatory landscape. They underpin essential infrastructure and emerging technologies and their classification under NIS2, CRA, and the AIA, as summarized in Table 1, reflects their strategic importance in ensuring resilience, cybersecurity, and safety across interconnected EU digital ecosystems. Furthermore, the selection is motivated by ongoing standardization efforts to face dual compliance demands from horizontals vs verticals, via presumption of conformity, such as Mandate M/585 for the CRA, ENISA and national authority recommendations to adopt the IEC 62443 series, and ISO/IEC 42001:2023 for AI governance under the AI Act.

These use cases are (UC1) Battery Storage Clusters for EVs Charging Station, (UC2) Robot Cybersecurity Inspection (Wi-Fi/5G) and (UC3) 5G/6G MEC Platform, and described in Sects. 4.2, 4.3, and 4.4, respectively. Each case is further analyzed for the following dimensions: (1) Vertical-specific safety/cybersecurity standards, (2) Risk assessment scope, and (3) Integration and compliance practices. Horizontal requirements are generically described in Sect. 3.

4.2 Battery Storage Cluster for EV Charging Stations

As the energy sector moves towards renewable sources, effective energy management becomes crucial due to the inherent variability of sources (e.g., fluctuation of wind and solar). To address this, battery storage technology serves as an innovative solution for fast charging electric vehicles (EVs), e.g., electric cars and e-bikes to ensure both grid stability and long-term energy reserves. The

Table 1. EU Risk-based Classification under NIS2, EU CRA, EU AI Act per UC

Use Case	EU Risk Classification
Battery Storage Cluster for EV Charging	**NIS2**: Essential entity (energy); **CRA**: Class II - firmware, controllers
Robot Cybersecurity In spection (Wi-Fi/5G)	**CRA**: Class II - AI-enabled, wireless; **NIS2**: for digital providers; **EU AI Act**: High-risk, semi-autonomous operation
5G/6G MEC Platform	**NIS2**: Important entity (edge cloud), Essential entity (electronic communications providers following EECC amendments); **CRA**: Class I or II - platform-level components; **EU AI Act**: Depends on hosted customer service

battery storage system (boosted charger + EV charging station) stores excess renewable energy to be fed back into the grid during shortages. However, complex electrochemical processes within batteries pose safety-critical risks, including fire hazards and potential chemical pollution.

High-Level Description. The industrial process depicted in Fig. 1 consists of operating locally and distributing industry-grade physical containers at the client's premises, subjecting them to security and safety obligations. It is supported by various industry partners that provide remote maintenance services, continuous monitoring of containerized equipment (e.g., battery health management, temperature & HVAC monitoring, and electrical power performance). In addition, an external aggregator handles charger payments through a process that authenticates the driver via RFID (accounting functionalities). The operator tracks physical conditions through PLC and HMI-based SCADA systems, ensuring that the parameters remain within safe operational limits. Commercial Off-The-Shelf (COTS) equipment is used and integrated with proprietary or legacy systems [31].

Use Case Requirements from Verticals. The system is engineered in accordance with IEC 62443 [23], applying Security Levels 2âĂŞ3 based on asset exposure. It enforces a layered security model separating IT and OT via network segmentation and defense-in-depth [30,31]. Product suppliers must follow secure development lifecycles (IEC 62443-4-1, 4-2) for components (PLCs, HMIs, sensors, network devices), ensuring authenticated firmware updates and encryption. System integrators (IEC 62443-2-4) must implement segmentation, secure protocols, and access controls, while asset owners (IEC 62443-2-1, 2-3) handle risk management, monitoring, and incident response. Shared SL targets and conformance criteria across suppliers and service providers enforce supply chain security. The battery infrastructure complies with IEC 61508 [20], using SIL 2-3 for critical functions (charge/discharge control, temperature regulation) based on hazard assessments. A full safety lifecycle—from requirements through validation and periodic review—mitigates risks like overcharge or overheating. It adheres to IEC 61508-3 parts [19], employing fault-tolerant architecture and

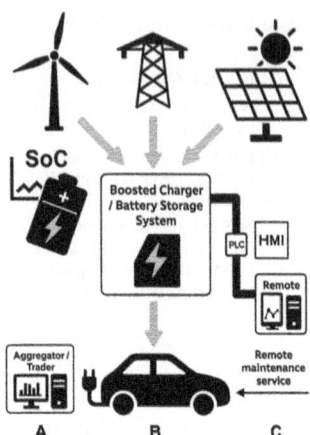

Fig. 1. Use Case 1 Architecture - Multi-party services A: Accounting, B: Operator, C: Remote maintenance

Table 2. Use Case Requirements from Vertical Standards

Key Requirements	Vertical Standard	Req. Type
Secure product development lifecycle for components (PLCs, HMIs, sensors)	IEC 62443-4-1/4-2 (Product Supplier)	Technical
Integration of secure communications, segmentation, and access control	IEC 62443-2-4 (System Integrator)	Technical
Cybersecurity governance and risk management during operation	IEC 62443-2-1/2-3 (Asset Owner)	Organiznl.
Supply chain security and third-party control alignment	IEC 62443 (General Supply Chain Requirements)	Organiznl.
Software design techniques supporting fail-safe behavior (e.g., over charge/overheat protection)	IEC 61508-3 (Software requirements for safety-related systems)	Technical
Structured safety lifecycle (hazard identification to validation)	IEC 61508 (Safety Lifecycle Process)	Procedural
Joint consideration of safety and cyber security in risk analysis	IEC TR 63069 (Co-engineering Framework)	Procedural
Coordination of safety and security responsibilities across stakeholders	IEC TR 63069 (Stakeholder Alignment)	Organiznl.
Identification of safety-induced vulnerabilities from predictable behavior	IEC TR 63069 (Cross-domain Vulnerability Analysis)	Technical
Assessment of security impacts on real-time safety-critical performance	IEC TR 63069 (Latency/Security Trade-off Awareness)	Co-Assurance

deterministic logic to ensure predictable and reliable responses under fault conditions or cyber-physical threats. To align these two domains, the principles of IEC TR 63069 [21] are applied in practice through joint risk assessment workshops, integrated architectural reviews aligning SIL and SL targets, and combined validation strategies. Safety and security teams coordinate assurance processes, ensuring fail-safe functions remain effective even under cyber threats, while shared governance structures and co-engineered documentation improve lifecycle traceability and co-assurance.

Table 2 outlines system requirements derived from specific IEC standards. Each requirement is clearly linked to its corresponding vertical standard (e.g., IEC 62443 [23], IEC 61508-3 [19], IEC TR 63069 [21]) and categorized by requirement type—Technical, Organizational, Procedural, or Co-Assurance.

4.3   Robot Cybersecurity Inspection

High-Level Description. As human-robot collaboration becomes increasingly integrated into critical infrastructure environments, ensuring their secure, safe, and compliant operation is vital. An agile dog robot (such as Spot), as a semi-autonomous, Wi-Fi/5G-connected platform, represents a cutting-edge solution for cybersecurity inspections that is capable of patrolling indoor and outdoor facilities, analyzing IoT sensor data, and detecting anomalies in real time. By combining mobility, AI, and sensor integration, the robot enables a proactive approach to monitoring system health and cyber resilience. However, its deployment in such environments (Human Robot Interaction, HRI) introduces a wide range of regulatory, safety, and privacy challenges that must be addressed to ensure its effective operation and efficiency.

The agile dog robot is part of an HRI indoor inspection system that greatly enhances operational efficiency but also opens up new cybersecurity and safety challenges. Securing both physical and digital elements, especially the autonomous or semi-autonomous robot, IoT sensors, and wireless communications, is essential to ensure the reliability and trustworthiness of safe inspections.

Use Case Requirements from Verticals. Although Spot is not a conventional industrial robot, safety remains essential when operating in dynamic human environments. During autonomous or semi-autonomous operation, Spot must comply with functional and collaborative robotics safety standards, including ISO 10218-1, ISO 13849, and ISO/TS 15066, through comprehensive risk assessments and fail-safe design. Secure operation requires adherence to NIST SP 800-82 for safe ICS communication and interaction. Spot must also implement cybersecurity controls such as network segmentation and access management in line with the IEC 62443 series.

Table 3 illustrates the vertical requirements that are relevant for the deployment of a dog robot capable of performing indoor cybersecurity inspections in different operational scenarios.

4.4   5G/6G Multi-access Edge Computing (MEC) in Industry 4.0

Multi-Access Edge Computing (MEC) in a 5G/6G context brings computing and storage resources closer to the network edge and allows Mobile Network Operators (MNOs) to tailor network characteristics to directly benefit vertical industries. This brings ultra-low latency for AR/VR, gaming, industrial automation, Vehicle-to-Everything (V2X) communications); high bandwidth for video

Table 3. Robot Cybersecurity Inspection: Regulation vs. Function vs. Challenges

Regulation (Code)	System Function	Key Requirements
ISO 10218 & ISO/TS 15066 (Robot Safety Standards)	HRI during patrols or inspections	Collision avoidance, physical safety measures, compliant force and speed limits
NIST SP 800-82 (Cyber security for ICS)	Real-time inspection of industrial control systems (ICS)	Ensuring the robot does not create ICS vulnerabilities or interfere with critical ops
IEC 62443 (Industrial Communication Networks - Security)	Cyber resilience in OT environments, anomaly detection	Hardening endpoints, managing network segmentation, authenticating devices

streaming and content delivery); and localized data processing (for enhanced privacy, compliance, and performance to process medical data or automated driving data) [27]. This adds to the current transformation in the telecommunications industry, where operators are shifting from monolithic network designs to Containerized Network Service Infrastructures (CNSIs) and disaggregated architectures (e.g., OpenRAN), borrowing IT technical know-how from cloud native technologies (virtualization, orchestration, and automation). This enables rapid deployment and flexible management of network functions (e.g., network slices leveraging Network Function Virtualizations (NFVs) [18], Software-Defined Networking (SDN), and advanced orchestration tools).

High-Level Description. The MEC architecture, illustrated in Fig. 2, features [27]:

– Distributed computing nodes (edge cloud): located near the Radio Access Network (RAN), in the 5G Core Network or in between
– Virtualized infrastructure (compute, storage, and network): containerization and orchestration technologies for customized on-demand network slices
– APIs: allowing application developers of various industries to integrate diverse services and tailor applications to specific business needs

Use Case Requirements from Verticals. From a network provider's perspective, delivering MEC services enables differentiated offerings and requires support for diverse applications with varying requirements. Vertical industries can transfer certain safety obligations to network providers by defining them as requirements and incorporating them into Service Level Agreements (SLAs) while security requirements are transferred into Security Service Level Agreements (SSLAs) [15]. Thus, safety and security are embedded into SLAs/SSLAs. For example, 5G teleoperated surgeries in the healthcare industry can transfer safety and performance obligations to network providers to obtain reliable and fast connections and computing resources. Other examples are illustrated in Table 4 following previously reported 5G MEC requirements [27].

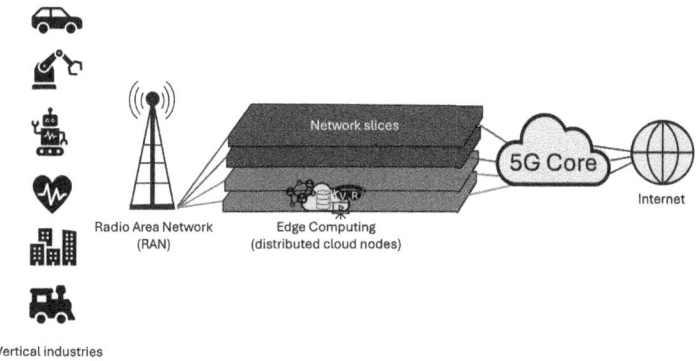

Fig. 2. Use Case 3 - 5G MEC Architecture. From left to right: vertical industries, RAN, MEC distributed node, network slices, 5G Core Network, Internet

Table 4. Examples of Security and Safety Req. for MEC Applications

Verticals	Examples	Security Threats	Safety Threats	Key Requirements	SLAs
Manufacturing	Robotic arms, AGVs	ICS compromise, supply chain attacks on IoT, ransomware	Worker injury, equipment damage	Process protection, sabotage prevention	Ultra-low latency, high reliability, isolation
Healthcare	Remote surgery, diagnostics	Medical device compromise, data breaches	Patient harm, privacy loss	Device/data security, file protection	High reliability, data privacy
Automo-tive	Autonomous driving, connected cars	Unauthorized vehicle access, V2X attacks	Passenger harm, vehicle damage	Secure access, safety assur ance	Low latency, high band width
Smart Cities/ Grids	Intelligent traffic man agement	Infrastructure disruptions, service outages	Cascade failures, public safety	Infrastructure security, resilience	Scalability, resilience
Banking	Mobile banking, fraud detection	DoS attacks	Economic disruption, citizen safety	Network/device security	Low latency, high reliability

In addition to supporting each vertical industry's unique constraints, 5G/6G MEC deployments must also address their own specific security challenges spanning the entire technological stack—from the radio link to core network components, including network slices, computing resources, and any elements of the infrastructure and software dependencies. Consequently, 5G/6G MEC deployments face a complex regulatory landscape that includes vertical-specific regulations and standards (e.g., EECC [7], 5G Toolbox [2], FFT [14], ETSI recommendations [12], SEVESO [5], DORA [10]) thus must provide enough flexibility to ensure compliance across all these verticals.

5   Discussion

5.1   Gap Compliance Analysis

Table 5 illustrates examples of gaps in risk management requirements from emerging cybersecurity regulations (horizontals) vs established safety and security standards (verticals). It is important to recognize that the level of maturity in jointly considering cybersecurity and safety varies significantly across sectors (e.g., from smart grids, autonomous robots, to remote-operated MEC services).

The complexity of sectoral regulations and industry-specific constraints prevents, under the current state-of-the-art, any possibility of automating this industrial risk management to reduce costly integration efforts, unpredictable risks and gaps, and legal and technical assurance. Another dimension of this complexity is related to the capacity of industry to continuously comply over time, independently of the evolution of sectoral regulations, with their constraints. Then, the concept of continuous certification could be introduced both at the level of each industrial infrastructure and at the level of critical infrastructures and products used by these industrial entities. If we approach these questions from the perspective of the vulnerabilities of the products and services used by these manufacturers, the CRA Directive is a first approach that still needs to demonstrate its realistic implementation (cost effective in time and efficiency) but also take into account the extra-territorial aspect required for its effectiveness (if a product or service is operated by a non-European legal entity). However, the CRA Directive cannot meet the identified sectoral needs, since it is focused on product vulnerabilities that are disconnected from industrial implementations, i.e. the risks specific to each user entity. The NIS2 Directive is focused on risk management specific to each industrial or legal entity; it cannot, as it stands, take into account the risk management of a complex ecosystem integrating several manufacturers both at the level of products and services delivered and at the level of infrastructures used and subject to the NIS2 Directive. These approaches can be perceived as antagonistic or independent: vulnerability management versus risk management and will therefore have disconnected life cycles, thereby preventing any industrial automation over composite environments

5.2   Future Work

A similar approach to that used in the common criteria composition mechanisms (in production for several decades for specific products) could then serve as a bridge between each of these manufacturers and allow them to delegate some of their security objectives to other industrial entities. Based on this hypothesis, the implementation of such a framework would require the following.

- A capacity to fine-tune these objectives when delegated to or managed by a stakeholder in the value chain (concept of contractualization and liability: SLA),
- A capacity to provide, at all times (continuously), a presumption of compliance with SLAs/SSLAs, both at the subcontractor level vis-à-vis the delegating industry, and at the national security authority level for each industry.

Table 5. Examples of Risk-centric Integration Gaps Across Use Cases and How PoPPs Harmonize Them

Aspect	Energy Use Case	Telecom Use Case	Manufacturing Use Case	PoPP Harmonization
Risk Granularity	Broad NIS2 classification vs. detailed SIL/SL in standards	NIS2 evaluates service-level risk; client verticals (e.g., DORA, SEVESO) vary in granularity	CRA and AI Act classify AI use cases at a high level; ISO 13849 applies numerical PL-based safety metrics	Defines asset-specific assurance mappings linking SIL/SL with NIS2 domains; aligns abstract AI risks to deterministic safety levels using traceability anchors
Risk Focus	NIS2/CRA target infrastructure-level impact; IEC 61508/62443 assess local system failure modes	NIS2 focuses on availability and platform stability; client verticals focus on data integrity, financial safety, or environmental hazards	EU AI Act emphasizes societal and ethical risk; ISO 13849 targets human injury and physical hazards	Harmonizes global regulatory risks with component-level safety/security claims across multi-domain systems
Risk Owners	Risk managed at the org. level (CISO, regulatory affairs) vs. system level (OT engineers, safety/security integrators)	NIS2 compliance sits with providers; enforcement of vertical-specific controls handled by client-side teams	Legal/AI governance teams manage AI Act obligations; safety is implemented by industrial engineers	Encodes stakeholder-specific roles and responsibilities using modular PoPP profiles with SLA/assurance context bindings
Compliance Logic	CRA/NIS2 require life cycle management and secure development governance; IEC standards focus on system and design assurance	NIS2's organizational controls are difficult to reconcile with technical diversity across customer use cases	AI Act demands traceability, oversight, and documentation across the lifecycle; ISO 13849 emphasizes deterministic system behavior and upfront design validation	Encodes abstract regulatory tags, lifecycle phases, and system design evidence into coherent, reusable assurance structures

- A capacity to abstract and model safety and cybersecurity requirements into structured interfaces that can be understood and negotiated by heterogeneous stakeholders across industrial, digital, and critical infrastructure domains,
- A capacity to optimize these delegations (or to orchestrate these delegations), integrating instantaneous cost dimensions, end-to-end latency, and geographical constraints, or time-limited contextual criticality requiring reinforced measures and services for a specific actor (independently of other industries present in the area or using the same services).

To cope with this complexity, we propose to model the constraints in a new concept called *Platform-oriented Protection Profile (PoPP)* inspired from Common Criteria and use a bottom-up and iterative approach on concrete use cases. Although Common Criteria are a strong foundation for cybersecurity assurance, it is not sufficient on their own for safety assurance. Thus, joint modeling of co-assurance artifacts (e.g., extended Protection Profiles), are needed to address cyber-physical systems holistically.

The PoPP ontology illustrated in Fig. 3 is designed to unify safety, security, and compliance to concerns of both horizontals and verticals for cyber-physical platforms by providing a machine-interpretable profile that links high-level regulations and detailed standard clauses to concrete system assets and security and safety objectives.

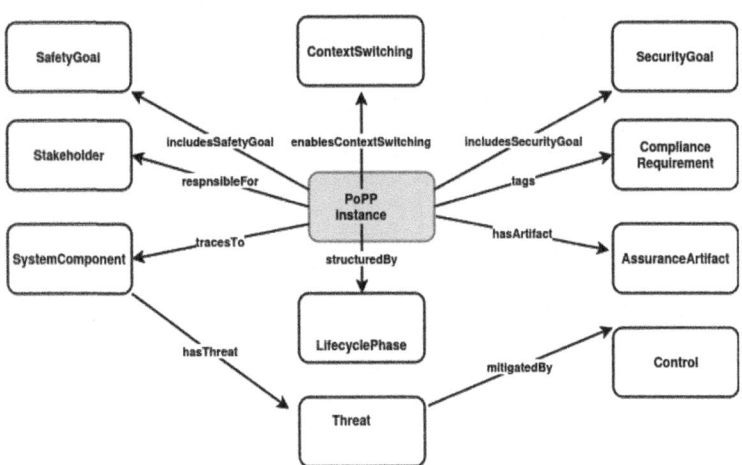

Fig. 3. PoPP ontology schema: classes and properties

It allows *ComplianceRequirement* instances to represent both broad horizontal requirements (e.g., NIS2) and detailed requirements of verticals (e.g., IEC 61508/SIL or IEC 62443/SL), with each instance linking to them via *popp:tags* and to specific objectives via *includesSafetyGoal* and *includesSecurityGoal*, thereby unifying high-level and fine-grained needs. Different risk domains are captured through distinct safety and security goal instances reflecting local failure modes or infrastructure impacts. *SystemComponent* instances denote assets, i.e., hardware/software units that implement these goals connected to the PoPP by *tracesTo* property and linked to platform-level requirements. Organizational and system-level ownership is modeled via the *Stakeholder* class with *popp:assignedTo* and *popp:responsibleFor*, e.g., *ex:CISO* or *ex:OTEngineer*. The lifecycle is structured with *popp:LifecyclePhase* and *popp:structuredBy*, enabling phase-specific compliance activities, and evidence is tied through *popp:AssuranceArtifact* to both phases and requirements. Finally, *popp:ContextSwitching* captures runtime modes (such as *MaintenanceMode* for safe updates under combined SIL/SL constraints) to ensure the correct compliance logic is enforced dynamically.

The next research step is to instantiate PoPP for specific use cases (e.g., UC1) with a minimal set of regulations and then incorporate standards and regulations on a case-by-case basis. This will pave the way towards a generic PoPP that would be too complicated to build from scratch.

6 Conclusion

EU regulations such as the CRA, the NIS2 Directive, and the EU AI Act—along with safety and cybersecurity sector-specific standards like IEC 61508, IEC 62443, and ISO 13849—adopt a risk-based approach. However, they differ substantially in their language, scope, and level of application. EU frameworks emphasize organizational accountability and horizontal compliance, whereas sectoral standards focus on technical system-level control, creating a disconnect in implementation. Safety and cybersecurity remain largely siloed in both practice and regulation, with divergent stakeholders, methodologies, and lifecycle models, which hinders integrated assurance. Insights from cross-sector use cases in energy, telecom, and manufacturing consistently highlight these tensions, especially when EU-level legislation introduces new horizontal duties atop mature vertical norms. To address this complexity, we introduce the concept of Platform-oriented Protection Profiles that refer to structured, adaptable, and liable templates for specifying joint cybersecurity and safety requirements at the level of industrial platforms, facilitating harmonized and continuous compliance with emerging EU regulations and verticals across complex, interconnected systems.

References

1. Bajramovic, E., Gupta, D., Guo, Y., Waedt, K., Bajramovic, A.: Security Challenges and Best Practices for IIoT (2019)
2. European Commission: Cybersecurity of 5G networks: Eu toolbox of risk mitigating measures (2020). https://ec.europa.eu/newsroom/dae/document.cfm?doc_id=64468. Accessed 23 Apr 2025

3. European Commission: Proposal for a regulation of the European parliament and of the council laying down harmonised rules on artificial intelligence (artificial intelligence act) and amending certain union legislative acts (2021). https://eur-lex.europa.eu/legal-content/EN/TXT/?uri=CELEX%3A52021PC0206 , cOM(2021) 206 final, 2021/0106(COD). Final adoption expected 2024–2025

4. European Commission And High Representative: the eu's cybersecurity strategy for the digital decade (2020). https://digital-strategy.ec.europa.eu/en/library/eus-cybersecurity-strategy-digital-decade. jOIN(2020) 18 final. Accessed14 Apr 2025

5. European Parliament And Council: Directive (EU) 2012/18 on major-accident hazards (seveso iii directive) (2012). https://eur-lex.europa.eu/legal-content/EN/TXT/?uri=CELEX:32012L0018. Accessed 23 Apr 2025

6. European Parliament And Council: Directive (EU) 2016/1148 on security of network and information systems (nis directive) (2016). https://eur-lex.europa.eu/eli/dir/2016/1148/oj . Accessed 23 Apr 2025

7. European Parliament And Council: Directive (EU) 2018/1972 establishing the European electronic communications code (EECC) (2018). https://eur-lex.europa.eu/eli/dir/2018/1972/oj. Accessed 23 Apr 2025

8. European Parliament And Council: Regulation (EU) 2019/881 on enisa and ICT certification (cybersecurity act) (2019). https://eur-lex.europa.eu/legal-content/EN/TXT/?uri=CELEX:32019R0881. Accessed 14 Apr 2025

9. European Parliament and Council: Directive (EU) 2022/2555 on cybersecurity (NIS 2 directive) (2022). https://eur-lex.europa.eu/legal-content/EN/TXT/?uri=CELEX:32022L2555. Accessed 14 Apr 2025

10. European Parliament and Council: Regulation (EU) 2022/2554 on digital operational resilience (dora regulation) (2022). https://eur-lex.europa.eu/eli/reg/2022/2554/oj/eng. Accessed 23 Apr 2025

11. European Parliament and Council: Regulation (EU) 2024/2847 on cybersecurity requirements for digital products (cyber resilience act) (2024). https://eur-lex.europa.eu/legal-content/FR/TXT/?uri=CELEX:32024R2847. Accessed 20 Apr 2025

12. European Telecommunications Standards Institute: MEC security: Status of standards support and future evolutions (2021). https://www.etsi.org/images/files/ETSIWhitePapers/ETSI_WP_46-_MEC_security.pdf. Accessed 23 Apr 2025

13. European Union Agency for Cybersecurity: 2024 report on the state of cybersecurity in the union. Publications office of the European Union, Luxembourg (2024). https://doi.org/10.2824/0401593

14. Fédération Française des Télécoms: Rézférentiel d'objectifs de sécurité en matière de fonctions réseau virtualisées (2018). https://www.fftelecoms.org/app/uploads/2021/02/fftelecoms_referentiel_objectifs_securite_virtualisation.pdf. Accessed 23 Apr 2025

15. Gaber, C.E.A.: The owner, the provider and the subcontractors: how to handle accountability and liability management for 5G end to end service. In: Proceedings of the 17th International Conference on Availability, Reliability and Security, pp. 1–7 (2022)

16. Gupta, D., Bajramovic, E., Hoppe, H., Ciriello, A.: The need for integrated cybersecurity and safety training. J. Nucl. Eng. Radiat. Sci. 4 (2018)

17. Guzman, N., Kozine, I., Lundteigen, M.A.: An integrated safety and security analysis for cyber-physical harm scenarios. Saf. Sci. 144, 105458 (2021)

18. Han, B., Gopalakrishnan, V., Ji, L., Lee, S.: Network function virtualization: challenges and opportunities for innovations. IEEE Commun. Mag. 53(2), 90–97 (2015)

19. International Electrotechnical Commission: IEC 61508-3:2010 on software requirements for functional safety, Edition 2.0 (2010). https://webstore.iec.ch/publication/5513. Accessed 23 Apr 2025
20. International Electrotechnical Commission: IEC 61508 on functional safety of electrical/electronic/programmable systems (2010). https://webstore.iec.ch/publication/5510. Accessed 23 Apr 2025
21. International Electrotechnical Commission: IEC 63069 on framework for functional safety and cybersecurity (2019). https://webstore.iec.ch/publication/64927. Accessed 23 Apr 2025
22. International Organization for Standardization: ISO 13849-1:2015 on safety of machinery and control systems design (2015). https://www.iso.org/standard/69883.html. Accessed 23 Apr 2025
23. International Organization for Standardization and International Electrotechnical Commission: ISO/IEC 62443 on industrial communication networks security (2018). https://www.iso.org/standard/80410.html. Accessed 23 Apr 2025
24. Link, J., Waedt, K., Ben Zid, I., Lou, X.: Current challenges of the joint consideration of functional safety & cyber security, their interoperability and impact on organizations: how to manage RAMS + S (reliability availability maintainability safety + security). In: 2018 12th International Conference on Reliability, Maintainability, and Safety (ICRMS), pp. 185–191 (2018)
25. Link, J., Waedt, K., Ben Zid, I., Lou, X.: Current challenges of the joint consideration of functional safety and cyber security, their interoperability and impact on organizations: How to manage RAMS + S (reliability availability maintainability safety + security). In: 2018 12th International Conference on Reliability, Maintainability, and Safety (ICRMS), pp. 185–191 (2018)
26. Nguyen, T.A., Sabaliauskaite, G., Khan, F.: A model-based approach for safety and security co-engineering. J. Syst. Architect. **122**, 102358 (2022)
27. Nowak, T.W., et al.: Verticals in 5G MEC-use cases and security challenges. IEEE Access **9**, 87251–87298 (2021)
28. Ramachandra, S., Vankeirsbilck, J., Boydens, J.: Challenges in the co-assurance of functional safety and cybersecurity in industry 4.0. In: 2022 6th International Conference on System Reliability and Safety (ICSRS), pp. 418–423 (2022)
29. Rushby, J.: Compositional verification for assurance cases. In: Computer Safety, Reliability, and Security (SAFECOMP), pp. 3–17. Springer (2019)
30. Schindler, J., Kirdan, E., Waedt, K.: Secure OPC UA server configuration for smart charging stations. In: INFORMATIK 2021 (2021)
31. Schindler, J., Watson, V., Waedt, K.: Interoperability of fast charging station with battery booster. In: INFORMATIK 2019: 50 Jahre Gesellschaft für Informatik – Informatik für Gesellschaft (Workshop-Beiträge), pp. 295–307. Gesellschaft für Informatik e.V., Bonn (2019)
32. Ylönen, M., Björkman, K.: Integrated management of safety and security (IMSS) in the nuclear industry – organizational culture perspective. Saf. Sci. **166**, 106236 (2023)

An Explainable Method for Malware Detection Through Convolutional Neural Networks

Francesco Mercaldo[1,2(✉)], Paul Tavolato[2], Antonella Santone[1], and Fabio Martinelli[3]

[1] Department of Medicine and Health Sciences V. Tiberio, University of Molise, Campobasso, Italy
{francesco.mercaldo,antonella.santone}@unimol.it
[2] Faculty of Computer Science, University of Vienna, Vienna, Austria
{mercaldof67,paul.tavolato}@univie.ac.at
[3] Institute of High Performance Computing and Networking, National Research Council of Italy (CNR), Rende, Italy
fabio.martinelli@icar.cnr.it

Abstract. Considering that current antimalware, typically based on signature-based approaches, are not able to identify threats whose signatures are not present in the antiviral database, in this paper we propose a method to identify malware based on deep learning, in particular on convolutional neural networks to identify whether an application is malicious. A distinctive feature of the proposed method is the ability to explain the reasons why the classifier predicts whether an application is malware or trusted, in fact in addition to the binary prediction, the proposed method is able to select the opcodes of the identified application that according to the model are symptomatic of the malicious behavior, thus providing a kind of explainability. Experimental results have shown satisfactory results, thus demonstrating the effectiveness of the proposed method.

Keywords: Malware · Deep Learning · Convolutional Neural Network · Explainability · Security

1 Introduction

Malware refers to any software intentionally designed to disrupt, damage, or gain unauthorized access to computer systems and digital devices, including personal computers, smartphones, and enterprise networks [18]. One of the primary objectives of malware is the extraction and exfiltration of sensitive information from victim devices. This stolen data often includes personal credentials, financial records, proprietary business information, or other forms of confidential content, which are then transmitted to the attacker without user knowledge or consent.

Over the years, malware authors have continually evolved their techniques to circumvent conventional detection systems, especially those relying on

B. Coppens et al. (Eds.): ARES 2025 Workshops, LNCS 15994, pp. 322–339, 2025.
https://doi.org/10.1007/978-3-032-00630-1_18

static signature-based methods employed by most commercial and open-source antivirus tools. Traditional signature-based detection involves identifying known malicious patterns within files, such as specific byte sequences or code snippets. While effective against previously identified threats, this method falls short in detecting new, unseen, or obfuscated malware variants [1].

To overcome signature-based limitations, malware frequently employs obfuscation techniques, in which the malicious payload is compressed, encrypted, or otherwise obfuscated within a wrapper to disguise its true behavior. This trend has given rise to malware particularly challenging to detect due to its ability to alter its external appearance while preserving its internal functionality. This is the reason why malware can bypass static analysis tools and evade heuristic detection by mimicking the behavior of legitimate software or by decrypting itself only at runtime.

Recently, deep learning, more generally artificial intelligence, is providing the possibility of training models, starting from data, to build classifiers [6]. Deep learning in particular, has demonstrated a great ability to generate models capable of obtaining very encouraging performances, especially in image classification [9, 11, 15, 16]. Unfortunately, one of the major obstacles to the adoption of deep learning is the lack of explainability behind a given prediction [5]. In fact, in order for the end user to have confidence in a model, it is essential to know the reasons why a model takes a given decision, or predicts a given label for an input instance.

Starting from these considerations, in this paper we propose a method for malware detection by exploiting deep learning. We represent an application under analysis in terms of an image, obtained from the opcodes extracted by disassembling the application. Furthermore, the proposed method, in addition to predicting whether an application is malware or trusted (i.e., we consider a binary classification task), is also able to provide which section of the application has resulted to be the malicious payload (from the point of view of the model). As a matter of fact, we adopt Class Activation Mapping (CAM) to generate a heatmap related to areas of the image that are of interest for the classification provided by the model [4]. Thus, the proposed method is not only able to say whether an application is malware, but it is also able to provide the reasons behind the prediction, in terms of the opcodes that, from the point of view of the model are related to the malicious payload.

The paper proceeds as follows: in the next section we describe in detail the proposed method for explainable malware detection; in Sect. 3 we present the results of the experimental analysis performed on real-world (malware and trusted) applications, aimed to show the effectiveness of the proposed method; in Sect. 4 we review the current state-of-the-art in malware detection by exploiting deep learning and, finally, in the last section conclusion and future research lines are drawn.

2   The Method

This section describes the proposed explainable image-based malware detection method, which exploits the opcode sequences extracted from both trusted and malicious Microsoft Windows files to generate RGB images used as input for a set of CNN models. Moreover, with the aim to provide a kind of explainability behind the model prediction, the proposed method incorporates explainability through CAMs, which provide insight into the decision-making process of a CNN model.

The proposed method is composed by two main steps i.e., the model training, whose workflow is shown in Fig. 1 and the model testing, whose related workflow is shown in Fig. 4.

In the follow we describe the model training step, composed by following key components:

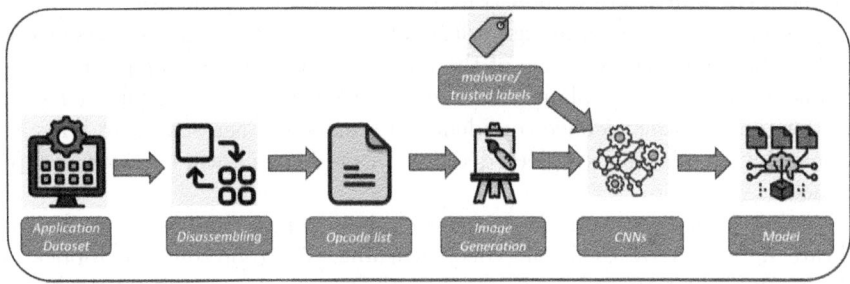

Fig. 1. The training step of the proposed method for explainaible malware detection.

Opcode-Based Image Construction: malware and trusted binaries are first subjected to extract opcode sequences from their disassembled code, thus we consider a static analysis. For this task we exploit the objdump disassembler[1], freely available on Linux-based operating systems. We consider the opcode sequences for each application, without the arguments.

To convert the opcode sequences into a visual representation, each opcode is mapped to an integer value and normalized to a red pixel value in the range [0, 255]. The opcodes are then arranged into a two-dimensional matrix to form an image. The width of the image is fixed, while the length is dynamically adjusted based on the total opcode count. The ratio behind the image conversion is to provide a transformation enabling the use of CNN from the domain of image classification to be applied directly to malware analysis, and also to provide explainability.

The code snippet 1.1 shows the Java code developed by the authors to convert an opcode sequence into an image.

---

[1] https://linux.die.net/man/1/objdump.

```java
public void imageGeneration(String filename) {

% Method declaration. Takes a filename as input.

    int width = 512, height = 512;

% Define the resolution of the output image: 512$\,\times
    \,$512 pixels.

    BufferedImage image = new BufferedImage(width, height,
    BufferedImage.TYPE_INT_ARGB);

% Create a blank ARGB image to store pixel data.

    List<String> opcodes = Arrays.asList("mov", "push", "
    pop", "add", "sub", ...);

% Define a list of known opcodes, each of which will be
    mapped to a unique color.

    List<String> lines = Files.readAllLines(Paths.get(
    filename));

% Read all lines (opcodes) from the input file.

    int x = 0, y = 0;

% Initialize pixel coordinates.

    for (String line : lines) {
        int index = opcodes.indexOf(line);
        Color color;
        if (index != -1) {
            color = new Color(index * 5 % 256, index * 3 %
    256, index * 7 % 256, 255);
        } else {
            color = new Color(0, 0, 0, 255); // Unknown
    opcode = black
        }
        image.setRGB(x, y, color.getRGB());
        x++;
        if (x >= width) {
            x = 0;
            y++;
            if (y >= height) break; // Avoid writing
    outside the image bounds
        }
    }

% For each opcode line:
```

```
43 % - Find its index in the known list
44 % - Map it to a unique RGB color using modulo operations
     for variety
45 % - Set the pixel color at position (x, y)
46 % - Increment x (column); wrap to next row when necessary
47 % - Stop if the image is completely filled
48
49
50     try {
51         ImageIO.write(image, "png", new File(filename + ".
     png"));
52     } catch (IOException e) {
53         e.printStackTrace();
54     }
55 } % Save the resulting image as a PNG file. Catch and
     print any IO exceptions.
```

Listing 1.1. Java code snippet for the image generation from opcode sequences.

Figure 2 shows two examples of images obtained from two malicious applications. Both applications are Trojans; the first having identification[2] in the Virus-Total report [3] and the second having identification[4] in the VirusTotal report [5].

Fig. 2. Two examples of images obtained from malicious applications.

---

[2] identified by the 52b9970cf2d50af70ad1938a77e44c41a334667fbcf6e08506b9a209cc1e
1d2d hash.

[3] https://www.virustotal.com/gui/file/52b9970cf2d50af70ad1938a77e44c41a334667fb
cf6e08506b9a209cc1e1d2d.

[4] identified by the 52e12f1e41fb8d7763a7c2966a53e6e7b7c3a9275a5942e9d7ff1cd84708
d9a6 hash.

[5] https://www.virustotal.com/gui/file/52e12f1e41fb8d7763a7c2966a53e6e7b7c3a9275
a5942e9d7ff1cd84708d9a6.

Figure 2 shows two examples of images obtained from two trusted applications. For the first application[6] hash, the Virustotal report is available[7] and also for the second one[8] hash there is the VirusTotal report available [9].

Fig. 3. Two examples of images obtained from trusted applications.

The rationale behind this conversion is that opcode distributions and patterns carry structural information about the behavior of the executable. As a matter of fact, as can be seen in Figs. 2 and 3, trusted and malicious samples can produce distinguishable image patterns, which can be effectively captured by CNNs.

CNN Classification: once the opcode-based images are obtained, they are used to train CNN models for malware detection with different architecture.

We conduct experiments with 10 different CNN architectures, listed below:

- LeNet: LeNet is one of the earliest CNN, introduced for handwritten digit recognition. It has a simple architecture with two convolutional and two fully connected layers, and serves as a foundational model for deep learning in computer vision.
- AlexNet: AlexNet significantly advanced the field of deep learning by winning the ImageNet competition. It consists of five convolutional layers followed by three fully connected layers, employing ReLU activations and dropout for improved training and generalization.

---

[6] identified by the 2d901bf0cb31995d596329a8406471c6e82671811c0d16255cfa02154e6 dd90b.

[7] https://www.virustotal.com/gui/file/2d901bf0cb31995d596329a8406471c6e82671811 c0d16255cfa02154e6dd90b.

[8] identified by the 4c77b3ecfe7ff1be8b05f7bc58d2360531c67997c3fae399f6f24132cb05 065a.

[9] https://www.virustotal.com/gui/file/4c77b3ecfe7ff1be8b05f7bc58d2360531c67997c3 fae399f6f24132cb05065a.

- VGG16 and VGG19: VGG16 and VGG19 are deep convolutional networks characterized by their uniform architecture, using $3 times 3$ convolution filters and increasing depth (16 and 19 weight layers, respectively). They are typically exploited for their intersting performances obtained in image classification tasks.
- ResNet50: ResNet50 is a deep residual network with 50 layers, introducing skip (residual) connections to mitigate the vanishing gradient problem and enable the training of much deeper networks. It achieves high performance by learning residual mappings instead of direct transformations.
- Inception: The Inception architecture, also known as GoogLeNet, incorporates multi-scale processing through parallel convolutional operations with different filter sizes within the same layer, enabling efficient feature extraction with fewer parameters.
- DenseNet: DenseNet connects each layer to every other layer in a feed-forward fashion, promoting feature reuse and mitigating the vanishing gradient problem. It achieves high accuracy with fewer parameters compared to traditional CNNs.
- MobileNet: MobileNet is designed for efficient inference on mobile and embedded devices. It uses depthwise separable convolutions to reduce the number of parameters and computational cost, while maintaining competitive accuracy.
- EfficientNet: EfficientNet introduces a compound scaling method that uniformly scales depth, width, and resolution using a fixed set of scaling coefficients. It achieves state-of-the-art accuracy with significantly fewer parameters and FLOPS compared to earlier models.
- Standard_CNN: The Standard_CNN model refers to a CNN developed by the authors, composed of a set of convolutional, pooling, and fully connected layers. More details about the Standard_CNN architecture can be found in [13].

Training Phase: the model training step begins with the preprocessing of raw executable files to extract opcodes and convert them into images. These images are then fed into a selected CNN architecture, where the model learns to differentiate between malicious and benign samples.

The second step, as previously introduced, is the model testing (shown in Fig. 4), which aims at evaluating the effectiveness of the model built in the previous step. It is composed of following key components:

Testing and Evaluation Phase: the testing phase involves applying the trained model to unseen samples. The test data undergoes the same preprocessing steps to produce opcode-based images. These images are then passed through the trained CNN to obtain predictions.

For each test image, the model outputs: the predicted class (malicious or benign) and the probability scores for each class.

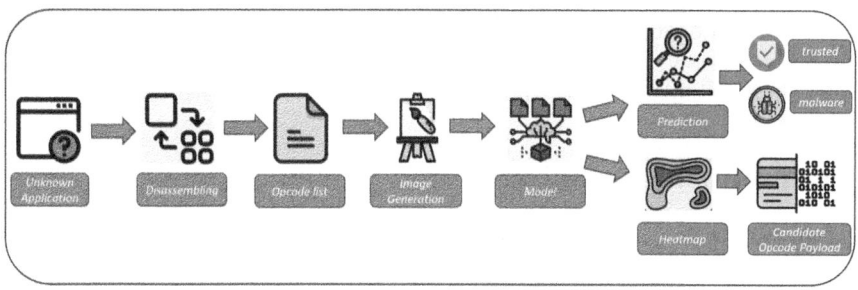

Fig. 4. The testing step of the proposed method for explainable malware detection.

Explainability via CAM: a distinctive aspect of the proposed method is its ability to provide visual explanations behind the model decisions. For this purpose, we resort to CAM, aimed to highlight the regions of the input image that contribute most strongly to the predicted class. This is achieved by projecting the weights of the final classification layer back onto the convolutional feature maps.

CAM is able to generate an heatmap for each prediction. These heatmaps are overlaid on the original malware images to visually indicate the discriminative areas that influenced the decision. This helps cybersecurity analysts in validating whether the model is focusing on meaningful opcode regions and not on irrelevant or noisy opcode patterns.

Incorporating CAMs ensures that the system is not a black box and can provide interpretable feedback.

In detail in this work we experiment with the Gradient-weighted Class Activation Mapping (i.e., Grad-CAM), a widely used post-hoc explainability technique designed to provide visual interpretations of CNN decisions. Grad-CAM generates coarse localization maps that highlight the important regions in an input image that contribute most significantly to the network's prediction for a given class. Unlike earlier class activation mapping methods that require architectural changes (e.g., replacing fully connected layers with global average pooling), Grad-CAM is compatible with a broad range of CNN-based architectures without requiring any modifications.

The method operates by computing the gradient of the target class score (i.e., the output of the softmax or final classification layer) with respect to the feature maps of a selected convolutional layer. These gradients are global-average-pooled to obtain importance weights for each feature map channel. The weighted sum of the feature maps, followed by a ReLU activation, results in a heatmap that highlights the discriminative regions used by the model to make its decision. The heatmap is then upsampled to the original image resolution and overlaid on the input for visual interpretation.

Grad-CAM is particularly valuable in domains such as medical imaging, where model transparency and trust are critical. It allows practitioners to assess whether the model is focusing on clinically relevant regions, facilitating error analysis, model debugging, and validation of learned representations. Moreover,

Grad-CAM can be extended to work with other tasks beyond classification, such as object detection and image captioning, making it a flexible and powerful tool for the explainability of deep learning predictions.

3   Experimental Analysis

To evaluate the effectiveness of the proposed method on real-world malware and trusted applications, we utilize a publicly available repository i.e., the Dike dataset[10], which offers a set of trusted and malicious files in Portable Executable (PE) and Object Linking and Embedding (OLE) formats. The malicious samples in this dataset are representative of the current malware landscape and encompasses a broad range of categories, including generic Trojans, Ransomware, Worms, Backdoors, Spyware, Rootkits, Encrypters, and Downloaders. For dataset balancing between trusted and malicious applications, we also considered a set of application and libraries provided from a Microsoft Windows 11 installation.

Thus, the full dataset is composed of the following 19573 applications:

- 8943 malware samples;
- 10630 trusted samples.

We consider as training dataset the 80% of the (malware and trusted) samples, as validation dataset the 10% of the (malware and trusted) samples and as testing dataset the remaining 10% of the (malware and trusted) samples.

With the 10 CNN models introduced in the previous section, we consider a set of 20 experiments (2 for each model).

Table 1 shows the details related to the hyperparameters we used for the proposed experiments, in particular we consider the image size, the learning rate, the epochs and the batch size considered in training.

Table 1 outlines the hyper-parameter configurations employed across 20 experiments involving a diverse set of CNN architectures, including both classical and state-of-the-art models such as AlexNet, LeNet, MobileNet, EfficientNet, DenseNet, ResNet50, Inception, VGG16, VGG19, and the STANDARD CNN developed by the authors. Each model was evaluated under two different learning rate conditions (0.01 and 0.00001) to observe the impact of learning dynamics on convergence and performance.

All models were trained for 25 epochs, with batch sizes set to either 16 or 32. A consistent image resolution of $224 times 3$ was used for most models to ensure comparability, except for ResNet50 and Inception, which were assigned their native input dimensions of $100 times 3$ and $299 times 3$, respectively, to retain architectural compatibility and optimal feature extraction.

This experimental design facilitates a systematic comparison by isolating the effects of model architecture and learning rate while controlling other training parameters. The dual learning rate setup is particularly useful for examining

---

[10] https://github.com/iosifache/DikeDataset.

Table 1. Hyper-parameters setting.

Exp.	Model	Image size	Learning rate	Epochs	Batch size
#1	AlexNet	224 × 3	0.01	25	16
#2	LeNet	224 × 3	0.01	25	16
#3	MobileNet	224 × 3	0.01	25	16
#4	EfficientNet	224 × 3	0.01	25	16
#5	STANDARD_CNN	224 × 3	0.01	25	16
#6	DenseNet	224 × 3	0.01	25	16
#7	ResNet50	100 × 3	0.01	25	16
#8	Inception	299 × 3	0.01	25	16
#9	VGG16	224 × 3	0.01	25	16
#10	VGG19	224 × 3	0.01	25	32
#11	AlexNet	224 × 3	0.00001	25	32
#12	LeNet	224 × 3	0.00001	25	32
#13	MobileNet	224 × 3	0.00001	25	32
#14	EfficientNet	224 × 3	0.00001	25	32
#15	STANDARD_CNN	224 × 3	0.00001	25	32
#16	DenseNet	224 × 3	0.00001	25	32
#17	ResNet50	100 × 3	0.00001	25	32
#18	Inception	299 × 3	0.00001	25	32
#19	VGG16	224 × 3	0.00001	25	32
#20	VGG19	224 × 3	0.00001	25	32

model sensitivity and generalization capabilities. Moreover, evaluating models with varying batch sizes (in the second configuration set) provides additional insight into the training stability and memory efficiency of each architecture.

Overall, the hyper-parameter settings were carefully chosen to balance fairness across models with practical considerations regarding the training of deep learning systems, enabling a robust benchmarking of model performance in the subsequent analysis.

Table 2 presents the experimental results obtained by evaluating various deep learning architectures across two distinct experimental phases (where the related hyperparameters are shown in Table 1). Each model is assessed based on following performance metrics: Loss, Accuracy, Precision, Recall, F-Measure and Area under the Curve (AUC). Moreover we add the Execution Time required for model testing.

As can be seen from Table 2, experiments #1–#10 exhibit really low performances. As a matter of fact in this setting, all models perform suboptimally, with Accuracy, Precision, Recall, and F-Measure values generally below 0.55,

Table 2. Experimental analysis results.

Exp.	Model	Loss	Accuracy	Precision	Recall	F-Measure	AUC	Execution time
#1	AlexNet	0.692	0.457	0.473	0.457	0.465	0.5	0:03:46
#2	LeNet	0.691	0.542	0.542	0.542	0.542	0.542	0:06:38
#3	MobileNet	1.203	0.466	0.466	0.466	0.466	0.496	0:22:56
#4	EfficientNet	0.711	0.542	0.542	0.542	0.542	0.542	0:13:41
#5	STANDARD_CNN	0.695	0.494	0.511	0.494	0.502	0.351	0:04:02
#6	DenseNet	0.859	0.384	0.384	0.384	0.384	0.335	0:15:08
#7	ResNet50	0.737	0.542	0.542	0.542	0.542	0.440	0:03:08
#8	Inception	0.692	0.541	0.541	0.541	0.541	0.548	0:48:44
#9	VGG16	0.683	0.542	0.542	0.542	0.542	0.612	0:03:02
#10	VGG19	1.00	0.457	0.457	0.457	0.457	0.639	0:03:07
#11	AlexNet	0.193	0.969	0.969	0.969	0.969	0.986	0:15:53
#12	LeNet	0.293	0.899	0.899	0.899	0.899	0.947	0:15:36
#13	MobileNet	0.158	0.975	0.975	0.975	0.975	0.987	0:41:56
#14	EfficientNet	0.331	0.872	0.872	0.872	0.872	0.933	1:08:22
#15	STANDARD_CNN	0.121	0.971	0.971	0.971	0.971	0.985	0:21:09
#16	DenseNet	0.100	0.984	0.984	0.984	0.984	0.990	1:14:49
#17	ResNet50	0.146	0.984	0.984	0.984	0.984	0.987	0:59:46
#18	Inception	0.519	0.981	0.981	0.981	0.981	0.977	1:18:27
#19	VGG16	0.122	0.979	0.979	0.979	0.979	0.989	1:27:36
#20	VGG19	0.160	0.981	0.981	0.981	0.981	0.991	1:14:51

and AUC scores peaking at just 0.639 (VGG19). This suggests a general lack of discriminative capability across models under these conditions.

Conversely, Experiments #11–#20 in Table 2 exhibit more interesting performance. All models in this phase exhibit significant performance improvements. Accuracy, Precision, Recall, and F-Measure values consistently exceed 0.87, with AUC scores reaching as high as 0.991.

From a performance point of view, the DenseNet model in the experiment #16 emerges as the best-performing model, achieving the highest values across all evaluation metrics with an accuracy, a precision, a recall and an F-Measure equal to 0.984 and AUC equal to 0.990.

These results indicate that the DenseNet model built in experiment #16 not only classifies with high precision but also maintains excellent balance between sensitivity and specificity, as reflected by the near-perfect AUC. ResNet50 (experiment #17) closely follows, matching DenseNet in Accuracy and F-measures (0.984), with a slightly lower AUC of 0.987.

To better understand the performance of the model obtained in experiment #16 in malware detection, in Fig. 5 we show the confusion matrix related to this model.

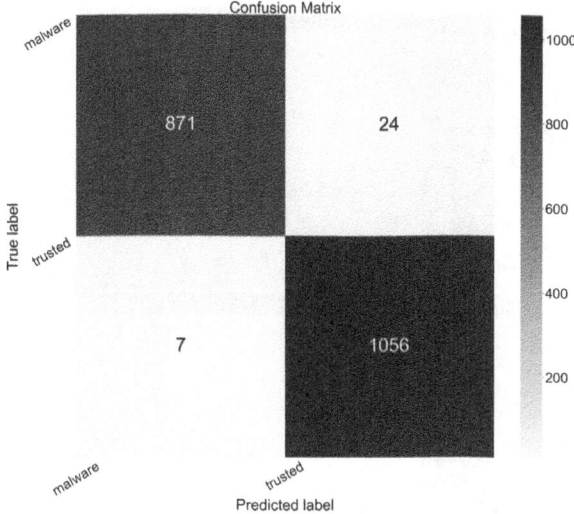

Fig. 5. The confusion matrix obtained with the DenseNet model in the experiment #16.

As shown in the confusion matrix in Fig. 5 the model correctly identifies 871 instances of malware and 1,056 instances of trusted files, while only misclassifying 24 malware samples as trusted and 7 trusted samples as malware, thus showing the model effectiveness.

Once identified the best model in malware detection, in the follow we provide several examples of explanations provided by the proposed method. To highlight the areas of interest from the model point of view we set the Grad-CAM algorithm to consider the Viridis colormap, where the color spectrum ranges from deep purple through blue and green, to yellow, moving smoothly through a single-hue gradient. Its perceptual uniformity means that the differences in color are consistently perceived across the scale: this is crucial when interpreting data based on color intensity or variation. In detail the yellow color highlights the areas of the image under analysis that are of great importance from the model point of view, the green color signifies the areas of medium interest and the purple color areas that are of no interest with respect to model prediction.

Figure 6 shows two examples of explainability related to two malicious applications.

For each application three figures are shown: the first is the input image, the second is the heatmap generated by the Grad-CAM, while the third image represents the overlap between the image representing the application and the heatmap, so that you can see the areas of the image highlighted by the heatmap (i.e. the yellow and green areas).

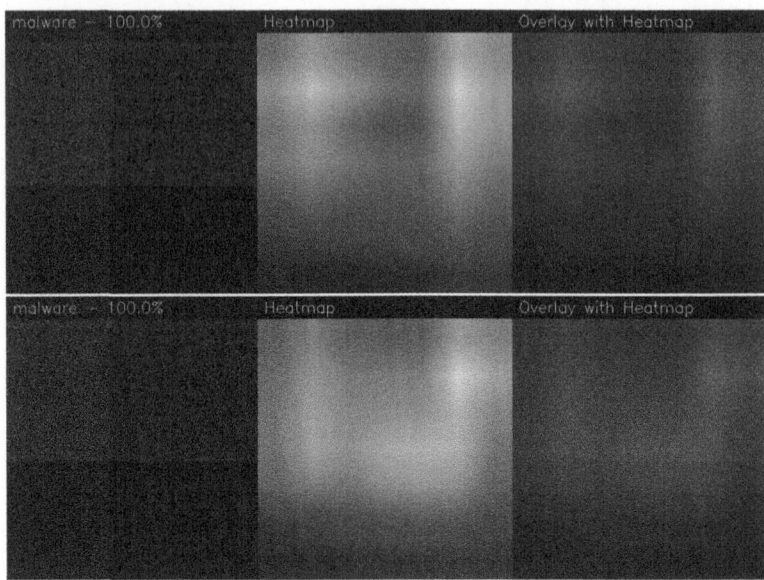

Fig. 6. Two examples of explainability provided by the proposed method.

In detail, with regard to the first application[11], whose VirusTotal report is available[12], we can note that there are two main areas highlighted in yellow, symptomatic for its maliciousness. With regard to the second application[13], whose report is available on VirusTotal[14] we notice that there are several areas of interest from the model point of view, this could indicate that the sample contains more malicious opcode sequences than the previous example.

In Fig. 7 we show (for space reasons) an excerpt of the opcode sequence obtained from the heatmaps related to the first application shown in Fig. 6.

Looking at Fig. 7 we note a jle (Jump if Less or Equal) opcode i.e., a conditional branch, likely part of a check (e.g., timing, environment, counter) to alter execution flow. That could be a check for a sandbox environment or control flow logic. Moreover, there is the presence of push/pop sequences, typically used to manipulate the stack, possibly to set up parameters for a function call or preserve/restore registers and also a "nop" code, often used for padding, anti-disassembly, or obfuscation. This could be trying to evade signature-based detection.

---

[11] *0ab06167cb7fd6d00a08079bbcd2d2ca05cbb5a9edaa943543dca37d7aaed05b* hash.

[12] https://www.virustotal.com/gui/file/0ab06167cb7fd6d00a08079bbcd2d2ca05cbb
5a9edaa943543dca37d7aaed05b.

[13] *0ae694c5332ae2c89f5cfb1e65ac6805c34e02c0b63b33197b5cb7f554c7cf76* hash.

[14] https://www.virustotal.com/gui/file/0ae694c5332ae2c89f5cfb1e65ac6805c34e
02c0b63b33197b5cb7f554c7cf76.

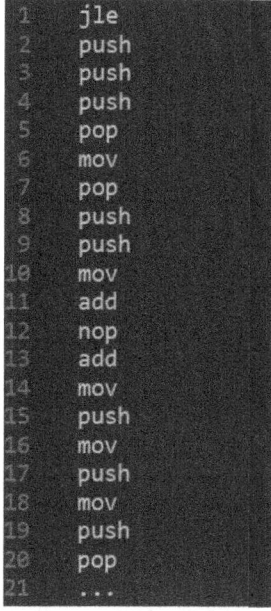

Fig. 7. An excerpt of the opcode sequence extracted from the heatmaps obtained from the first application shown in Fig. 6.

In Fig. 8 we show (for space reasons) an excerpt of the opcode sequence obtained from the heatmaps related to the second application shown in Fig. 6.

In the opcodes list shown in Fig. 8 we note the presence of call/add/pop/ret pattern i.e., a classic shellcode trick known as the "Call-Pop" technique, used to get the current instruction pointer (EIP/RIP): call next_instruction pushes the address of the next instruction onto the stack, pop reg retrieves that address and add adjusts it (e.g., to point to shellcode/data offset). Then ret could be used to transfer control, possibly via return-oriented programming (ROP) or to jump to shellcode.

4 Related Work

This section reviews recent literature focused on malware detection by exploiting deep learning.

Devi et al. [8] proposed a technique for malware detection in a Windows environment. They considered two datasets comprising 4,075 executable files, including 2,954 malicious and 1,121 benign samples. Classification algorithms were applied using the Weka tool to assess the models' performance. Unlike their approach, which relies on classical machine learning techniques, our method leverages deep learning and transforms each executable into an RGB image.

In another study, Biondi et al. [3] explored the detection of malware using machine learning classifiers, including Naive Bayes, Decision Tree, and Random

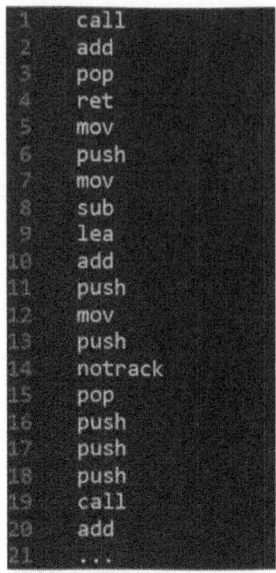

Fig. 8. An excerpt of the opcode sequence extracted from the second application shown in Fig. 6.

Forest with Extra Trees. Their approach relies heavily on manual feature extraction. In contrast, our method employs an end-to-end deep learning pipeline that automatically learns features from image-based representations of executables.

Kim et al. [14] presented an experimental framework to detect malware using machine learning. They extracted 13 features from 28,807 Windows PE files and trained several classifiers, including KNN, Logistic Regression, SVM, Random Forest, and Multilayer Perceptron.

Gao et al. [10] introduced MaliCage, a deep learning-based framework for malware detection. Their approach used Generative Adversarial Networks to generate fake-packed samples to mitigate underfitting. They achieved an accuracy of 0.916 using samples and 0.978 when including GAN-generated data. Our method also utilizes deep learning and malware but the main difference are the better accuracy we obtained and the possibility to provide explainability.

Rabadi et al. [17] proposed a malware detection technique based on API call analysis in Windows executables. They developed two feature extraction methods: one where each API call and its argument list are treated as a single feature, and another where each element of the arguments is treated separately. While their results were promising, the approach diverges by forgoing traditional feature engineering entirely. Instead, we transform entire executable files into images and use deep learning models for automatic feature extraction and classification by providing explainability.

Ciaramella et al. [7] focused on classifying ransomware, general malware, and trusted applications using deep learning. In contrast, we not only employed VGG16 but also evaluated a broader set of CNNs and provided explainability.

Huang et al. [12] developed a hybrid malware detection technique combining static and dynamic analysis. Their method used the Cuckoo Sandbox to produce dynamic behavioral data, which was visualized and processed using a VGG16-based CNN. Although they also converted executables into visual representations, our method differs in its exclusive reliance on static analysis. We evaluated ten CNN architectures, offering a comprehensive comparison across multiple configurations.

Azeez et al. [2] conducted malware detection experiments in the Windows environment using both traditional machine learning and deep learning. While their deep learning experiments involved adjusting the number of neurons in dense and 1D-CNN layers, their best performance was achieved using the Random Forest algorithm. In contrast, the proposed method emphasizes fully image-based deep learning analysis across ten CNN architectures, by also providing prediction explainability.

5 Conclusion and Future Work

Traditional antimalware solutions, which primarily rely on signature-based detection, are often ineffective against new or unknown threats whose signatures are not yet included in their databases. In this paper, we introduce a novel method for malware detection that leverages deep learning, specifically CNNs, to classify applications as either malicious or benign. A key strength of the proposed approach lies in its explainability: beyond delivering a binary classification, the model highlights specific opcode sequences that contribute to its decision, offering insights into the behavior that led to the classification as malware. We performed 20 different experiments, aimed to find the CNN obtaining the best accuracy value (i.e., the DenseNet one with an accuracy equal to 0.984). Moreover we discussed from two malicious applications, an example of explainability, by showing opcode sequences extracted from the heatmaps generated by the Grad-CAM algorithm, demonstrating that the proposed method can be considered also to provide insight for malware analysts, too.

As future work we will consider more CAMs algorithms, for instance Grad-CAM++ and Score-CAM, with the aim to compare the opcode sequences obtained from the same application but using different CAMs, with the aim to provide a kind of robustness behind the explainability provided by the CAMs. Moreover, we will perform family classifications, to detect malicious categories (for instance, ransomware), too, instead of a binary classification only.

Acknowledgment. This work has been partially supported by EU DUCA, EU Cyber-SecPro, SYNAPSE, PTR 22-24 P2.01 (Cybersecurity) and SERICS (PE00000014) under the MUR National Recovery and Resilience Plan funded by the EU - NextGenerationEU projects, by MUR - REASONING: foRmal mEthods for computAtional analySis for diagnOsis and progNosis in imagING - PRIN, e-DAI (Digital ecosystem for integrated analysis of heterogeneous health data related to high-impact diseases: innovative model of care and research), Health Operational Plan, FSC 2014-2020, PRIN-MUR-Ministry of Health, Progetto MolisCTe, Ministero delle Imprese e del Made in Italy, Italy, CUP: D33B22000060001, FORESEEN: FORmal mEthodS for attack dEtEction in autonomous driviNg systems CUP N.P2022WYAEW and ALOHA: a framework for monitoring the physical and psychological health status of the Worker through Object detection and federated machine learning, Call for Collaborative Research BRiC -2024, INAIL.

References

1. Almobaideen, W., Abu Alghanam, O., Abdullah, M., Hussain, S.B., Alam, U.: Comprehensive review on machine learning and deep learning techniques for malware detection in android and IOT devices. Int. J. Inf. Secur. **24**(3), 1–34 (2025)
2. Azeez, N.A., Odufuwa, O.E., Misra, S., Oluranti, J., Damaševičius, R.: Windows PE malware detection using ensemble learning. Informatics **8**, 10 (2021)
3. Biondi, F., Enescu, M.A., Given-Wilson, T., Legay, A., Noureddine, L., Verma, V.: Effective, efficient, and robust packing detection and classification. Comput. Secur. **85**, 436–451 (2019)
4. Borgli, H., Stensland, H.K., Halvorsen, P.: Better image segmentation with classification: guiding zero-shot models using class activation maps. In: International Conference on Multimedia Modeling, pp. 105–111. Springer (2025)
5. Chander, B., John, C., Warrier, L., Gopalakrishnan, K.: Toward trustworthy artificial intelligence (tai) in the context of explainability and robustness. ACM Comput. Surv. **57**(6), 1–49 (2025)
6. Chen, X., et al.: Deep learning-based software engineering: progress, challenges, and opportunities. SCI. CHINA Inf. Sci. **68**(1), 1–88 (2025)
7. Ciaramella, G., Iadarola, G., Martinelli, F., Mercaldo, F., Santone, A.: Explainable ransomware detection with deep learning techniques. J. Comput. Virol. Hacking Tech. **20**(2), 317–330 (2024)
8. Devi, D., Nandi, S.: Detection of packed malware. In: Proceedings of the First International Conference on Security of Internet of Things, pp. 22–26 (2012)
9. Di Giammarco, M., et al.: A robust and explainable deep learning method for cervical cancer screening. In: International Conference on Applied Intelligence and Informatics, pp. 111–125. Springer (2023)
10. Gao, X., Hu, C., Shan, C., Han, W.: Malicage: a packed malware family classification framework based on DNN and GAN. J. Inf. Secur. Appl. **68**, 103267 (2022). https://doi.org/10.1016/j.jisa.2022.103267, https://www.sciencedirect.com/science/article/pii/S2214212622001296
11. He, H., Yang, H., Mercaldo, F., Santone, A., Huang, P.: Isolation forest-voting fusion-multioutput: a stroke risk classification method based on the multidimensional output of abnormal sample detection. Comput. Methods Programs Biomed. 108255 (2024)
12. Huang, X., Ma, L., Yang, W., Zhong, Y.: A method for windows malware detection based on deep learning. J. Sig. Process. Syst. **93**, 265–273 (2021)
13. Iadarola, G., Martinelli, F., Mercaldo, F., Santone, A.: Towards an interpretable deep learning model for mobile malware detection and family identification. Comput. Secur. **105**, 102198 (2021)

14. Kim, J.W., Namgung, J., Moon, Y.S., Choi, M.J.: Experimental comparison of machine learning models in malware packing detection. In: 2020 21st Asia-Pacific Network Operations and Management Symposium (APNOMS), pp. 377–380. IEEE (2020)
15. Martinelli, F., Mercaldo, F., Petrillo, L., Santone, A.: Security policy generation and verification through large language models: a proposal. In: Proceedings of the Fourteenth ACM Conference on Data and Application Security and Privacy, pp. 143–145 (2024)
16. Qu, Y., et al.: CGAM: an end-to-end causality graph attention mamba network for esophageal pathology grading. Biomed. Signal Process. Control **103**, 107452 (2025)
17. Rabadi, D., Teo, S.G.: Advanced windows methods on malware detection and classification. In: Proceedings of the 36th Annual Computer Security Applications Conference, pp. 54–68 (2020)
18. Rabitti, G., Khorrami Chokami, A., Coyle, P., Cohen, R.D.: A taxonomy of cyber risk taxonomies. Risk Anal. **45**(2), 376–386 (2025)

Securing the Additive Manufacturing Process Chain

Nikolai Puch[1,2]($\boxtimes$) (iD), Stefan Dopfer[1,2], and Leon Birkel[1,2]

[1] Technical University of Munich, Garching bei München, Germany
[2] Fraunhofer Institute AISEC, Garching bei München, Germany
nikolai.puch@aisec.fraunhofer.de

Abstract. Additive Manufacturing (AM), commonly known as 3D printing, is a manufacturing process that creates parts layer by layer. This innovative technique is increasingly utilized across various applications, ranging from rapid prototyping to the production of safety-critical components. Today, the process chain has become digitalized and distributed across multiple organizations, allowing for highly efficient manufacturing. Consequently, this has created a need for security measures to protect these process chains against attacks. For this reason, we propose a holistic concept for securing the AM process chain.

We have developed a comprehensive model for the process chain that encompasses all relevant steps and stakeholders involved. By mapping common proactive and reactive security measures specific to AM to these stakeholders, we derive the first holistic security concept that fully covers the process chain. Our primary focus is protecting against sabotage and intellectual property theft while ensuring traceability throughout the process. In particular, we introduce a custom file format for secure exchanges of design and manufacturing files, a Public Key Infrastructure for managing trust between stakeholders, and describe supplemental measures, like side-channel analysis and watermarks, to specifically secure the manufacturing step and final part. To demonstrate the feasibility and usability of our security concept, we have implemented a proof of concept based on widely used open-source 3D printing applications.

Keywords: Additive Manufacturing · Supply Chain · Security Concept · Secure File Exchange

1 Introduction

In 2024, the total Additive Manufacturing (AM) market grew by 9.1 % and reached a volume of 21.9 billion US$s [23]. Today, not only are prototype parts routinely produced using AM, but also safety-critical components like turbine blades. It is expected that the adoption of AM and, consequently, the market will continue to grow. This growth is largely facilitated by the digitalization of the manufacturing process chain, which allows more granular and productive operation. Furthermore, this digital transformation allows for high efficiency on-demand production models, like Manufacturing-as-a-Service (MaaS). However, the increase in digitalization has opened up the AM process chain to attacks.

B. Coppens et al. (Eds.): ARES 2025 Workshops, LNCS 15994, pp. 340–358, 2025.
https://doi.org/10.1007/978-3-032-00630-1_19

For example, the *dr0wned* study by Belikovetsky et al. [10] showed how a small defect introduced into the design file can lead to catastrophic failure later on; in this case, a propeller of a drone breaking during flight. Thus, it is essential to find suitable security measures to protect the process chain while minimizing the impact on the process and the productivity. To the best of our knowledge, we provide the first holistic security concept for the whole AM process chain from design to the final part. We map traditional and AM specific security measures to the chain to derive a security concept which fulfills the specific requirements of the process chain. To demonstrate the feasibility of the concept, we have implemented the core features in a Proof of Concept (PoC).

The remaining sections are structured as follows. In Sect. 2 and Sect. 3 we introduce AM and relevant security measures. Next, Sect. 4 introduces our concept for a secure AM process chain, whose PoC is shown in Sect. 5

2   Additive Manufacturing

2.1   Additive Manufacturing Process Chain

In contrast to traditional subtractive manufacturing, AM, colloquially referred to as 3D printing, works by building a part layer by layer. This allows for different geometries, like internal cooling channels, and reduces overall waste [40]. The production of a part starts with the design in the Computer-Aided Design (CAD) phase, where a designer creates a 3D object. This phase is often an iterative process, which utilizes simulation methods for part strength and deformation testing, like Finite Element Analysis (FEA) [7], to fulfill the technical requirements. For AM Standard Tessellation Language (STL) files are the default design file format [32], which describe the surface geometry with tessellation via triangles. The STL files are then converted to machine instructions in the Computer-Aided Manufacturing (CAM) step. This step usually entails slicing the model into layers, creating infill, and adding supports for the printing process. CAM highly depends on the manufacturing method and machine, as different methods require different approaches, and different machines have different optimal parameters. For example, Powder Bed Fusion melts metal powder via a laser, while Fused Filament Fabrication (FFF) extrudes thermoplastics through a nozzle to build up the layers, resulting in different procedures. The instructions are usually transmitted in a G-code file and then executed by the Computerized Numerical Control (CNC). In this step, the machine builds the part layer by layer, which is sent to the customer after optional post-processing and quality control. Figure 1 illustrates the CAD-CAM-CNC process chain. Increasingly, all steps are not performed by a single source, but instead, the files are exchanged across company borders to benefit from increased specialization.

2.2   Threat Categories in Additive Manufacturing

Increased digitalization has exposed the AM process chain to attacks, which Yampolskiy et al. [43,45,46] group in their taxonomy into the following four categories.

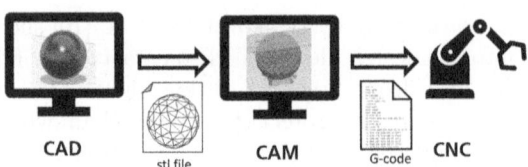

Fig. 1. AM process flow from CAD to final part. The design is transmitted as a STL file and the machine code as G-code.

Theft of Technical Data. Attackers may try to extract sensitive information from the AM process. This can be part specifications like its geometry or manufacturing process specifications like temperature. To achieve their goals, attackers may compromise equipment to steal information or reverse engineer the part from side-channel information [35].

Sabotage Attacks. The goal of sabotage attacks is to achieve real-world physical effects. The target can be the manufactured part, the AM equipment, or the environment. AM has quite a wide attack surface in regard to sabotage attacks, for example, an attacker may change the parts' geometry. Large geometry changes can lead to scrap production, but even small changes in the part specification or AM process can lead to drastic changes in part strength. It may lead to unexpected failures, as shown by Belikovetsky [10]. Insecure settings can damage the AM machine or even create unsafe conditions for workers.

Illegal Part Manufacturing. Illegal part manufacturing concerns the manufacturing of export-controlled or prohibited parts. The first prominent example is the Liberator gun, a simple pistol built from mostly 3D printed parts. The blueprint was quickly downloaded over 100 000 times before the US State Department demanded to take them down [20]. Similarly, on a nation-state level, nuclear proliferation may be a problem if, e.g., parts for enrichment are distributed. Nevertheless, this threat is hardly researched.

Data Ex-/Infiltration. Data ex- and infiltration is a new threat category introduced by Yampolskiy et al. in 2021 [45]. The idea is to add additional information to STL files without changing the printed part via steganographic methods. An attacker may use this method to extract sensitive information from a corporate network or embed a malicious payload to sabotage the production.

3   Related Work and Security Measures

3.1   Related Work

We investigate a secure file format and approaches for secure file exchange in AM, which commonly utilize blockchain.

3D Manufacturing Format - Secure Content Extension. 3D Manufacturing Format (3MF) [2] is an open-source file format designed for AM, with support from companies like Autodesk. Next to supplemental information like material, color, or thumbnails, the format includes a secure content extension [1], which supports end-to-end encryption. The extension uses a two-layered encryption scheme, where a random symmetric key, called Content Encryption Key (CEK), encrypts the sensitive content. The CEK is then encrypted with an asymmetric Key Encryption Key (KEK) and wrapped into the 3MF file. The key handling is not specified by 3MF, and the structure requires prior knowledge of the destination. Additionally, if there are multiple recipients, the CEK must be encrypted with a distinct KEK for each recipient. By definition, the 3MF format focuses solely on secure file exchange and does not address other types of attacks, such as machine manipulation. Moreover, public key management is outside the 3MF specification. We adopt a broader approach that considers trust relationships and supplemental measures.

Blockchain. Multiple approaches use blockchain to secure parts of the AM process chain. They range from storing design file hashes in a blockchain to prevent tampering [39] to more complex solutions with multiple file storage and transfer processes. One such approach provides traceability for AM-produced spare parts by tracking transactions between stakeholders in an Ethereum smart contract. The actual files are stored in InterPlanetary File System due to their large size [6]. Another approach for a marketplace is proposed by Tapas et al. [37]. They describe a rigid flow consisting of an evaluation and a feedback phase traced in smart contracts. In the first phase, the model is shared for free to solicit verification, which is further confirmed in the feedback phase. The concept is based on a mathematical trust model utilizing rewards and penalties.

The blockchain provides, first and foremost, traceability in the process chain. Asymmetric cryptography is still often required for authenticity and integrity of the design files. A method to handle reputation is often integrated to mitigate malicious members. Whether a blockchain is required in this use case can be evaluated by the methodology described by Wüst et al. [42]. In all AM use cases, information is written by multiple writers to the blockchain. All writers typically are known in the AM process chain, as they are linked to real-world processes, which favors a permissioned blockchain. Often, the crucial question is whether all those writers can be trusted. Executing someone's machine code on a CNC usually requires a level of implicit trust, as the slicing step can lead to unintended errors if knowledge about the machine is lacking. In extension, this is also often true for design files and their creators. Additionally, many AM supply chains have a strong central entity like a marketplace provider, which could serve as an online trusted third party, making a blockchain unnecessary.

3.2   Cybersecurity Countermeasures in Additive Manufacturing

We differentiate cybersecurity countermeasures into proactive and reactive measures. Proactive measures make attacks more difficult or outright prevent them.

Reactive measures make attacks more detectable so that potentially affected parts might be sorted out or affected operations stopped.

Proactive Measures

File-Based Cryptography. Cryptographic countermeasures usually come in the form of signatures or encryption. They prevent attackers from manipulating or reading sensitive design files. Additionally, the receiving digital identity can be bound to a hardware Trusted Platform Module (TPM), so only the target printer can decrypt the manufacturing file [33]. As a rule, well-established ciphers like AES or ECC are used here, but the emerging field of Post-Quantum Cryptography (PQC) is transforming this space and getting much attention. Due to the long lifetime of industrial equipment, PQC or the ability to easily exchange cryptography should be considered when designing for AM. As they only protect the files they are only usable to protect the transmission and not the slicing and manufacturing step. They are also the foundation for other measures like secure boot, but we will discuss them in detail later.

Secure Data Transmission. Secure data transmission standards vary between Information Technology (IT) and Operational Technology (OT). In IT, Transport Layer Security (TLS) [31] is the widely adopted standard for transport encryption, primarily known as a part of HTTPS. It is also used by QUIC, which has spread in recent years due to its performance increase. The OT field is notably more heterogeneous, incorporating both general IT protocols like TLS and HTTPS, along with industry-specific protocols such as OPC UA [30]. OPC UA provides the security modes *None*, *Sign*, and *SignAndEncrypt*. Alternatively, MQTT is often used to create publish-subscribe architectures. MQTT lacks built-in security, but *secure-mqtt* incorporates TLS to ensure transport security. Notably, secure versions of protocols in industrial networks have significantly less proliferation than in the IT [16]. Thus, one should not rely solely on the secure data transmission in such networks, but instead add security features directly to sensitive files.

Hardening Against Side-Channel Attacks. As mentioned in Subsect. 2.2, side-channel attacks can be used for theft of Intellectual Property (IP). Here, an attacker monitors sound [4,14], magnetic [35], or thermal imaging [5]. The collected information is then usually processed via Machine Learning (ML) and post-processed to correct for artifacts and obtain the original G-code. Multiple hardening measures were proposed to prevent such attacks. Chhetri et al. [15] propose to monitor for potential information leakage already in the CAM step and then reduce the impact by modifying machining or part parameters, like orientation and speed. They tested their approach for vibration, acoustic, magnetic, and power side-channel of a FFF printer. For their test case, they observed an average reduction of the G-code reconstruction success rate of 8.74 %. Liang et al. [25] proposed a defense against optical side-channel attacks in 2022. They projected optical noise, based on different algorithms, onto the build plate to obscure the movement. Their proposed state randomization algorithm can defend even against an advanced attacker aware of the defensive measure. This measure focuses mainly on the theft of IP in the CNC step.

Software Hardening and Traditional Security Measures Multiple standards and guidelines exist for security best practices. ISO/IEC 27001 [21] is an international standard for establishing, implementing, maintaining, and continually improving security. It focuses largely on organizational measures like corporate structure, planning, and risk assessment. National standards like NIST SP 800-53 [28] go into more detail for the threats, systems, and controls. These range from access control and incident response to supply chain risk management. In addition to general best practices, specific measures such as source code audits for CAD and CAM systems should be implemented. Other measures include system encryption and strong authentication. The standards primarily focus on organization-wide security and provide some measures for secure file transfer. However, most measures pertain to hardening systems, which can be applied to CAD and CAM systems.

OT Security Measures. The same measures should be used for the OT as well. However, many older OT are only functionally designed and do not support such security measures. Thus, accompanying measures are required, with national standards providing guidance [29]. For example, many CNC machines come with default users and credentials, which should be deactivated in favor of individual accounts. The OT network should be separated and segmented using firewalls and data diodes to limit access, especially from IT networks. This can be supplemented with Intrusion Detection System (IDS) and anomaly detection, which harnesses cyber-physical effects to link network anomalies to effects [41]. Finally, tailored cryptography and authentication should be used to reduce the burden on constrained OT devices. [27] In addition to using the TPM for protecting the file, Safford et al. propose using it to verify soft- and firmware during boot and runtime [33]. The OT measures work similar to the IT, just focussing more on industrial applications like the CNC step.

Reactive Measures

Physical Properties Based Printer or Part Tracking. The goal is to use small, involuntary differences in a part, caused by deviations in a specific machine, to identify the printer or trace objects back to a manufacturer in, e.g., forensic investigations. This approach is similar to Physical Unclonable Functions (PUFs), which leverage unique physical variations in semiconductor manufacturing to create a secure and unique identifier for each device [36]. *PrinTracker* [24] uses branding (spacing of printing lines) and infill attachment to edge patterns as distinguishing features, which are captured with a scanner. They employ a support vector machine classifier to match such a fingerprint to the printer with high confidence. Other properties, such as the temperature curve during pre-heating, can be used to derive a unique fingerprint for a printer [19]. Song et al. [34] follow a similar approach and measure variance in embedded QR codes. They were able to find thresholds for the earth-mover-distance between features by different printers and thus can identify genuine QR codes. The fingerprints cannot only be used to differentiate printers but also to differentiate instances of the same object. One can use existing material structure characteristics [18], like grain or pores, or introduce, e.g., additional particles and use the microscale patterns caused by Brownian motion as an entropy source for PUFs [22].

Watermarks. Additional information can also be embedded into the part as a watermark instead of relying on existing properties. For example, different slicing parameters like infill pattern or line width can be used to create a parameter space large enough to identify individual instances of an object [17]. A common approach is to embed tracking or QR codes into the parts themselves and read them via spectral scanning, like CT-scanning. Splitting the QR code into parts and distributing it over different layers reduces the impact on mechanical properties [12]. As an alternative encoding method, the layer height can be varied to embed data bitwise [19]. A special variant of a watermark to prevent counterfeiting are security features embedded in the CAD model, which weaken the final part significantly if the object is not sliced correctly. One example uses curvature and internal surfaces in combination with tessellation to create security features that require a specific workflow and printing orientation [13].

Machine Code Analysis. Another method is to analyze the machine code for malicious commands before executing it on the printer. The challenge lies in identifying changes that may not appear malicious without the original design as a reference. For example, increasing the size can alter part fit while still using standard production instructions. One approach to address this problem is to reconstruct the STL file and run it through FEA to detect stress points caused by attacks [38]. Alternatively, one can use statistical modeling or ML to identify anomalies in the G-code [9]. As a third option, a digital twin of the machine can be used to emulate the planned operation and detect anomalies or attacks before running the task on the actual machine [8].

Side-Channel Based Anomaly Detection. Side-channel based anomaly detection adopts the methods of the side-channel based theft of IP as an out-of-band anomaly detection method. Usually, a fingerprint of a verified good print is created, and emissions of consecutive prints are compared against the fingerprint by a ML model. Fingerprint creation can place an additional burden on quality control. The methods in cybersecurity and quality assurance are pretty similar; security looks at deliberate errors, and quality assurance looks at random errors. They often use machine learning, image processing, or statistical approaches to detect process anomalies like voids, print speed variations, or toolpath manipulations. They used acoustic emissions, electric current, thermal emissions, optical, or vibrations as the side-channel for monitoring. [3]

Table 1. For proactive measures, **S** indicates that the AM process chain is secured against sabotage, and **T** marks protection against theft of IP. For reactive measures, corresponding marks are placed if such attacks are detectable. **part** denotes partial or secondary protection.

Countermeasure	CAD	—	CAM	—	CNC	Product
Proactive						
File-based cryptography	No	S&T	No	S&T	No	No
Secure data transmission	No	S&T	No	S&T	No	No
Cryptography (blockchain)	No	S	No	S	No	No
Hardening vs. side-channel attacks	No	No	No	No	T	No
Traditional IT security measures	S&T	part	S&T	part	No	No
Traditional OT security measures	No	No	No	part	S&T	No
Reactive						
PUF based part / printer tracking	No	No	No	No	No	S
Watermarks (design feature)	No	S	S	S	S	No
Watermarks (CAM tag)	No	No	No	part	part	S
Machine code analysis	S	S	S	S	No	No
Side-channel based anomaly detection	S	S	S	S	S	No

4   Secure Digital Additive Manufacturing Process Chain

4.1   General Process Chain

In this section, we outline the scope of our process chain, define the process chain and its stakeholders, and then derive security requirements based on this model. As the focus lies on the digital side of the Cyber-Physical System (CPS), we focus on the CNC software instead of the machine itself. Additionally, we do not consider testing after the production. Real-world design typically follows a multistep process, where feedback from sources such as FEA is integrated into the design. We simplify this to a linear model, but our proposed solution could easily be extended to accommodate cyclic structures.

First, we define the following seven roles a stakeholder can possess:

- *Design Producer* is responsible for generating design files. Additionally, they may improve their designs via FEA.
- *Design Provider* is responsible for distributing the design files. This may be in the form of a centralized system or decentralized peer-to-peer networks.
- *Slicer Operator* is responsible for creating machine code instructions from the design file.
- *Machine Operator* is responsible for executing the machine code on the machine and monitoring the process.
- *Manufacturing File Provider* is responsible for distributing manufacturing files

– *Equipment Manufacturer* produces the necessary hard- and software.
– *Customer* receives the final part.

Design, slicing, and machining require different, often highly specialized, hard- and software systems. We abstract these setups as CAD, CAM, or CNC Systems. Between the roles, different types of data or objects are transmitted. *Design Files* contain the geometry of the to-be-produced part and are sent via the design provider to the slicer operator. Here, they are transformed to *Manufacturing Files*, which are sent to the machine operator. We consider *.stl* and *.gcode* files as exemplary design and manufacturing files due to their vendor-agnostic nature and widespread prevalence. Finally, the instructions are transferred into physical actions by the CNC to produce the final *Part*, which can be delivered to the customer. Both the design and manufacturing file providers act as intermediaries for file exchange. The design provider usually operates between organizations, while the manufacturing file provider functions within an organization and can be as simple as a USB stick or fileserver. However, in scenarios like MaaS, more complex machine administration and file distribution systems can be employed. Additionally to this data, some knowledge has to be shared between different roles [44]. *Part Specifications* contain additional information like the part's required mechanical load capability. This information informs the slicing step, as manufacturing methods and material significantly impact the final part's properties. Another information in the slicing and machining step is the *Manufacturer's Institutional Knowledge*. This includes, for instance, the parameters required to operate the machine at peak efficiency. This knowledge can either be institutional knowledge, especially if roles are shared in an entity, or has to be exchanged as supplementary information, typically in the form of PDFs. Alternatively, some information can be added to manufacturing files. For our requirements and security concept, we assume that the knowledge is integrated into design or manufacturing files or, if exchanged in a non-standardized format, secured otherwise.

The complete proposed process chain with all roles, exchanged objects, and knowledge can be found in Fig. 2. Real-world stakeholders like e.g. designers or 3D-printing-as-a-Service providers can encompass multiple roles. In such cases,

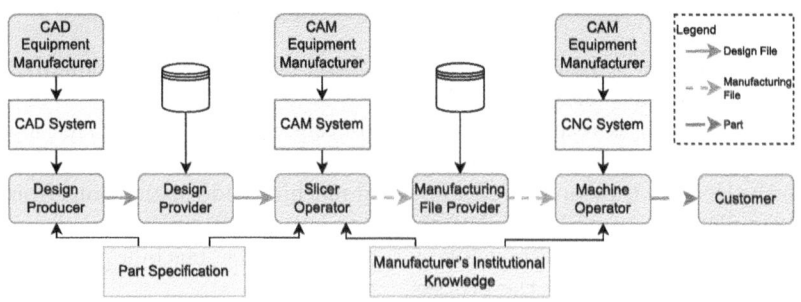

Fig. 2. Proposed AM process chain with roles, systems, exchanged files, and knowledge.

the security model might be simplified as there is implicit trust within the same stakeholder.

4.2   Requirements

We analyze all roles and objects in the model with the threat taxonomy by Yampolskiy et al. as outlined in Subsect. 2.2. Theft of technical data and sabotage are the primary threats, with data ex-/infiltration as an enabler for both. We exclude illegal part manufacturing because it is closely tied to legal issues and thus cannot be addressed alone with technical solutions. Initially, we define three overarching goals: first, most roles have sensitive IP, which they want to protect. This may be the design producer who wants to disclose their design only to paying customers or the slicer operator whose institutional knowledge to slice optimally gives them a competitive edge. The second goal is that the customer wants a functional part to their specification without any malicious defects. Additionally, the slicer and machine operator want to protect their equipment against sabotage. The final goal is traceability of the process chain for the customer, as they not only require a non-defective part but also the correct one. The goal of protecting everyone's IP against theft leads to the requirement to keep files confidential for all the participants in the process chain (*R1, R4*). However, in cases like open-source designs, protecting IP may be unnecessary, allowing for the removal of corresponding measures. The same is true for the integrity of design and manufacturing files (*R2,R5*), as every role can be affected by, e.g., regression claims based on *G2*. Design and manufacturing file provider have no own data worth protecting but must act as a secure intermediary for other roles to avoid liability (*R10*). As a manipulated software basis can lead to both theft of technical data and sabotage, protection of the corresponding software is required

Table 2. Requirements and goals for securing the process chain. Operator is shortened to *OP*.

ID	Role	Requirement
G1	Design producer, slicer & machine OP	Protect sensitive technical data against theft
G2	Slicer & machine OP, customer	Protect equipment and parts against sabotage
G3	Customer	Traceability for the manufacturing process chain
R1	Design producer	Protection against theft of design files
R2	Design producer	Protection against sabotage of design files
R3	Design producer	Security of CAD/FEA system
R4	Design producer, slicer & machine OP	Protection against theft of manufacturing files
R5	Design producer, slicer & machine OP	Protection against sabotage of manufacturing files
R6	Slicer OP	Security of CAM system
R7	Machine OP	Security of CNC system
R8	Customer	Verify manufacturing process chain
R9	Design producer, slicer & machine OP	Unobtrusive and usable security
R10	Design & manufacturing file provider	Secure intermediary for file transfer

by each role (*R3, R6, R7*). To ensure *G3*, the customer requires the capability to verify the whole process chain (*R8*). In conjunction with the *R2,R5* this means that authenticity of files is required as well. As the primary task of everybody in the process chain is to create functional parts, security should not obstruct the normal workflow and should be kept in the background where possible. Where user interaction is required, it should be designed in a usable manner (*R9*). A summary of the stated goals and requirements is given in Table 2.

4.3   Security Concept

We propose a security concept for the AM process chain consisting out of a file format for secure data exchange, a Public Key Infrastructure (PKI) for trust management, and supplement measures to provide traceability and harden systems.

Secure Data Exchange in the Process Chain. We attach cryptographic security measures directly to the files to facilitate secure data exchange. To ensure integrity and authenticity, we require signatures for the design and manufacturing files. Additionally, encryption should be used to maintain confidentiality. We prefer a sign-then-encrypt scheme for file distribution, as final recipients may be unknown when files are initially sent to a provider and only forwarded later. Unlike transport encryption, the signature is retained during storage and can still be verified later by the final recipient. This simplifies operations for providers acting as intermediaries. Additionally, this approach reduces the communication overhead in Peer-to-Peer (P2P) networks, as key exchanges for session keys between peers are reduced. Transport encryption should still be employed as part of a defense-in-depth strategy, especially where it can be easily implemented, such as on central servers. To address the inefficiency of asymmetric cryptography with large, high-resolution design files, we utilize a hybrid encryption scheme that encrypts a symmetric key with the recipient's public key. The design file contains the .STL file, if necessary metadata, and the designer's signature. The manufacturing file contains the G-code, all required metadata for the slicing process, and the design file signature. The slicer operator then signs all the data. To keep the data confidential, both containers are encrypted

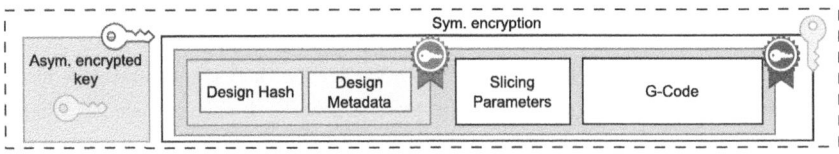

Fig. 3. Secure manufacturing file exchange format for the message slicer to the machine operator, containing a G-code file and additional metadata. Blue is the designer's, and red is the slicer operator's signature. The symmetric key is encrypted with the machine operator's public key.

using the hybrid scheme. If the specific scenario does not require confidentiality, the encryption layer may be dropped. A symbolic representation of the resulting manufacturing file is shown in Fig. 3. This approach is similar to the 3MF secure content extension, but we drop the additional features, like images, as they increase complexity and enlarge the attack surface. However, adaption would be easy if required, as the remaining security concept is compatible with 3MF.

Trust in the Process Chain. The secure data exchange relies on trust between the different roles, typically realized via asymmetric cryptography in the form of certificates. Because of the reasons outlined in Sect. 3.1, we prefer not to use blockchain. In centralized systems, the most straightforward method for handling certificates is a PKI. We propose an issuing Certificate Authority (CA) for each role, i.e., the design producer CA would handle issuing all the certificates to the design producers. Intermediate CAs are proposed, depending on the mapping of roles to real-world stakeholders. For example, if an AM service provider offers both slicing and manufacturing as a service, they should operate an intermediate CA in addition to their slicer and machine operator issuing CA. As the CAM step requires machine-specific knowledge and thus is often executed by the machine owner, this setup is often present in practice. The ideal place for the central root CA depends on the real-world use case. However, in a MaaS scenario, placing it with the AM service provider or an external entity, such as an industry association, may be more advantageous. Web of Trust (WoT) can be a decentralized alternative, especially if there is no strong and trusted entity in the scenario. But removing the central CA brings additional key management effort to the individual entities participating in the network.

In the centralized system, the trust between different organizations has to be handled via the root CA and intermediate CAs. For example, if a design provider starts distributing malicious designs, the corresponding intermediate has to handle the certificate revocation. For the decentralized WOT, an additional trust scoring system has to be implemented, which at least allows certificate revocation. It should be noted that trust is always required for the roles, particularly for the machine operator, as physical control over a machine and the final part enables reverse engineering without interacting with the design or printer [35]. An example of a PKI structure for a central marketplace and an AM service provider is provided in Fig. 4. Machine-specific manufacturing files are directly transmitted, eliminating the need for a manufacturing file provider CA. Design producers are registered at the marketplace. To shorten the certificate chain, and since only one certificate is needed, the example does not use a dedicated CA for the design provider. This approach benefits PQC by accommodating the larger signatures and certificates.

4.4   Supplemental Measures

While these measures secure transmission between process chain entities, they do not protect the entities themselves, necessitating additional security measures.

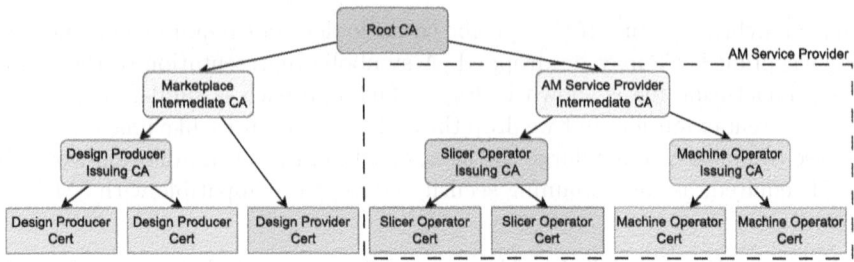

Fig. 4. Example PKI with a central marketplace and an AM service provider responsible for slicing and manufacturing.

Traditional security best practices, such as those outlined by NIST [28], should be adhered to, especially for systems running CAD and CAM software, as these are typically integrated into a traditional enterprise IT network. Additionally, providers should adhere to best practices relevant to their specific technology, whether it be a web- or fileserver. Security measures differ slightly for CNC software managed by a Programmable Logic Controller (PLC) or motion controller within OT. The overall concepts and approach, like defense in depth, stay the same, but the application may differ [26]. Often OT relies more heavily on network segmentation and air gaps, while baked in access control has been problematic [11]. Consequently, it is advisable to supplement the OT with additional security measures. Side-channel analysis can detect attacks on the machine itself and previous malicious changes but relies on known good parts. For FFF, acoustic emissions can be easily adopted and provide good results. The described measures only provide security up to the final part. To extend the protection and provide traceability, watermarking should be considered. Physical properties can be used to derive a unique ID for the part to link it to its manufacturing file. However, managing and tracking these IDs in, e.g., a blockchain requires additional administrative effort. Thus, we prefer to embed a signature and hash over the G-code, including all its metadata, into the final part. In the case of regression claims, this hash can then be used to check if the by the machine operator used manufacturing file matches the customers' expectations. This way, traceability is not focused on documenting every step in logs but instead on providing methods to verify the manufacturing chain retroactively. Finally, usability should be emphasized in any implementation. Since the main task of all roles is to design and manufacture parts, security should not interfere with this process. Operations should be automated and require minimal user interaction whenever possible. When interaction is necessary, clearly communicate the state and possible courses of action, along with their consequences, to the user.

5   Proof of Concept

We provide a PoC for our solution, focusing on the secure data transmission. The PoC does not aim to provide a production solution but instead aims to show our concept's feasibility and limited usability impact. We implement a marketplace and extensions for a slicer and the printer. For our PoC, we choose a centralized system. For the data transfer, we decide to both encrypt and sign the designs and thus define a *.secstl* file format. The data is stored in Extensible Markup Language (XML) format to reduce the overhead introduced by encoding. We decide to place our root of trust in the marketplace.

5.1   Marketplace

We implement our marketplace to provide designs akin to popular maker platforms, where slicer operators can sign in and download designs. For the secure file exchange, they can deposit their operator certificate. In addition to the design files in our custom *.secstl* format, the marketplace offers the corresponding design producer certificates. We provide scripts to the design producers to convert their designs into our *.secstl* file format before uploading it to the marketplace.

5.2   Slicer Plugin

As a CAM software, we choose the slicer UltiMaker Cura[1]. It is highly popular with over a million users worldwide and is backed by UltiMaker, a FFF printer manufacturer. Additionally, being open source and supporting custom plugins allows for easy extension. Consequently, we implement a plugin for UltiMaker Cura version 5.8.1 for the secure process chain. The plugin allows the slicer operator to import STL files and export G-code, which are signed and encrypted as specified in the concept. In addition, the plugin provides traceability by adding the SHA-256 hash of the imported files and slicing parameters to the G-code. The hash is generated and temporarily stored to track multiple STLs in the same printing job. Cura has access to the slicer operator's private key to decrypt files and sign G-code, as well as the certificates of the design producer to verify the origin. The plugin adds the custom file type *.secstl* to the list of importable files. The plugin's file reader acts like a preprocessor, which handles all cryptographic operations before handing the file to the UltiMaker Cura's STLReader. The export works similarly and is an extension to Cura's GCodeWriter. The plugin appends all properties from the previously traced files to the beginning of the G-code as a comment, the slicing parameters are also added via the machine settings. The resulting G-code is signed and then encrypted for a predefined Machine Operating. The control flow of the slicer plugin is shown in Fig. 5.

---

[1] https://ultimaker.com/de/software/ultimaker-cura/.

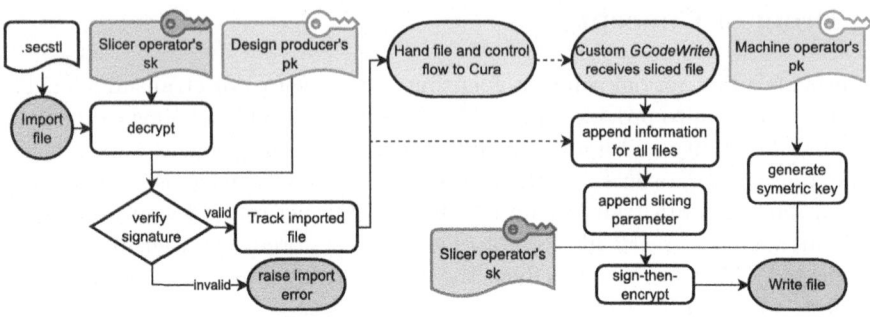

Fig. 5. Flowchart for importing, slicing, and exporting the resulting file in Cura. **sk** is the private and **pk** the public key.

5.3 Printer Plugin

For the printer operator, we decided to extend the popular printer management software OctoPrint[2] with our secure G-code upload plugin. The plugin was developed for OctoPrint version 1.10.2. OctoPrint sends G-code commands directly to an Ender 5 Plus via a USB serial connection, enhancing the CNC functionality with a user-friendly management component. Additionally, OctoPrint can easily be extended with custom plugins. The plugin processes uploaded signed and encrypted G-code files. For this, the plugin hooks into the preprocessing of all files. Our preprocessor then handles all files with a *.secgcode* extension. It first decrypts the contents, if encrypted, using its private key to decrypt the symmetric key. Next, the plugin verifies the signature against the slicer operator certificates it can access and informs the user about the results. The G-code is then, if the verification is successful, uploaded to OctoPrint for printing.

Table 3. Fulfilled requirements ●, partially fulfilled requirements ◐, not fulfilled ○. For the concept, it is shown which measure fulfills which requirements.

Requirements	R1	R2	R3	R4	R5	R6	R7	R8	R9	R10
Concept	●	●	●	●	●	●	●	●	◐	●
Secure file exchange	●	●	○	●	●	○	○	●	◐	●
IT/OT security	◐	◐	●	◐	◐	●	●	○	○	●
Side-channel analysis	○	●	◐	○	●	◐	●	○	○	◐
Watermarks	○	○	○	○	○	○	○	●	○	○

---

[2] https://octoprint.org/.

6   Conclusion

We evaluate whether our solution and PoC can fulfill the stated requirements. Our concept focuses primarily on securing the exchange of information, fulfilling requirements R1, R2, R4, and R5 with our proposed data exchange format. These requirements are fully implemented in the PoC as well. The format allows the providers to serve as secure intermediaries (R10). We give some security best practices for CAD-CAM-CNC systems, which we supplement with additional measures like side-channel based analysis. However, due to the complex interplay of such systems, these measures cannot provide the same level of certainty as cryptographic measures, and thus, we can only partially fulfill R3, R6, and R7. We decided against hardening our PoC in this regard and are leaving it for future work. R8 is fulfilled as the whole AM process chain is traceable via the signature chain in the files and the QR code in the final part. Finally, while we aim to minimize the impact on users, operations may fail due to security concerns, affecting the user experience and, thus, only partially fulfilling requirement R10. We strive to keep the PoC usable but have not fully optimized the user experience because of its exemplary nature. The results are summarized in Table 3.

This paper presents a comprehensive security framework for the AM process chain, addressing critical threats introduced by digitalization. Our proposed concept encompasses security measures tailored to each phase, from CAD to the final part, emphasizing the importance of protecting IP and ensuring product integrity. We incorporate proactive and reactive countermeasures, such as file encryption, digital signatures, and side-channel anomaly detection, to securely link the physical and digital worlds, thus enhancing the robustness of the manufacturing process. By implementing a PoC, we demonstrated the feasibility of secure data exchanges within the AM ecosystem, significantly reducing the risk of data theft and sabotage. Future work will focus on refining these security measures and exploring additional technologies, such as adopting watermarking and PUF to other manufacturing technologies, to further bolster traceability and accountability in AM. Risk assessment can be used to further detail the threats for AM and thus refine the requirements for specific case studies. As the industry continues to evolve, ongoing research will be essential to keep pace with emerging threats and ensure the secure advancement of AM technologies.

Acknowledgments. This work was supported by the German Federal Ministry of Research, Technology and Space (BMFTR) under Grant No. 16KIS1847 (ALPAKA).

Disclosure of Interests. The authors have no competing interests.

References

1. 3MF Consortium: 3MF secure content extension (27/02/2025). https://github.com/3MFConsortium/spec_securecontent/blob/master/3MF%20Secure%20Content.md
2. 3MF Consortium: 3MF specification (27/02/2025). https://3mf.io/spec/

3. Ahsan, M., Rais, M.H., Ahmed, I.: SOK: side channel monitoring for additive manufacturing - bridging cybersecurity and quality assurance communities. In: European Symposium on Security and Privacy (EuroS&P), pp. 1160–1178 (2023)

4. Al Faruque, M.A., Chhetri, S.R., Canedo, A., Wan, J.: Acoustic side-channel attacks on additive manufacturing systems. In: International Conference on Cyber-Physical Systems (ICCPS), pp. 1–10 (2016)

5. Al Faruque, M.A., Chhetri, S.R., Faezi, S., Canedo, A.: Forensics of thermal side-channel in additive manufacturing systems. CECS Technical Report (2016)

6. Alkhader, W., Alkaabi, N., Salah, K., Jayaraman, R., Arshad, J., Omar, M.: Blockchain-based traceability and management for additive manufacturing. IEEE Access **8**, 188363–188377 (2020)

7. ANSIS: What is finite element analysis (2025). https://www.ansys.com/simulation-topics/what-is-finite-element-analysis

8. Balta, E.C., Pease, M., Moyne, J., Barton, K., Tilbury, D.M.: Digital twin-based cyber-attack detection framework for cyber-physical manufacturing systems. IEEE Trans. Autom. Sci. Eng. **21**, 1695–1712 (2024)

9. Beckwith, C., et al.: Needle in a haystack: detecting subtle malicious edits to additive manufacturing g-code files. IEEE Embedded Syst. Lett. **99**, 111–114 (2022)

10. Belikovetsky, S., Yampolskiy, M., Toh, J., Gatlin, J., Elovici, Y.: dr0wned – cyber-physical attack with additive manufacturing. In: Workshop on Offensive Technologies (WOOT) (2017)

11. Biham, E., Bitan, S., Carmel, A., Dankner, A., Malin, U., Wool, A.: Rogue7: rogue engineering-station attacks on s7 simatic plcs. BlackHat (2019). https://api.semanticscholar.org/CorpusID:201702777

12. Chen, F., Luo, Y., Tsoutsos, N.G., Maniatakos, M., Shahin, K., Gupta, N.: Embedding tracking codes in additive manufactured parts for product authentication. Adv. Eng. Mater. **21**, 1800495 (2019)

13. Chen, F., Mac, G., Gupta, N.: Security features embedded in computer aided design (CAD) solid models for additive manufacturing. Mater. Des. **128**, 182–194 (2017)

14. Chhetri, S.R., Canedo, A., Faruque, M.A.A.: Confidentiality breach through acoustic side-channel in cyber-physical additive manufacturing systems. ACM Trans. Cyber Phys. Syst. **2**, 1–25 (2018)

15. Chhetri, S.R., Faezi, S., Al Faruque, M.A.: Information leakage-aware computer-aided cyber-physical manufacturing. IEEE Trans. Inform. Forensics Secur. **13**, 2333–2344 (2018)

16. Dahlmanns, M., Lohmöller, J., Pennekamp, J., Bodenhausen, J., Wehrle, K., Henze, M.: Missed opportunities: measuring the untapped TLS support in the industrial internet of things. In: ACM Asia Conference on Computer and Communications Security (ASIA CCS), pp. 252–266 (2022)

17. Dogan, M.D., et al.: G-ID: identifying 3D prints using slicing parameters. In: Conference on Human Factors in Computing Systems (CHI), pp. 1–13 (2020)

18. Eisenbarth, D., Stoll, P., Klahn, C., Heinis, T.B., Meboldt, M., Wegener, K.: Unique coding for authentication and anti-counterfeiting by controlled and random process variation in L-PBF and L-DED. Add. Manuf. **35**, 101298 (2020)

19. Gao, Y., Wang, W., Jin, Y., Zhou, C., Xu, W., Jin, Z.: ThermoTag: a hidden id of 3D printers for fingerprinting and watermarking. IEEE Trans. Inform. Forensics Secur. **16**, 2805–2820 (2021)

20. Greenberg, A.: 3D-printed gun's blueprints downloaded 100,000 times in two days (with some help from kim dotcom). https://www.forbes.com/sites/andygreenberg/2013/05/08/3d-printed-guns-blueprints-downloaded-100000-times-in-two-days-with-some-help-from-kim-dotcom/ (2013)

21. ISO/IEC: Information security, cybersecurity and privacy protection—information security management systems—requirements (2022). https://www.iso.org/standard/27001

22. Ivanova, O., Elliott, A., Campbell, T., Williams, C.B.: Unclonable security features for additive manufacturing. Add. Manuf. **1–4**, 24–31 (2014)

23. Jamshid, M., Huff, R.: Wohlers Report 2025. ASTM international (2025)

24. Li, Z., Rathore, A.S., Song, C., Wei, S., Wang, Y., Xu, W.: Printracker: fingerprinting 3D printers using commodity scanners. In: Conference on Computer and Communications Security (ACM SIGSAC), pp. 1306–1323 (2018)

25. Liang, S., Zonouz, S., Beyah, R.: Hiding my real self! Protecting intellectual property in additive manufacturing systems against optical side-channel attacks. In: Network and Distributed System Security Symposium (NDSS) (2022)

26. López-Morales, E., Planta, U., Rubio-Medrano, C., Abbasi, A., Cardenas, A.A.: SOK: security of programmable logic controllers. In: USENIX Security Symposium (2024)

27. Mekala, S.H., Baig, Z., Anwar, A., Zeadally, S.: Cybersecurity for industrial IoT (IIoT): threats, countermeasures, challenges and future directions. Comput. Commun. **208**, 294–320 (2023)

28. NIST: Security and privacy controls for information systems and organizations (2020)

29. NIST: Guide to operational technology (OT) security (2023)

30. OPC Foundation: OPC UA reference (2024). https://reference.opcfoundation.org/

31. Rescorla, E.: The transport layer security (TLS) protocol version 1.3. RFC Editor (2018). https://www.rfc-editor.org/info/rfc8446

32. Rossel, J.: Usage statistics of 3D printing file formats (2022). https://upb-syssec.github.io/blog/2022/3d-printing-file-format-usage/

33. Safford, D.R., Wiseman, M.: Hardware rooted trust for additive manufacturing. IEEE Access **7**, 79211–79215 (2019)

34. Song, C., Li, Z., Xu, W., Zhou, C., Jin, Z., Ren, K.: My smartphone recognizes genuine QR codes! In: Proceedings of the ACM on Interactive, Mobile, Wearable and Ubiquitous Technologies, pp. 1–20 (2018)

35. Song, C., Lin, F., Ba, Z., Ren, K., Zhou, C., Xu, W.: My smartphone knows what you print: exploring smartphone-based side-channel attacks against 3D printers. In: Conference on Computer and Communications Security (ACM SIGSAC), pp. 895–907 (2016)

36. Suh, G.E., Devadas, S.: Physical unclonable functions for device authentication and secret key generation. In: Conference on Design automation (DAC), p. 9 (2007)

37. Tapas, N., Belikovetsky, S., Longo, F., Puliafito, A., Shabtai, A., Elovici, Y.: 3D marketplace: Distributed attestation of 3D designs on blockchain. In: International Conference on Smart Computing (SMARTCOMP), pp. 311–316 (2022)

38. Tsoutsos, N.G., Gamil, H., Maniatakos, M.: Secure 3D printing: reconstructing and validating solid geometries using toolpath reverse engineering. In: Zhou, J., Damiani, E. (eds.) Proceedings of the 3rd ACM Workshop on Cyber-Physical System Security - CPSS 2017, pp. 15–20. ACM (2017)

39. Wang, Y., Yang, Y., Suo, S., Wang, M., Rao, W.: Using blockchain to protect 3D printing from unauthorized model tampering. Appl. Sci. **12**, 7947 (2022)

40. Wohlers Associates: What is additive manufacturing? (2020). https://wohlersassociates.com/terminology-and-definitions/additive-manufacturing/

41. Wu, M., Moon, Y.B.: Intrusion detection of cyber-physical attacks in manufacturing systems: a review. ASME (2019)

42. Wüst, K., Gervais, A.: Do you need a blockchain? In: Crypto Valley Conference on Blockchain Technology (CVCBT), pp. 45–54 (2018)
43. Yampolskiy, M., Gatlin, J. (eds.): Springer Handbook of Additive Manufacturing: Security Threats in AM. Springer Handbooks, Springer International Publishing, Cham, 1st ed. 2023 edn. (2023)
44. Yampolskiy, M., Gatlin, J., Yung, M.: Myths and misconceptions in additive manufacturing security: deficiencies of the CIA triad. In: Workshop on Additive Manufacturing (3D Printing) Security, pp. 3–9 (2021)
45. Yampolskiy, M., Graves, L., Gatlin, J., Skjellum, A., Yung, M.: What did you add to my additive manufacturing data?: Steganographic attacks on 3D printing files. In: International Symposium on Research in Attacks, Intrusions and Defenses, pp. 266–281 (2021)
46. Yampolskiy, M., et al.: Security of additive manufacturing: attack taxonomy and survey. Additive Manuf. **21**, 431–457 (2018)

Author Index

The manufacturer's authorised representative in the EU is Springer
Nature Customer Service Centre GmbH, Europaplatz 3, 69115 Heidelberg,
Germany. If you have any concerns regarding our products, please
contact ProductSafety@springernature.com

Printed and bound by CPI Group (UK) Ltd, Croydon, CR0 4YY
24/04/2026
02096367-0013